WOMEN DRUG TRAFFICKERS

Diálogos Series

Kris Lane, Series Editor

Understanding Latin America demands dialogue, deep exploration, and frank discussion of key topics. Founded by Lyman L. Johnson in 1992 and edited since 2013 by Kris Lane, the Diálogos Series focuses on innovative scholarship in Latin American history and related fields. The series, the most successful of its type, includes specialist works accessible to a wide readership and a variety of thematic titles, all ideally suited for classroom adoption by university and college teachers.

Also available in the Diálogos Series:

Searching for Madre Matiana: Prophecy and Popular Culture in Modern Mexico by
Edward Wright-Rios

Africans into Creoles: Slavery, Ethnicity, and Identity in Colonial Costa Rica by
Russell Lohse

Emotions and Daily Life in Colonial Mexico edited by Javier Villa-Flores and
Sonya Lipsett-Rivera

Native Brazil: Beyond the Convert and the Cannibal, 1500–1900 edited by Hal Langfur

The Course of Andean History by Peter V. N. Henderson

Masculinity and Sexuality in Modern Mexico edited by Anne Rubenstein and
Víctor M. Macías-González

Modernizing Minds in El Salvador: Education Reform and the Cold War, 1960–1980 by
Héctor Lindo-Fuentes and Erik Ching

A History of Mining in Latin America: From the Colonial Era to the Present by
Kendall Brown

Slavery, Freedom, and Abolition in Latin America and the Atlantic World by
Christopher Schmidt-Nowara

Cuauhtémoc's Bones: Forging National Identity in Modern Mexico by
Paul Gillingham

For additional titles in the Diálogos Series, please visit unmpress.com.

WOMEN DRUG TRAFFICKERS

Mules, Bosses, and Organized Crime

ELAINE CAREY

University of New Mexico Press · Albuquerque

Library of Congress Cataloging-in-Publication Data

Carey, Elaine, 1967–
Women drug traffickers : mules, bosses, and organized crime / Elaine Carey. —
First Edition.
pages cm. — (Diálogos Series)
Includes bibliographical references and index.
ISBN 978-0-8263-5198-2 (pbk. : alk. paper) — ISBN 978-0-8263-5199-9 (electronic)
1. Drug dealers—Mexico—History—20th century. 2. Female offenders—Mexico—
History—20th century. 3. Drug traffic—Mexico—History—20th century. 4. Drug
abuse and crime—Mexico—History—20th century. I. Title.
HV5840.M6C37 2014
363.45082'0972—dc23
2014002206

Cover photograph: Woman in a Sinaloan marijuana field.
Photo by José Carlos Cisneros Guzmán.

Cover design by Catherine Leonardo
Text composition by Felicia Cedillos
Composed in Minion Pro 10.25/13.5
Display Type is Asphaltum WF and ITC Franklin Gothic Std

CONTENTS

Acknowledgments
vii

INTRODUCTION
Selling Is More of a Habit: Women and Drug Trafficking, 1900–1980
1

CHAPTER ONE
Foreign Vices: Drugs, Modernity, and Gender
14

CHAPTER TWO
Mules, Smugglers, and Peddlers: The Illicit Trade in Mexico, 1910s–1930s
53

CHAPTER THREE
The White Lady of Mexico City: Lola la Chata and
the Remaking of Narcotics
91

CHAPTER FOUR
Transcending Borders: La Nacha and the "Notorious" Women of the North
126

CHAPTER FIVE
The Women Who Made It Snow: Cold, Dirty Drug Wars, 1970s
158

CONCLUSION

Gangsters, Narcs, and Women: A Secret History
194

Notes
205

Bibliography
255

Index
281

ACKNOWLEDGMENTS

And we were too young to be hippies
Missed out on the love
Turned to a teen in the late 70s
In the summer of the drugs

—VICTORIA WILLIAMS

IN 1982, I RETURNED TO THE UNITED STATES FROM EUROPE TO FINISH high school. I arrived just in time for the escalation of Ronald Reagan's war on drugs. The "Just Say No" campaign of his wife, Nancy, connected to the sleepy beach and military town of Pensacola, Florida, in a number of ways: signs around schools claimed the establishment of "Drug Free Zones," while, inside, locker inspections for marijuana became common. Overhead, the sounds of low-flying aircraft could be heard, routine aerial surveillance of Florida highways and rural areas. During this period, some of my friends disappeared from school, their parents sent to prison and their homes sold at auction after a series of cocaine arrests in the early 1980s. As the war on drugs raged, I became more familiar with the consequences of addiction and criminalization. When a friend became an intensive-care foster parent, I held the HIV-positive crack-addicted babies that she fostered, most of whom never lived beyond three years of age. My friend, a former Peace Corps volunteer and nurse, routinely provided information about safe sex to the mothers of her foster children; she was their only HIV counselor in a time when few existed anywhere.

Pensacola is known for its laid-back Florida lifestyle combined with brimstone evangelical Christianity, and I frequently returned there, avoiding the latter but relishing the former. In 2003, I discovered that one of my favorite beach bars, the Sandshaker Lounge and Package Store—home of the original Bushwacker—became the site of a federal sting. Operation Sandshaker ensnared wealthy and successful business owners along with resident beach bums.[1] All had entered the business of cocaine, running it from Miami to Pensacola for personal use and for distribution within the Florida Panhandle and the greater Gulf Coast region. Operation Sandshaker and the loss of a favorite haunt happened just as I began to envision this book project. Federal agents arrested more than thirty people, but most intriguing to me were the women: lawyers, business owners, and even the creator of the Bushwacker and owner of the Sandshaker.[2] Was the risk worth it, I wondered? And for successful women, why did they take such a risk? Was it the money, the glamour, the adventure, or just simply timing? I cannot separate my experiences growing up in Florida during the war on drugs from my interest in the history of narcotics.

Over the years, that interest in gender and the history of drugs led me to seek out others with similar research agendas. Even though historical academic writing often lacks creativity, it is a collaborative process, and collaboration adds creative elements. As this book progressed, I traveled across borders in an effort to uncover the lives of women whose business models, and whose very lives, rested upon their anonymity and ability to avoid detection. Many people—scholars, librarians, archivists, journalists, filmmakers, and former police officers—in the United States, Mexico, Colombia, and Canada have assisted in this project since I began the initial research in 1997. Thus, I would like to thank a number of people who have influenced my own conceptualization of the history of Latin America, narcotics, and crime by offering their time, analysis, and criticism: Felipe Aljure, Peter Andreas, Luis Astorga, Sam Brunk, Nancy Campbell, Isaac Campos, Ric Curtis, George Díaz, Roxanne Dunbar-Ortiz, Sterling Evans, David Fahey, Richard Friman, Michelle García, José Guarnizo, Joe Heyman, Hermann Herlinghaus, Lyman Johnson, Regnar Kristensen, Fernando Lebrija, Victor Macías-González, Dan Malleck, Andrae Marak, Marcel Martel, Jocelyn Olcott, Diego Osorno, Tony Payan, Pablo Piccato, Margaret Randall, Joe Spillane, Barry Spunt, Elijah Wald, and Glenn Weyant. W. Clark Whitehorn has long been a proponent of this project. Jennie Erin Smith shared information about Griselda Blanco's final days. Howard Abadinsky, a St. John's University colleague whom a Mexican student recommended that I seek out, helped me understand the complexities of organized crime and various structural models. I also benefited from many contacts in the New York Police Department who helped me understand the evolution of police work with respect to narcotics control. In particular, I would like to thank Kathy Burke, Paul Chu, and Thomas Ong for their insight.

Throughout this project, I worked more closely with librarians and archivists than I had in the past. All expressed interest in the project, provided guidance, and pushed me in directions that I had not considered. I would like to thank a number of archivists and librarians: Gene Morris, Fred Romanski and John Taylor at the National Archives and Records Administration (NARA), College Park, Maryland; Jessica Schmidt at NARA, Kansas City, Kansas; Joe Sanchez at NARA, San Bruno, California; Monique Sugimoto at NARA, Riverside, California; and Christopher Wright at NARA, Fort Worth, Texas. Kyle Ainsworth at the East Texas Research Center graciously went through files looking for information regarding Alvin Scharff and Garland Roark.

Closer to New York City, my early work with Karen Anson, Robert Parks, and Marc Renovitch at the Franklin D. Roosevelt Presidential Library and Charlotte Strum at the Rockefeller Archive Center proved to me that this topic was feasible. Barbara Traub, Astrid Emel, and Bill Manz at St. John's Rittenberg Law Library gave me crash courses in legal research for this project. Dorothy Beck at St. John's University Library provided a regular fix of books and materials acquired through interlibrary loans. Ismael Rivera-Sierra and Alyse Hennig at STJ's Davis Library introduced me to the concept of social history through insurance claims, something I now refer to as "Insuring Addiction." Jim Quigle at the Special Collections at Pennsylvania State University is an expert on the history of narcotics in the United States and assisted me with the Anslinger papers. I met Idilio Peña in his role as the chief archivist of the Dominican Studies Institute and Archives at the City University of New York while working on another research project. Previously, he was the deputy commissioner of the New York City Municipal Archives. He introduced me to the rich collection in New York that had transnational ties. At the Lloyd Sealy Library of the John Jay College of Criminal Justice, Larry Sullivan, Ellen Belcher, and Ellen Sexton, experts on crime, endlessly discussed the history of crime with me and gave me an "office" in the city.

The Stephen A. Schwarzman Building at the New York Public Library has become a second home. My former student Ray Pun helped me find resources and revise chapter 1. He also advised me about sources regarding the anti-Chino movement in Mexico. More significantly, Pun and I have worked closely together on historical methods classes for St. John's University students. Working with an embedded librarian led me to reconceptualize my research methodologies, offered me an opportunity to know libraries and archives at a different level, and challenged me to continually mine sources whether ephemera, documents, or material culture. In the summer of 2013, we participated in the NCC Team Building Workshop on Japanese resources at Harvard University. The librarians and scholars at the workshop introduced me to an array of materials and methods that allowed me to pursue global networks within the history of narcotics, which will have an ongoing impact on my research.

The librarians, archivists, and curators of the NYPL had a profound impact on this project. Jay Barksdale has offered his insight into the workings of the NYPL and the beauty of silence in the Wertheim Study. Anne Marie Belinfante assisted in my better understanding of the Jewish community of Shanghai during the interwar years. Jessica Pigza and Tal Nadan introduced me to the vastness of the Rare Books and Manuscripts and Archives divisions, which offered another realm of material on narcotics, drugs, and crime. Katherine Cordes demonstrated the importance of maps in the study of transnational flows. Paul Friedman explained the black, green, red, and blue (as well as other hues) books that line the walls of the Rose Reading Room. Sachiko Clayton's introduction of genealogical research assisted me in developing the familial past of U.S.-based drug traffickers. Ross Takahashi humorously described the realm of business and the unique collections of the Science, Industry, and Business Library. Michael Cambre and Gwinith Evans introduced my class to another place to find secondary sources and a quiet place to work on the fifth floor at the mid-Manhattan branch.

The final chapter of this book could not have been finished without the assistance of archivists and staff at the National Archives in New York. I particularly want to thank Sarah Pasquello, Trinia Yeckley, Angela Turdico, and Doug Cantelemo. Greg Plunges explained docket numbers, told me who to contact at the local courthouses, and tracked down complex legal cases that had been consolidated under one docket number. All explained the organization of legal documents (the difference between red and blue) and held materials for months while I read through the case files.

For the past three years, I have met a growing community of colleagues through the American Historical Association and its Tuning Project. They have had a profound impact on my teaching but also on my scholarship through their research, writing, and advocacy for the historical profession. Their examples led me to return to this manuscript with a more critical and focused eye.

In Mexico, the staff and activists at the Archivo General de la Nación (AGN), in particular José Zavala of Referencia, Arturo Librado Galicia of Galeria 2, and Raymundo Alvarez García of Galeria 3, were invaluable. All three were helpful in this project and also had interesting anecdotes about working in the archive. At the Fototeca Nacional del Instituto Nacional de Antropología de Historia, Patricia Muñoz Arteaga, Pedro Edgar Guerrero Hernández, Diana Sanchez, and Mayra Mendoza assisted in the acquisition of images. They, too, pointed me in directions I had not considered. I would also like to thank the staff at the archive of the Secretaría de Salud. Carmen Juárez of the Biblioteca del Estado de Hidalgo "Ricardo Garibay" assisted in searching for material on local drug peddlers and smugglers. Lastly, at the Secretaría Relaciones Exteriores Archivo Histórico Genero Estrada, archivists Oscar Aquirre L and Hugo Martinez ran numerous searches, allowed me to use the phone, and let me photograph documents that will be part of my research for years to come.

Over the years, I received funding from two St. John's University Faculty Summer Fellowships in 2004 and 2008; the Beeke-Levy Research Fellowship, Franklin and Eleanor Roosevelt Institute, New Hyde Park, New York, 2005–2006; a Fulbright–García Robles Fellowship, COMEXUS and CIES, Mexico City, 2007–2008; and lastly a Lloyd George Sealy Research Fellowship at John Jay College of Criminal Justice, 2008–2013.

I have also benefited from the scholarly community at St. John's University. My students read the chapter on Lola la Chata and endlessly tolerated my ongoing discussion about women and dope, particularly Andrés Bermudez, Tiffany Bal, Ray Devries, Pablo López del Oro, Kevin Lubrano, Tiara Moultrie, and Candace Rowser. Sharmina Akhtar, Elise Barbeau, Jennifer Caputo, Daniel Kelly, Greg Lubrano, Josh Powers, and Xiaochun Wang helped me with the digital images, finding materials, communication, and photocopying documents. Yesenia Bran graciously and humorously watched narco B-flicks and explained the Salvadoran angle to me. Melvyn Threatt Peters, my research assistant, read through many of the court cases, digitized countless documents, and wrote brief biographies of people and summaries of complex conspiracy cases. My colleagues have tolerated ongoing dope conversations, contributed their own ideas, and assisted in translations or explanations on an array of information: Dolores Augustine, Mauricio Borrero, Tracey-Anne Cooper, Betsy Herbin, Flora Kesheshian, Jeff Kinkley, Tim Milford, Phil Misevich, Susie Pak, Nerina Rustomji, Susan Schmidt-Horning, Kathy Shaunessy, Ben Turner, Konrad Tuchscherer, and Lara Vapnek.

I have benefited from a large group of scholars, writers, and writing workshops. The outline for chapter 5 began at the Faculty Writers Retreat in Rome, Italy, in 2007. I would like to thank Derek Owens, Harry Denny, Anne Geller, and Tom Philopose for coordinating the retreat, for their feedback, and for the great tours, company, and food. Additional sections were further developed through the Faculty Writer Initiative; a big thanks to Maura Flannery and Anne Geller for numerous writing retreats. I would also like to recognize the members of the Colloquium on the History of Women and Gender in Mexico, the New York City Latin American History Workshop, and the St. John's University Junior Faculty Research Colloquium participants who contributed comments on earlier drafts. Jonathan Ablard, Howard Campbell, Nancy Campbell, Bob Chessey, Froylán Enciso, Paul Gootenberg, Lyman Johnson, Andrae Marak, Alejandro Quintana, and Joe Spillane read and commented on drafts. Evelyn Schlatter, a comrade for over twenty years, makes me yearn to be a better writer, and I long for the day when I can jot down a jingle, joke, sentence, paragraph, essay, or monograph like her. Harrison Reiner's interest in my research, his crash courses in creative and screenplay writing, as well as his input on the manuscript and "the story arc" inspired, I hope, a better style. Through our friendship, he has demonstrated his skills as an exceptional historian.

For their hospitality, I want to thank the extended Alvarez Isasi family, particularly my father-in-law Javier, the Ruiz Morales family, Roger Magazine, Lucia Rayas Veleasco, and José Agustin Román Gaspar. Enrique Semo and Margarita Arévalo continue to be advocates of my research and work, and offer insight into Mexico. My work with Sinaloan ethnographer José Carlos Cisneros Guzmán further expanded my knowledge about contemporary women in the drug trade, and his research and our collaborative project forced me to make modern connections.

My trips to Pensacola have also been a joy as the family grew. Andrea, Dan, Brian, Erin, Sophelia, Xavier, Roardan, and Jeremy have offered good company and hospitality, and their location in Pensacola inspired the broader work. My extended family in New York and New Jersey has participated in the entire project with humor and jokes, particularly offering feedback on cover art. I owe a special thanks to Ryan Carey for perusing contracts and giving me legal advice. My Queens family have added their own takes on the subject: Angelina Petiton McKenna and Alexia Eroglu; Michele, Dana, and Danielle Viscosi; and the Bellerose-Floral Park Wine and Book Club: Trish Deely, John Kouri, Gigi Lavaud Gately, Kathy Mavrikakis, Kathy O'Malley, Karen Reiter, Carolyn Telesca, and Rex Whicker. Javier Alvarez Isasi continues to be a source of support, good humor, and wisdom, if not an occasional voice of trepidation that I only pretend to ignore. Lucas accompanied me into the field and to libraries and archives with an inspiring sense of wonder and awe.

This book is dedicated to my maternal grandparents. From Spanish murmurs, songs, poems, jokes, and political conversation and for his continued support and interest in my work on Latin America and even the feminist "stuff," this book is dedicated to my grandfather James Gerard Stofer. He represents the greatest generation: a multilingual high school dropout and a survivor of Pearl Harbor and the Battle of Midway who evolved into a Wharton man and a corporate warrior. He was also a theater collective member, actor, and lover of art, music, and history. His life companion, also from Fort Greene, Brooklyn, the late Marie Joan Curley Stofer, my grandmother, too was part of that greatest generation: working as an accountant in factories during World War II, crossing the country to see her Brooklyn boy when he was stateside, and supporting my grandfather while he pursued his education and career. She explained to me that during the war she held her best job as a financial officer at an armaments factory, a job she never held again. After the war, she worked in banking but continually trained men who went on to take the jobs that in another time and place would have been hers. Their examples have taught me about perseverance.

INTRODUCTION

SELLING IS MORE OF A HABIT

Women and Drug Trafficking, 1900–1980

ON FRIDAY, SEPTEMBER 29, 2007, MEXICO CITY POLICE CAPTURED Sandra Ávila Beltrán while she was driving her BMW in a plush part of the city. Dubbed "la reina del Pacífico" (the queen of the Pacific) after the title of Arturo Pérez-Reverte's best-selling novel *La reina del sur* (*The Queen of the South*), her shocking personal tales of cocaine trafficking, sexual conquests, and the kidnapping of her child were followed by the press.[1] That she came from drug royalty only added to the titillation, since her power derived from her familial network. Ávila is the niece of both Miguel Ángel Félix Gallardo and Juan José Quintero Payán, two of Mexico's most prominent drug traffickers.[2] According to newspaper and television reports, Ávila sashayed about the police station wearing tight jeans and demanding time to fix her hair and makeup for her mug shot. Her beauty and numerous conquests seemed more fiction than reality. Prior to her arrest, she had been wed to several high-ranking police officers while carrying on affairs with prominent drug traffickers. Journalists reported that her ex-husbands, the police officers, always ended up dead.

A couple of weeks after Ávila's arrest, a spokesperson for the attorney general of Chihuahua, Mario Ruíz Nava, stated that the police had killed "la güera polvos" (Snow White), Rosa Emma Carvajal Ontiversos, on October 7, 2007. The police in Ciudad Juárez, El Paso, and southern New Mexico were familiar with Carvajal, who operated from Palomas, Chihuahua, which borders Columbus, New Mexico.[3] Carvajal trafficked cocaine and people through that

1

major overland port with impunity. She had sealed her notoriety in 2004 when she led a group that ransacked the police station in Palomas.

In 2007, these two high-profile incidents occurring within two weeks of each other suggested a disturbing shift in the world of drug trafficking in the dawn of the new century: women were important to the drug trade. The two women displayed distinct forms of agency within the world of narcotics. Ávila had gained her power due to her familial and communal contacts with founders of what became known as the Sinaloa cartel. Her ties to such men allowed her to benefit financially, but she also created legitimate business ventures such as nail salons and clothing boutiques. Carvajal was a female boss who led a group of men along the U.S.-Mexico border.[4] She, too, had gained access to power due to her relations with men, but she had taken the extraordinary step of showing her power over men within her organization as well as within a local police force. La reina del Pacífico fits the image of the sexy lover, wife, or companion of numerous drug traffickers and police agents, yet she is also a member of a notorious crime family.[5] These familial relations gave her access to resources and power that most women never enjoy, but her connections ensured her desirability among men, who viewed her as a conquest or business partner. Carvajal rose to prominence in illicit trade, not as a child of a criminal family but as a means to survive and raise herself and her children out of poverty. Both biographies demonstrate the quotidian practices within the trade and the complexities by which women participate in illicit flows of narcotics.

The sensationalism that surrounds such cases distorts the trade at its most basic element. Women have always been part of the drug trade despite their fetishized representations in popular culture, such as in the television series *Weeds*. There, doe-eyed Mary-Louise Parker plays Nancy, an upper-middle-class housewife who resorts to drug peddling when her husband dies. Melodramatic films like *María Full of Grace*, *Traffic*, *Blow*, and *Scarface* offer female protagonists, often as secondary characters who reinforce popular notions of women as mules or as lovers of prominent drug lords. In *María Full of Grace*, Catalina Sandino Moreno as María Álvarez escapes poverty by serving as a cocaine mule to provide for her family. In *Traffic*, Catherine Zeta-Jones plays a wife left destitute when her husband is implicated in drug trafficking. She turns to his business to make ends meet. Mirtha Jung, played by Penélope Cruz in *Blow*, is similar to Ávila, a reina with ties to the Colombian drug oligarchy. In the 1983 *Scarface*, Michelle Pfeiffer depicts the beautiful lover, Elvira Hancock, who is lured by the wealth and lifestyle of Tony Montana.[6]

Earlier studies of narcotics and drug trafficking that emerged in the 1980s and early 1990s rarely mentioned women, but a few scholars considered how women were connected to the trade as addicts, mules, lovers, or victims.[7] More recently, scholars of the present—anthropologists, criminologists, and sociologists—have begun to systematically study women as important actors with a multiplicity of roles in the global flows of drugs.[8] Women play key roles as bosses, money launderers, and couriers as well as mules and addicts.

In this study, my approach to women and drug trafficking is historical. Rather than interviewing women or observing them over a period of years, I sought them in written records. This involved a consistent mining of sources in an array of archives in Mexico and the United States. Thus, my methods differ from those undertaken by anthropologists, sociologists, and criminologists, who are active observers and ethnographers. Yet, I speak to their disciplines' growing body of literature on women and drugs by explaining historical change over time and across spaces as essential to illicit flows whether in urban spaces, rural borderlands, or urban ports of entry.[9] Through a historical approach, I explore the roles of women in all areas of the drug economy, from mules to bosses. I engage the historiography and policy studies on drug trafficking in North America by expanding its dimensions to consider the historical complexities of gender, race and ethnicity, and class as these intersect with drug trafficking in North America.

U.S. Customs agents along the U.S.-Mexico border noted the growing prominence of women bootleggers and narcotics smugglers as early as 1914. By the early 1920s, those officials stationed in Mexicali-Calexico estimated that women may have been responsible for 60 percent of the drug flow across the border. As bootleggers, women became experts in peddling tequila and mescal; as mules, they hid narcotics under their skirts, in their clothing, or even in their bodies. One official complained: "It is not at all easy for men engaged in the work of trailing these agents to seize and search women."[10] The reason for their inability to seize and search women was due to a lack of female agents. U.S. Customs officials and smugglers along borders were engaged in a struggle, with women serving as the mules of choice because they were less likely to draw suspicion and be searched.

By the early 1930s, with the end of Prohibition in the United States, the role of women in illicit trade in North America was made more explicit in the newspapers and was ever more disturbing for police, customs officials, Foreign Service officers, philanthropists, and narcotics warriors on both sides of the border. With the greater attention of law enforcement, smugglers grew more sophisticated and adept, demonstrating a fluidity to avoid capture and use new forms of technology whether in banking, communications, or transportation long before the media and academic scholarship began to focus on the globalization of crime.[11]

The professionalization of drug controls emerged in the early 1900s when countries led by the United States began to meet in an attempt to regulate the flows of opiates from Asia. With the formation of the League of Nations, the United States, although never a member of the league, found a venue in which to work closely with other countries to further attempt to stem the flows. In turn, narco-infused tales of deviancy, destruction, miscegenation, crime, and systemic dangers circulated and transgressed national borders. These narratives of vice crossed borders and intersected to construct and reinforce national tales of woeful criminality. These tropes have informed the popular imagination, forging shifts in political, medical, economic, cultural, and social practices. Moreover, drug economies coexisted with traditional economies but were more evident in marginal places of alleged violence such as inner cities and the border regions. These also exist in sites of profit, legitimate business, and political ambition, and they create socioeconomic advancement for those on either the margins or the apex of society, regardless of citizenship.[12] Like the drugs themselves, narconarratives and narcoculture crossed socioeconomic boundaries of class, ethnicity, gender, and physical space. Just as today, drug money bought power, technology, and expertise as well as conspicuous consumption, which in turn structured identities and social hierarchies.[13]

From the rise of drug trafficking in the early 1900s to its present manifestations, a century of narconarratives have flowed across borders. Scholar Hermann Herlinghaus argues that narconarratives designate a multiplicity of dramas expressed in antagonistic languages and articulated along the border through fantasies that revolve around the depravity and deterritorialization of individual and communitarian life.[14] Many examples are evident, including the rise of narco-corridos, music that celebrates the exploits of drug traffickers. The U.S.-Mexico border has served as a common site for such analysis, but narconarratives expand beyond national borders because drug trafficking is a global enterprise tied to localized markets and forms of production; in *Andean Cocaine*, Paul Gootenberg explains how Peruvian officials, medical doctors, and industrialists saw cocaine as a commodity for medicinal purposes that could help modernize and industrialize the country.

Even after cocaine became an illicit commodity, the Peruvian market for the drug continued to thrive.[15] Moreover, these narratives, like all such creations, change over time to reflect shifts in laws, technology, and politically and criminologically infused popular interpretations. In the twentieth century, narconarratives crossed borders but also genres, whether political speeches, journalistic exposés, music, art, or film.

In North America, border regions served as sites of illicit trade that offered women a place to conduct business, whether as suppliers, couriers, contacts, or clients.[16] Certain women gained financially from the smuggling and peddling of narcotics, and they were often intimately involved in the planning and execution of the business. Women joined men in the establishment of chief narcotics ports along the U.S.-Mexico border beginning in the 1910s and 1920s. Moreover, these participants deployed new forms of technology, from concealment contraptions to airplanes, to supply customers in the major narcotics hubs of New York City, Chicago, Seattle, Los Angeles, and Toronto; cities far from Calexico-Mexicali, Tijuana, Ciudad Juárez, and Mexico City, or from Buenos Aires and Medellín. They sought and struggled to consolidate their businesses and power.

Scholars Itty Abraham and Willem van Schendel warn against the belief that all nation-states are engaged in a valiant struggle against the transnational flows of crime and vice. Instead, these authors adopt a non-state-centric approach that makes a distinction between what nation-states deem to be legitimate (i.e., legal) and what different groups of people think is legitimate (i.e., licit).[17] In keeping with this point of view, I utilize the state for its resources—since few traffickers have left their papers to an archive or library—while also highlighting how informal social networks developed throughout the twentieth century. I firmly reject the state's framework regarding the drug trade that usually employs tropes of good versus evil. This story is far more complex.

To uncover the stories of women's, men's, and their children's involvement in the drug trade, I accessed a wide selection of materials including international diplomatic documents, medical and public welfare studies, letters, reports, correspondence between drug czars, newspapers, and prison and hospital records. Those women who flourished in the drug trade relied on their abilities to circumnavigate systems of constraint constructed by politicians and civil authorities. Public awareness of their existence and their participation brought financial difficulties and ruin to women peddlers and traffickers. Thus, I discuss in detail those who entered into the historical public record while acknowledging that countless others slipped through due in part to their ability to remain hidden. Beginning in the 1910s, these women established their own definitions of "legitimate" in their businesses that contradicted what national governments considered "legitimate." Women in urban and rural settings saw the drug economy as a vehicle to making a viable living—like their other forms of informal work such as street vending or prostitution.[18]

To find women involved in the drug trade decades ago involved tried and true historical methodology. Initially, I noticed that William Burroughs had mentioned Lola la Chata, a Mexico City drug boss, in his novels and short stories. In Mexico City, I read newspaper coverage of her while working on my dissertation on a completely different topic. Since then, in order to demonstrate the important role some women played in the drug trade, I have continued to seek women and build upon the methodologies of Luis Astorga, Nancy Campbell, Paul Gootenberg, Joe Spillane, and William Walker III to further analyze women's illicit transnational businesses.[19] I read newspapers from across the United States and Mexico looking for women involved in transnational drug enterprises. If the coverage was substantial enough, I pursued them in official documents and other public sources to develop a greater understanding of them and their eras, their lives, and their relationships with various forms of state and local power structures. Like these women, I, too, moved across borders in pursuit of sources in both the United States and Mexico. Many times, I pieced together their histories from evidence I found in various archives and libraries. At times, their stories abruptly ended due to death, imprisonment, or diminished stature in the trade, or they simply disappeared from the public record.

These sources show that women, men, and children peddled and smuggled opiates, cocaine, and marijuana from and through Mexico, but also Colombia and Argentina, into the United States from 1900 to the 1980s. Upon examination, their lives complicate the accepted masculine constructions of the narcotics trade that predominate in journalistic coverage, policy studies, and popular culture. More importantly, these narratives have long been "open secrets"—a cultural dynamic where much is known but little is publicly acknowledged.[20] Borrowing from the work of Avery Gordon, I agree that drugs have haunted the Americas, exhibiting seething presences, acting on and meddling with assumed realities not only on the border but throughout the hemisphere.[21]

By analyzing peddling and trafficking, I thus construct a new understanding of the intersection between gender and the transnational concepts of crime, nation, political economy, modernity, and globalization from the early 1900s. More importantly, I demonstrate how women and men, whether traffickers, peddlers, or policing agents, concocted and contextualized the role of women in the trade in response to diverse shifts throughout time. Historian Nancy Campbell has suggested that drugs became codified as a threat particularly to white women, who held an ambiguous status in the United States due to their lack of political and financial independence during the early years of efforts to stem the flow of narcotics trafficking. Significantly, Campbell argues that drugs "threatened civilization by working to level the naturalized hierarchy of the distinction between the sexes and the state."[22] Women addicts neglected their duties as mothers and wives to acculturate children and maintain a stable home. Instead, they pursued their addiction. As peddlers, dealers, and traffickers, they further threatened civilization by challenging the view that women were "unfit" to hold positions in the upper hierarchies of the drug economy, just as they were considered "unfit" to play a role in the upper levels of the formal economy. Drug trafficking has traditionally been perceived as a man's world by both male and female scholars and policy makers.[23]

As drug use shifted from elite, white, female iatrogenic (doctor-assisted) addicts in the late nineteenth century to urban, lower-class, male criminal addicts, certain women exploited lucrative career paths.[24] They accessed one of the few spaces in the economy left open to them: the informal market. Women have frequently used this market to build capital and, at times, personal and economic influence in their communities. Building upon the illicit trade routes created by bootleggers along the U.S.-Mexico border during the early 1900s, women found that narcotics smuggling paid more than peddling food, drinks, or their own bodies. Accustomed to working in the informal economy or the secondary labor market, they used a prescribed gender role—their feminine wiles—to advance their positions in this business. Women in Mexico, along the U.S.-Mexico border, and in other parts of the world were able to develop sophisticated networks of trafficking.

Many women smugglers had male partners who furthered their careers, but a few were the architects of their own transnational crime syndicates.[25] More commonly, women served as complements to the trafficking businesses of their husbands, fathers, or brothers. While men moved drugs across borders, women controlled local distribution, particularly to other women. To ensure the continued success of their enterprises, women resorted to co-optation, bribery, manipulation, and, if necessary, violence.

They also embraced stereotypical, gendered rhetoric to avoid imprisonment by exploiting tales of victimization. More often, their exercise of power ensured the attention of political and police figures throughout North America due to their notoriety in the trade. Women traffickers, then as today, were sensationalized as sexual deviants. In turn, these women informed policy, policing, and political practices, but more significantly they transformed cultural and social assumptions.[26]

This work also intersects with the emerging body of literature on the history of crime and narcotics in the Americas.[27] The rise of the Mexican narcotics trade and the first drug war came during the apex of the Mexican Revolution in the 1920s, and the trade flourished in the 1930s. In the wake of the revolution, Mexico sought to revitalize the economic, social, political, and cultural life of the nation. Despite the rhetoric of revolutionary change, Mexican officials abandoned certain Porfirian ideals about crime and punishment while embracing others—particularly those that dealt with race. Certain attributes became associated with certain races particularly regarding shiftlessness, laziness, and criminality. They passed laws regulating certain practices such as public drunkenness and prostitution, which they deemed dangerous to the health of the nation.[28] By the mid-1920s, the governments of Álvaro Obregón (1920–1924) and Plutarco Calles (1924–1928) included the regulation of narcotics as part of revitalization of the nation and the means by which to build new citizens.[29] This shift occurred because of the global pressure to curtail drug trafficking, use, and addiction that heightened during the 1920s. Moreover, illicit trade undermined domestic production in Mexico and hampered the growth of the legitimate economy. Policy makers thus tried to address the problem through cooperation with the United States, which was demanding that Mexico exercise greater control over narcotics and criminalize consumption.

Recent scholarship on illicit flows and globalization has recognized the overlapping consequences of the market in a global environment. Due to Mexico's shared and often unregulated border with the United States, a space of trade existed. As Carolyn Nordstrom has written, markets are everywhere, concurrently central and peripheral in a global economy, and the relevance of the moral state is redefined particularly in border regions where laws, capital, and commodities flow. Movements of people and culture are constantly renegotiated.[30] Since I pay close attention to border regions and the transnational flows of drugs, I note a frontier ambiance of freedom, danger, and profit that men and women experience equally.[31] Here, people continually navigate between diverse spaces—whether between one country and another, one set of laws and another, or the illicit versus the licit. This continued renegotiation of markets, laws, and cultures ensured flexibility in relationships and social status, including gender. Outside border zones, men and women recognized gaps in policing or state control of certain spaces, such as in cities and even rural areas. They took full advantage of the economic and social openings available to them by engaging in behavior that in certain sectors was deemed illicit but in others widely accepted and even encouraged. Drugs thus operated within varying definitions of "legal," depending on the environment in which business was conducted.

Moreover, women in the trade ruptured the normative expectations of what it meant to be a woman by using limited and constrained forms of feminine power to build criminal empires at a time when most other women were galvanized by the revolutionary ideals in Mexico to work in education or public health. Some women took on greater public roles, but other poor and illiterate women did not have the good fortune to be selected for such campaigns. For instance, in chapter 4 I discuss Lola la Chata, who created a transnational drug trafficking organization that operated from the 1930s until her death in the 1950s. In analyzing revolutionary and postrevolutionary Mexican history, historians have discussed how women mobilized to teach in schools, organized feminist meetings (although they did not receive the vote until 1953), entered professions, and became politically engaged.[32] They became instrumental in the creation of revolutionary ideals by their own zeal, yet women such as Lola la Chata, poor, illiterate, and mestiza, remained on the margins of these revolutionary ideas.

Compared to the elite social spheres, women of the lower classes had a vastly different experience during the revolution and in the postrevolutionary process of modernization. While some readily worked for the modern nation, many were not selected or motivated to become the foremothers of revolutionary ideals. Instead, for women such as Lola la Chata and others mentioned in this book, the revolution brought upheaval and displacement. And yet this same upheaval also provided them with hands-on education in transnational trafficking along the border or within internal urban spaces in conflict that could serve as sites of peddling. During the apex of revolutionary zeal in the 1930s, a time that also witnessed global depression and an increased demand for drugs, certain women seized opportunities to consolidate narcotics empires by taking advantage of the weaknesses inherit in a state in transition.

By examining women as central figures in the drug trade, I interrogate the "public secret" of drugs, modernity, and nation.[33] Women and men of elite and lower classes and from diverse nations entered the trade, yet so too did the middle class. I argue that traffickers created cross-class and cross-ethnic alliances across the globe long before the term "globalization" even emerged.[34] Women adopted certain cultural and gendered roles to construct prominent criminal enterprises and crime families, but they also employed strategic essentialist arguments about gender and maneuvered to resist, undermine, manipulate, or co-opt police and government authorities.

Ironically, the family played a key role in smuggling alcohol and narcotics.[35] Parents trained and educated their children in the trade particularly to sell in places where adults would have been conspicuous, such as schools and playgrounds. As Nordstrom has noted, and many scholars of Latin America have confirmed, women are the center of the family and construct the basic elements of society and culture and, in turn, the nation.[36] Women create families whether men are present or not. Men have enjoyed more fluidity and movement historically and socially, but women forge the basic links of society: they produce food, provide daily necessities, and establish communal networks and market systems. The ability of women to do so ensures their and their children's survival. Their ability to forge substantial familial and communal networks ensured that certain women traffickers and peddlers remained in the trade for decades longer than many men. Thus the role of family as an integral part of both the informal and formal social networks that facilitated narcotics peddling is crucial.

In the first chapter, "Foreign Vices: Drugs, Modernity, and Gender," I examine the emergence of the shared narconarratives regarding race and moral degeneration in North America that created a transnational language of "vice." With the end of the Mexican Revolution and the rebuilding of the nation, public health drew considerable attention from new national leaders. With the establishment of the Secretaría de Salud (Department of Health), Mexican leaders attempted to modernize the nation and its people.

Due to its proximity to the United States, Mexico has played a key role in the smuggling of alcohol and drugs and as a site of transshipment of Asian and European opiates. Instead of recognizing drugs as both an internal and an external problem, Mexican revolutionary rhetoric and zeal became a tool wielded against immigrants. Mexican citizens' letters and organized groups led by men and women employed the language of the revolution and that of the new national goals to target internal enemies, who were blamed for the degeneration of the race (*la raza*).

On both sides of the border, government officials blamed foreign enemies within their midst for the introduction of narcotics and drug use. National leaders turned against their own citizens, constructing a national narrative of deviancy that they directed at various groups at different times. These campaigns targeted certain immigrants (whether legal or illegal) such as German and Chinese immigrants who were seen as collaborators in "racial tainting." Nationalist, racist, and gendered rhetoric fueled such campaigns, creating a collusion between policy and popular culture that spawned images of "users," "addicts," "sellers," and "victims."

In chapter 2, "Mules, Smugglers, and Peddlers: The Illicit Trade in Mexico, 1910s–1930s," I address smuggling, which created a controversy on both sides of the border in the context of the first war on drugs that emerged in the 1930s. I consider the transnational transformation of narcotics policing, peddling, and trafficking from the passage of the Harrison Narcotics Tax Act in the United States in 1914 to the rise and fall of Prohibition (1919–1933), which brought an even greater focus on narcotics. Beginning in the 1910s, the role of women in contraband, from the smuggling of certain items usually associated with women's traditional work such as sewing and cooking items to their role in the creation of chief narcotics ports along the U.S.-Mexico border and the establishment of transnational networks, drew more and more scrutiny from customs and police agencies.

Examining female bootleggers and the emergence of narcotics mules and smugglers in the wake of the Harrison Act, I explore how the shifting terrain of drug trafficking offered women economic opportunities. The U.S. and Mexican governments, particularly customs agents, responded to these shifts by collaborating in key international cases such as that of Maria Wendt, an infamous mule, whose arrest in California led to the dismantling of a global opium trafficking network based in Mexico City that extended across three continents.

In chapter 3, "The White Lady of Mexico City: Lola la Chata and the Remaking of Narcotics," I introduce a crime boss based in Mexico City. In 1945, President Manuel Ávila Camacho issued an arrest warrant for "public enemy number one" Lola la Chata (María Dolores Estévez Zuleta). She emerged as a heroin peddler par excellence in Mexico City and operated from the 1930s until her death in 1959. Her story was central to the struggle between narcotics peddlers and traffickers and the government. Her contacts within the Mexican police and government revealed the extent of her power, and her "golden arms" extended from Mexico to Toronto, where Canadian organized crime peddled Mexican heroin during a time when heroin abuse was allegedly declining due to World War II, a conflict that severed the heroin routes from Asia and Europe. Her career helped create the modern image of the Mexican drug trafficker as a prevailing threat, an image more commonly associated with men.

I examine the U.S.-Mexico border as a site of vice and danger in chapter 4, "Transcending Borders: La Nacha and the 'Notorious' Women of the North." Another famous trafficker and contemporary of Lola la Chata, Ignacia Jasso la viuda (widow) de González, also known as la Nacha, operated in Ciudad Juárez. La Nacha and other women of the border exemplified an ongoing negotiation of drug war policies along the U.S.-Mexico border. What makes la Nacha even more fascinating is her position as a transnational narcotics dealer whom the U.S. government attempted to extradite for violation of the Harrison Act in 1942 even though she had not been arrested in the United States.

La Nacha and her supporters successfully fought the extradition order and continued to operate as suppliers for peddlers in the United States. By the time of her death in the early 1980s, she, like Lola la Chata, had spawned a multigenerational peddling and trafficking family whose ties reached throughout Mexico and into the United States. Her life further illuminates the role of women as wives and mothers in the trade who created family-based enterprises.

In chapter 5, "The Women Who Made It Snow: Cold, Dirty Drug Wars, 1970s," I consider the shift of political and national focus in North America from heroin to cocaine. In 1975, the Drug Enforcement Administration (DEA) proclaimed "no antiwoman job bias in the narcotics trade," in response to key arrests of women from Argentina, Chile, Mexico, Colombia, and Venezuela who were involved in the trafficking of cocaine into the United States.

Beginning in the 1960s, Mexico served as a site of cocaine transshipment for the U.S. market, and women were key to that development. As the United States focused on the flow of heroin coming across the border from Mexico, new routes to move heroin emerged. The focus on the heroin trade ensured a shift from heroin to cocaine. Collaboration between U.S. and Mexican drug enforcement agents at the border disrupted flows from the south to the north and undermined certain organized crime trafficking families such as the Hernández organization in Tijuana. Those policing efforts led to a shift to other locations and the emergence of new players such as the Chilean Yolanda Sarmiento, who played a significant role in recentering the heroin market, demonstrating a transnational cross-ethnic alliance. "The Godmother" Griselda Blanco also emerged as a central transnational cocaine boss, who led DEA agents on a chase that lasted over ten years.

In the conclusion, "Gangsters, Narcs, and Women: A Secret History," I return to contemporary depictions of women in the drug economy as it flows across borders, to contextualize the representation of women in relation to depictions of masculinity. Male traffickers and narcotics agents are celebrated in song, literature, film, and other media. The victimization of women and children remains tangential to the encomiums of performative masculinity whether by drug traffickers, policing agents, bankers, or politicians.

CHAPTER ONE

FOREIGN VICES

Drugs, Modernity, and Gender

IN THE 1920S AND 1930S, MEXICAN OFFICIALS STRUGGLED TO UNITE people under new ideas of nationhood in the wake of the Mexican Revolution. That search for identity would come at the expense of Mexico's foreign-born population, who would become linked in the public mind—often falsely—to crime and drugs. Racializing crime occurred in the United States and Canada as well, and, in the 1920s and 1930s especially, foreign residents and citizens in all countries endured the public's fears of drugs and vice. Foreign men and women served as vehicles to construct arguments of deviancy but also new conceptions of nation. Chinese immigrants bore the brunt of these ideas, due to racism and because native-born and mestizo Mexicans perceived that they presented economic competition. Foreign-born men and women who used or trafficked drugs or who were perceived to have done so were sensationalized as threats to the emerging Mexican nation. In turn, immigrant doctors, businesspeople, pharmacists, and countless others found themselves labeled by their neighbors, including local and national politicians and bureaucrats as well as ordinary citizens, as the architects of vice and depravity. In other words, certain people associated other citizens or immigrants as illicit and dangerous to the emerging nation.

In April 1935, Juan de Dios Bojórquez, the secretary of the interior for the Mexican state of Durango, received a letter from M. Durán, a concerned citizen. In the letter, the author complained about his neighbor, Vida Nahum Altaled. He wrote:

YBP Library Services

CAREY, ELAINE, 1967-

WOMEN DRUG TRAFFICKERS: MULES, BOSSES, AND
ORGANIZED CRIME.
                              Paper   295 P.
ALBUQUERQUE: UNIV OF NEW MEXICO PRESS, 2014
SER: DIALOGOS.

AUTH: ST. JOHN'S UNIVERSITY. HISTORY OF WOMEN
INVOLVED IN DRUG TRADE FROM MEXICO TO US.
LCCN 2014002206
  ISBN 0826351980   Library PO# FIRM ORDERS

                              List   29.95 USD
  8395 NATIONAL UNIVERSITY LIBRAR   Disc   .0%
  App. Date 11/11/15   SOPS   8214-08 Net   29.95 USD

SUBJ: DRUG DEALERS--MEXICO--HIST.--20TH CENT.

CLASS HV5840   DEWEY# 363.45082097 LEVEL GEN-AC

YBP Library Services

CAREY, ELAINE, 1967-

WOMEN DRUG TRAFFICKERS: MULES, BOSSES, AND
ORGANIZED CRIME.
                              Paper   295 P.
ALBUQUERQUE: UNIV OF NEW MEXICO PRESS, 2014
SER: DIALOGOS.

AUTH: ST. JOHN'S UNIVERSITY. HISTORY OF WOMEN
INVOLVED IN DRUG TRADE FROM MEXICO TO US.
  LCCN 2014002206
  ISBN 0826351980   Library PO# FIRM ORDERS

                              List   29.95 USD
  8395 NATIONAL UNIVERSITY LIBRAR   Disc   .0%
  App. Date 11/11/15   SOPS   8214-08 Net   29.95 USD

SUBJ: DRUG DEALERS--MEXICO--HIST.--20TH CENT.

CLASS HV5840   DEWEY# 363.45082097 LEVEL GEN-AC

In this town [Durango] lives a woman of Turkish origin whose name is Vida Nahum Altaled who owns an establishment called the TIPTOP precisely in the main square, the source for most Durango addicts who require that which is indispensable to mitigate the effects of withdrawal.

Ms. Vida Nahum Altaled lives in a love relationship with her brother, and they make frequent trips to bring—as they say "new blood"—young women that they exploit in this city. . . . In the house of Nahum, people gamble and drink, and she provides drugs and women to her friends. She has never been punished due to the complicity of the Durango police that has to do with the police commander. Besides, this lady has entry papers to the Republic and then she has Izquierdo [the chief of police] to defend her when questioned. I hope these facts serve to help the work of moralization.[1]

Bojórquez pursued this citizen's complaint by forwarding the letter to the governor of the state of Durango. In turn, Bojórquez initiated a criminal investigation of Nahum and her brother Sam. When, how, or who conducted the investigation remained undocumented. Yet, by June 21, 1935, the investigation ended with Leopoldo Alvarado, the subsecretary of the state of Durango, concluding that Nahum Altaled "lived an honest life and was dedicated to her business of selling clothes." Moreover, she and her brother were not lovers, but Sam was living with her while he was getting a divorce.[2] Thus, the state of Durango closed the case.

Despite the brevity of the investigation, the siblings Vida and Sam Nahum illuminate the complex intersections between modernity, gender, alcohol and drug abuse, prostitution, and financial gain in ways that contrast with the ideals of a new nation with its focus on hygiene, sanitation, political order, and legal economic growth. The brother and sister drew the suspicion of their neighbors for a number of reasons. First, they were foreigners in a highly nationalistic postrevolutionary Mexico. Originally from Turkey—a country known for its production of opium—they made frequent trips abroad to conduct and support their clothing retail business. Their success as entrepreneurs appeared to have fueled the suspicions of their native-born neighbors.

Their perceived economic success, their country of origin, and their physical mobility drew concern from a fellow citizen at a time of heightened nationalism during the 1930s and growing concern over vices that might undermine the social health and hygiene of the nation. The Mexican government embarked on a campaign to improve social hygiene and people's health after years of revolution and economic stagnation. Its leaders turned to controlling vices such as selling and using drugs that they perceived degenerated the society and undermined the concepts of the new nation and the modernization efforts to rebuild the battered country.

After the revolution, Mexican elites relied upon and embraced certain narratives of European superiority that had circulated during the Porfiriato and the early years of Mexican modernization to set them apart from the lower classes.[3] Yet, these tropes grew complicated with evolving concepts of crime and nation. Thus, the Nahums' ability to accumulate wealth and establish a business that allegedly thrived on vice led the state government of Durango to undertake an investigation initiated by a single letter of complaint. The Nahums' ties to the police, asserted in the denunciation, also revealed an increasing local concern over police corruption in the postrevolutionary period. The perceived ability of foreigners to bribe and manipulate certain police officers for financial gain or protection led to considerable numbers of investigations and speculations. Moreover, Durán, the letter's author, suspected Vida, a successful immigrant woman, of sexual deviancy with her brother, buying into the era's rhetoric of xenophobic nationalism. One can only suspect that Durán may have owed her money or had an ongoing argument with the Nahums over disputed property or some other matter.

In the 1930s, after years of civil war and violence, the Mexican government tried to rebuild the nation and modernize. No easy task. From 1926, the Mexican revolutionary government encountered the Cristeros, a counterrevolutionary faction that protested many new anticlerical laws. Peasants and elites challenged the revolutionary government in other ways, undermining attempts to rebuild the nation.[4] Mexico endured years of upheaval that were then followed by efforts to rebuild and modernize the nation. During the revolutionary and then the Cristero fighting, the United States militarized its border with Mexico due to the flows of people fleeing the violence. Ironically, in the midst of this militarization, the United States embarked on its first war on drugs. As the violence subsided in Mexico, both nations became increasingly concerned about the impact of drug addiction on the health of their citizens—Mexicans and Americans—associating physical health with the general health of their respective nations.

The intersections between nation building and narcotics that arose from the 1910s to the early 1930s informed gender, race, nationalism, and modernity.[5] Mexico's official government policy shifted in step with that of the United States. These coordinated moves reveal the interconnectedness of policies on both sides of the border, a scenario that created shared narco-narratives. Rather than providing an extensive policy history, I will examine these themes through the quotidian experiences of people who transgressed certain spaces in the pursuit of profit. Their personal movements across borders and their passage through diverse social spaces generated similar discourses and ideas about drugs among both the elites and the emerging middle classes, and how they envisioned the lower classes and immigrants. In this era, from the 1910s to 1936, people were highly mobile, and their mobility illustrated a period of rapid change. Sources and documents from the era demonstrate how policy makers contextualized a shared language, experience, and rhetoric of narcotics that reflected concerns of "foreign contagion."[6] As elites adopted moral codes of conduct in North America, they constructed a gendered language of deviancy as it pertained to drug use, trafficking, and addiction.[7] In Mexico and the United States, immigrants—whether from Europe, Asia, or elsewhere in the Americas—became targets of repression and were depicted as a threat to the moral and physical health and the general good of the nation. The development of the "other" as a "contagion" shadowed national policies. Conversely, Mexican women in the drug trade, although lacking modern methodology and technology, were relentless in their entrepreneurial pursuits. Informed by Edward Said's *Orientalism*, I consider how the United States and Canada applied these internal constructs of deviancy to control their more exotic neighbor to the south, Mexico.[8]

A BRIEF HISTORY OF MEXICAN DOPE

The use of narcotics and mind-altering substances has a long history in Mexico. Fray Bernardino de Sahagún wrote about intoxicating mushrooms, or *teonánacatl* (flesh of the gods), in the sixteenth century.[9] Despite their interest in documenting the use of previously unknown plants, Spanish colonists in Mexico attempted to abolish the use of mind-altering substances among Amerindians in religious ceremonies. Their practices undermined the Spanish clergy's evangelization efforts.[10] Although ingesting psilocybin, the toxin found in certain mushrooms, remained common, the Spanish associated these practices with indigenous religious beliefs that were deemed offensive to the Catholic Church. Spanish clerics documented three separate types of psychoactive mushrooms, but there were actually many more—over fifty have now been identified.[11]

The struggle to control the use of mind-altering substances (such as mushrooms and other plants), narcotics (opiate derivatives such as morphine and heroin that induce sleepiness), and marijuana led to continued struggles and growing concern for scholars, medical professionals, and politicians that has continued into the modern period. By the Porfiriato, Sahagún's initial list of psychoactive plants of the sixteenth century had greatly expanded. Beginning in the 1700s, European travelers came to believe that marijuana was indigenous to Mexico because of its ubiquitous presence.[12] The idea that marijuana was indigenous to Mexico continued to circulate into the twentieth century, informing policy arguments in the United States to the present day. Marijuana actually is native to Asia, not the Americas, and the Spanish introduced marijuana (hemp) during the colonial era for the purpose of making rope. Yet, even scholars of narcotics associated marijuana with Mexican workers who allegedly introduced it to the United States.[13] Thus, marijuana usage became associated with Mexicans of working-class or lower-class origin, and the plant's origin itself remained an accepted "truth" about Mexico.

Notwithstanding, the cultivation of poppy and the production of opium and its derivatives grew in Mexico, although poppy too is not indigenous to the Americas. By the early 1800s, poppy had been introduced in Mexico, particularly in the northern states, by Chinese immigrants who grew it for medicinal and personal use. In the late 1800s and early 1900s, poppy was grown in Sinaloa, Chihuahua, and Durango, and it later spread to Tamaulipas and Veracruz.[14] By the 1870s, poppy could be found in Michoacán, Nayarit, Oaxaca, Chiapas, and Guerrero, as well as northern Guatemala.[15] Mexico as well as Guatemala provided an excellent environment for poppy cultivation due to the soil and to mostly full sun exposure for much of the year.

Travelers to Mexico in the 1800s circulated the belief that the Mexican people were especially prone to vices and alcoholism, but few travelers directly and specifically discussed the use of narcotics or marijuana.[16] Their journals documented the exotic aspects of Mexico, accounts similar to narratives written about Asia and Africa. Marijuana, opium, and cocaine could be found, but their intoxicating features only entered the popular imagination of Mexicans by the mid- to late 1800s. Narratives of drug use and alcoholism came to be associated with Mexicans. In Mexico, people found items such as cocaine cordials and opiate derivatives such as morphine and heroin on the shelves of local pharmacies, just as they did in the rest of North America. Yet that availability was reduced in the 1910s and 1920s due to the revolution, which cut off supply lines.

Mexico's role in Andean cocaine and Asian heroin flows emerged early in the 1900s, much to the consternation of officials influenced by the concerns of northern diplomats, ministers, politicians, and policing agents. At international meetings prior to the Mexican Revolution, politicians, ministers, and medical doctors gathered to construct policies to stem the flow of narcotics. The United States became increasingly concerned about opiate use during its occupation of the Philippines after the Spanish-American War. The prevalence of opium use in the Philippines troubled missionaries, who in turn reported their findings to U.S. government officials.[17] For example, Episcopal minister Charles H. Brent traveled to the Philippines, where he noted the use of narcotics; his experience there led to his global campaign against narcotics, which was adopted by the United States.[18]

By the early 1900s, Brent's influence on the question of narcotics and trafficking had taken hold. Controlling international drug flows led to a growing interest in Mexico. In their report to the U.S. Senate, the American delegates to the International Opium Conference, Bishop Brent, Hamilton Wright, and Henry J. Ford, reported a growing crisis south of the border that they believed would continue to have serious implications.

> A recently enacted Canadian statute not only forbids the importation of this form of the drug, but its manufacture, transshipment, or exportation. The Attorney General has held that under our opium-exclusion act of February 9, 1909 prepared opium may not be imported into the United States for immediate transshipment. Mexico has no law on the subject. The result is that the great mass of Macanise opium is brought to San Francisco and immediately transshipped by sea to Western Mexican ports, from whence it is added to the direct Mexican import, is mostly smuggled into the United States across the Mexican border.[19]

Although Mexico produced opiates, in the early 1900s it also served as a site of transshipment of Asian contraband, whether opiates or Chinese workers, to the United States. Lack of oversight in Mexican ports drew suspicion from the country's northern neighbors. With the emerging drug war and the inflammatory rhetoric that surrounded drug abuse and criminal trafficking, U.S. officials and social reformists demanded greater control over the Mexican ports.[20] In the end, Mexico's northern neighbors would have to wait more than a decade for an improvement in Mexican law enforcement, due to the outbreak of the Mexican Revolution.

Along with growing international concern about the lack of port security, the issue of drug use also caused concern among Mexican criminologists during the Porfiriato. Carlos Roumagnac, in his well-analyzed and historicized work *Los criminales en México: ensayo de psicología criminal* published in 1904, documented the use of marijuana among male and female prisoners.[21] He wrote:

> Marijuana . . . is well known; it is a grass that is smoked and causes a delirious drunkenness. The "drunken" marijuana user becomes a lunatic; and once he has contracted the vice, he delivers himself to it until he succumbs. It is, along with *pulque*, one of greatest and terrible national dangers. Therefore its sale must be rigorously prohibited.[22]

Roumagnac's work may have created an early version of "reefer madness," an illogical fear of marijuana that swept the United States in the 1920s and 1930s. In his interviews, prisoners discussed their use of marijuana, but few reported psychotic outbreaks, and marijuana then, like today, served as a form of currency in prisons. Using a variety of means, prisoners' friends and families routinely smuggled it inside. Roumagnac found that women braided it into their hair, passed it to prisoners in baskets of fruits and vegetables, or hid it in food products like tamales. Some men and women visiting their imprisoned friends and family members stuffed the heels of their shoes with marijuana and passed tobacco cigarettes that were in fact marijuana or laced with marijuana.[23] Despite Roumagnac's claim that the Porfirian regime prohibited the formal sale of marijuana, men, women, and children sold it openly on the streets and in markets. It even appeared in songs, in the early 1900s, that told of its uses and pleasures.

Despite Roumagnac's pragmatic views about the formality of the law, the internal marijuana trade within and beyond prison walls carried on as usual. Those legal regulations and controls had to be reintroduced after the Mexican Revolution. More significantly, as an early criminologist, Roumagnac's studies of crime and criminal behavior intersected with his own racialized and

Figure 1. Basket of confiscated goods. Serie Mariguana, opio, y drogas, ca. 1935, 142917, Casasola, Mexico City, Fototeca Nacional del Instituto Nacional de Anthropología e Historia (INAH), Pachuca, Hidalgo.

elitist views of criminal behavior. His early work did not disappear with the Mexican Revolution; instead, it found a growing audience that considered crime and criminality a detriment to progress and development. As Mexicans struggled to redefine national identity after the Porfiriato, a new narrative that associated depravity with race and ethnicity inserted social hygiene as a central component of nation building. Ironically, despite views that the Porfirian era triggered excesses and vice, many of the proponents of social hygiene programs employed similar ideas and concepts from the era that they criticized. In the midst of the chaos of war, certain Mexican states attempted to control the production and consumption of narcotics and alcohol. In the wake of the 1912 International Opium Conference, Mexican leaders too sought to respond to the global shift to control production. By 1916, the Constitutionalists, who had gained control of the government, issued the first federal laws controlling narcotics distribution and use.[24] President and leader of the Constitutionalists, Venustiano Carranza, decreed it illegal to produce, consume, and sell narcotics throughout Mexico. The

newly formed Departamento de Salubridad (Department of Health) held the
only rights to import and distribute morphine, heroin, and cocaine for medicinal purposes. The department also maintained control of particular substances produced in Mexico: marijuana and opium.[25]

In 1917, the delegate to the Constitutional Convention from Coahuila,
Dr. José María Rodríguez, requested the creation of the Consejo de
Salubridad General (Department of Public Health) to support and expand
public health initiatives to facilitate modernization. Initially, the Department
of Health focused its efforts on fighting diseases such as yellow fever and
sleeping sickness through the use of vaccinations. Its social workers also
struggled to remove raw sewage from public streets in many cities. Through
research and international conferences and communication, the department
sought new models that had been adopted in Europe and the United States,
and it reported them to the federal government, issuing studies and propos-
ing projects that could be adopted in Mexico. In 1919, Rodríguez petitioned
the Mexican president and Congress to fight syphilis by implementing educational campaigns to promote effective condom use and by issuing a certificate of health to couples who married.[26] These requests mimicked those
reforms advocated by the Bureau of Social Hygiene in the United States,
funded by John D. Rockefeller. Rockefeller, too, was gravely concerned about
drug abuse, since it contributed to illness, undermined workers' ability to
perform their jobs, and ultimately destroyed the lives of men and women.[27]

Like in the United States, Rodríguez's department also issued statements
that reflected a growing public concern about drug and alcohol abuse. He
suggested that the Department of Public Health should "correct this sickness
of the people (la raza) principally provoked by alcoholism and medicinal
drugs such as opium, morphine, ether, cocaine, and marijuana." As a medical professional, he recognized that such substances were necessary for medicinal purposes, but when abused, they contributed to the degeneration of
the people and ran counter to nation building. Later, the department would
focus on alcohol abuse, but also opium, marijuana, heroin, and cocaine
abuse, because drug use had spread across class and ethnic lines.[28]

CONTROLLING THE DEGENERATES

By 1920, Edmundo G. Aragón, the secretary-general of the Department of
Health, implemented restrictions and limitations on the cultivation and

distribution of products that "foment vice and that degenerate the people." The federal government required that the Department of Health grant permissions and maintain records of businesspeople and medical professionals who wished to import opium, morphine, heroin, or cocaine. These products could only be imported for medicinal purposes issued by medical doctors and pharmacists. Previously, the United States and Canada had passed similar laws.

By 1921, provisional president Adolfo de la Huerta's administration further considered the problem of narcotics trafficking. The Department of Health submitted a report to the president summarizing U.S. controls on narcotics and the history of Mexico's involvement in international agreements and meetings.[29] Enclosed in the report was a Spanish translation of the 1912 International Convention on Opium. Federico Gamboa represented Mexico at The Hague for the conference. Delegates debated and formalized a treaty to control the distribution of raw opium "to limit exclusively to medicinal and legitimate purposes the manufacture, sale, and use of medicinal opium, morphine, cocaine, and heroin and all new derivatives of these products."[30]

Gamboa signed the agreement, but the Mexican Senate never approved it, nor did the president at the time sign it.[31] Because of the political instability of the revolutionary period, the Mexican government did not consider the opium convention to be a priority. This changed ten years later in 1923 when the Department of Health asked the president to ratify the convention in order to establish better control over opium.[32] In the 1920s, debates in Mexico about narcotics control illustrated shifting disagreements about modernization and nationalism in the country. With the requests from the Department of Health, President Álvaro Obregón (1920–1924) finally signed the 1912 Opium Convention and prohibited the import of opium (morphine and heroin) as well as cocaine in 1923, except for medicinal purposes. The United States and Canada, however, pressured the Mexican government to enact additional restrictions in the 1920s.

Legal changes in the United States began in 1906 with the passage of the Pure Food and Drug Act and evolved with the 1914 Harrison Narcotics Tax Act, the 1922 Narcotic Drugs Import and Export Act, and the 1924 Heroin Act; however, actual drug enforcement was meager. The Pure Food and Drug Act dismantled the patent remedies industry in the United States, in which consumers easily found opiates and cocaine in everything from gripe water (treatment for colic in children and toddlers) to love potions and

asthma treatments. These American initiatives as well as the increasing
number of medical studies on narcotics use helped determine the legislative
agenda in Mexico after 1920. Druggists and doctors on both sides of the
border did not welcome many of these legislative restrictions and vigorously
fought them, questioning whether politicians should legislate how doctors
treated their patients. Patients feared that the laws would render their accustomed relief-giving prescriptions illegal.[33]

In the 1920s, American druggists maintained patients in violation of the
law by selling items such as Dover's Powder (which contained opium) in
places like Elmira, New York, and Mobile, Alabama. They sold Godfrey's
Cordial (which also contained opium) over the counter to addicts, although
its use had originally been for colicky babies.[34] Some infants died from
opium poisoning due to such remedies. In 1927, legally supplied addicts could
be found in cities across the United States, much to the chagrin of social
workers and narcotics officers. Treatment remained a viable option for these
addicts, rather than criminalization. Congressman Stephen G. Porter, chair-
man of the Foreign Affairs Committee and the American delegation to the
Geneva Opium Convention of 1925, criticized the new drug laws by arguing
that

> they contain no measure calculated to relieve those unfortunates
> who, through their own weakness of otherwise, have become vic-
> tims of drug addiction, and to place them in a position where they
> may once again assume the responsible duties of citizenship. The
> treatment of those given to drug addiction, important as it is from
> a humanitarian standpoint, is equally, if not more, important in its
> relation to the clandestine and illicit traffic of narcotics.[35]

These types of complaints led to the development of "narcotics farms" for
men and women to treat their addictions while prohibiting ambulatory care
for addicts.[36] Narcotics farms in the United States treated addicts in a resi-
dential setting. Of course, the farms also served as laboratories for scientists
to study narcotics addiction and use.

Because international borders facilitated addicts' ability to access drugs,
reformers focused on more effective means of policing. In Tacoma,
Washington, the Bureau of Social Hygiene reported that addicts traveled to
Vancouver, British Columbia, where they allegedly purchased as much heroin and morphine as they wanted.[37] Despite Canada's own early drug war

and the imposition of control that began prior to similar action in the United States, Canada, like Mexico, captured the imagination of U.S. reformers as a source of supply and transshipment beginning in the 1920s. That idea continues to the present, with fears of Colombian drug lords exchanging cocaine for crystal meth in the 1980s or American psychologist Timothy Leary potentially convincing Canadian youth to "turn on, tune in, and drop out."[38]

Coastal cities and those along the U.S.-Canada and U.S.-Mexico borders were key ports for transshipment. Borders also served as sites where the United States' constructs of deviance grew more rigid, particularly with regard to the southern border in the wake of Prohibition (1920–1933). Along the borders, zones of tolerance welcomed U.S. business travelers and tourists to border towns where Americans could freely drink and engage in sex tourism. Cities such as Tijuana, Ciudad Juárez, and even Windsor, Ontario, became associated with vice. Parents' organizations and women's groups challenged the zones of tolerance that flourished on both borders.

In the 1920s, U.S. public health professionals wondered whether Mexican drug addiction and deviance was more a myth than a reality. Charles Edward Terry, who worked for the Bureau of Social Hygiene and conducted its 1927 study on narcotics use, claimed that in El Paso, few Mexicans consulted medical doctors and few used narcotics. Instead, he wrote,

> The poverty of the patient and the disinclination of Mexican physicians to prescribe narcotics make for a very low Mexican legal per capita use. It is noticeable that prescriptions including narcotics issued to Mexicans, were in the large majority of cases, written by American physicians. It was also noted that the number of prescriptions was considerably less in the Mexican drug stores in proportion to their other trade than in the American drug stores, and that ratio of narcotic prescriptions to the general file of prescriptions in the Mexican drug stores was about one-half that obtaining in the American drug stores, although both Americans and Mexicans patronized Mexican drug stores. This feature was so outstanding that it is believed the legal use of narcotics for Mexicans was practically negligible.[39]

Terry appeared to blame American medical doctors for encouraging legalized addiction among Mexicans even though U.S. public health officials and narcotics policing agents ignored their historically low rates of drug use. Their nation's low numbers of addicts compared to the United States was not lost on Mexican officials. Terry argued that Mexicans in El Paso turned to traditional methods to treat illnesses rather than seek out opiates. Even the U.S. Internal Revenue Service noted that the lowest levels of drug use in the 1920s occurred in those southwestern American states that directly bordered Mexico. The two coasts harbored the largest number of addicts: California and Washington in the West and Massachusetts, New York, New Jersey, Maryland, and Virginia in the East. States along the Mississippi River also had more addicts than those states that bordered Mexico.[40]

Along with signing the conventions in the 1920s, Mexican officials also recognized that its trade policies regarding alcohol and drugs had to shift due to events that took place in the north. With the passage of the Eighteenth Amendment inaugurating Prohibition, the United States purportedly went dry, and the U.S. temperance movement did not go unnoticed in Mexico.[41] In Mexico, alcohol and distilleries remained legal, but the flow of its legal commodities across the U.S.-Mexico border, always a moderately lucrative trade, now generated greater profits. Prohibition created new organized crime networks in the United States that spread to cities and other locations where there had earlier been little evidence of organized crime. The growth of organized crime also triggered an increase in policing within the Department of the Treasury. That period of history continues to feed the popular imagination with films, television series, and books. The prohibition of alcohol in the United States triggered arrangements among various parties with regard to the trafficking of alcohol, but it also facilitated the rise of transnational criminal networks that later adapted to other revenue streams once alcohol was made legal again in 1933.

Upon attaining an agreement with Canada for greater control over the smuggling of booze, the United States sent a document to the Mexican president as well as a cover letter suggesting a similar agreement with Mexico.[42] Mexico agreed to work closely with the U.S. Treasury Department in 1925 to prevent the illegal exportation of alcoholic products into the United States. Perhaps sensing business opportunities and revenues, government officials also allowed former U.S. distilleries and brewers to reincorporate in Mexico. For its part, the Canadian government refused to provide assurances to the U.S. government that it would prevent ships loaded with legally produced goods that were illegal in the United States to leave Canadian ports.[43] Mexican and U.S officials met and established an agreement that regulated a variety of items including alcohol, narcotics, food products, and people. The two governments planned to cooperate with one another through customs to control narcotics.

As a signatory to the opium conventions, the Mexican government received reports about international seizures of opium and drugs from the League of Nations. Many of these took place in China and Europe, particularly in Germany.[44] Although it is difficult to ascertain whether these reports played any role in the crackdown on foreigners in Mexico, by 1925 President Plutarco Elías Calles (1924–1928) had ordered the police department to arrest all narcotics users and dealers. He also demanded the immediate deportation of all foreigners in Mexico who were involved in trafficking and consumption.[45] Calles also responded to U.S. ambassador James Rockwell Sheffield's request to limit the importation and movement of Asian opium through Mexico and into the United States by smugglers, whether Chinese, American, or Mexican.[46] In turn, on April 10, 1926, *Diario Official*, the official publication of Mexico's executive branch, announced cooperation with the United States to control the importation of illegal items, including narcotics, and illegal immigration. Moreover, *Diario Official* reported:

> It is the obligation of the U.S. and Mexico to prevent the smuggling of prohibited goods and to authorize that strict levees in accordance with the agreements of both parties be included in the prohibition of narcotics that can not be imported into Mexico, but under conditions that preserve our Health Act.[47]

Mexico participated in international conferences in which officials described the country's legislative and punitive changes. At the 1926 First World Conference on Narcotic Education in Philadelphia, Consul Don Basilio Bulnes reported to the delegates that the importation of narcotics into Mexico was illegal except with special permission and only for medicinal purposes. Those who sought to import had to apply to the Department of Health for permission and maintain strict records. Drugs could only be imported through six ports: Progreso and Veracruz on the Gulf of Mexico; La Paz and Mazatlán on the Pacific coast; and through the land ports of Nogales and Nuevo Laredo.[48] He clarified that any products not collected from the customhouse went to auction, but only those with permission from the Department of Health could bid and purchase.

With regard to drug use, Bulnes reported that *Cannabis indica*, or "Indian hay," was used only by "the lowest and worst type of people, and for that reason, perhaps, is the cause of many crimes."[49] Participants at the conference asked about the poppy that flowed north. Bulnes stated that he had heard of poppy cultivation in Sonora within the "big colony of Chinamen," but that the government prohibited its cultivation and had stopped all opium production within the country.[50] Perhaps to tweak the noses of those who blamed Mexico for the proliferation of opium, marijuana, and cocaine, Bulnes stated that he had heard that there had been attempts to cultivate poppy in New York's Central Park. He stated: "So, in a place favored with such marvelous police protection as you have in New York, is it to be wondered that down in Mexico, in the desolation of our state there, that men can succeed in growing things against the law, and that the opium poppy can be cultivated there in defiance of the law? It is really unlawful in Mexico to cultivate, import, export, or manufacture opium."[51]

Although Mexico had begun to control the flows of alcohol and drugs into and out of the country, the policies that it implemented in the 1920s continued to draw criticism from the United States. U.S. officials complained that prominent government officials had been involved in growing and producing drugs since the 1910s. U.S. customs agents reported that the governor of Baja California, General Esteban Cantú (1914–1920), had granted leases to opium producers and smugglers. He and his brother José, who worked for Mexican customs, as well as his father-in-law all financially benefited from revenues generated by opium traffickers.[52] Cantú's financial wealth from drug trafficking ensured that U.S. customs and treasury inspectors and officials routinely questioned the involvement of those in power with the drug trade.

To stem the introduction of narcotics and perhaps to dispute the public image of corruption, the Mexican government reported to international monitoring organizations that drugs on import licenses not claimed within the proper time were to be sold at public auction by the Importation Customhouse in Mexico City. Confiscated drugs illegally imported were also sold in the same manner.[53] Mexican officials reported that fines from 25 to 5,000 pesos were imposed. At that time, the government did not require jail time, as opposed to the Harrison Act in the United States, which imposed a fine of $2,000 ($25,900 in 2012 dollars) and imposed a five-year prison term.[54] The lack of an eradication policy for legal and illegal narcotics in Mexico as well as a lack stringent penalties for distribution of narcotics continued to be a source of ire for U.S. officials.

Mexican officials and scientists struggled against a host of problems that hindered nation building including syphilis, alcoholism, prostitution, and drugs. Politicians and social welfare activists continued to seek ways to lower rates of addiction and avoid producing more addicts. In universities and among medical professionals, nationalism infused the scientific community in its search for answers and treatments. On December 21, 1927, Dr. Demetrio López submitted a report to the Department of Health titled "Manifesto on Narcotic Substances That Are Not Habit Forming and Do Not Contribute to the Degeneration of the People" in which he outlined analogous pharmaceutical drugs that could be used in place of cocaine or opiates in medical settings to avoid addiction.[55] Using the language that circulated in the rhetoric of the executive government and the Department of Health about the degeneration of the races, López's research sought to improve the nation by using substances to treat illnesses that avoided provoking addiction among the people. The doctor recognized the need for narcotics to treat a host of ailments, but he, like most public health officials, saw addiction as contributing to a feeble nation. Like social workers and public health officials, people such as López sought to treat the ill to improve the collective social hygiene of the nation. Of course, attempts to seek analogous drugs often simply swapped one addiction for another, such as using heroin as a step down from morphine addiction.

Mexican authorities addressed the continued flow of drugs from a public health stance and to improve Mexico's diplomatic standing in the world by modernizing the nation's narcotics laws. But nation building and narcotics enforcement took on a potentially dangerous tone when race was injected into the public discourse. Public health officers studied the laws, policies, and changing criminological studies that were being promulgated worldwide. Criminologists, medical and public health professionals, and politicians debated revisions to Mexican policies in the pages of such publications as *Eugénica: Boletín de la Sociedad Eugénica Mexicana para el Mejoramiento de la Raza*, *Eugenesia: Higiene y Cultura Física para el Mejoramiento de la Raza*, and *Criminologia*.[56] These academic publications connected narcotics use, race, and public health in the popular imagination of the educated and the elite.

Eugenics and drug use reinforced one another in North America. Experts argued that weaker races were far more prone to drug use, which thus endangered the health of the nation. The United States, in particular, informed much of this debate. The U.S. Treasury and later the Bureau of

Narcotics placed greater pressure on the Mexican government to clean up its country, pushing notions of degenerate drug users. The concept of "degenerate" in Mexico mimicked the definitions used north of the border, infusing racialized social hierarchies.

FOREIGN MENACE

Tightening the laws regulating the production and distribution of narcotics did not stem the possibilities for economic advancement by some Mexican citizens willing to take risks. On both sides of the border, many could not resist the potential profits to be derived from illegal alcohol and drugs. By the 1920s, traffickers had found that, due to the upheaval of Mexico's revolution and the lack of oversight at central ports, Asian opium easily entered Mexico and then could be moved north to supply the growing demand in the United States. In all three places, race, drug use, and trafficking easily reinforced one another.[57]

In the United States and Canada, drug use and criminal behavior reinforced concepts of "nation," leading to a tightening of immigration laws during the 1920s. Ideas and theories about racial degeneration provoked by Chinese immigration and their alleged ability to intoxicate native-born Americans, Canadians, and Mexicans encouraged anti-Chinese sentiment as well as the equation of drug use with deviance. These tropes flowed across borders and informed policy and public health campaigns. In turn, all three countries began to associate drug use with the "otherness" of certain foreign immigrants, who, it was believed, brought their vices to North America and undermined nation building.

As in the United States and Canada, Mexicans were not immune to these racialized ideas that portrayed certain people as not part of their nation or its goals. Beginning in the 1920s, Mexican nativists associated Jews, Middle Easterners, and Chinese with deviance, drugs, and prostitution. These tropes infused scholarly and political debates. As the elite and ruling classes circulated racist and xenophobic narratives of deviance in their diplomatic and public health meetings, citizens' groups embraced these discourses and developed their own campaigns against "the other." Significantly, Mexican women appeared as both the victims of foreign degenerates and collaborators with them in the tainting of the nation when they married and bore children with foreign men who injected the nation with crime and vice.

As an example of these shared narconarratives of deviance, consider the following. In the United States, the passage of the Harrison Act in 1914 led to a crackdown on drug trafficking and traffickers. Some of these busts demonstrated that women were heavily involved in drug trafficking. In 1917, the *Los Angeles Times* reported that police had dismantled the largest transnational drug smuggling ring operating in the United States for violation of the Harrison Act.[58] Police had earlier arrested Oscar Kirshon and Max Singer, two smugglers in New York City, who turned state informants by offering evidence. Their testimony led to the dismantling of what was claimed to be one of the most lucrative dope rings on the east and west coasts.[59] That million-dollar-a-year (2012: $18,072,000) bicoastal enterprise moved heroin and opium from Canada and Mexico into California. With cooperation from the New York smugglers turned informants, authorities in California reported that they had taken into custody Charles Cohn, Louis Bernzaft, Max Steiner, Joseph Smith, Sam Levy, Alexander Gladstone, Max Silverstein, and Mrs. Eva Silverstein. During a raid of the Silversteins' apartment, police discovered $60,000 (2012: $1,084,000) worth of morphine and heroin. The police reported that the drugs originated in both Canada and Mexico. The arrest of Eva Silverstein—the lone woman—garnered major media attention, and she was labeled the "queen" of the ring.[60] The *Los Angeles Times* reproduced only her image, and not those of her colleagues. Using a portrait probably found during the raid, the newspaper showed Silverstein dressed in a shirt coat while resting her head to the left on her index finger, with her hair in tidy buns on either side of her head. She appeared more a union leader or a working-class suffragette than an international drug smuggler. Speculation about Silverstein's role in narcotics trafficking led to the supposition that her husband was an addict, or perhaps she herself was.[61]

Another woman, Sadie Stock, developed a lucrative transnational business in the 1920s by using an emerging seaport in Baja California to traffic opiates from Mexico to the United States.[62] By land, limited amounts of heroin and other opiates could be hidden under women's skirts or strapped to their legs. Stock, a successful businesswoman, demonstrated a technological and entrepreneurial innovation that yielded far greater profits, using Mexican ports to transship contraband to the United States by sea. U.S. federal agents arrested Stock and her chauffer, Oscar Dusel, on August 4, 1924, in San Diego.[63] In their search, agents seized large amounts of narcotics, jewelry, and $22,000 (2012: $297,000) in cash. Stock insisted that she planned to use the money to pay her income tax, but to no avail. With Stock's arrest, agents reported that they had dismantled one of the most successful narcotics syndicates in the United States. She had ties in Europe, Asia, and Mexico, and she received her shipments of opium from Asia through ports in Ensenada, Mexico; she also received shipments of other drugs from Germany.[64] From Ensenada, she moved her merchandise into the United States, where she supplied much of the heroin consumed in California and the Pacific Northwest. Immediately after her arrest, Stock posted a $15,000 bond. Her attorney paid Dusel's $5,000 bond. Later, Stock went to trial, but she was released on a technicality that was not publicly disclosed. Calexico-Mexicali as a central narcotics port was overshadowed by Tijuana–San Diego toward the end of the 1920s, due to the activities of women such as Stock. In the 1930s, Stock had not given up her involvement in drugs. She appeared to still be trafficking, working with a Mexican partner through the Calexico-Mexicali port.[65]

Both Silverstein and Stock served to reinforce xenophobic and gendered notions of drug trafficking. As immigrants, they drew suspicion and bolstered preconceptions that certain immigrants were prone to such behavior.[66] Furthermore, the fact that women had been heavily involved as either a partner, in the case of Silverstein, or a boss, in the case of Stock, reinforced assumptions that foreign women were apt to behave badly. This further created suppositions about masculinity, that foreign men lacked the ability to control their women or, alternatively, that they forced women into criminal acts that undermined the women's physical and moral health and also that of their adopted nation. The reference to Silverstein as a "queen" in the drug trade marks a recurring rhetorical device in reference to women in the trade that is now a century in use. Queens like Silverstein used illicit businesses to get rich, simultaneously undermining their adopted nation by poisoning its citizens.

During the 1920s, California ranked third among the states for convictions for narcotics traffickers under the Harrison Act. Consequently, state officials became increasingly concerned about drug use.[67] In 1926, the California legislature estimated that addicts in their state spent $6.00 a day (2012: $78.00) on average on drugs. State officials in California and elsewhere viewed addicts as a criminal and financial drain on state resources. The report from the California legislature proclaimed: "These addicts prey upon the state to the extent of from $4,300,000 to $7,000,000 per year without estimating the indirect cost of crime, the strain on our law enforcement system, our police, our judiciary, our penal institutions, jails, and prisons."[68] Recidivism also reinforced perceptions of addicts as costly criminals in many state and federal reports.[69] It seemed to state officials and the public that drug addicts could not be cured.

Narcotics garnered more and more attention from politicians, public health workers, the police, criminologists, and medical professionals in the 1920s. At international, national, and state meetings in the United States, Mexico, and Canada, attendees searched for a means to treat addicts and to punish traffickers and peddlers. Ideas ranged from complete isolation of addicts, to narcotics farms, to imprisonment. These meetings intersected with an ongoing interest in eugenics in all three countries. Cases like those of Silverstein and Stock fueled xenophobic attitudes and incited attacks in the United States.

In Mexico, officials echoed American rhetoric and denounced the plague of foreigners, whom they blamed for introducing drugs and trafficking in Mexico. Significantly, the constructions of alleged criminality of certain groups and their alleged association to narcotics flowed across borders just as narcotics and people did. As traffickers and couriers serendipitously moved opiates and cocaine across international boundaries, those battling against narcotics met in various venues to decry this scourge of the modern age and to introduce, exchange, and perpetrate their criminological and racialized ideas.

In the 1920s, Mexican president Plutarco Calles, a native of Sonora, brought certain racial ideas with him to national office. Sonora had a history of anti-Chinese sentiment that was as long as Chinese immigration to Mexico itself. Since the seventeenth century, Asian men had migrated from the Philippines to Mexico City to conduct commerce.[70] In Mexico City, Chinese men developed businesses. After the passage of the Chinese Exclusion Act in the United States in 1882, many Chinese laborers went south and settled in Baja California and Sonora in Mexico.[71] There, immigrant communities developed with transnational links to China but also to the United States, Canada, Cuba, and other parts of the Americas. These communities fostered entrepreneurial partnerships in company towns that served mines and railroads, many owned and operated by Americans.[72] Thus, Chinese immigrants operated laundries, restaurants, and other businesses that served miners and railroad workers. Regardless of the contributions of Chinese immigrants to North America, anti-Chinese sentiment traveled across borders, circulated in the press and literature, and was popularized through jokes and caricatures.

On a global scale, Mexico's entry under Calles into the diplomacy associated with narcotics control further exacerbated xenophobia and led Mexicans to target nationalities that were consistently mentioned in League of Nations narcotics reports: Chinese, Middle Easterners, and Jews. Negative depictions of immigrants circulated in the press. Moreover, Mexican citizens', workers', and women's groups viewed their foreign-born compatriots with suspicion whether they were German pharmacists, Middle Eastern merchants, or Chinese businesspeople. They would often "report" suspected violations to authorities. Thus, Mexicans of foreign birth increasingly found themselves the subjects of police investigations for narcotics violations and raids whether they were laborers or professionals, including doctors and pharmacists.

Like in the United States and Canada, Mexican officials demanded that doctors and pharmacists accept greater oversight due to their obvious associations with narcotics and cocaine. Official reports from all three countries demonstrate the vast discrepancies in prescribing practices among medical professionals, even veterinarians. Early debates over addiction and peddling included discussion of medical professionals, who were sometimes characterized as addicts themselves or as unprofessional dope doctors who simply sought to turn a profit at the expense of citizens, thus contributing to the degeneration of the nation, whether in the United States, Canada, or Mexico. Drugs, eugenics, and sexuality combined to create narratives of vice that relied upon racist narratives.

In the mid-1920s, the laws in Mexico regarding the import and distribution of narcotics changed as they had in the United States and Canada. Like their northern colleagues, doctors and pharmacists in Mexico now had to maintain stricter accounting procedures for opiates and cocaine. Just as in the United States and Canada, Mexican authorities were gravely concerned about the role that professionals played in the distribution of narcotics. In turn, part of the Penal Code, the Código Sanitario y los Reglamentos, was rewritten to abide by many of the demands of the United States and other Western powers.[73] Abiding by the changing laws, pharmacist Lamberto Hernández, the proprietor of Droguería Mexicana in Mexico City, listed all the narcotics he had in his pharmacy in 1927, and Emilio Kentler, owner and pharmacist of Droguería y Farmacia Iturbide in Mexico City, also sent a list of his inventory to the Department of Health.[74] Both pharmacists listed inventories of over eleven kilos of medicinal opium and less than two kilos of cocaine.

Figure 2. Public officials with doctors probably associated with drug
trafficking. Serie Mariguana, opio, y drogas, ca. 1935, 142911, Casasola,
Mexico City, Fototeca Nacional del Instituto Nacional de
Anthropología e Historia (INAH), Pachuca, Hidalgo.

Like in the United States and Canada, Mexico's Department of Health
compiled lists of doctors arrested for distribution of opiates and cocaine.
In all three countries, health professionals felt attacked by people who were
not part of the medical profession even as debates regarding maintenance
programs for addicts flowed across borders. What has been less frequently
addressed in the historiography is interprofessional squabbling over drugs.
Foreign medical professionals in Mexico came under attack from their native colleagues. Medical colleagues and associates wrote letters of complaint about each other, as in 1929, when Julio M. González testified that
Hugo Schroeder engaged in the drug trade in Mexico City. He stated:

Dr. Hugo Schroeder is dedicated to prescribing narcotics to addicts.
. . . He gives recipes in which he prescribes morphine sulfate

accompanied by various other substances to be taken in the form of pomade or spoons, but he also gives them [addicts] prescriptions written in German and typed on a typewriter, signed by himself and directed to Herr Markenson, owner of the pharmacy on Avenida Juárez. The message written in German recommends the pharmacist to fill the recipes that include morphine or heroin.[75]

González's letter embraced xenophobia but also questioned other aspects of Schroeder's professional standards. Schroeder's use of technology and language drew criticism. The use of German ensured that the pharmacist who filled the prescriptions would have to be literate in German as well as Spanish. Thus, the pharmacist who filled the prescription was most likely another German speaker. Rather than believing that the doctor was merely offering economic support to another business within the German immigrant community, from one professional to another, González saw Schroeder's actions as potentially criminal. Schroeder used a typewriter rather than handwriting to give specific directions on how to mix the concoction, and gave directives on how to avoid detection by public health, police, and medical authorities, González charged. According to González, Schroeder and the pharmacist Markenson were conspiring to sell illegal drugs. For authorities to detect the crime, they would have to be literate in German and have a highly sophisticated knowledge of chemistry or pharmacology. Cases like this, in which medical professionals reported on each other to the authorities, were commonplace in this dense atmosphere of suspicion.

In another case in 1931, Dr. A. Perales Vega demanded that the Health Department investigate Dr. C. L. H. Medici de Birón for the illegal distribution of morphine. Perales attached an example of one of Medici's prescriptions to prove that he was a notorious dope doctor. Perales also enclosed a signed statement from one Señora Sara Valdívar stating that Medici had given her a *papelito* of morphine. Perales alleged that Medici not only distributed morphine and heroin but was an addict himself. Perales, like other citizens, used the charge of addiction to bolster his call for action against those—especially foreigners—who drugged not only themselves but vulnerable women who were seeking medical help.[76] Perales's letter to the Health Department captured the fear that fellow doctors could taint the entire profession with their scandalous acts.

In both cases, observations of doctors' prescription pads, their office technology, their chosen pharmacists, and their patients suggested that the authors of these letters may actually have been competitors who, out of envy perhaps, used a language of exceptionalism and nationalism to sully the reputations of other doctors. The construct "dope doctor" relied on a subtext: foreign doctors intoxicating a population that struggled to throw off one form of oppression (a dictatorship) only to be bound by another, addiction, which also would retard national progress and modernity.[77]

The association of foreign men with diverse technologies and in positions of authority or in jobs associated with modernity was repeated in the official text and likewise marked by suspicion. For example, in 1925 the newly formed Department of Health arrested a man named Felice Bonaudo. Investigators found Bonaudo in possession of 1.5 kilos of cocaine. The fact that he had that much cocaine was cause for alarm, but public officials expressed greater concern that this Italian immigrant was an airplane mechanic for Mexico's Secretariat of War and Navy.[78] Through his employment, Bonaudo had access to airplanes, which he could potentially utilize to distribute cocaine. Airplanes, a technological innovation and symbol of modernity, were being put into use for illicit means. Bonaudo's arrest may be interpreted in one of two ways. First, he personally used a lot of cocaine. Or second, in a country that had yet to harness aviation to a significant degree in the private sector, Bonaudo was, per se, a narcopioneer, demonstrating an early use of airplanes to traffic cocaine into and throughout Mexico.

Women, too, found themselves targets of the Department of Health, but their association at this point had little to do with technology and modernity. Domestically, the emergence of the Department of Health and the professionalization of public welfare led to internal questions about health that targeted women and their traditional work as antithetical to the concepts of modernity. As in the United States, traditional female healers and midwives had to be regulated out of existence in order to professionalize the practice of medicine.[79] Of course, women mobilized to work in public health campaigns to promote hygiene and better health; they became nurses and social workers.[80] Yet, *curanderas* (female traditional healers) remained figures of suspicion. They came under scrutiny not only from public health officials but also from their neighbors. As foreign men were marginalized within their chosen professions, women in the healing arts also encountered new roadblocks with the greater professionalization of medicine in Mexico.

In 1931, in a list of arrested medical doctors involved in illegal narcotics distribution, a curandera, Felipa Castillo, was also included. Originally from Texas, the thirty-eight-year-old lived in Villa Acuña, Coahuila. She was

arrested for possessing 1.64 kilos of marijuana. Her neighbors submitted
signed statements to the authorities attesting that Castillo grew and distributed marijuana, providing it to those who suffered from illness and injury.[81]
Like many female healers in Mexico who used marijuana to treat a host of
illnesses, Castillo provided it for oral ingestion, smoking, or application as a
salve, often used to treat arthritis and rheumatism. These aliments called for
a tincture or salve, which the healer prepared by soaking marijuana in alcohol and then rubbing it onto the afflicted areas, relieving the pain.[82] For
women like Castillo, the fact that their traditional healing methods were now
seen as illegal caused difficulties. Healers competed with medical doctors,
who sought to regulate and control other kinds of practitioners. Significantly,
women healers appeared to be the antithesis of modernity and progress.
They cared for people in their homes rather than in hospitals or clinics, and
they used herbs and plants rather than narcotics or analogous substances.
For a nation trying desperately to be accepted as part of the modern world,
Mexican public health officials wanted to do away with its traditional medicines, particularly in the cities.

While medical professionals and pharmacists of foreign birth were targets
of the authorities, many defended themselves by following Mexican laws and
keeping meticulous records of the narcotics they dispensed. Native female
healers did not have this option because their trade was unregulated and un-
recognized by a broader agency. In turn, a two-front battle was waged. On one
hand, medical and public health officials sought to modernize the nation by
questioning Mexican traditional medicine and practitioners who undermined
their goals. On the other hand, organized citizens' and professional groups
protested the presence of foreign nationals in the medical and pharmaceutical
fields who were seen as contributing to the degeneration of the race and undermining the nation. Doctors, particularly of foreign birth, in Mexico, the United
States, and Canada drew considerable condemnation as peddlers of dope.
Although some doctors were legitimately arrested for violating the laws, others
came under attack due to economic competition rather than their being involved in the illegal distribution of narcotics or cocaine.

CREATING AN ENEMY: THE ANTI-CHINO MOVEMENT

In part, commercial competition fed the anti-Chinese movement in Mexico
as it simultaneously fed suspicions about foreign-born doctors and

pharmacists. In 1925, anti-Chinese sentiment intensified with citizens' groups, newspapers, and zealous governors leading the attacks in public debate, police action, and violent assaults, despite the fact that U.S. officials questioned the involvement of Chinese in large-scale drug peddling and smuggling.[83] In 1927, U.S. consul Henry C. A. Damm wrote: "The large Chinese population on the Mexican West Coast would undoubtedly offer a market for a large quantity of opium produced, but this consulate has not heard of any attempts to smuggle the drug of Sonora origin into the United States directly across the border."[84]

Despite U.S. perceptions that Chinese immigrants in Mexico engaged in drug trafficking only infrequently, the evidence suggests that some did in fact smuggle drugs across the border, as did native Mexicans. However, the anti-Chino movement associated all Chinese with narcotics and blamed this small community for trafficking, addiction, and crime. Diplomatic correspondence contrasted greatly with internal policies. Initially, Mexican leaders actively recruited Chinese laborers to the country's "hot zones" because they were perceived as able to withstand the climate, which was similar to that of parts of China.[85] Later, beginning in the early 1900s, Mexican officials sought to control immigration from China.[86] At that time the Chinese, who were not well represented in the medical profession in Mexico, had a difficult time defending themselves and their families against allegations that they were dope peddlers. This situation led to numerous attacks on the Chinese in Mexico, which continued through the 1920s and into the 1930s with Mexican nationals publicly denouncing Chinese businesspeople as dealers, pushers, and traffickers. In turn, the state investigated Chinese businesses and in some cases moved toward deporting business owners. Moreover, the anti-Chinese movement created a fervor over police corruption and racial tainting through intermarriage.

Although the study of the anti-Chinese movement has focused on the state of Sonora, the movement spilled across state borders and moved south to the Gulf Coast region, another "hot zone."[87] The governors of Durango and Tamaulipas, for example, both led campaigns against the Chinese in 1930. In September 1930, José Román Valdez, the governor of Durango, sent a telegram to the secretary of the interior requesting permission to deport first twenty-three, then an additional seventy-six Chinese men from his state. Police had arrested all ninety-nine targeted men at a private home where they were allegedly gambling and smoking opium. During the raid, police confiscated only 180 pesos as well as some playing cards, but Román

Figure 3. Pipes and opium. Serie Mariguana, opio, y drogas, ca.1935, 142913, Casasola, Mexico City, Fototeca Nacional del Instituto Nacional de Anthropología e Historia (INAH), Pachuca, Hidalgo.

requested permission to deport all the men. The arrest papers specified that all the men hailed from Canton, but this was only the port city from which they had left China and may not have been their hometown. Half of them were married. Only one out the ninety-nine had a previous arrest, for gambling. The other ninety-eight displayed *buena conducta* (good conduct), which meant that they had no criminal records, were hard working, and owed no debts.[88]

Earlier in Tamaulipas, the arrests of Juan Lee, Enrique Lee, José Wong, and Manuel Ham exemplified the intersection of race, nationalism, and modernity in Mexico. They were arrested in September 1925 in an opium den, and they had all been arrested previously on similar charges. What made the case different was that it had been initiated in part by complaints sent to Governor Enrique Medina and the secretary of the interior by the Sindicato Nacional Pro-Raza (Pro-race National Syndicate, SNPR). In one letter dated August 20, 1925, the syndicate claimed:

The anti-Chinese leagues of this port and town of Cecilia in consid-
eration of our society are justly alarmed and indignant at the continued cases of criminal opium dens that have been uncovered. We
respectfully ask the Minister of the Interior that Juan Lee, Enrique
Lee, José Wong, and Manuel Ham be expelled from our country.
They bring shame to us and to all respectful citizens.[89]

The syndicate closed its letter by demanding the deportation of all vice-
ridden classes that they believed to be degenerating the Mexican race. At that
time, the state of Tamaulipas had the largest Chinese population among the
Gulf States, but still it was a mere 2,918.[90] Throughout the 1920s, the SNPR and
other leagues demanded the expulsion of all Chinese from Mexico. In 1925,
after the arrest of José Chiu, Rafael Leg, Manuel Chioke, and Chong Pérez, the
SNPR demanded their expulsion, blaming the men for trafficking "huge
quantities" of cocaine, heroin, morphine, liquid opium, and opium paste. The
organization's ads in newspapers became increasingly racist as they embraced
the language of eugenics. One ad placed by the Liga Nacional Pro-Raza (Pro-
race National League) and the Comité Feminil Anti-Chino de la Región
Petrolera (Women's Anti-Chinese Committee of the Petroleum Region)
demanded a region-wide boycott of all Chinese businesses. The anti-Chinese
campaign generated by these racist organizations created a hierarchy of
acceptable foreign-owned businesses. Directing their statements to organized
workers, these organizations argued that native-born, Spanish, and French
business owners supported Mexican workers' demands, while Chinese
businessmen only wished to extend their "sick tentacles" to oppress Mexican
workers.[91] The fact that state governments responded to these tactics reflected
the growing ties between bureaucrats and racist organizations.

Anti-Chino organizations posited a schizophrenic interpretation of
Chinese masculinity that played out in popular culture. As discussed by historian Evelyn Hu-DeHart, Mexican nationalists cast Chinese men as "effemi-
nate," since they replaced women in certain areas of work; however, that work
at times contributed to economic advancement for the men and their community. In the north, that work led to certain men finding success in the dry goods
business, but the association with allegedly feminine work and Chinese contact with local women who patronized their stores led to rampant allegations
of predatory sexuality. This appears contradictory since, on one hand, the men
were described as feminine, but on the other they were portrayed as sexual

predators who enticed women into prostitution. Both Robert Chao Romero and Hu-DeHart document that these portrayals also concealed jealousy over the economic success enjoyed by segments of the Chinese community. Wealthy Chinese offered lines of credit to young and newly arrived entrepreneurs, a common practice in all immigrant communities.[92]

By the late 1920s and early 1930s, the anti-Chinese movement in Mexico had grown in the number of both organizations and publications. The press in the northern and Gulf states associated the Chinese with drugs, addiction, and disease. The Chinese consul in Tampico, Tamaulipas, found himself under attack by a highly organized citizens' group that had the ears of many politicians and the resources to take out ads in newspapers. In 1927, the Liga Nacional Pro-Raza placed an ad, "La bestia amarilla," in newspapers. The ad was surrounded by the phrase "mujeres no degeneres tu raza" (women do not degenerate the race).[93]

Written as a song, "La bestia amarilla" refers to Mexico's illustrious past, invoking the names of Cuauhtémoc, the Aztecs, and Hernán Cortés. In the text, the Chinese are responsible for all the travails of Mexico. They are "yellow beasts" who bring disease to the country through their drug use and addiction, creating "fetid bastions of misery."[94] Referring to an elusive, glorious past that ironically associated Cortés with Aztec rulers reflected a profound misreading of the national history that was propagated by the government. This revisionism supported the government's rhetoric that created an external threat and focused attention on the enemy within.

As Canadian historian Catherine Carstairs notes, the moral panic surrounding drugs led to Canada's passage of the Chinese Immigration Act of 1923, which was designed to keep unwanted immigrants out of Canada.[95] This act predates the height of the anti-Chinese movement in Mexico. Thus, there is a correlation with regard to the exchange of information in North America about drugs. North American governments attempted to link drugs to foreigners. The anti-Chinese movement that emerged in all three countries in the 1920s demonstrates a shared narconarrative of vice and race. In policy papers drafted by the three governments and even by the League of Nations, officials created an enemy that embodied internal vice and, further, contributed to the degeneration of the predominant race in each respective society. In North America, Chinese immigrants became that enemy.

Mexican women who associated with Chinese men became targets for "rehabilitation" by women's organizations, public health officials, and politicians as fears of miscegenation fueled the anti-Chinese movement. Newspaper editorials, slogans, cartoons, and popular culture further maligned Chinese immigrants and their families.[96] Some images showed native (although European in representation) women cast as slaves, tethered to plows, or trapped in the house. Mass arrests of Chinese men revealed a distinct narrative that differed from what the anti-Chinese leagues portrayed. Wives and other family members wrote to governors begging that their loved ones not be deported. In one appeal, a wife discussed how her husband had come to Mexico as a child. He no longer spoke Chinese and now had children and grandchildren born in Mexico. She explained that her husband was Mexican, that he supported the community and engaged in civic life. In other words, he was a good husband and a good citizen.[97]

Chinese officials in Mexico also took action. The Chinese consul, M. M. Chen, sent a letter of complaint to the secretary of the interior in 1930 about the continued arrests of Chinese immigrants in the cities of Tampico and Villa de Cecilia in the state of Tamaulipas. Chen's letter only raised the ire of pro-Raza Mexicans, though, because he had dared to complain about the arrests, harassment, and poor treatment. More significant is how the letter became public. In his letter, Chen argued that the police illegally detained Chinese men, and, contrary to reports, they were not arrested for illegal entry into Mexico. Rather, Chen alleged, their homes were raided purely from information provided by citizens' groups. Then, after arresting the Chinese men, the police withheld food and water for over twenty-four hours.[98] The rhetoric of pro-Raza groups together with the growing awareness of the racial overtones of targeting immigrants as evidenced by Chen's complaint led to a diplomatic problem in the Mexican government. The secretary of the interior circulated the letters to the governor and other officials since he himself was uncertain what to do. As in Canada and the United States, Chinese nationals and diplomats defended their compatriots against allegations that they associated with drugs.[99]

Chen's letter provides an opportunity to investigate anti-Chinese sentiment. In their mass arrests, the police confiscated few opium pipes or decks of playing cards and very little money. In photographs taken of arrested men, some were posing with a pipe or two, but one wonders if the photos had been staged by the police and social workers. The fact that one-half of the men arrested were married, whether to Chinese or Mexican women, demonstrates that they were not criminals but that they were part of the fabric of the nation. Furthermore, most likely their wives were present in Mexico. Their ages

Figure 4. Public officials and Chinese men who had been detained. Serie Mariguana, opio, y drogas, ca. 1925, 142899, Casasola, Mexico City, Fototeca Nacional del Instituto Nacional de Anthropología e Historia (INAH), Pachuca, Hidalgo.

ranged from quite young (teenage) to elderly. The lack of evidence of wrongdoing suggests that the raids and arrests took place in clubs or aid societies that pro-Raza groups easily identified rather than in shady alleged opium dens. The lack of drug paraphernalia also casts doubt on claims of rampant Chinese drug use. Thus, Chen and other diplomats had to defend not only those who had left China, but China itself from charges that it was a nation of opium addicts, white slavers, and shifty businesspeople setting out to exploit native masses around the world.

MUTUAL AID SOCIETIES AND POLICE CORRUPTION

Mexican government officials focused on the Chinese community because they blamed the immigrants for introducing poppy production and addiction to Mexico in the late 1800s. For many years, those Chinese who cultivated poppy in Mexico and extracted opium paste did so quietly and mostly for private consumption. As the demand for opium and its derivatives—whether legal or illegal—grew, so did the growing and processing of poppy.

In postrevolutionary Mexico, opium use moved far beyond the nation's Chinese communities. With the U.S. government's anti-immigration legislation directed at the Chinese and its greater surveillance of the Pacific coast, many Chinese immigrants made their way to Mexico. The Mexican government encouraged such immigration and worked closely with tongs (organized crime groups) to recruit and bring workers to Mexico. Historian Robert Chao Romero has discussed how Mexican officials sought labor and worked with the tongs to acquire men to work in a host of industries, whether agriculture, railroading, or mining. Vice-President Ramón Corral worked with the Chee Kung tong in San Francisco to recruit and acculturate Chinese workers.[100] Chee Kung also organized Chinese businesspeople in both the United States and Mexico. Of course, that also opened up Mexico to Chinese organized crime in the areas of prostitution, gambling, and opium peddling. In the 1920s, a tong war emerged between Guo Min Dang and its Mexican affiliate, Lung Sung, who hoped to gain control of the drug trade from Chee Kung.[101] More significantly, the competition between the tongs spilled over into other parts of Mexican society. In some ways, the tong wars fueled anti-Chinese sentiment.

Revolutionary rhetoric, concepts of nationalism, and xenophobia reached levels that made life increasingly difficult for Chinese immigrants and their families in Mexico. Moreover, Chinese businesspeople and the groups they formed to combat attacks also became suspect. The cases of the Chee Kung tong (frequently transcribed as Chee Quen Towan) and Lung Sung (which also appears as Lung Sing), affiliated with Guo Min Dang, reflected an internal struggle within the Mexican Chinese community for power. The two organizations had distinct ideological differences. The Chee Kung tong was more conservative than the Lung Sung, and its goal was to organize different business enterprises.[102] These struggles in Mexico reflected power struggles that were taking place between Chee Kung and Guo Min Dang in China. Hence, the political infighting in China continued in Mexico. The power struggles between tongs fueled the anti-Chinese movement and served as an early narconarrative about police corruption in Mexico and its association with organized crime. More importantly, the tongs' activities demonstrated Mexico's centrality to the growing transnational criminal organizations, which were operating with greater impunity.

In 1927, J. Meza Terán, a government official, drafted a classified document in which he claimed that Chinese owners of grocery stores, cafes, bakeries, and other business establishments had formed a mutual aide society, the "Chee Quen Towan."[103] He argued that in Sinaloa, men who had become wealthy from selling drugs also established their own organization, Lung Sung. Lung Sung's members hailed from Tampico, Veracruz, San Luis Potosí, and the Federal District. Meza Terán argued that Lung Sung aimed to control the opium trade and gambling houses in major cities throughout Mexico.

Meza Terán went on to explain that Lung Sung viewed Chee Quen Towan as a potential threat to their business enterprises throughout Mexico. That threat crystallized when Chee Quen Towan expelled members who had ties to Lung Sung. Meza Terán argued that the Chinese had turned on each other, behavior that was common of their race, he explained. Meza Terán's racialized views of the tongs' fighting blinded him to other realities, such as long-standing political and ideological differences that were imported to the nation. While Mexican authorities had confiscated materials from the tongs, it appears that many of their Chinese-language books and documents were never translated into Spanish, since few translations exist in the archives. Despite Meza Terán's lack of knowledge regarding the Chinese, he did gather information about their important alliances with non-Chinese, an important feature in organized crime.[104]

After a raid on a Lung Sung establishment by Raúl Camarago, chief of the narcotics police of Mexico City, Lung Sung made Camarago an offer he couldn't refuse. Meza Terán recounted that members of Lung Sung asked Camarago to work for them. In turn, Camarago arrested members of Chee Quen Towan for drug trafficking and demanded their expulsion from Mexico. Thus, Camarago accepted a bribe to expel principal members of Chee Quen Towan, who had never been involved in drug trafficking. Chee Quen Towan members protested the arrests and expulsions, but to no avail. How could the words of an immigrant stand up against those of the chief narcotics officer? Meza Terán also accused Camarago of working for other prominent drug dealers who were native-born Mexicans. Camarago helped Lung Sung gain control of various enterprises such as gambling dens and drugs. In his conclusion, Meza Terán lamented the immoral practices of his colleague, and he recommended that Camarago be placed under surveillance.

In 1929, Camarago was arrested for corruption, and his case revealed that ties existed between the police and drug traffickers beginning in the 1920s regardless of the hysteria and antidrug rhetoric then sweeping the nation.[105]

Camarago, like other police officers at the time, could be bought. Significantly, he played an important role in the early cross-ethnic alliances that were emerging in the world of drugs. Camarago's job put him in contact with drug dealers and traffickers all the time. Men such as Camarago had an impact on the perceptions of Mexicans and their ability to police drugs and drug trafficking, since cases such as his not only were widely reported in Mexico but also became part of a transnational narrative of police ties to drugs.

FOREIGN VICES AND THE CREATION OF MEXICAN DEVIANCY IN THE 1930S

While Mexicans used the Chinese as scapegoats for the scourge of drugs and vice, a competing narrative of vice, danger, and disease in the United States cast Mexicans in a similar position. Like Chinese workers who came to Mexico to fill a labor void, Mexicans moved across their own northern border in search of work and to engage in trade and commerce. Despite the Mexican government favorably responding to its northern neighbors' demands to tighten regulations regarding the distribution of narcotics and cocaine, 1930s images and rhetoric about drugs in the United States and Canada painted a different picture. While Mexicans looked to foreigners as undermining their nation, Mexicans themselves were seen as the foreign distributors of vice and disease by Americans and Canadians north of the border.

American nativists who feared the influx of immigrants and temperance crusaders who abhorred drunkenness realized that certain people sought to profit from Prohibition. The Mexican government, too, recognized that profits could be gained due to Prohibition. As men and women from the United States crossed the border in search of alcohol and entertainment, their demand created a lucrative border market. Thus, Mexican mayors and governors created "zones of tolerance" where foreign businesspeople could convene in border cities and enjoy alcoholic beverages. The border zones evolved into havens for Americans seeking a good time.

Despite the convenience of these zones of tolerance, economic problems in the United States ignited fervor against Mexicans. With the advent of the Great Depression, Mexican immigrants in the United States found a harsher social environment north of the border. Many Americans saw Mexican immigrants as competitors for scarce jobs and a drain on social welfare systems. In January 1928, prior to the collapse of the economy, C. M. Goethe published

"The Influx of Mexican Amerinds" in *Eugenics: A Journal of Race Betterment*. He decried the growing migration of poor and working-class Mexican "peons" to California: "It is doubtful whether ten percent of Mexico's say 15 million are free from Amerind blood. Eugenically as low-powered as the Negro, the peon is from a sanitation standpoint a menace. He not only does not understand health rules: being a superstitious savage, he resists them."[106] Mexicans, he argued, lowered wages for native-born workers. More significantly, they brought disease and vice and engaged in miscegenation. They had more children than native white women. He argued that, although Ellis Island may have closed, a back door to the United States existed that also needed to be closed. Goethe's views and others like them, although extreme, found a growing audience in the United States in the 1920s and 1930s.

Mexican government bureaus and social agencies, worried about increasing tensions with their northern neighbor, sought to recall workers, vagrants, and citizens in the United States and repatriate them to Mexico.[107] Repatriation took place when the newly formed U.S. Federal Bureau of Narcotics began taking a greater interest in Mexico. The rhetoric of deviance increased because of economic competition, decline, and problems along the border that resonated within the social policies of the United States with regard to Mexico. As a supplier and transshipper of narcotics, Mexico informed U.S. government policy but also spawned tales of horror printed in the sensationalist press and escalated a narrative of deviance associated with Mexico and Mexicans in the popular imagination. The categories of deviance that had been embraced in North America to target Chinese shifted to other supposedly dangerous groups, due in part to successful immigration controls that stemmed the influx of Chinese workers.

Harry J. Anslinger became a primary vehicle for such propaganda. He elaborated images of foreignness to portray a country under attack by external forces. Anslinger dredged up twenty-year-old narratives of "reefer madness," which he claimed was afflicting Mexico. Newspaper reports and medicinal studies of the early 1900s argued that "Mexican" marijuana was a cause of grave concern. Ridiculous claims ensued. Some journalists wrote that the Empress Carlota had succumbed to insanity because of her penchant for marijuana.[108] Other reports argued that Belem Prison was full or marijuana addicts, that soldiers freely used the plant, and that miners who were intoxicated on it killed their American managers.[109] All these tales added to increasing fears that Mexico was trying to push addictions on its northern neighbor.

Newspapers reported on "freak outbursts of madness" among Mexicans in both rural and urban areas.[110] In another sensational case, a distraught mother fed her children marijuana, which caused the entire family to engage in outbursts of "crazed laughter" before they went insane.[111] These reports came at the time that Mexico embarked on its first eradication of poppy and its first ban on marijuana cultivation.[112] Regardless of such positive steps, Mexico and Mexicans became increasingly associated with drugs, smuggling, and madness.

One of Anslinger's most poignant examples was that of Victor Licata, a Mexican American arrested for the murder of his entire family in Tampa, Florida.[113] Licata allegedly murdered his family after he smoked marijuana.[114] Documents released at the time suggested that Licata had a long history of mental illness prior to his 1933 arrest. Later he was admitted to the Florida State Hospital, where he murdered a fellow inmate and eventually killed himself in 1950. Licata's Mexican background is also subject to debate, but his case served as ammunition to highlight the dangers of

Figure 5. Public prosecutors posing with confiscated packages of marijuana.
Serie Mariguana, opio, y drogas, ca. 1935, 142908, Casasola, Mexico City,
Fototeca Nacional del Instituto Nacional de Anthropología e
Historia (INAH), Pachuca, Hidalgo.

marijuana and foreigners. Despite the lack of clear evidence about Licata's actual state of mind, not to mention his ethnicity, Anslinger made Licata's case central to the reefer madness hysteria. The violence that came to be associated with marijuana smoking became part of a new narrative that blamed Mexicans for the distribution of drugs and vice. Anslinger, who was commissioner of the Federal Bureau of Narcotics from 1930 to 1962, first associated Mexicans with drugs and violence in his speeches as early as 1933, and he sensationalized these claims in a published report in 1937, in which he wrote:

> Marijuana was introduced into the United States from Mexico, and swept across America with incredible speed. It began with the whispering of vendors in the Southwest that marijuana would per-form miracles for those who smoked it, giving them a feeling of physical strength and mental power, stimulation of the imagina-tion, the ability to be "the life of the party." The peddlers preached also of the weed's capabilities as a "love potion." Youth, always adventurous, began to look into these claims and found some of them true, not knowing that this was only half the story They were not told that addicts may often develop a delirious rage during which they are temporarily and violently insane; that this insanity may take the form of a desire for self-destruction or a persecution complex to be satisfied only by the commission of some heinous crime.[115]

Whether poppy or marijuana, Mexico became associated with the dan-gers, sexual allure, deviance, and political destruction that ensued from drugs, despite the low use of drugs among Mexicans—even as documented by American organizations like the Bureau of Social Hygiene. The United States, often working with Canadian officials, sought to influence internal Mexican affairs through a narrative of vice and deviance. This narrative, however, incorporated a xenophobia that flowed across borders and in-formed international as well as domestic policies. Just as the United States had little stake economically in China at that time, American officials saw an opportunity to gain influence by sponsoring the International Opium Conference in 1909. In 1911, the United States continued the initiative at the meeting in The Hague, where they were joined by other countries in favoring regulation.

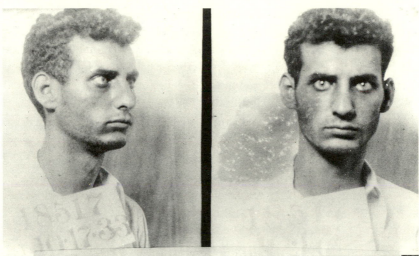

THE MOST HEINOUS CRIME OF 1933

Victor Licata, Tampa, Florida, on October 17, 1933, while under the influence of Marihuana, murdered his Mother, Father, Sister and Two Brothers, WITH AN AXE while they were asleep.

Figure 6. Victor Licata. H. J. Anslinger Papers, box 14, folder 5, image 228, Eberly Family Special Collections Library, Pennsylvania State University, University Park, PA.

From 1900 to the 1930s, Mexico remained a country in struggle, first with the revolution and then in building a new nation. That difficult transition and the ensuing instability offered the United States an opportunity to create a narrative of Mexican culpability in the increasing use of marijuana and later heroin. The early international drug meetings set the stage for continued confrontations between the neighboring countries. Internally in Mexico, the transitory nature of the state led to attacks on foreigners, who served as scapegoats for drug trafficking and drug use—the same role that Mexico itself was saddled with in global meetings on narcotics. Mexican public welfare officials and politicians developed their own language of deviance; thus a shared narconarrative was generated, resulting in cross-border sting operations that predate the founding of the Federal Bureau of Narcotics (FBN) and later the Drug Enforcement Administration (DEA). More importantly to this study, women would emerge as central antagonists in these cross-border collaborations and sting operations. These women could reside in the shadowy underworld as low-level players. Once they moved beyond that role, they drew attention, speculation, and transnational interest. Like men, women worked in all levels of the drug trade, whether selling from their homes or in the street or trafficking large quantities of drugs across international borders. More significantly, women of all backgrounds regardless of class, ethnicity, or national origin entered the trade. They, too, became involved in organized crime, since drug trafficking is an organized crime, and they, too, created transnational alliances.

CHAPTER TWO

MULES, SMUGGLERS, AND PEDDLERS

The Illicit Trade in Mexico, 1910s–1930s

IN 2004, THE ROLE OF WOMEN AS DRUG MULES ENTERED THE POPU-
lar imagination with the release of the film *María Full of Grace*, which depicts the life of a young Colombian woman who swallows sealed packets of
cocaine and smuggles them into the United States.[1] María Álvarez, played
by Catalina Sandino Moreno, passes through the port of entry at New
York's John F. Kennedy Airport, a present-day Ellis Island. In the film,
María also works in one of Colombia's other leading export industries,
flower production. She resorts to muling after she loses her job and finds
herself in a precarious economic situation. Young, unemployed, and pregnant, she enters the trade seeking to improve her life. Instead, she predict-
ably encounters additional difficulties. She sees her friend die from
poisoning when a cocaine-packed condom ruptures in her stomach while
she's in transit. After she arrives at JFK, Immigration and Naturalization
Service (INS) and customs agents interrogate her because she cannot pass
through the X-ray machine due to her pregnancy. She then meets her contact, who detains her until she is able to expel the cocaine. Abandoned in
Corona, Queens, with few friends and few economic prospects, she eventually finds assistance within New York's Colombian community.

María Full of Grace gained recognition because it placed women in a
masculine world. María and her fellow mules are instrumental in the transnational flow of products, whether legal carnations or illegal cocaine. In
2004, when the film was released, she was not the stereotypical feminine

image found in films about drugs. Women in this genre tended to play sultry sirens to drug lords, junkies, or whores in freak houses. The film portrays María's physical and economic vulnerability and places her in a global context. As portrayed, the men aren't necessarily to blame as much as the neoliberal economic structures that force far too many men and women into illicit trade. Rarely have women appeared as instrumental to the economics of the narcotics trade as the character María. Circumstances force a sympathetic protagonist into the shadowy world of drugs.

The contemporary image of María, sensational as it may be, positions women within the transitional drug trade, yet the film also dramatizes the internal drug industry in Colombia. Trafficking and peddling narcotics have long served as profit-making enterprises. Both men and women have sought opportunity in the field, but the role of the female mule was particularly troubling both for Colombia and for destination countries. Women demonstrated an agility to circumnavigate surveillance because officials did not expect women to engage in the trafficking of contraband at this level. Of course, smugglers recognized that women were less prone to searches, so they hired them to move drugs and other commodities. The activities of mules ranged from small-time border smuggling to transnational multimillion dollar trafficking businesses. Smuggled items included durable goods, arms, cattle, food commodities, clothing, and personal hygiene products as well as drugs and alcohol. Women sought profit in illicit products, using their bodies, fashion accessories, and luggage to conceal contraband. As burros or mules, they facilitated the transnational movement of goods, narcotics, and money, whether physically on their persons or on a larger scale as couriers of narcotics, commodities, or cash.

Female smugglers, local peddlers, and international drug mules were and remain important players in the international drug chain. While they may not appear as dangerous as male suppliers and drug lords, one must consider that their involvement in illegal flows has continually altered the policing of borders and flows of people and goods. This chapter opens with what may be described as a "glocal" approach in which women intersect with the transnational drug trade by creating and working in local markets as peddlers and mules.[2] In the early twentieth century, women appeared as the victims of the international drug trade, pernicious doctors, and indifferent politicians. Yet, as policing agents discovered, women were also involved in selling and trafficking illegal commodities such as alcohol (during Prohibition) and drugs. Of course, these women did not identify with the modern-day mantra "think globally, act locally," but their illicit work reflects their ties to global markets, whether for the purpose of expanding their own trading networks or profiting from the illicit flows. Their peddling, muling, and smuggling led to societal repercussions, because women as small-time smugglers and mules moved through cities, controlled spaces, and crossed borders. In turn, their involvement in contraband and vice created new professions for noncriminal women whether along the border, in communities, or in prisons.

To expand the discussion from the glocal to the global drug trade, the most famous transnational mule of the 1930s, Maria Wendt, exemplifies the role of mules as essential to an international trafficking organization; her case allows for a glimpse of a highly sophisticated global trafficking organization that defies many contemporary stereotypes. The case exhibits early transnational cooperation between policing agencies on both sides of the U.S.-Mexico border. Although Wendt portrayed herself as a mule, she had a tremendous impact on popular culture in the 1930s and 1940s, and her case informed policy in both Mexico and the United States. Fifty-six years before *María Full of Grace*, Wendt became the first transnational mule whose story was told in celluloid.

ILLICIT FRONTIERS

The historical role of women as mules feeds the contemporary imagination through sensational photos of detained women with kilos of uncut heroin and cocaine taped to their thighs.[3] From the early 1900s, the detained mule emerged in popular culture as a victim, penitent, or deviant. During Prohibition and in its wake, as female mules grew more and more prominent in illicit trade, the U.S. and Mexican governments made adjustments to border strategies and public health policy to address the troubling criminology of women. Customs and other agencies on both sides of the border began hiring women as agents and inspectors to better cope with the new trend in an ironic twist of traditional views of gender in law enforcement.[4]

The reality of the mule serves as a vehicle to understanding shifts in policy on both sides of the border. The mule as a primary although subservient agent remains a conscribed, passive role that has been viewed as suitable exclusively for women. Smuggler and mule have distinct meanings. One moves goods for her own enrichment or benefit, while the other is merely a vessel for transportation controlled by others. The latter is exploited by the former. It is the role of women as mules and, to a lesser degree, as smugglers that has compelled governments to hire women in customs and policing agencies.[5]

Scholars such as Tammy Anderson, Eloise Dunlap, Bruce Johnson, and Ric Curtis recognize that women play key roles in the drug trade. They provide housing and sustenance to male peddlers and traffickers, and they subsidize those who are at the low end of the trade.[6] They also engage in selling and buying. Frequently, women addicts exchange sex for drugs, and prostitutes use drugs to perform their work.[7] In other contemporary examples, women use their drug vending to maintain aspects of a middle-class life such as a decent apartment and tuition for their children's private schools.[8] Additionally, women (and children) can provide an excellent cover for men in their family to engage in the drug trade, furnishing legitimacy in the form of a genuine family life. By having a family, the male drug dealer can be a doting father who is active in his community.[9] The 2000 film *Traffic* demonstrates this in the character Helena Ayala, played by Catherine Zeta-Jones.[10] In Ayala's case, she took up trafficking to maintain her lifestyle after the arrest of her husband.

Anthropologist Howard Campbell interviewed women on the U.S.-Mexico border over a period of several years. His research expands the roles of women in the drug trade beyond those of addict and enabler to male drug peddlers. He found that women entered the drug trade for a host of personal, social, and economic reasons.[11] Campbell argues that some woman are victimized by the trade. Some resort to working as mules to pay off the debts of their lovers, husbands, fathers, or sons. Others, however, find empowerment in the drug trade. By running drugs, women such as Cristal, whom Campbell interviewed, found a socioeconomic ladder to climb in an industry that is far more lucrative than traditional jobs available to them.[12]

Contrary to popular culture, for most of the twentieth century women served as the drug couriers of choice because they drew less attention from the authorities than their male counterparts.[13] In the contemporary period, women are important economic actors in the trade as mules, but they have received scant attention.[14] Although considered minor players, mules make up the majority of transnational actors in drug trafficking. Bosses, whether of small-time gangs or international cartels, rarely risk their own safety, security, and profit to go through international ports of entry with a stash hidden in a false compartment in a gas tank or stuffed in a bra, girdle, or panties. Even fewer bosses are willing to ingest condoms stuffed with coke or heroin.

In reconstructing the history of mules and couriers, written evidence is slight because most of the mules were successful, avoiding detection and detention, and they do not appear in the official documents. For the most part, they remain nameless to history.

For transnational mules and drug smugglers to emerge, a market had to exist that demanded the products they carried. Scholars of narcotics have argued that the 1914 Harrison Act marked the beginning of increased demand in the United States. With greater controls placed on pharmacists and medical doctors, demand shifted from legal outlets to illegal, thus altering the landscape in urban America, all along the U.S.-Mexico border, and in port cities throughout the North American continent. The act required physicians and pharmacists to register with the Treasury Department, maintain records of the narcotics they prescribed or dispensed, and pay taxes on sales they made.[15]

Historians and medical scholars argue that the Harrison Act, followed by the Supreme Court's 1919 antimaintenance interpretation of the law, contributed directly to the increase in illicit trade and an explosion of addiction, since it essentially cut off supplies to iatrogenic addicts. The Supreme Court ratified the Harrison Act in a case brought before it regarding a Memphis-based physician who provided a morphine maintenance program to long-time patients.[16] Prior to the passage of the Harrison Act, most opiate addicts were women because doctors prescribed it to treat a host of "feminine illnesses."[17] Doctors have historically treated men and women with various complaints, whether cough, dysentery, asthma, neuralgia, or neurasthenia, with opiates and their derivatives, thus creating a class of addicts. Some doctors treated female members of their own families with opiates, known of course for their calming effect.

Medical professionals first introduced heroin as a substitute for other opium derivatives such as codeine and morphine that had proven to be addictive. Doctors and pharmacists prescribed heroin for a host of ailments, and it became a common treatment for respiratory illnesses.[18] Administered orally in pill form or as an elixir, only small amounts of heroin needed to be consumed to alleviate wheezing and to relax the bronchial tubes. Heroin was first introduced as a treatment for respiratory infections in U.S. prisons. Having experienced the euphoric effects of the narcotic, prisoners sought the drug on their own once outside prison walls. Former prisoners became the first large group of male addicts in the United States. Once heroin entered society's mainstream, whether for treatment or recreational use, it evolved into a problem.[19]

In 1903, U.S. physician George Pettey caused a stir when he contradicted conventional wisdom and noted that heroin was indeed habit forming.[20] Doctors in the United States took note of his warning, and by the 1910s were prescribing less heroin. Just when the U.S. government was forcing pharmaceutical companies, pharmacists, and medical professionals to comply with changes in the law, heroin entered the general population as a replacement for other narcotics because of its ability to maintain its euphoric effect when adulterated; thus, it was the least expensive of the narcotic drugs.[21]

The shifts wrought by the Harrison Act in the United States also contributed to the criminalization of drugs along the border, coinciding with the violence of the Mexican Revolution, which pushed people toward the northern border.[22] With the population shifts from the South, U.S. military and customs officials on the border realized that this invisible line in the sand had become a site of dangerous pleasures and a space for criminality. For most of the first third of the twentieth century, Mexicans and Americans freely moved across the border for the purpose of trade and commerce. The population in northern Mexico was sparse, as was that of the southwestern United States. With growing concern, U.S. military and customs officials noted the border's permeability in that people, alcohol, and other commodities easily flowed into the United States. For those on the border trying to survive in a difficult economy, smuggling became a viable economic opportunity although one fraught with danger, including dealing with policing agencies and military forces. Often, law enforcement officers became the smugglers' customers. By 1916, U.S. soldiers stationed along the border had developed a taste for tequila and mescal, and Mexican smugglers were more than happy to oblige their vices. As journalist W. D. Hornsday noted:

> One of the many interesting and strange phases of the animated military life upon the long strip of United States territory that fronts Mexico is the native bootlegger and smuggler, who in some mysterious unaccountable way, manages to cross the boundary line without detection and through confederates on this side, place the contraband fiery intoxicating liquors within purchasing reach of some of the camps of soldiers.
>
> Ever since the Rio Grande became the dividing line between the United States and Mexico, mescal smuggling has been a fine art with many of the brown skin natives of the border. It is more or less a family vocation with them. In the old days it was regarded as an honorable

though somewhat hazardous method of earning a livelihood. Mescal smuggling is not confined to men but many Mexican women are adept in the business. . . . It is petty lawlessness that the border customs officers and their guards have never been able to suppress.[23]

Hornsday's 1916 article about alcohol smuggling was a harbinger of greater profits to come with drug smuggling. Smuggling to avoid paying customs, in turn yielding greater profits, gave men and women of the border region during a time of economic instability a means to make a living. Even before Prohibition in the United States, Mexican bootleggers created the paths and ports of entry that would serve their successors in the trade of marijuana and opiates. Bootleggers learned early on that customs officials and border agents were few and far between, and that they could bypass fees and duties by smuggling their goods over the border to gain greater profits. In 1963, the U.S. Department of the Treasury estimated, for example, that it had intercepted only 5 percent of the narcotics smuggled into the United States from Mexico.[24]

The role of women and the Mexican family in transnational bootlegging, which Hornsday recognized early on, evolved into an essential characteristic of the illicit trade of narcotics, although not unique to Mexico.[25] As early as 1916, Hornsday challenged expected gender roles in Mexico and their emphasis on *marianismo* and machismo.[26] These stereotypical concepts assumed that women are self-sacrificing, private, and submissive to the male members of the family, who are public and more prone to violence. In Hornsday's piece, men and women are observed to engage in bootlegging with equal success. For many women, street vending was one of the few economic opportunities open to them, but bootlegging served as a more lucrative extension of selling beverages, whether alcoholic or not. In the United States, women of all backgrounds found a revenue source before and during Prohibition from the "cooking," selling, and distribution of alcoholic beverages.[27] They and their children collected and cleaned bottles that were used in speakeasies; they sometimes even managed speakeasies; and they bootlegged alcohol whether selling it from their own homes or trafficking it across international borders.[28] During Prohibition, the number of women arrested for bootlegging surged, whether on the U.S.-Mexico or U.S.-Canada border, in both cities and rural areas.[29] Bootlegging gave women another area of work, whether as sellers or distributors, whether acting as lookouts, couriers, assistants, or small business owners. Historically, women dominated the informal economic sector whether selling

food, drinks, or their own bodies. In many ways, they created a separate economic sector for themselves since they were unable to work in the formal economy. Immigrant women in the United States turned to making homemade
wine or bathtub gin to supplement their income. As one Italian bootlegger who
had immigrated to the United States wrote in 1932:

> We see our Federal Courts filled with young and old, men and
> women, mothers of families. We see these mothers convicted, dis-
> graces, and broken for selling a small amount of wine, a glass of
> whiskey, a bottle of beer to clothe their children, feed their babies,
> to keep a roof over their heads. We are taught the doctrine, and the
> law so holds it, that it is far better and less blameful for these moth-
> ers, these American women to become prostitutes, scarlet women
> in the streets of our cities than for them to dare sell a glass of wine.[30]

The majority of working and lower-class women have always had to sub-
vert societal gendered expectations by being public and engaging in commerce in order to survive and support their families. Women of the lower
classes have worked in factories, labored as domestics in the homes of the
middle and upper classes, served food and beverages in restaurants and bars,
sold items on the street, taken in piecework, and prostituted themselves. In
most studies of Prohibition, scholars have focused on the Woman's Christian
Temperance Union (WCTU). While some working-class women joined the
WCTU, most women involved were from elite or middle-class backgrounds,
and they had little experience supporting a family. While the saloon, pub,
bar, and, in Mexican-American areas, cantina took money away from women
and children because men frittered away their wages on drinks, as the
WCTU argued, the private and localized vending of spirits maintained many
families.

In major U.S. cities, Italians, Irish, Jews, Germans, Poles, and other immigrants sought socioeconomic advancement through bootlegging and
smuggling. In the Southwest and California, Mexican immigrants captured
much of the whiskey market. Scholars like José M. Alamillo and George Díaz
have depicted how bootlegging became associated with masculinity among
Mexicans, leading to masculine competition over the market.[31] Bootlegging
and smuggling in immigrant communities gave men, like women, a vehicle
to economically survive and, in some cases, thrive. Many men in the these
communities found that they could not secure loans from banks to open

businesses, so they resorted to illicit means to generate income that funded both legal and illegal business ventures.[32] The image of the successful bootlegger established ideals of proper masculine behavior for men who found little opportunity for economic advancement through legitimate means. During Prohibition, this demonstration of masculinity often came at a dangerous price.

As Díaz has documented, competition between men for valuable smuggling routes into the United States emerged. Those with greater access to new forms of technology such as cars, trucks, and firearms displaced those bootleggers who still relied on mules and more peaceful means to navigate the desert terrain. With Prohibition, attacks on Mexicans by Anglo Americans increased along the border because of suspicion that they were making, selling, and drinking alcohol; attacks on immigrants in northeastern cities were also on the rise.[33] While Mexicans along the border encountered violence due to their alleged association with bootlegging, the Mexican embassy in Washington ensured that cases of whiskey, tequila, sherry, and wine cleared U.S. Customs for use in the embassy.[34] Moreover, the Man in the Green Hat scandal emerged, ensnaring various U.S. congressmen in a sting operation. The man, George L. Cassiday, regularly delivered spirits to members of Congress and other Washington dignitaries, demonstrating that the Prohibition laws were really meant for certain classes of people and not applicable to all. A World War I veteran, Cassiday found bootlegging to be far more lucrative than other jobs for which he was qualified, and he found excellent customers among the very same congressmen who supported Prohibition.[35]

Less often discussed but still observed was the extended role of women in bootlegging. Journalist Hornsday had observed a common phenomenon in the informal economic sector, whether legal or criminal: a family business passed from generation to generation, and both men and women participated in it equally. The family, thus, served as an instrumental institution for social acculturation and economic maintenance. Families not only passed on their cultural and social practices, but they also bequeathed economic practices.

In Mexico, a country where informal markets flourished, street vending and peddling provided far greater profits than traditional jobs.[36] Along the border in a time of economic crisis and massive social upheaval due to the Mexican Revolution, Prohibition, and the global economic depression of the 1930s, such economic activities sustained families that had experienced

Figure 7. Public prosecutors examining drugs. Serie Mariguana, opio, y drogas, ca. 1935, 142937, Casasola, Mexico City, Fototeca Nacional del Instituto Nacional de Anthropología e Historia (INAH), Pachuca, Hidalgo.

displacement through violence or been deprived of their traditional means of earning a living. The traditional work of women may have been valued within the family, but contraband became a way to economically survive. It is no mystery why or how women engaged in illegal trafficking.

Along the U.S.-Mexico border, numerous cities served as central ports of entry, and these developed further due to the flows of alcohol and money during Prohibition: Laredo–Nuevo Laredo, Brownsville-Matamoros, and El Paso–Ciudad Juárez in Texas; Douglas–Agua Prieta in New Mexico; Nogales in Arizona; and Calexico-Mexicali and San Diego–Tijuana in California. Sleepy border crossings became important transit sites for experienced smugglers and their North American partners. Smugglers treated these cities as central points of trafficking whether they were moving cattle, people, goods, tequila, or mescal. Despite their focus on alcohol, U.S. customs agents grew concerned about narcotics that entered the United States and Mexico along the California and Baja California coasts.[37] By the 1930s, certain cities in Mexico long known as illegal alcohol ports were transformed into transit stations for heroin and marijuana. The U.S. Department of the Treasury shifted its focus to narcotics after the passage of the Blaine Act and the Twenty-First Amendment in 1933 that ended Prohibition and again legalized alcohol consumption, distribution, and sales. Heroin and marijuana use, however, had increased during that same period in the United States.[38]

By the end of Prohibition, both marijuana and opiates had moved beyond their traditional users. U.S. officials asserted that Mexicans in the Southwest gravitated toward marijuana whereas Chinese, sailors, and bohemians preferred opiates. By the 1930s, marijuana and opiate use had spread to the major cities of the United States, far from the ports of California and Baja California and the border states. Relations between the United States and Mexico grew strained due to narcotics because the United States sought to control opiate smuggling from Asia, and Mexico was a convenient trafficking point.[39] By the early 1930s, Mexican and U.S. authorities resolved to collaborate in their antinarcotics efforts, since the transit routes already existed.[40]

SMUGGLERS, MULES, AND PEDDLERS

With the beginning of the first U.S. war on drugs in the 1930s, Mexico was forced to respond to the internationalization and Americanization of narcotics enforcement in Mexico.[41] The century-long interaction between Mexico and the United States challenges the assumptions that the internationalization of narcotics enforcement is something that emerged only with the formation of the Drug Enforcement Administration in 1973.[42] Instead, it had followed the ebb and flow of policy initiatives on both sides of the border that corresponded to one another. The realities of transnational trafficking challenge conventional wisdom regarding the image of mules as portrayed in contemporary scholarship focusing on the United States and Mexico.[43] It is far more complex and fluid. Modernization and changing policies in the United States and Canada have had dramatic effects on Mexico. Beginning in the 1910s, the United States controlled drug trafficking locally, with the states having the authority to pass laws at the local level. In the 1920s, Prohibition in the United States further strengthened enforcement powers for both local officials and those in the Department of the Treasury. The Treasury's Prohibition Unit stationed agents in ten countries to control the illegal flow of alcoholic beverages to the United States. The use of agents and controls established during Prohibition served as a model for U.S. drug enforcement efforts in the following decades. In the 1930s, with the end of Prohibition and the establishment of the Federal Bureau of Narcotics (FBN) within the Department of the Treasury, official focus shifted toward drugs.[44]

In Mexico, nation building and the push to reestablish domestic businesses that promoted Mexican manufactured products led to increased monitoring of smuggling along the nation's northern and southern borders. The government viewed contraband, even of legal products, as a threat to the growth and development of new business. Mexico and the United States thus engaged in further agreements regarding trade, for vastly different reasons. Those trade agreements evolved into a relationship between the United States and Mexico about the issue of narcotics in the 1930s. With heightened U.S. attention to narcotics, Mexico responded with its own investigations, which led to greater transborder cooperation. For many residents of the borderlands, the lure of smuggling, whether drugs, alcohol, or licit products, was a risk worth taking regardless of the penalties and fines, and regardless of nationalistic rhetoric condemning such activity.

Cases along the border reveal that women smuggled almost anything, and they used various crossing points. In 1936, for example, Mexican customs agents in Nogales detained forty-eight-year-old Luisa Primero Mendoza, a widow from Guadalajara. She had attempted to smuggle clothing and cleaning products from the United States for her profession as a washerwoman in Mexico. She was found guilty of carrying contraband and received a sentence of one year in prison and a thirty-peso fine. Although poorly educated, she wrote a letter to President Lázaro Cárdenas demanding her early release in order to care for her children.[45]

Primero Mendoza was one of countless women and men who smuggled legal as well as illegal items into Mexico. To border agents, they were avoiding taxes and defrauding the state. In the eyes of the Mexican federal government, contrabandists of all stripes undermined the progress of the nation through their fraud. Sales of Mexican products, and the collection of taxes on the transactions, were important to rebuilding the economy. Primero Mendoza, however, in transporting clothes and cleaning products, sought greater economic stability for herself and her children.[46]

For the most part, women acquired and smuggled items associated with their work. Thus, they smuggled clothing—such as undergarments, socks and stockings, baby clothes, purses, shoes, and dresses—as well as food products, face creams, hair products, soaps, dishes and crockery, cloth, thread, and linens. They packed their own clothing with the contraband items or layered them one on top of the other and stuffed their pockets, bags, and suitcases. Customs officials even reported bolts of cloth as contraband. Once detained, women argued that they had brought the items for their own personal use, with no intention of reselling for profit. The amount of material that could be transported on one's body without drawing attention was minimal, but women attempted to pass enough items to stock a small shop.

In 1937, Anastasia Serna Mendoza la viuda de Mendoza walked across the border from Laredo, Texas, to Nuevo Laredo, Tamaulipas, wearing or otherwise carrying six brassieres, various dresses, forty-eight pairs of stockings, and other items.[47] In 1939, also in Nuevo Laredo, Eloisa Cárdenas Benavides de Guerra smuggled a wedding dress, four pairs of gloves, undergarments, three large spools of thread, three pairs of stockings, an ordinary dress, and two necklaces.[48]

Rarely did officials denote in their documentation that the women worked as *comerciantes*, or professional vendors. Instead, inspectors listed their employment as housewife, housekeeper, laundress, or unemployed. And yet, the agents relied on their own interpretations of what the women told them. Of course, a woman who was smuggling for profit would never mention that she was going to resell the items. Agents, however, noted that the items were to be sold from their homes or in their hometowns. Despite working in the secondary market and providing for their families, women opted not to state their own work in documents and self-reported their employment as housewives. This discrepancy ensured that the women received smaller fines and shorter sentences. Also, it demonstrates their own ability, whether conscious or not, to manipulate customs agents and the law.

Customs officials often detained Mexican women who crossed international ports of entry on foot; other, more affluent or better-connected women, however, used automobiles. In their cars, they packed clothing, dishes, cloth, foods, and other items inside the seats or under the floorboards. By embracing more sophisticated means of transport that enabled greater profits, these women appeared to be entrepreneurs. For example, Natalía Ortíz Ramos la viuda de Cerda from Ciudad Juárez crossed the international bridge from El Paso in 1937. Customs official Manuel Peralta found in the seat of her truck clothing for men, women, and children, plates and cups, glassware, and salt.[49] In 1939, Manuela Ortíz Rodríguez de Caballeros drove her children in her Plymouth across the international border. Under the seats, she had packed thirty-six dresses and other clothing. At times, children within the family assisted in smuggling items.[50] In 1936, Carmen Cantú de Garza, a forty-seven-year-old housewife from Monterrey, smuggled clothing while accompanied by her two daughters and a friend. The inspectors checked them because they appeared to be wearing clothing that was too heavy for a spring day in Nuevo Laredo.[51] Upon inspection, the officials found that the four had hidden automobile parts under their skirts. In addition to the auto parts, they also had layered clothing on their bodies, no doubt appearing quite bulky and even bowlegged.

Cantú's case demonstrates a couple of significant aspects of smuggling. Like other women, she employed her children. Children served a number of roles in the flow of contraband. Their presence in a car or as companions to their mothers or sisters on foot may have influenced whether inspectors searched a car or a group of pedestrians. Parents coached their children to assist them. Crying, whining, or complaining provided an excellent distraction for a distraught mother, who sought to divert attention from her smuggling. Children's behavior could also disrupt customs agents trying to inspect a car or search a child's mother. Children also served as carriers. If a woman such as Serna Mendoza was attempting to smuggle forty-eight pairs of stockings among other items on her own, a woman with a child would be able to cross with even more merchandise. Thus, children were instrumental to their mothers' enterprises.

In addition, Cantú's smuggling of automobile parts, even on foot, suggests that she sought greater profit than what she could make from traditional items that women smuggled. Automobile parts, cars, guns, hardware, and livestock provided far more profit than clothing and food items. Men were far more involved than women in the smuggling of cars, car parts, guns, livestock, and heavy durable goods. Significantly, Cantú and her daughters may have been mules who smuggled such items for a man.

The evidence also suggests that women traveled long distances to smuggle legal goods from the United States into Mexico. In 1937, Raquel Katz de Frenkel, a twenty-three-year-old married Polish immigrant who lived in Mexico City, was arrested in Nuevo Laredo with suitcases filled with clothing purchased in the United States.[52] In 1936, Emilia Fabris Guica, a fifty-year-old Yugoslavian immigrant who lived in Mexico City, was arrested in the port of Veracruz attempting to smuggle new European clothing that she had hidden in dirty laundry.[53] Soledad González Sandoval, a fifty-year-old single woman from Guanajuato, was arrested in Nogales for contraband activities. She, like the other women, was searched by a woman, in this case María Leonor Páez la viuda de Madrid.[54] The movement of women from various parts of Mexico through international ports of entry, whether by land or sea, suggests that the risk of getting caught weighed less than the profit one could make. Moreover, it reflected an entrepreneurial spirit that enticed these women to take the risk.

Like women, men also smuggled an array of commodities. In the documents, men appear more involved in the smuggling of higher-end commodities such as cattle, horses, and guns. However, they too used innovative means to smuggle less lucrative items. In 1936, Daniel Curiel Rodríguez, a twenty-three-year-old day laborer from Tamaulipas, used a launch to smuggle various food products from the United States into Mexico. Men, more than women, commonly employed launches and used the river system in the border area to smuggle animals and food across the border.[55] One could smuggle far more on a launch than under one's clothing. On Mexico's coastlines, inspectors regularly detained fishing vessels and their crews to ensure that they were not smuggling. Men controlled the fishing industry, as they still do.

Men dominated key areas of smuggling, particularly the smuggling of guns, which has been a lucrative trade in the twentieth century. Mexican government officials, Mormons, cowboys, bandits, and individual opportunists all smuggled guns into Mexico during the revolution using an array of innovative methods.[56] But even in the midst of this masculine business, as historian Elizabeth Salas has documented, women have played a role.[57] Like today, women drew less attention, and their clothing served as an excellent cover for weapons, which could be tied to their legs hidden by their skirts. Ammunition could be sewn into hems and hidden pockets or stashed into bags that women carried.

The smuggling of legal goods to avoid paying fees and taxes reflects a long history of transnational commodities flows.[58] Women employed children, adopted various forms of new technologies, and traveled long distances to engage in smuggling. Those whom inspectors detained, questioned, and prosecuted represent a small number of those who crossed the border on a regular basis weighted down with illegal clothing, makeup, or food. Often, punishment for such crimes was sporadic and minor. Smugglers generally received fines of forty to one hundred pesos and the loss of the merchandise.[59] Those who smuggled on a larger scale with greater ingenuity—for instance, using an automobile—received greater fines and prison sentences.

For example, Guadalupe Navarro de Cons, a forty-three-year-old vendor, was arrested with her driver in 1936, receiving a sentence of six months in jail and the impounding of her car.[60] In 1937, Ola McDonald, a forty-two-year-old married woman from Eagle Pass, Texas, received a sentence of six months to two years. She was fined seven hundred pesos for smuggling tires into Mexico, which was a large fine for the time.[61] As a U.S. citizen, McDonald could not have been smuggling for her own personal use in Mexico. She and other U.S. citizens involved in smuggling appeared to pay heavier fines than their Mexican peers.[62] Cigarette smugglers, once detained, paid only a minor fine, and their property was confiscated. Most were quickly released.[63]

The extent that women engaged in transnational contraband ensured that other women would be recruited on the enforcement side of customs and border patrolling. Women, it was thought, were better suited to search other women and children to avoid allegations of sexual impropriety. Male customs agents oversaw and monitored the people, animals, cars, and trucks moving through the ports of entry. They questioned and studied people, they searched vehicles, and if necessary they detained people. Women agents conducted the searches of suspected women and children on both sides of the border. With women on their staff, federal agents became more comfortable searching, seizing, and arresting women who they believed were involved in contraband.

As women used their bodies as vessels for smuggling, customs agencies needed to employ not only women inspectors and matrons but also medical doctors and nurses to search suspects. In *María Full of Grace*, a female customs agent selects María for further inspection. Due to her pregnancy, the customs agent is unable to x-ray her. In reality, body searches could be far more brutal.

Over the years, policing has become more sophisticated and now employs more professionals and a greater range of technology. Women and their bodies have attracted growing attention as vessels for contraband. Few cases exist that document brutal body cavity searches for drugs, but a couple of examples do stand out. The 1940 case of Winnifred Chapman of Vancouver illuminates the medicalization of inspections and the escalation of violence used. Police agents suspected Chapman of selling opium. Although she and her partner, Henry Sherman, were Anglo, they maintained cross-ethnic alliances with the Vancouver Chinese community, who were their suppliers and their customers. They sold in cafés and teahouses frequented by both Anglos and Chinese. On July 31, 1940, in an undercover sting operation, a Vancouver constable took Chapman and Sherman into custody.[64]

The agents separated Sherman and Chapman. First, they strip-searched Sherman, finding nothing. Believing then that Chapman held the opium, the matron and narcotics agents told her that she could give up the drugs voluntarily or that a police officer who was also a surgeon would search her. Chapman, described as "a girl of large physique hardened by her mode of living," denied that she carried drugs on or in her body.

The matrons and doctor escorted her to a doctor's office that contained only a white examination table. With Chapman's refusal, the surgeon offered her another opportunity to give up the drugs voluntarily in front of him and three matrons. She again refused. They obtained leather straps and forced her onto the table. Chapman struggled for more than thirty minutes. The doctor was unable to use any surgical instruments, but after half an hour he extracted two fingerstalls secured with rubber bands that contained a total of forty decks of opium (a deck may contain anywhere from one to fifteen grams).[65] Fingerstalls are rubber finger or thumb coverings that were used by pharmacists, bank tellers, cashiers, and doctors, and they were used to transport narcotics and cocaine before the widespread adoption of condoms for that purpose.

Chapman's physical if not brutal body search demonstrates heightened panic on the part of enforcement agencies about drugs, and also a growing willingness to permit physical force. The bodies of women involved in selling were subject to scrutiny and search. Because of her working-class background, Chapman was readily subjected to a violent gynecological search, an indignity that an upper-class drug dealer or user would never have to submit to. The fact that a doctor, a police sergeant, and three prison matrons spent more than thirty minutes conducting a vaginal search demonstrates the power that officials could display over a criminal. Moreover, women using their bodies as vessels for contraband caused panic but also titillation. Why did the Vancouver authorities share this piece of evidence with the U.S. Federal Bureau of Narcotics? Despite the brutality of the search, Chapman did not disclose her supplier. She reported to the police that she had every intention of resuming peddling drugs in Vancouver once released.[66] Obviously, the intrusive search that was a form of punishment did not deter her.

As cross-border trade in illegal substances grew, so did the underground trade in legal contraband. The fact that people traveled great distances to smuggle clothes and soap reflected the growing demand for "foreign"—whether U.S. or European—goods, despite nationalistic rhetoric; one explanation is that domestic goods often cost more than their foreign equivalents.

That demand fueled trade in contraband, just as the demand for drugs in the United States and Canada fueled the flow of opiates and marijuana from Mexico northward.

In the late 1920s, the Bureau of Social Hygiene interviewed the five hundred women at the Alderson, West Virginia, prison for women. Of these prisoners, officials listed 317 as either drug users or drug sellers; 70 were sellers only. Their case studies depict the fluidity and mobility of young women involved in drugs. Some reported becoming addicted due to the men in their lives, some due to family members, and others due to their employers. One anonymous case highlighted transnational flows of drugs from Mexico to the United States.

Jane Doe was born in 1891 in Texas, and her father was a newspaperman. She attended convent schools until she went to the University of Texas and majored in journalism.[67] The summer of her sophomore year, she went to visit "a group of wild friends of hers," and ended up dropping out of college and going to New York, where she fell in with Lefty Louis (Louis Rosenberg) and the Lenox Avenue Gang. Members of the gang went to jail for a murder in 1912 in which they killed a bookmaker, Herman Rosenthal, at the request of Police Lieutenant Charles Becker. Rosenberg's sentence was execution.[68] In 1912, "Jane" took a prolonged spring break in Mexico, placing her in the midst of the Mexican Revolution.

She told social workers that she had fallen in love with a Mexican engineer who was an opium addict, and by the age of twenty she was as well. He eventually went straight but died fighting in the Mexican Revolution. Jane then embarked on a second relationship with a medical doctor who supplied her addiction. They divorced in 1922, and she returned to the United States, settling in California. There, she fell in with another gang that specialized in stealing furs, selling narcotics, and smuggling. She also served as a steerer, or "confidence worker" as she put it.[69] Essentially, Jane worked with crooks to rob people. Her job was to ensure that targeted individuals came to trust her and her associates, in order to facilitate the fraud. In 1927, she was arrested on a narcotics charge, check forgery, and mail fraud, convicted, and sent to Alderson.

Jane shares a number of commonalities with contemporary female drug peddlers and traffickers. An addict, she relied on her husband and lovers to supply her, and she saw crime as a means by which to supply her addiction. Her divorce from the Mexican doctor forced her to return to the United States. There, she fell into crime to support her habit. However, she returned to organized crime, where she previously had been a moll, a woman who associates with and works for the mob, a role she had played with the Lenox Avenue Gang.[70] What is remarkable about Jane is that she could very well have established an opiate connection between a Mexican supplier and organized crime in the United States. In her statement, she argued that in Mexico she had been an addict, but she had moved in organized crime circles both in New York before moving to Mexico and later in Los Angeles. While living in Mexico, her opium would have been acquired locally, whether it had originated in Mexico or Asia. She would have gained access to and knowledge of the internal market as well as the larger Asian opium trade. As someone who moved across borders, she also would have been able to identify the lack of oversight and the inadequate policing on the border. Once she returned to the United States, she became involved in various criminal activities, but she only reported that she sold narcotics.

Women as drug mules, whether smuggling for themselves or for someone else, operated as central components of the trade. Their bodies, accessories, and clothing—their femaleness—became tools for smugglers, whether of licit products such as clothing and automobile parts or of illegal products such as drugs. At times they worked for men, or they worked independently to support themselves or their families. Some women turned to smuggling because of their own addictions. Women such as Jane, who was an addict, also provided important skills. She worked as a partner within organizations and may have assisted men in identifying markets and suppliers.[71]

While Jane's case seemed sensational due to her transnational movements and her ties to organized crime in the 1910s and 1920s, by the 1930s and 1940s women who functioned as partners of men were drawing increasing recognition from customs and FBN officials. Margarita Rosas Trejo's association with drug dealers drew the attention of the FBN. Harry Anslinger wrote in 1940:

> Trejo married her while drunk then left her. She lives with a drunkard Francisco Nunez, a smuggler of drugs. He takes drugs to San Diego and Solano Beach . . . and they smuggle marijuana. . . . Do not allow them to enter as they are dangerous, also Jose Rosas who recently entered the US without permission. His sister Josefina Perres Chica lives in Solano with Juan Santoya . . . and she smuggles marijuana and other drugs. . . . She is always in Tijuana. . . . Consult with people in Solano Beach and they will tell you the kind of person she is. . . .

Francisco Nunez the drunkard ask in Tijuana and Mexicali as to his smuggling activities. Jose Rosas lived over there (Ex. US) without permission with the man his sister lives with, his sister is fat and has two children. . . . She lives there in Tijuana and has immigration permission.[72]

ILLICIT FLOWS IN CONTROLLED SPACES

The flow of contraband did not only occur across borders. Illegal commodities flowed from cities into rural areas, through local controlled spaces. Women introduced illicit substances into controlled spaces such as prisons. In Mexico, and in many other parts of the world, families were expected to provide food, clothing, and other items to their family members who are imprisoned. If there were no family members who fulfilled such obligations, charities such as the Catholic Church donated needed items. During family visits, people also passed drugs. In 1931, Josefina Lara Paredes, a thirty-nine-year-old single woman, went to the prison in Tampico to visit her lover. She hid marijuana in the bags of fruit that she passed to him. Upon inspection, guards confiscated the marijuana, and she was later found guilty and sentenced to two years in prison.[73]

In 1938, thirty-year-old Antonia Rodríguez Ávila hid marijuana in a false bottom of a bottle of milk she brought for her husband in prison.[74] She, too, was arrested at the prison. With food items, women demonstrated their creativity. They used tamales, fruit, and newspapers and other reading materials as vessels to conceal contraband from the prison staff. Women also mixed marijuana with tobacco and rolled cigarettes, thus passing drugs into the prison. María Albina Flores, a thirty-five-year-old domestic worker, was arrested in 1936 for passing marijuana that she disguised as other herbs to help alleviate her imprisoned husband's suffering due to "the chronic sickness in his legs."[75]

In 1940, prison guards arrested Manuela Rodríguez Sánchez, who had traveled from Veracruz to Santiago Tlatelolco prison in Mexico City to visit her husband, Pablo Campuzano Torres.[76] Campuzano had committed homicide so his prison sentence was long. At the time of her arrest, Rodríguez said that she knew that her husband enjoyed fruit, but he was more partial to "Juanita." So she had prepared a basket of tropical fruits and hid marijuana

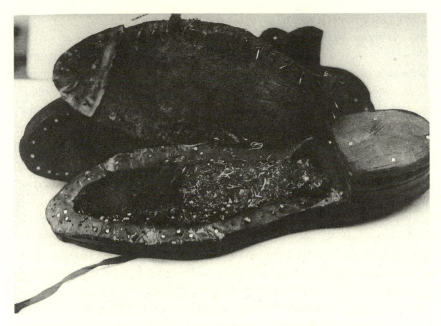

Figure 8. Shoe with marijuana. Serie Mariguana, opio, y rogas, ca. 1935, 142927, Casasola, Mexico City, Fototeca Nacional del Instituto Nacional de Anthropología e Historia (INAH), Pachuca, Hidalgo.

in her clothing. Guards arrested her for concealing and then transferring marijuana. She was aware that it was illegal to pass this plant to her imprisoned husband, given that she had taken the trouble to hide it.

In prison, men and women both sold and used drugs to gain power, to obtain privileges, and to make money. In both Mexico and the United States, family members of male inmates have played the role of sympathetic visitor but have also acted as fronts for the inmates' internal drug businesses by smuggling in supplies. As in the early 1900s, women passed drugs to their imprisoned men not only to help them assuage the slow passage of time, but also to allow them greater access to power within prison that drug possession provided. Prisoners sometimes worked alongside prison guards and even wardens to profit from drug trading both within and beyond the prison.

Drug use and vending in prison became a growing problem in Mexico in the 1930s, causing tensions within communities that surrounded prisons and in relations with the United States. In April 1935, C. Zepeda Morantes, a concerned citizen, wrote to Juan de Dios Bojórquez of the Secretariat of the Interior about Alejandro Lazy, a prison director in Mexico City, who allowed alcoholic drinks as well as heroin and other drugs to be widely consumed. Zepeda wrote that a conspiracy of vice existed between Lazy, a lawyer named C. J. Guadalupe, and the commander of the guards, Rodolfo H. Vivanco.[77] He argued that male and female prisoners used drugs and alcohol that they purchased from a small store maintained by the prison director's lover, Soledad Rodríguez Prado, whom he routinely met at the house of a prison guard, Mercedes Moreno, who lived in the neighborhood. In turn, Lazy, Guadalupe, Vivanco, and Rodríguez conspired to sell drugs to the prison population. Rodríguez's store served as a front for drug distribution. Conspiracies like this document that prisoners, prison directors, attorneys, and guards alike felt the lure of drugs as a means to make money.

Despite the overall lower addiction rates in Mexico compared to the United States, Mexican health authorities recognized that prisons presented a growing problem with regard to drug trafficking.[78] In 1938, U.S. Treasury agent Alvin Scharff met with Mexico's chief of alcohol and narcotics service of the Department of Health, Dr. Leopoldo Salazar Viniegra, to discuss the problem. Salazar worked closely with addicts. He told Scharff that there were some four hundred addicts in the various jails and penitentiaries in the Federal District who had been securing supplies of drugs for their personal use from people who smuggled the drugs into the jails. Salazar argued that it had been impossible to prevent smuggling into the prisons because of lax conditions and strong demand.

Differing dramatically from policies favored by the United States, Salazar advocated a medical response that would provide addicts with morphine so that the heroin and opium traffickers' fortunes would wane and they would lose influence in the prisons.[79] Moreover, Salazar alluded to the fact that the drug trade flourished in part due to the corruption of government officials who too were involved in the trade.[80]

Outside prison walls, the relationship between women and drug peddling was also complex. Women peddled drugs in the street as they sold fruit, cigarettes, and other items. Cases from the 1930s demonstrate that women sold marijuana cigarettes on the street, sometimes hidden in fruit baskets, while other times, in certain neighborhoods, more prominently displayed but still hidden from inspectors. For example, María Dolorez Cruz Hernández, a forty-five-year-old woman, drew suspicion in the Plaza Fray Bartolomé de las Casas in Mexico City. Police reported that she appeared to be a lower-class street vendor who became nervous when they approached her. On inspection, the police discovered that she had a number of well-rolled marijuana cigarettes. In the interrogation, she told the police that she secured her supply from a dealer from the Tacubaya neighborhood and had just finished her day's work.[81] She had apparently sold a substantial number of marijuana cigarettes in the plaza.

Localized vending among women was common in many major cities around the world. In New York City in the 1910s, narcotics peddling among the nonelite demonstrates an emerging narconarrative of vice. In 1914, Lulu Hammond stood trial for violation of the Harrison Act. She had allegedly sold "a deck of cards [cocaine]" to a man posing as her client. Hammond, an African American widowed single mother, argued that she was a laundress who did not sell drugs, as alleged, from her apartment, where she lived with her daughter, a roommate, and a dog. In the court transcripts, Hammond is described as wearing an Asian kimono at the time of her arrest. Her kimono, her living circumstances, and the testimony of her own daughter, who told the court that her mother owned a gun, ensured that whether she had sold the cocaine or not, she was destined for jail. The attorneys and detectives were fascinated by the spectacle of a black woman wearing a kimono, which they believed signified that she was probably a prostitute. She argued that it had been a gift from a merchant marine boyfriend, which only fueled speculation that she worked as a prostitute. Stereotypes of the time suggest that an armed African American woman, wearing a kimono and selling cocaine to a white man, was a threat.[82]

Hammond may have been a small-time peddler, but other women involved in the drug trade developed sophisticated selling practices that continue today. In 1923, narcotics agent Walter C. Smith arrested Alice Hurley for selling cocaine in Philadelphia.[83] In his interview, she told him that she worked a particular area of the city on commission for a male dealer. Smith documented that women like Hurley worked on commission or held franchises from other dealers. Hurley appears to have worked on commission for a man affiliated with organized crime.[84] Cases such as these from the 1920s, although few, document that female street vendors had a multidimensional relationship with the selling of drugs.[85] Women served as steerers, lookouts, runners, jobbers, and fronters for drug sales; as fronters, they purchased drugs for other people and perhaps smuggled them into prisons.[86] Through maintaining franchises, selling on commission, or serving as steerers by bringing customers to dealers, women had a degree of autonomy from male authority because they sold independently on the street or from their homes. In those cases, they controlled the ebb and flow of their business.

Many women also sold for their husbands and lovers. Those familial connections to a prominent bandit or drug peddler ensured that certain women would continue to draw police attention. For instance, Ana María Barrera de Urquito was the wife a bandit. When she was arrested with her lover, Elpidio Miravete, a member of another family of imprisoned bandits, the Mexican press reported that the two became insulting and adopted a challenging and insolent attitude toward authorities. Ana María declared: "Since you were unable to bother my husband . . . you now endeavor to hurt me saying that I sell drugs. . . . That is not true!"[87] Police often assumed—and probably rightfully so—that a woman's connections indicated her likely involvement in drug selling.

The peddling of narcotics mimicked the vending of alcohol. Women began selling drugs to support their families, and they used family networks to sustain their work. Bingham Dai, in his work on opium addiction in Chicago during the 1930s, documented that of the 672 women addicts he studied, 14 percent were nonaddicted peddlers who had been arrested and sent to either the Women's Reformatory at the Dwight Correctional Center or the Keeley Institute, both in Dwight, Illinois.[88] These women made up the portion of those arrests who were in fact vendors who sought profit, not access to drugs. Among the other women, Dai also noted the high rate of venereal disease among women addicts compared to male addicts, a result of women's additional work as prostitutes.

Drug use, however, caused concern that women were acting beyond their acceptable gendered roles in society. Smuggling and peddling, although a form of commerce, in many ways undermined expected gendered norms. Women who bought and sold drugs transgressed beliefs about the role of women within the illicit labor market. While prostitutes often used mind-altering substances to perform their work, other women may have used drug selling as a way to move beyond prostitution, or they simply opted to sell drugs rather than turn tricks. Both occupations were dangerous, subjecting women to police harassment, personal attacks, and physical deprivation. However, the transgressions of street vendors, *contrabandistas*, and smugglers ensured the scrutiny of policing agents on both sides of the border. Prostitution, on the other hand, was simply an internal Mexican problem that rarely led to the sharing of information with U.S. law enforcement officers.

In 1939, the Mexican newspaper *Excélsior* reported that a woman, Teresa Sánchez Velázquez, had gotten into a heated argument with Alejandro Aguilar Luna in a saloon. This incident caught the attention of Harry Anslinger at the FBN. Aguilar Luna, an addict, had apparently bumped into Sánchez, which triggered a dispute. Sánchez was described as having "hair on her chest and a revolver in her belt." When Aguilar bumped into her, she "abused him" for his lack of gentility. He picked a fight with her, and she shot him in the foot.[89]

What remains striking is why the U.S. embassy in Mexico City would share such a minor news report with the FBN. Perhaps Sánchez's use of force clearly showed how drug use, whether by an addict or by those who come into contact with one, works to undermine social hierarchies between the sexes.[90] Sánchez frequented an establishment where addicts were present, and her perceived physical appearance as masculine further supported the threatening view that drug use altered the social order, even between men and women and masculinity and femininity. Sánchez's act of self-defense also raised questions about what she was doing in a cantina, traditionally a male establishment. Incidents like this yielded considerable discussion among public health officials about drugs and women. These fears flowed across borders and contributed to transnational cooperation.

THE GLOBAL MULE: THE TRANSNATIONAL CASE OF MARIA WENDT

Internal flows of drugs created domestic problems for Mexico. As the country tried to rebuild and modernize, drug selling and use undermined those efforts. However, internal drug use in Mexico was beginning to draw global attention; a growing number of international cases involving multiple actors reached far beyond the arms of Mexico's policing and state agencies and created a huge dilemma for the country. In the 1930s, technological advancements wrought by modernization allowed men and women involved in criminal behavior to expand their activities by using air travel, telephones, and banking wires. In the wake of the collapse of the Mexican economy in 1929, many people found the means to make money through narcotics beyond localized smuggling along the border or simple peddling. The case of Maria Wendt (also referred to as Molly Maria Wendt) can serve as an example of women used as transnational mules by international criminal syndicates. Wendt was exceptional because her ties to one of the era's most prominent drug trafficking rings helped create a partnership between the United States and Mexico. Her arrest led to the dismantling of one of the world's most famous global opiate rings. More importantly, she and the men that she worked with provide keys to understanding the supply of Asian opium to Mexico.

In 1933, Harry Anslinger wrote to Francisco Vásquez Pérez at the Department of Health about a suspected trafficker, Jorge Halperin, aka Mechel Halperin, who was operating in Mexico City.[91] In October and November 1934, Anslinger sent Vázquez Pérez three letters in which he argued that Halperin worked for Naftali Loeffelholz-Brandstatter (also referred to as Norbert), the head of a company called the Machinery and Engineering Corporation based in Shanghai.[92] Anslinger alleged that this business served a front for a notorious transnational opium trafficking ring that operated from Shanghai, Los Angeles, Mexico City, Havana, and Berlin.[93] Anslinger also claimed that Halperin had exchanged telegrams with George Dorande of Shanghai, an agent for Loeffelholz-Brandstatter; Dorande demanded money from Halperin and told him to use an agent, Albert Rosenbaum, at a particular Mexico City bank to wire the money to Shanghai.[94] Anslinger's cryptic messages to Vásquez Pérez never specifically outlined what the Mexican public health official should look for, but he asked Vásquez Pérez to put Halperin under surveillance. Anslinger was convinced that Halperin was involved in narcotics smuggling.

As discussed in chapter 1, Mexican officials had already shown great concern about the illegal activities of foreign nationals. This case had extraordinary repercussions. The early cooperation that emerged between Mexico and the United States was unprecedented. With Anslinger's encouragement, Mexican officials gathered information about Halperin, who lived with his wife, Ethel, and two sons, Otto and Rodolfo. Halperin, of German origin but a naturalized "Central American citizen" (no country specified in the documents), worked as a businessman who sold decals (calcomanías) and as a real estate agent for properties owned by Americans in Mexico.

In a handwritten, unsigned letter to Anslinger, an agent for the Department of Health asked if the FBN knew whether the drugs would come by ship or by parcel to Mexico. Officials in Mexico believed that a large shipment was due to arrive soon. But neither Mexican nor U.S. officials knew when, where, or how that shipment would arrive.[95]

The surveillance of Halperin demonstrated cross-border cooperation in an attempt to stem drug trafficking. It also illustrates the impact of modernity on drug trafficking, and those who worked to stop it. Anslinger and his agents had observed Loeffelholz-Brandstatter, intercepted various telegrams, and sent that information to Mexican authorities, although it is unclear how the FBN secured telegrams sent from Mexico to China.

Halperin used telegrams to communicate with his contacts in Shanghai and received his instructions from Dorande the same way. Moreover, the ability to wire money to another country reflected an innovation in banking technology that enabled traffickers to often dispense with physical couriers. FBN agents, perhaps operating illegally in Mexico, intercepted communications and instructions and passed those on to Mexican authorities. The evidence suggests that Mexican authorities never questioned how Anslinger acquired the telegrams—which is rather suspicious, since all were sent from Mexico City directly to Shanghai, though they may have been routed via the United States. Instead, they followed his request to place Halperin under continuous surveillance, which revealed little except that his family life and daily activities did not seem that unusual or threatening.

In 1936, the investigation of Halperin and his ties to Loeffelholz-Brandstatter took an advantageous turn. On August 5, U.S. Customs agents detained Maria Wendt when she disembarked from the Japanese ship MV *Heiyo Maru* after it docked in San Pedro, California.[96] Customs inspectors grew suspicious of her and searched her baggage. Initially, they thought she was a silk smuggler because her wardrobes were full of silk, but these only served as a front for her true cargo. Upon closer inspection, customs officers found secret compartments in her trunks that yielded fifty-four pounds (862.75 ounces) of pure heroin valued at $100,000 (2012: $1,652,000). Once cut, it had a value of over $1 million (2012: $16,518,000). Federal officials arrested her. At that time, it was one of the largest narcotics hauls ever apprehended from a mule.[97]

Once arrested, the twenty-three-year-old confessed that she was supposed to deliver the heroin to a man dressed in black on a certain day in a certain place in Los Angeles. During their investigation, agents found that the heroin originated in Shanghai. Daniel Bailey, the customs agent in charge, reported "that the deal for this shipment of narcotic was consummated in Mexico City between Anton Wurthmueller of Mexico City and Norbert Lefenholtz Branstatter of Shanghai, China and unknown parties from New York City."[98] He alluded to the fact that Wendt may have been present at the meetings in Mexico City in which the group planned to move the heroin to its final destination in New York.[99] Bailey's communication confirmed that the organization had been under surveillance in Mexico City, most likely due to the earlier surveillance of the Halperin case. Loeffelholz-Brandstatter lived in exile in Shanghai and based his business there; Anton Wurthmueller lived in Mexico City, overseeing an operation that shipped agricultural and engineering equipment from Germany to Mexico and Central America. Hidden away in that equipment, he smuggled heroin. In 1935, he was believed to have smuggled four hundred pounds of heroin into the port of Veracruz in a single shipment.

When arrested in San Pedro, Wendt confessed that she had been asked to deliver the heroin to a man she had planned to meet. In her testimony, she stated that Mr. and Mrs. Francis Rossendahl (also appears as Rosendeal) hired her to accompany Mrs. Rossendahl from China to San Francisco.[100] She had met Mr. Rossendahl, a stockbroker, at a café in Shanghai.[101] Wendt was to accompany his wife as a nurse. After arriving in San Francisco, Wendt argued, Rossendahl asked her to travel to Los Angeles on her own to deliver some trunks. After that, she would travel to Mexico City.[102]

After Wendt was taken into custody, officials held her, hoping to nab her accomplice. They planned to hold her for a few days and allow her to make the drop so that they could arrest others. Trusting Wendt to work with them, they housed her at the Rosslyn Hotel in Los Angeles rather than the country jail; however, their plan failed because Wendt escaped from the hotel. Her escape led to a crisis in the Treasury Department; a woman who was the key to a two-year-long investigation had slipped through the fingers of agents. Officials proclaimed that "her own friends" must have kidnapped her. On August 12, 1936, Thomas Gorman of customs reported to Henry Morgenthau, secretary of the treasury, that Wendt had fled from his officials in Los Angeles. However, he stated that they detained the fugitive that morning in New York City boarding the SS *Deutschland* to sail for Germany. Morgenthau became enraged over the incompetence of his LA agents, and he called for disciplinary action against the employee or employees responsible for Wendt's escape.[103]

Of course, Morgenthau didn't know that her escape and recapture was far more complicated than the story reported by Gorman. After leaving the hotel, Wendt hailed a cab and went to the Los Angeles airport. There, she boarded a United Airlines flight to New York. Gorman reported that a man who agents assumed was Japanese had purchased her ticket. B. W. Thomas, the taxi driver, confirmed that Wendt had hailed his cab and asked him to drive her to the airport. They made no stops until arriving at the airport.

However, since they were early, Thomas drove her around the neighborhood surrounding the airport until ten minutes before the plane was scheduled to depart, at 11:00 a.m.[104] Moreover, a stewardess on the flight argued that Ms. Wendt seemed agitated during the flight, but she flew alone and did not speak with any other passengers.[105] No one ever demonstrated how Wendt came to have enough cash to purchase her plane ticket or how she had otherwise obtained the ticket. The reports of a Japanese man helping her were never proven. Upon her arrival to New York, how a fugitive without a passport could board a ship bound for Europe further complicated the tale.

Indeed, how did Wendt, a fugitive, pass through Customs and Immigration and board a ship when an all-points bulletin had been issued for her arrest? During her trial, Wendt testified that upon her arrival in New York she met a Chinese American man named Wong and married him. Once married, she applied for a passport and was issued one under the name of Mayline Wong. She argued that she had met Mr. Wong in a restaurant in New York and that he was the one who had proposed marriage. She accepted, took his name, and acquired a passport under her married name.[106]

Whether Wendt married Wong for a passport or whether Wong was part of her network of contacts or even one of her handlers remains a mystery. Yet, it permitted her to gain access to a passport and to board the SS *Deutschland* bound for Europe. She boarded the ship, and it set sail. Before long, the agents realized their mistake and feared the loss of their jobs.[107] They worked with the Coast Guard to intercept the ship and force it back to New York. Customs agents detained Wendt and sent her back to Los Angeles for further questioning. In the U.S. press, Wendt was cast as a mere pawn for a Japanese trafficking ring, while the documentary evidence suggests that she played a key role in the enterprises of Loeffelholz-Brandstatter and Wurthmueller.[108]

By the time Wendt returned to Los Angeles, Treasury agent Alvin Scharff had begun to interrogate Sam Schwartz, an accomplice, seen with Wendt on the ship from Shanghai. With both Wendt and Schwartz in custody, customs agents began to piece together an outline of this transnational trafficking organization, but it was Schwartz who told agents that the organization was not based in Shanghai, as it first appeared, but rather in Mexico City. Always unorthodox in his demeanor and policing techniques, Scharff decided to return immediately to Mexico, and he invited Schwartz to travel with him as far as El Paso. During this train trip, Schwartz provided the testimony that Scharff gave

Mexican authorities and that led to multiple arrests in Mexico City and New York in 1936 and 1937. Despite Anslinger's earlier efforts, it was Al Scharff, his competitor and foil, who broke the Loeffelholz-Brandstatter ring, one of the largest drug trafficking organizations to that point, and who rose to prominence in the Department of the Treasury.

Scharff's life story is as infamous as those of the traffickers whom he tracked. Like Anslinger, he remained a prominent figure in the early war on drugs from the 1930s into the 1960s.[109] In his preface to Scharff's biography, Philip Nichols Jr., the commissioner of customs, wrote: "It is apparent that another Al Scharff could not possibly be admitted to the Customs Service today. By his own account, Al had smuggled, rustled cattle, peddled counterfeit money, filibustered, and committed fornication on numerous occasions."[110] Scharff's biography reads like a picaresque account of border life. However sensationalized, his life attested that he knew and understood Mexico, the border, and transnational crime better than most crime fighters.

Like many young men, Scharff went west to seek his fortune. He came of age on the border, where he worked in mining, counterfeiting, and even smuggling. Scharff ended up in a Mexican prison after he traveled across that country passing counterfeit pesos. A U.S. consul secured his release, recognizing Scharff's shrewdness and his knowledge of Mexico. During World War I, German U-boats challenged the United States in the Pacific.[111] The FBI suspected that there was a wireless station in Mexico being utilized by the Germans, and they recruited Scharff as a special employee to target and destroy it.[112] In what reads almost as a fictional account, Scharff set out on the mission accompanied by his guide, Red Slippers, and four Yaquis. In the Sonora Mountains they found and destroyed the wireless station and also killed two German agents.[113]

While in Mexico during World War I, Scharff developed sophisticated networks of personal relations in Mexico City and along the border. After the war, he returned to his life of legal and illegal activities. Like many borderlanders, Scharff had a different interpretation of licit living. He was a cattle rustler working both sides of the border to support his fledgling attempts to establish a gold mine. Eventually, his transborder crimes drew the attention of U.S. customs officials, who offered him a chance to put his skills to work for the government or go to jail. As a customs agent, Scharff immediately distinguished himself in the 1920s by breaking up an infamous rum-running organization operating through Galveston, Texas.[114] In Galveston, he used informants tied to organized crime to penetrate criminal rings. In the 1930s, the department stationed Scharff in Mexico City to ascertain the duty values to be placed on Mexican handicrafts exported to the United States. Despite tariff laws stipulating that Mexican products must be assessed the same taxes, customhouses in the United States assigned different values. Thus, Scharff returned to Mexico to study and assess different Mexican handicrafts and commodities.

As Garland Roark established, Scharff made great use of his time in Mexico City. He befriended the U.S. ambassador, Josephus Daniels, who had grown increasingly concerned about narcotics and Mexico's seeming lack of control along its border with the United States. Scharff also befriended a number of prominent Mexicans in the government, including Dr. José Siroub, the director of the Department of Health, Luis Franco, the head of alcohol and narcotics, and Attorney General Ignacio Téllez. He also made numerous contacts among the Mexican elite, the business classes, and the growing Jewish community. These networks of friends in positions of power assisted him in his investigations, but he reciprocated their value to him by sharing information.

Unlike his Mexican colleagues and friends who enjoyed Scharff's antics, straitlaced U.S. bureaucrats like Anslinger grew annoyed and frustrated with him. With his southern twang, cowboy boots, and colorful past, Scharff had broken the Loeffelholz-Brandstatter ring almost singlehandedly. He used his extensive contacts within the embassy as well as in

Figure 9. Alvin Scharff in Sonora, Mexico. Garland Roark Papers, East Texas Research Center, Stephen F. Austin University, Nacogdoches, TX.

Figure 10. Alvin Scharff in a Texas marijuana field. Garland Roark Papers, East Texas
Research Center, Stephen F. Austin University, Nacogdoches, TX.

Mexican society. Moreover, he continually argued that narcotics and drug
smuggling must remain within the domain of Customs, not the FBN, thus
threatening Anslinger's position. Although Anslinger had informed the
Mexican government about Loeffelholz-Brandstatter in 1933, the case was
broken in Mexico. Journalist Douglas Valentine argues that Scharff generated the leads and informants and did not share them with anyone in the
FBN.[115]

Documents in Mexico suggest that this was indeed true. Scharff provided information to Secretary of Health Siroub and to the Mexican government; in 1936, Scharff controlled the case because he had developed the leads
and was working directly with the Mexican authorities, bypassing
Anslinger.[116] What Scharff uncovered in Mexico led to the arrests of Judas
Fustenberg, Icek Katz, Majick Salve, and Mochen Eghise. Scharff stated that
the people operating in Mexico coordinated with those who worked in
China, including Wurthmueller, Matt Kattwinkel, Mirecea Lepescu, Curt

Smith, Albert Rosenbaum, and José Buchawald; all of these worked with Loeffelholz-Brandstatter as well as Will Seigel, based in New York City.

All those arrested in Mexico City provided the government with depositions. These, along with Scharff's deposition, outlined a global organization that moved drugs and money that Scharff had been tracking from the United States and Mexico since the early 1930s.[117] Scharff noted that the capture of Wendt, who was to travel to Mexico after arriving in Los Angeles, triggered the collapse of the organization.[118] Scharff explained in his deposition that, once Wendt was arrested, her colleagues used various forms of communication to determine what had happened, leading to her escape from the Los Angeles hotel. Once they realized that she had been captured again in New York, they began to liquidate assets and hide their business dealings.

After her capture in New York, Wendt was returned to Los Angeles by authorities on August 14, 1936. Because of her previous escape, two agents traveled with her from New York, and eight agents met her plane in Los Angeles. She was arraigned and held on a $25,000 bond to stand trial. Since she could not make bail, she awaited trial in the county jail. While incarcerated, she explained to agents that her escape from the Los Angeles hotel had been facilitated by an American woman who had visited her in the hotel and given her travelers checks and a plane ticket.[119] While in prison, she became very ill with advanced tuberculosis and underwent surgery. Because of her illness, she repeatedly requested to be deported to China, because she assumed that she would be sentenced to jail time. Despite these appeals, Wendt stood trial and was found guilty of violation of the Harrison Act. She received a sentence of ten years at the federal women's prison in Alderson, West Virginia. Newspaper coverage of her trial portrayed her as a petite woman in stylish clothes. Journalists identified her ethnicity as Eurasian or Chinese German.

Wendt's ethnic background and that of her collaborators fueled speculation on both sides of the border about who held responsibility for increased heroin trafficking in the 1930s. Customs agent Bailey reported that Mexican officials blamed expatriate Germans and Chinese in Mexico as responsible for the new heroin-processing laboratories that had sprung up in the 1930s. In the United States, customs and FBN agents repeatedly discussed the influence of the Japanese in drug trafficking in North America, due to their already documented involvement in Asian drug trafficking.[120] Additionally, the ship that Wendt sailed on to the United States was a Japanese vessel. Wendt and the men associated with her bolstered all these perceptions. Her contacts in Mexico included Germans, Poles, and Jews. Plus, she was of Chinese and

Questioned in Smuggling

Marie Wendt, reportedly the daughter of a wealthy Chinese official and being investigated on charges of silk smuggling, is shown here with a customs agent as she was fingerprinted in the United States marshal's office. Times photo

Girl Smuggler Suspect Escapes From Guards

Maria Wendt, held for investigation in connection with silk smuggling charges by customs officials, made a sensational escape from her guards in a downtown hotel last night. While she was being questioned one of the guards stepped from the room, when she returned Miss Wendt was gone. The hotel immediately was blockaded by radio police and Federal officers.

When a customs inspector chanced to jab a knife into a suspicious-appearing rounded corner of trunk, some white powder trickled out.

That powder was smuggled heroin, with a potential retail value of 1,000,000—easily one of the largest seizures of illegal narcotics ever made in the United States.

Collector of Customs Alfred A. Cohn last night thus summarized the sensational discoveries made upon the docking of the N.Y.K. liner Heiyo Maru from the Orient.

TWO TRUNKS SEIZED

Two American-made trunks were seized. Both had the ingeniously devised rounded inside corners. Concealed under the corners were silk bags holding the unadulterated heroin.

The combined seizure totaled fifty-three pounds, worth $107,000 in its present undiluted form. When diluted, it will have a value of $1,000,000.

Customs Inspector Mickle discovered the powder in probing with his knife. As a result, customs agents yesterday had a sweeping investigation in progress, hoping to identify members of a powerful dope smuggling ring operating between Shanghai and Japan and the Pacific Coast.

COUPLE RELEASED

Meantime, but with no connection to the case last night, Simon Harris, war veteran, and Maria Wendt, 23 years of age, said to be the daughter of a wealthy Shanghai official, were arraigned on silk-smuggling charges.

Harris, whose bail earlier had been set at $5000, and Miss Wendt both were released on their own recognizance by United States Commissioner Head upon recommendation of customs inspectors. Their hearing was set for August 17. Both deny the charges against them.

German descent. U.S. officials continued to argue that a Japanese agent had also purchased her ticket for the SS *Deutschland*. Wendt thus embodied the national rhetoric of degeneracy on both sides of the border. She was of partially Asian decent and was involved in drug trafficking with a cross-ethnic organization. She also complicates the narrative.

As a woman, Wendt maintained that she was simply a mule—"a tool"—who had been "abandoned by those who used me."[121] She argued that she had been arrested on her trial run, and that she had never previously engaged in smuggling. Because she was a woman, she could reiterate certain stereotypes of a "victim," hoping to sway perceptions in her favor. She was a pawn in a scheme concocted by two men: Loeffelholz-Brandstatter and Wurthmueller. However, the fact of her well-placed contacts in China and elsewhere cast doubt on her story. From the time of her arrest, journalists reported that she hailed from a well-connected Chinese family and that she was a cosmopolitan, multilingual, world traveler. One journalist noted that an agreement had been reached with the court not to disclose her family's name.

Figure 11. Maria Wendt: "Girl Smuggler Suspect Escapes from Guards." *Los Angeles Times.*

In 1936, Wendt's identity came to light when she was listed as the daughter of the governor general of Tibet.[122] But it was not until 1938, in a *New York Times* article about the new government and national anthem in Japanese-occupied Nanking, China, that a journalist reported the name of Wendt's family. Maria Wendt was the daughter of Wen Tsung-Yao, the minister of justice in the new Nanking government.[123] Prior to the 1911 Chinese revolution, he also served in the government in Tibet. Thus, since her childhood, Maria Wendt had moved in sophisticated circles. Moreover, her name remains a mystery. Did she carry her mother's name or create a Europeanized surname based on her father's name? Wendt exhibits early on the use of the pseudonym, which remains a common practice among men and women involved in the drug trade. With her multicultural background and powerful father, she was highly educated, urbane, Westernized, and well traveled. She easily moved from one country to another.

Wendt used certain stereotypical characterizations of women to undermine and resist the authorities in the United States. In California, this worked. Her strategic essentialist argument that she was a pawn was further complicated by the suicide of Naftali Loeffelholz-Brandstatter. U.S. Customs agents had tracked his movements through the 1930s from Shanghai to Mexico, to Cuba, and then to Europe. Wendt's detention led to the eventual arrest of Loeffelholz-Brandstatter, allegedly her business partner, in Cuba.[124] Deported from Cuba to New York in late August, he committed suicide en route while in the custody of U.S. Treasury officials.[125] His belongings revealed clues that other women had assisted the organization in addition to Wendt. A photograph of a blond woman was found; on the back of it was a code of some sort. Following Wendt's arrest and Loeffelholz-Brandstatter's suicide, police in Los Angeles, New York, and Mexico City conducted numerous raids and arrests resulting from information gathered from Wendt and those arrested in Mexico.

The evidence shows that Loeffelholz-Brandstatter and Wurthmueller definitely transshipped Asian heroin through Mexico to the United States, demonstrating practices of contemporary transnational criminal organizations. The group took full advantage of modern technologies to communicate with one another via telegram, the postal service, and telephone. They used various forms of transportation to move legitimate products, but also to move heroin. They employed ships, planes, and mail services, as well as human couriers. However, the heroin deliveries that law enforcement agencies were able to document are likely only a fraction of the total deliveries made by the group from the early 1930s to its collapse in 1936. If Wendt brought in fifty-four pounds, given the networks of contacts, bank employees, and operators on three continents, how much heroin altogether was moved by the organization is difficult to document.

The Loeffelholz-Brandstatter case substantiates much of the contemporary analysis of illicit transnational flows and globalization. As Moisés Naím and Michael Kenney have argued, technological advancements have facilitated illicit trade, and the organization took advantage of a country that was in transition.[126] Mexico of the 1930s, under the administration of President Lázaro Cárdenas, became more welcoming to foreign immigrants from all over the world as they fled fascism. His period of office coincided with both heightened nationalism and expanded integration and relations with the outside world. Mexican cultural life drew artists from Europe and the Americas, including many seeking refuge from the Spanish Civil War and the rise of Nazism.

The people involved with Loeffelholz-Brandstatter could easily blend into a changing Mexico, particularly in Mexico City as it was becoming more cosmopolitan. All came from educated and fairly prosperous backgrounds: they were all professionals. Those from Shanghai had worked in engineering and medicine. In Mexico, merchants and bankers joined the narcotics organization as well. All spoke multiple languages and lived transnational lives, due in part to the mass displacements that occurred during the interwar years. Meetings between people of diverse backgrounds routinely took place in Mexico City, among artists, intellectuals, and politicians. Thus, in such a cosmopolitan and evolving city, gatherings among expatriate European professionals such as engineers, bankers, and medical professionals who also happened to be involved in drug trafficking never drew suspicion.

Despite their level of education and professional experience, or perhaps because of that, they were attracted to profits in opium and heroin trafficking. From the evidence, the Loeffelholz-Brandstatter group had extensive contacts in the banking industry. They also recruited skilled agents who assisted them wherever they were. As scholars Itty Abraham and Willem van Schendel have argued, "individuals and social groups that systematically contest or bypass state controls do not simply flout the letter of the law; with repeated transgressions over time, they bring into question the legitimacy of the state itself by questioning the state's ability to control its own territory."[127] Thus, the Loeffelholz-Brandstatter organization challenged policing agents, national borders, and government regulation by working across a number of regulated spaces such as banking and communications.[128] Their ability to respond rapidly to a problem almost ensured that local investigations were inconclusive and the organization remained intact. How else to explain the ease with which the organization was able to purchase a plane ticket for Wendt? Group members mobilized to communicate across multiple borders, and in turn moved money to facilitate Wendt's escape from Los Angeles in a matter of hours.

The arrest of Wendt triggered numerous arrests of members of her organization and led to additional transnational cooperation among policing agencies, but the case also had a profound impact on popular culture. Wendt, Loeffelholz-Brandstatter, the "blond" woman, and the others served as the basis for the 1948 film *To the Ends of the Earth*. Some of those involved became more famous, such as Harry Anslinger, who plays himself in the opening scenes of the film. The screenplay depicts Anslinger and the FBN as central to breaking the case. Customs agent Alvin Scharff is not present, but the protagonist, Michael Barrows, played by Dick Powell, works with narcotics agents in different countries, much like Scharff did.

To the Ends of the Earth is the first film to document transnational drug smuggling and the role of women as key in this enterprise, well before the sensationalist images of women in *Scarface* or *Traffic* or *María Full of Grace*.[129] The film challenged censors in the immediate post–World War II era with its edgy topics of drug and human trafficking and interracial sexual attraction. The censors relented and allowed the release of this story about international police fighting the narcotics epidemic as well as transgressive sexual desire. The Loeffelholz-Brandstatter group had not only challenged the crime fighters of Mexico and the United States but also contributed to a provocative shift in popular culture in the post–World War II era. The film challenged censorship rules by depicting lurid topics, but it also portrayed transnational policing and investigation. These depictions, however, had a purpose: to educate viewers about the evils and dangers of drugs.[130]

Maria Wendt was an exceptional mule due to her education and her transnational and familial ties that stretched across continents. These attributes, enhanced by her cosmopolitanism, added to the pop culture titillation that resulted in the production of *To the Ends of the Earth*. Women, traditionally thought of as marginal to the drug trade, are in fact instrumental to illicit flows whether they act as small-time peddlers or transnational mules. Wendt is remarkable because of her ties to a transnational drug ring. Her significance lies in her ties to men who had gamed the system to such a degree that they came to be viewed as threats to the security and physical health of the United States and Mexico. Although initially Wendt, like most women in the drug trade, appeared to play only a small role, she was in fact a nexus between the drug traffickers and policing agents, between East and West, between educated and uneducated, between men and women.

Wendt's case offers some similarities to women operating today in the global drug market. For whatever reason, she embarked on a career as a mule, whether for excitement or for profit. Many women who did not have the education or access to networks that Wendt enjoyed were forced to seek innovative means for economic survival, and carried drugs out of necessity. Indeed, most women who engaged in drug peddling and trafficking did so at a small level, often with family members, and over various periods of time. Similar to prostitution, women moved in and out of drug vending. The buying and selling of illegal drugs allowed certain women to survive in a time when they had few economic options. Whether Wendt entered the trade as an equal partner, as an entrepreneur seeking greater economic mobility, or as a thrill seeker, she had peers who resorted to smuggling and peddling for all these reasons. Some women, though, took their role a step further, competing directly with men in the higher levels of organized crime or even at the highest levels of political power.

CHAPTER THREE

THE WHITE LADY OF MEXICO CITY

Lola la Chata and the Remaking of Narcotics

ON APRIL 27, 1945, MEXICAN PRESIDENT MANUEL ÁVILA CAMACHO issued a presidential decree that waived constitutional guarantees in cases of narcotics trafficking and permitted the immediate detention of peddlers and smugglers at the federal penitentiary at Tres Marías without trial in the Mexican courts.[1] Moreover, he issued a second decree ordering the minister of the interior and all police agencies throughout the country to arrest "public enemy number one": the infamous narcotics trafficker Lola la Chata.

In the United States, Federal Bureau of Narcotics (FBN) director Harry J. Anslinger received word from a "special employee" working in Mexico in the 1940s about the pending arrest of this prominent criminal. Anslinger immediately passed the information on to the director of the FBI, J. Edgar Hoover. He attached a history of la Chata. Because her growing narcotics empire had been a concern for Mexican as well as U.S. officials since the early 1930s, these actions were culminations of earlier decisions.

Ávila Camacho's presidential decree followed by Anslinger's correspondence to Hoover highlighted the perceived transnational threat of Lola la Chata's drug empire. La Chata's career demonstrated a more insidious threat compared to a woman such as Maria Wendt. Wendt worked as a mule for an organization controlled and operated by men. La Chata greatly differs from Wendt because she emerged as a dominant figure in the illicit narcotics trade during a time when the United States and Mexico were collaborating on narcotics arrests. During her era, criminologists, policy makers, and international women's organizations all reacted against an emerging epidemic of narcotics abuse that victimized men and women and that threatened society on both sides of the border, weakening the social fabric through disease, economic difficulty, and crime.[2] As a boss rather than a mule or small-time smuggler, la Chata serves as a representative of and predecessor to the emerging popular-culture manifestations of traffickers, lieutenants, and bosses.[3] From localized peddler to international trafficker, her role in the business of narcotics reveals that the trade could offer similar rewards to women that it did to men.[4] La Chata and women like her complicate popular masculine constructions of the illegal drug business, particularly in urban settings. Her role disrupts the view that women were passive and naïve victims of the trade, lured and tricked into drug trafficking by the vices and whims of male peddlers.[5] Or, that women were limited to the lower echelons of drug trafficking. Neither a victim nor a small-time peddler, Lola la Chata was an opportunist who became wealthy and well respected in the informal economic and criminal underworld. She eventually led an organized crime family that extended throughout Mexico.

This chapter documents la Chata's thirty-year career as a heroin peddler, trafficker, and crime boss. It also considers the efforts of police, government officials, and diplomats on both sides of the border to undermine her, while using her to justify shifts in policy in both the United States and Mexico. Like her counterparts, whether male or female, la Chata was seen as a threat to civilization, since her involvement in illicit trade brought her wealth but also access to power, defying all expectations for a woman of her race and class. Differing from Wendt and small-time smugglers, peddlers, and mules, la Chata endangered perceptions of Mexican and U.S. societies because she ruptured the normative expectations of what it meant to be a woman and to be civilized by using limited and constrained forms of feminine power to become a transnational threat.[6]

Like her mother before her, who had sold morphine and marijuana in an open-air market in Mexico City, la Chata used the space of the open street market—a feminine economic site—as the basis of her enterprise. She relied on her own familial relations as well as informal networks to circumnavigate structures of constraint placed upon her because of her sex and class.[7] In turn, she and her successors reoriented the social and economic positions of their families within the illicit market. She revealed her fluidity and flexibility when confronted with government policy changes as well as changes wrought by modernization. Her actions threatened the Mexican government by exposing it to inspection and ridicule by the United States. Mexican officials were mocked at international narcotics meetings, as they had been criticized in the past for the country's growing drug addiction problem. The Mexican government was cast as corrupt and inept. This scorn further translated into direct action whereby the FBN violated Mexico's national sovereignty by issuing demands and placing agents in the country.[8] More importantly, the FBN targeted certain Mexican researchers, particularly Leopoldo Salazar Viniegra, who countered Anslinger's tales of "reefer madness" with scientific studies that concluded that marijuana did not trigger violent criminal acts. La Chata's success serves as a lens through which the North American drug czars viewed the alleged incompetence of Mexican authorities. Despite la Chata's threat and her extended influence, policy makers continued to view her femininity and her ethnicity as potential weaknesses as they struggled to undermine her.

SELLING WOMEN: A GIRL FROM LA MERCED

Lola la Chata—María Dolores Estévez Zuleta—was born in 1906 and grew up in La Merced barrio in Mexico City.[9] La Merced was notorious for its "quantity of thieves" and its poverty.[10] During la Chata's lifetime, La Merced grew due to an influx of migrants from the provinces and its ever-increasing formal and informal economic activities.[11] It was and continues to be a hamlet of thieves but also a vigorous market of both legal and illegal commodities.[12] Today, as in the early twentieth century, vendors and peddlers in the district ply crockery, food, clothing, live animals, lotions, potions, herbs, powder, spells, and other substances to help alleviate virtually any human ailment. Any type of sexual act can also be purchased. Thus, the barrio provides the perfect educational environment for a budding trafficker. Young Estévez worked in her mother's food stall selling *chicharron* (pork rinds) and coffee. Later, her mother expanded to more lucrative markets: marijuana and morphine. At the age of thirteen, Estévez entered the trade working as her mother's mule, running drugs from the stall in La Merced to customers.

Young Lola and her mother were not unique in the buying and selling of marijuana. Women and men sold these illegal commodities in the streets of Mexico City for local consumption.[13] Street-vending children like Estévez moved through the city with this contraband in open or covered baskets.[14] Just as smugglers employed their children as vessels of transportation or as foils to distract customs agents, small-time drug peddlers used their own children to sell marijuana in areas where they would be less conspicuous to

Figure 12. María Dolores Estévez Zuleta walks on the street with plates of food. Serie Mariguana, opio, y drogas, ca. 1935, 14834, Casasola, Mexico City, Fototeca Nacional del Instituto Nacional de Anthropología e Historia (INAH), Pachuca, Hidalgo.

the authorities, like schools and playgrounds. The fact that parents induced their children to sell marijuana and other illegal substances led to shock and outrage on both sides of the border.[15] Parents acculturated their own children into the life, ensuring that the practices of addiction and selling passed from one generation to the next.[16] Newspapers and official reports decried this use of children, and public health authorities blamed parents for their children's addiction and selling.[17]

Most likely, Estévez's work as a child mule for her mother helped her learn the local terrain of peddling; the Mexican Revolution forced her to learn quickly and further her skills. The chaos of war led people to migrate around the country to escape the violence, seek work, or emigrate to the United States for greater economic opportunity. Estévez was no exception. Through her work as a mule in La Merced, she met Castro Ruiz Urquizo, who may have also been a street dealer.[18] With Ruiz, she went to Ciudad Juárez, where she learned the skills of transnational trafficking from one of the most prominent trafficking families on the border.[19]

Her time in Ciudad Juárez expanded her future career in both personal and professional ways. There, she gave birth to two daughters, Dolores and María Luisa, who appear to have been the daughters of Ruiz.[20] Her daughters ultimately followed her into the trade, creating a business matriarchy of sorts. In Ciudad Juárez, Estévez would have been introduced to transnational trafficking. Ciudad Juárez served as a main port for illicit trade with the United States, whether alcohol or narcotics. Her education on the border

ensured that her destiny would not remain localized in small-time drug peddling. Eventually, she made her way back to Mexico City, and, like her
mother, she ran a market stall that sold cheap lunches as her legitimate business cover. From that stall in La Merced, Lola la Chata began to build her
marijuana, morphine, and heroin empire in the 1920s.

La Chata went unnoticed by the authorities for much of the 1920s. By the
late 1930s, her name appeared in official documents in both the United States
and Mexico. Her success coincided with government policy shifts that led to
greater scrutiny of narcotics smugglers by the U.S. government. As discussed
previously, in 1933 the Eighteenth Amendment to the U.S. Constitution over-
turned Prohibition. With the end of Prohibition, government agencies
turned their attention from alcohol to the menace that was sweeping across
the country's southern border: narcotics.[21] As demonstrated with the case of
Maria Wendt, U.S. drug policy toward Mexico became more focused in the
1930s with the establishment of the Federal Bureau of Narcotics (FBN)
housed in the Treasury Department.[22]

In the United States, Harry Anslinger became somewhat of a celebrity
in regard to the decadence and decline of an America that was allegedly
under attack by Black, Latino, and Asian hordes who brought their vices to
the United States.[23] Anslinger was known for his use of racist language in
describing drug dealers. Secretary of the Treasury Henry Morgenthau disci-
plined Anslinger for releasing an all-points bulletin that described a suspect
as a "ginger-colored nigger."[24] This reference enraged Morgenthau, who
called Anslinger to his office and considered having him removed from his
position. Anslinger, using racist language, also tended to associate marijuana
distribution and use with African Americans and Mexicans. Anslinger
claimed that he originally became interested in narcotics control due to the
overwhelming numbers of female addicts prior to the passage of the Harrison
Act, and he remained gravely concerned about female drug use.[25] In
Anslinger's mind, drug use led white women to engage in miscegenation and
turn to prostitution to support their addiction.

Women, too, fit into these constructs of deviance that Anslinger detailed
in his books, articles, and speeches at public meetings and other venues.
Women, he argued, were more prone to addiction to narcotics such as heroin
and laudanum. Female criminal addicts often used poisons to kill their husbands and partners. And they also engaged in drug trafficking. Anslinger
recalled a case in 1942 centered on Jack W. Morse and Sallie Elsie Morse, an
Anglo couple who relocated to San Diego from Norfolk, Virginia. Sallie had

accumulated over $40,000 (2012: $564,000) from what Anslinger character-ized as "antisocial activities." With that money, the Morse couple bought opium from Enrique Diarte, who was a supply source for Tijuana. Anslinger described Diarte as "one of the most flagrant smugglers" operating out of Tijuana and Mexicali. He worked with another husband-and-wife team, Jesús Velázquez and Consuelo Landeros de Velázquez, who were arrested transporting 175 ounces of opium and 20 ounces of pure heroin.[26] Anglo and Mexican women often worked alongside their partners in the drug trade. In *The Traffic in Narcotics*, Anslinger argues that the Morse and Velázquez cases are similar. However, Sallie managed to raise a substantial sum of money for a major buy; Consuelo and her husband appear to be lower-level mules rather than distributors or suppliers.

Anslinger remained concerned about Mexico. He made frequent trips to the country, communicated with Mexican authorities, and exchanged infor-mation. However, despite his efforts to forge fruitful relationships with Mexican officials, Anslinger grew frustrated with Mexico's divergent re-sponses to drugs. Many Mexicans disagreed with Anslinger's assertion that addicts, sellers, and traffickers were all merely criminals; these Mexicans tended to view drug addiction as a disease. In turn, Anslinger never tried to understand the Mexican view of narcotics or the country's efforts to stem the flow of narcotics trafficking and addiction.[27] Rather, in the United States as well as in Mexico, he continued to assert his position that drug use was a crime, not a sickness. He disagreed with the approach of medical doctors in both countries who studied addiction and saw it as a medical problem that deserved treatment rather than imprisonment.

With the end of the Mexican Revolution, the government began to act on its mounting concerns about the rise of narcotics abuse in the cities. As discussed in chapter 1, Mexican officials grew concerned about the vices of foreigners, particularly Chinese immigrants, who were perceived as a threat to the nation by introducing disease as well as economic competition.[28] The condemnation of foreigners in Mexico—regardless of their national origin—as responsible for the increase in drug trafficking stemmed from xenophobic and feminized discourses that painted them, especially the Chinese, as a danger to the Mexican nation, very similar to arguments developed in the United States.[29]

Despite the creation of a public enemy who could be blamed for the in-troduction of opium and the rise in drug trafficking, by the 1930s the chief of alcohol and narcotics service of the Department of Health, Dr. Leopoldo

Salazar Viniegra (1938–1939), realized that drug addiction and peddling were no longer minor problems associated exclusively with the Chinese or with students, bohemians, and sailors. Salazar documented drug use in Mexico City among prostitutes, the poor, and other vulnerable populations. His work as a medical doctor challenged views held by early Mexican criminologists such as Julio Guerrero and Carlos Roumagnac.[30]

In 1938, Salazar published the results of a fourteen-year study on marijuana use that he conducted in the hospitals of Mexico City. In "The Myth of Marijuana," he argued that marijuana was less dangerous than tobacco.[31] He also claimed that only in the United States did marijuana seem to provoke crime. In conclusion, he suggested that drug addicts should receive medical care rather than be treated as criminals.[32] A medical doctor rather than a criminologist, Salazar viewed addiction from a medical perspective. His research led him to express sympathy for addicts, and he ultimately blamed peddlers, not addicts, as the criminals.

Notwithstanding his differences with Anslinger over addiction, Salazar considered peddling and smuggling part of growing crisis that threatened the nation and complicated its relations with the United States.[33] Consequently, la Chata's growing success brought her unwanted attention from officials on both sides of the border that had potentially damaging repercussions to her business.[34] Both in Mexico City and in the provinces, la Chata's mules covertly moved her heroin in small packets with religious stamps on the front or in the bases of yoyos. In the 1930s and 1940s, heroin was routinely sold in small packets, or papelitos. The religious stamp on the packets may have been some sort of brand that identified her heroin. Toys have also been a common vessel for transportation because of a perception that they are harmless items associated with children. Yoyos have bases and wooden bodies that can be hollowed out and filled with heroin. La Chata built her empire in the way she knew best, as understood by women: through familial and sexual connections.[35] She married an ex–police officer, Enrique Jaramillo, whose auto mechanic shop in Pachuca, Hidalgo, served as a distribution center and whose police contacts provided invaluable networks and protection. Although they were rumored to have divorced to suppress criticism of impropriety, her "marriage" to the police force provided alliances with police officers, bureaucrats, and politicians, many of whom she paid for information and protection.[36]

Her relationship with Jaramillo provided some cover for her business, but Mexican and U.S. authorities soon recognized him as a successful trafficker as well. La Chata appears to have enjoyed a tremendous amount of respect, more than what women in Mexico or elsewhere might have expected at that time or even today. Barbara Denton has argued that women in the drug economy are seen as "personally unfit," and, like the upper echelons of the formal economy, the illicit trade has always been seen as "a man's world."[37] La Chata appears to have figured out that family alliances enable women to compete in the man's world of drugs. The family ties of women in the drug trade have garnered greater attention in the contemporary media, but la Chata and others used their social networks at sophisticated levels decades before scholars noted the patterns.

When considering a woman in Mexico in the 1940s and 1950s, what explains her power within the drug economy, compared to women in that business today? Perhaps the fact that women on the margins of society who sought economic advancement in the illicit market, like men in the same position, enjoyed a certain level of respect if they were able to develop clientelist networks that mimicked those of more powerful members of society, whether among revolutionary generals, politicians, or criminals. What made la Chata's power unique among women in the trade was her ability to grow her business and have it endure until her death in 1959. Significantly, la Chata, like some others in the drug business, filled a void in La Merced and beyond by performing "good works" in her community.[38]

Drug traffickers and dealers rely on the people who surround them. They provide food, shelter, social services, and informal banking through loans to budding drug entrepreneurs who may not be able to access such funds through legitimate means.[39] La Chata recognized the fragility of power and nation during a time of crisis in Mexico, and she filled a void in her poor neighborhood by operating as a "godmother" to the people of La Merced. In the 1930s and 1940s, the economy was improving from that of the 1920s, but social services and economic structures continued to lag behind political developments. The fissures of the state and the instability of state control, whether due to revolution or the ensuing conflict, may have offered women opportunities to emerge as bosses. As history has demonstrated, in extraordinary times women take on greater nontraditional roles, such as becoming military leaders during a revolution.[40] Both Anslinger and Salazar saw la Chata as an equal if not superior trafficker and dealer to Jaramillo. Although both drug warriors studied and analyzed her relationship to Jaramillo and other men in her criminal organization, they recognized her as a primary threat, as detailed in their internal memos.

Despite la Chata's widely acknowledged ties to those in power, the police and government officials arrested and imprisoned her seven times from 1934 to 1945. Whether imprisoned in Lecumberri, Cárcel de Mujeres, or Islas Marías, she endured her prison terms in style. She maintained her own servants while in prison, including a woman who came once a month to do her hair. Similar to Pablo Escobar and Joaquín "El Chapo" Guzmán, she hosted numerous visitors to the prison, many of whom came to ask for favors. Like any other "godfather," she offered advice and assistance to those in need. As with other prisoners on Islas Marías, la Chata's daughters visited her for extended periods of time. However, she was reported to have built a hotel and an airplane runway on one of the penal colony's islands, so her daughters would find their visits easy and comfortable.[41]

In 1957, police arrested Lola la Chata for the last time at the age of fifty as she was processing heroin in her home.[42] Described in the press as a "famous international narcotic trafficker," she had been captured after eluding police for two years. Her elusion necessitated that she live under heavy guard in her home, in some ways similar to El Chapo Guzmán. The early-morning raid captured her and her "cohort Luis Oaxaca Jaramillo," as well as ten servants described as her agents. In the search of her mansion, investigators found twenty-nine million pesos in cash ($9,000; 2012: $73,600), expensive jewelry, and equipment for drug processing, as well as firearms and ammunition.

In an interview with the press while in jail, la Chata made one statement: "Yes, I'll talk, but first question all the police agencies. . . . All they wanted to do was arrest me and get me out of the way. However, don't implicate any more innocent people. I am the only responsible one for [the] narcotics traffic and business that I established."[43] Accepting full responsibility, she made a strategic—if not honorable—move, disassociating her deputies and agents from her crimes. Protecting those men, whose responsibility had been to protect her, she challenged bourgeois concepts of the patriarchal family in which the men dominated and protected the women.[44] Her statements to the press confirmed that she was the boss of the organization, not her husband or the other men associated with her. She did not hide behind the men of the organization; instead, she was openly public about her power. There is also an important criminal aspect to her assertion. She most likely hoped that some of her associates would not be sentenced to jail so that they could continue the business.

La Chata routinely broke with prevailing gendered norms; however, she was a product of a violent society in transition. She transgressed physical space within Mexico City and throughout the country. Although there is little evidence to suggest that she crossed into the United States, her heroin did cross borders. She moved beyond the dictates of gender that present organized crime in the 1940s and 1950s as a masculine endeavor. Instead, she established that the shadowy world of the informal market offered women viable options and public recognition, whether welcomed or not. After being found guilty and sent back to Cárcel de Mujeres, la Chata died in September 1959 of coronary failure. It was rumored that she had died of a heroin overdose, but her admirers acknowledged that she had ongoing heart problems. Despite her arrests and imprisonments, an estimated five hundred people attended her funeral, over one-third of whom were rumored to be police.

WOMEN BOSSES AND FAMILY TIES

La Chata's success came during a time when officials in the United States and Mexico were becoming increasingly worried about the impact of narcotics on national goals, and on the dangers of narcotics, specifically behaviors such as sexual lasciviousness that such substances allegedly caused. La Chata's drug empire stretched from Mexico to Canada. Her reach exceeded those of many other narcotics smugglers, and her power and networks proved effective in combating those who fought to undermine her.

What is striking about la Chata is that she was not the only woman in North America who led a transnational trafficking family in the 1930s and 1940s. Women worked alongside their husbands and lovers to sell and distribute drugs. As Anslinger tried to battle women such as la Chata, he also sought to undermine women in the United States who created crime families. In Texas, the Beland family had been a concern for local Fort Worth officials and federal treasury agents since the 1920s.[45]

Joe H. Beland and Lucy Beland headed the drug trafficking clan. Joe was a machinist who worked for the railroad until his death in 1925; he and Lucy had six children.[46] Born in 1871 in Georgia, Lucy Beland headed a crime family of "thieves, robbers, burglars, and drug addicts" who began to appear in documents in the early 1910s.[47] Joe Beland frequently was portrayed as the poor, suffering husband who endured his wife's eccentricities and criminality, which

Figure 13. Leavenworth mug shot of Charles Beland. Record Group 129, National Archives at Kansas City.

she passed on to their children. After Joe's death in 1925, it was alleged that Lucy worked with her children Charlie, Joe Henry, Annice Beland Hamilton, and Willie, along with their wives and husbands. Their drug operation grew in the 1930s and 1940s, and they distributed and sold heroin, both Asian and Mexican. Like la Chata, they created cross-class alliances that spread across the United States. They had connections to Jewish and Italian organized crime that sold their heroin in the major cities.[48]

Initially, the Belands appeared to be a family tormented by problems and tragedies. In 1911, the eldest son, Charlie, eleven years old at the time, appeared in newspapers for the first time when he stabbed his thirteen-year-old playmate and was put on probation. After that, his sister Willie was repeatedly arrested for shoplifting, first dresses from local dry goods stores and later silk kimonos. After her first arrest at the age of fifteen, she was described as a "stunningly pretty girl" who refused to talk to police officers. When questioned about one particular dress that she stole, she simply remarked that it was pretty.[49]

By 1921, Charlie Beland was serving a sentence in Fort Leavenworth for violation of the Harrison Act. Charlie and his younger brother Joe both did time in Leavenworth for narcotics charges.[50] Charlie's mother Lucy and his siblings were arrested twice in a period of three weeks for selling narcotics, even though they had attempted to avoid arrest by stashing a can of opium with some hens they kept.[51] Willie Beland told a journalist that only her father and one married older brother, George, had avoided morphine addiction. Willie blamed schoolyard drug pushers for her family's use of morphine, which had landed her brother Charlie in jail and her sister Cora (also referred to as Coral) in the morgue. Willie argued that her sister died from an unsupervised morphine withdrawal after she was arrested.[52] Cora died in 1917, at the age of eighteen.[53] In her prison interview in 1921, Willie argued that her and her sisters' addiction contributed to the entire family becoming addicts, due to the affordability of morphine, which she claimed cost only twenty-five cents for a large bottle. In defending herself in court, she declared that morphine addiction was a horrible torture to which most of her siblings had succumbed.

In 1936, the family reached prominence as drug traffickers due to the arrest of their primary competitors, the Ginsberg-Kayne-Gordon faction, which was also based in Texas. Anslinger's FBN destroyed the organization, allowing the Belands to simply take over their transnational trafficking business.[54]

The Beland family presented a classic case of recidivism. Lucy served her first prison sentence in 1921 but returned to jail in 1926 and 1938. Charlie was sentenced for violation of the Harrison Act in 1920, 1926, 1934, 1940, and 1942. Joe Henry, too, racked up convictions in 1926, 1934, 1938, and 1947.[55] Willie Beland James had numerous arrests from 1931 to 1947. Many times she received probation only to be rearrested on another narcotics violation. The reason for this was that the criminal sentencing of women involved in narcotics was far lighter than that of men. The wives of Charlie and Joe Henry, Esther and Jacqueline, respectively, had numerous arrests as well. The husbands of Annice and Willie worked closely with their wives, and they too were arrested and violated their paroles. The Belands, like la Chata, also maintained legitimate businesses that covered up their trafficking. Charlie Beland reported to prison authorities in 1951 that he had a trucking company, and approximately $20,000 (2012: $177,000) in property and investments.[56] By the 1950s, a granddaughter was operating package stores in Texas; she, too, remained under suspicion of drug trafficking, and the names of various Beland offspring continued to appear in congressional hearings.[57]

In the few U.S. sources that mention Lucy Beland, she is a sensationalized criminal who hooked her children to ensure that she maintained control over them. This appears unlikely from the documents. When her eldest, Charlie, was first arrested, he was viewed as the mastermind of the criminal family. In interviews, Lucy's children claimed that she never used.[58] They argued that she became involved in the drug trade due to their own addictions and that because of their addictions she began to sell drugs. After her husband's death in 1925, it is possible that she turned to selling

Figure 14. Leaven-
worth mug shot
of Joe Beland.
Record Group 129,
National Archives
at Kansas City.

drugs to supplement her income, particularly during the economic depression of the 1930s.

The Belands would be intimately involved in drug trafficking. Charlie's
arrests in the 1940s revealed that he traveled to New York for the purpose of
acquiring heroin, yet he also appeared to have sources closer to home. He and
Joe would live their lives in and out of prison. Charlie Beland died on
November 26, 1955, in Alcatraz, at the age of fifty-five. He had been moved
from Leavenworth to Alcatraz due to his drug smuggling in prison.[59] In his
prison record, he told officials that he mainlined heroin and got hooked because "he was a wild and crazy kid."[60] At the time of his death, he had been
in prison since 1944 on a narcotics charge. Lucy Beland died on December 30,
1952, at home in the same small town outside Fort Worth where she had lived
most of her life. At the time of her death, two of her sons were imprisoned and
two of her children were dead.

It is difficult to ascertain if some of the heroin that the Belands distributed
came from Lola la Chata. Their location in Fort Worth places them on a direct
transportation line, the eastern Pan-American Highway, sometimes referred
to as the Inter-American Highway, which stretches from Mexico City to
Pachuca to Monterrey to Nuevo Laredo to San Antonio to Fort Worth, in Texas
the I-35 interstate corridor.[61] What officials learned about Charlie Beland while
he was at Alcatraz was that he had contacts with Mexican organized crime for
the purpose of acquiring illegal drugs.[62]

In the 1940s, la Chata gained greater and greater recognition as her ties to
this transportation route became more evident. In 1944, S. J. Kennedy, treasury

representative in charge, requested information from Mexican officials about narcotics smugglers operating in Mexico. Mexican authorities informed Kennedy about one of la Chata's illegal laboratories, which highlighted her connections to powerful men and the reach of her trafficking in Mexico and beyond. The lab operated in the basement of the Hotel Imperial in the northern industrial city of Monterrey. La Chata, Jaramillo, and Enrique Escudero Romano, all successful traffickers, held interest in the lab, but so too did Gastón Vaca Cordella, the former chief of the sanitary police and a local politician.[63]

La Chata was not unique in operating laboratories and working closely with men. Mexican and U.S. officials documented other women from both countries involved in processing. For example, in 1949 U.S. and Mexican officials arrested Carmen Nuñez Reza along with her accomplice Juan Valdés Ham in Guadalajara. Despite the co-occupancy of Valdés Ham, Nuñez Reza held the property rights to the house where they were arrested processing heroin.[64] Women involved in processing heroin who owned the houses or establishments where they were arrested were also found in Ciudad Juárez, Guadalajara, Mexico City, Monterrey, and Tijuana.

La Chata's partnership with Gastón Vaca Cordella, the former chief of the sanitary police serves as another example of the collusion of civil authorities and civic and state leaders in drug trafficking. Vaca Cordella had been the chief narcotics agents for the city of Monterrey. His corruption and that of other federal agents charged with policing drug use and distribution continues to draw attention.[65] From the evidence, la Chata had labs not only in Mexico City but also in other Mexican cities. This demonstrates a series of overlapping networks across the country and into the border region that served to move heroin from different locals in Mexico into the United States. Moreover, la Chata's power coincided with more frequent investigations of governors and ex-governors as subjects in the smuggling and production of drugs.

Ávila Camacho's presidential decree demanding the arrest of drug traffickers triggered a North American search for fugitives María Dolores Estévez Zuleta and Enrique Escudero Romano. On June 16, 1945, the Mexican government sent a cable to the U.S. and Canadian governments asking for assistance in capturing the fugitives. Under separate cover, they sent photographs and fingerprints.[66] Unlike the newspaper snapshots of la Chata, María Dolores Estévez, in the photos provided by the Mexican government, appeared with her face completely uncovered and without sunglasses. She looked youthful, her hair curling around her forehead and with

Figure 15. Mug shots of María Dolores Estévez Zuleta and Enrique Escudero Romano, U.S. Department of Justice, Federal Bureau of Investigation, María Dolores Estévez Zuleta, Freedom of Information / Privacy Act request 1150736-001.

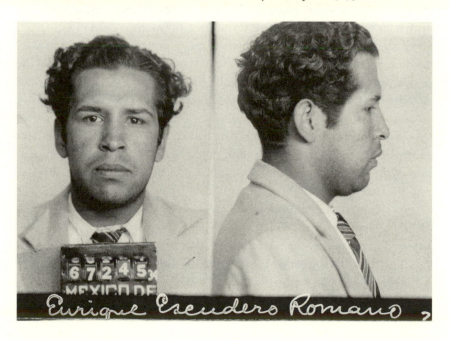

ornate gold earrings. Escudero appeared in a summer suit with his head
slightly cocked to one side.

Anslinger wrote to the chief of the Canadian Narcotics Division, Colonel
C. H. L. Sharman, about the case against la Chata.[67] Anslinger told Sharman
that arrest warrants had been issued for la Chata and Escudero, and they
were known to be traveling and transporting heroin to Canada in either a
1942 Cadillac Sedanette, a 1938 Dodge, or a 1942 blue and gray Sedanette.[68]
Over the next three weeks, INS agents in various cities including Los Angeles,
El Paso, San Antonio, and Philadelphia searched for the fugitives. A Puerto
Rican informant who had been in Laredo and El Paso told U.S. officials that
the wanted pair had been in Ciudad Juárez and had crossed the border into
El Paso en route to Canada.[69] The informant had worked for Mexican Secret
Service agents in Monterrey who had been trying to arrest la Chata and
Escudero. The State Department civil attaché told police agents that both
should be considered dangerous.

The San Antonio INS office sent information to the FBN that Escudero
had been arrested in Sanderson, Texas, in October 1940. At that time, he had
two U.S. Selective Service cards in his possession: one in his name and one
in another person's name. The Sanderson sheriff questioned him and later
released him with no charges. However, evidence that Escudero had been in
the United States and that he probably held proper documentation fueled the
search for him and la Chata. As it turned out, the man arrested in Sanderson
was actually Manuel Quintero, who had spent time in the Mendocino State
Asylum for the Insane and remained estranged from his family. Thus, the
Sanderson arrest turned out to be a false lead. U.S. authorities pressed their
search for la Chata and Escudero in the hopes of capturing them before they
reached Canada.

With the information about la Chata's and Escudero's alleged presence
in the United States, James E. Ruffin, special assistant to the attorney general of the United States, analyzed the treaties between the United States
and Mexico as they might relate to Lola la Chata. He concluded that her
crimes were extraditable under the Supplementary Extradition Convention
of July 1, 1926, which stipulated that "crimes and offenses against the laws
for the suppression of the traffic in and use of narcotic drugs" were extraditable. The 1926 agreement also stipulated that "crimes and offenses
against laws relating to the illicit manufacture of or traffic in substances
injurious to health or poisonous chemicals" were extraditable. Ruffin then
outlined U.S. codes, citing Section 651 of Title 18. He quoted that if a treaty

or convention truly existed between the U.S. government and any foreign government,

> upon complaint made under oath, charging any person found within the limits of any State, District, or Territory with having committed within the jurisdiction of any such foreign government any crimes provided by such treaty or convention, issue his warrant for apprehension of the person so charged that he may be brought before such justice, judge, or commissioner, to the end that the evidence of criminality may be heard and considered. If on such hearing, he deems the evidence sufficient to sustain the charge under the provisions of the proper treaty or convention, he shall certify the same, together with a copy of all the testimony taken before him, to the Secretary of State, that a warrant may issue upon the requisition of the proper authorities of such foreign government for the surrender of such person, according to the stipulations of the treaty and convention; and he shall issue his warrant for the commitment of the person so charged to the proper jail, there to remain until such surrender could be made.[70]

It was then concluded that if la Chata was found in the United States, she would be charged with violation of the Harrison Act.[71]

If the FBN, FBI, or any other policing agents apprehended la Chata and Escudero, the federal government wanted to ensure that they would be able to hold them in custody while the United States pursued extradition, even if they were found without narcotics in their possession. Despite the legal preparations and a manhunt that extended across North America, Lola la Chata and Escudero were ultimately arrested in a hideout in Mexico City on July 5, 1945. Over the next few days the investigation in the United States wound down.[72] The fact that Anslinger, Hoover, and others believed that la Chata had traveled through the United States to deliver heroin as far away as Canada demonstrates a misreading of her role. As many scholars have demonstrated, those who create the greatest amount of distance between their product, in this case heroin, and the actual sale are the most successful. In 1945, la Chata was not a mule. At the same time, the fact that the FBN ignored the connections between her lab in Monterrey, her ties to men in positions of power, and her status in the trade suggests an ongoing misreading of the importance of overlapping networks that helped distribute her heroin beyond Mexico City. Although la Chata sold in La Merced, she, like present-day drug bosses, would not have risked crossing the border with a load of heroin in her car even if she was not the driver. Like her contemporaries, she surely paid people to move her product, transfer it across the border, and deliver it to those who could effectively sell it in distant regions, far from where she sold to her local customers. Why would a boss drive from Mexico City to Canada when she was surrounded by numerous police officers and politicians who were on her payroll?

Despite her arrest in 1945, she fought the presidential decree. Special employee Salvadore Peña noted that U.S. Treasury officials and Mexican officials were closely observing la Chata's supporters. Peña had worked closely with Mexican authorities in searching for la Chata when it was believed that she had crossed into the United States. He wrote:

> A close watch was kept by agents of the Federal Narcotics Police of the Department of Health and Assistance and by this office over people who tried to help her by using their influence with the authorities. This was done in order to keep check on possible connections between this subject and any prominent Mexicans who might have some interest in the illicit traffic of narcotics.[73]

Both Anslinger's memo to Sharman and Peña's letter to U.S. Customs reveal the complexity of the networks that surrounded la Chata. Anslinger saw her threat extending well beyond her stronghold in Mexico City. Evidence the she had laboratories throughout Mexico, particularly in states that bordered the United States, further contributed to fears about her enterprises. As la Chata evolved from a successful local peddler to a transnational trafficker, Peña made it clear that she had powerful friends who facilitated her business.

Despite her powerful friends, in 1945 Mexican officials sent la Chata to the Islas Marías federal prison colony off the western coast of Mexico. In a letter to President Ávila Camacho, la Chata's daughter requested her transfer to a prison in Mexico City, arguing that her mother was simply a businesswoman who had worked hard to accumulate a small bit of wealth. La Chata wrote to the president and his wife, Soledad Orozco, in a letter probably dictated to her daughter from prison.[74] La Chata argued that she was a hardworking businesswoman who performed good works for the community of La Merced. She wrote that she provided shoes and clothes for the community's children as well as candy and toys during the holidays. Moreover, she claimed that she regularly assisted her neighbors with sugar and coal and other household necessities.

Her letter to Orozco suggests that she thought the president's wife might be more sympathetic to her struggle as a mother and as a good Catholic woman. Just like the *damas* in Catholic organizations, la Chata established her own programs of public welfare without any institutionalized support from the Church, the state, or the elites of society.[75] Thus, she filled the void of the state by offering public welfare where such did not exist. Her entreaties echo those of present-day drug traffickers whose generosity builds the social networks that expand their businesses and ensure protection and surveillance within a localized neighborhood. La Chata's appeals to the president's wife for a transfer back to Mexico City did not appear to be successful. Within a few months after her arrival at the island prison, however, she received a medical transfer that brought her back to Mexico City, where she continued peddling.

Although Anslinger acknowledged that women profited from the sale of narcotics, he saw that other women were vulnerable and in need of protection from dope dealers and addicts. Popular perceptions held that women served to perpetuate societal standards. As mothers, they acculturated children into the family, the community, and the nation. Addicts, on the other hand, pursued their own self-interest at the expense of their children and families. Their individual pursuit to feed their addiction and thus encourage criminality disrupted their families, their communities, and the nation.

Anslinger, with his discursive views of addiction as foreign and criminal, became particularly concerned about drug use and prostitution when he heard stories about rich Westchester County (New York) matrons who shuffled from their affluent suburban homes to Harlem for a fix. He concocted an image for the public of a young "flaxen-haired eighteen-year-old girl sprawled nude and unconscious on a Harlem apartment tenement floor after selling herself to a collection of customers throughout the afternoon, in exchange for a heroin shot in the arm."[76] Once addicts, these especially vulnerable and weak women fell into the grips of prostitution, often leading these white housewives and teenagers to engage in miscegenation.[77]

According to Anslinger, narcotics abuse was one of the four horsemen of the apocalypse. The white suburban addict was to be pitied for her weakness. How could she, a lowly woman, stand up against the communist, "oriental," African, or "Central American" conspiracy against the United States that plagued not just women as victims, but also men? In public, Anslinger liked to elaborate on the potential sexual connection between suburbanites and urbanites, casting suburban women as the prey of urban men. He recognized that women, too, sold narcotics, but this fact also took on a sensational aspect that endangered "real" Americans.[78] When he portrayed the Latin American woman in the drug trade, he cast her as the stereotypical Latina "firecracker." According to Anslinger, with a sexy swish of her hips and a slip of a packet packed with heroin, a Latina dealer could intoxicate any good (white) American man with her feminine wiles and her drugs.[79]

Despite the sexuality of the Latina, which Anslinger used to titillate his audiences in the United States, Lola la Chata complicated his narratives of deviance. In 1945, when Anslinger received a report about la Chata's attempt to flee to Canada, he circulated his own report that described her as short and fat (180 pounds), with a "Negroid" complexion and features and with gold-capped teeth.[80] By describing her as "Negroid," Anslinger highlighted what differentiated her from other Mexican peddlers and traffickers, who many times were listed in documents as "white" or with a "dark complexion" by agents operating in Mexico. Anslinger's continued exploitation of race, drugs, and the danger thereof continued. La Chata as black posed a far greater threat to the United States than if she had been light-skinned. Anslinger's use of racially tinged rhetoric sought to ensure greater funding and wider authority for his agency to hunt traffickers. His reference to her race circulated to each of the FBN's offices in Atlanta, El Paso, Los Angeles, and Philadelphia, as well as to the headquarters of the Royal Canadian Mounted Police in Ottawa.

In photos published in the Mexican press after her arrest, la Chata did not smile to reveal her gold-capped teeth, and she demurely covered her head in a silk rebozo. During her trial, she reiterated her Catholicism and devotion to good works for the poor, as she did in her appeals to the first lady of Mexico. For Anslinger, who enjoyed titillating the crowds that came to hear him speak on the perils of drugs and foreigners who turned good men and women into addicts, a short, squat, religious, grandmotherly figure seemed an unlikely seducer of men. Perhaps that was what made her all the more dangerous.

La Chata obviously was not a stereotypical Latina firecracker, but her physical appearance drew considerable attention from men in positions of

Figure 16. Lola la Chata: "Fin al trafico del drogas en México." *La Prensa.*

authority on both sides of the border.[81] The focus on the feminine as a site of danger to men, children, and other women was not new in drugs. The danger associated with women users, pushers, and peddlers was continually reiterated in correspondence between narcotics warriors.

Dr. Leopoldo Salazar wrote an open letter in 1938 to la Chata and those who were protecting her. Addressing the letter to the "White Lady," he seized upon the concept of beauty as an aspect of a culture of restraint. He wrote:

I was certain that you, Chata, I mean Lola, were a young, beautiful, and seductive woman, and really I was worried about the time you would finally be brought to me and would try your wiles upon me in an effort to obtain my complicity because, and I tell you this very confidentially, I am susceptible to feminine charms.

Later, I discovered—and you need not worry about me now—that you were not born under the sign of Venus and further that the years, the sale of quick lunches, the drug traffic, police persecution—of which it must in all honor be stated has always been cordial and affectionate—had inexorably rounded your figure.[82]

Both Anslinger and Salazar saw Lola la Chata's body and physical attributes as a site of danger and obsession.[83] They also make reference to her lack of beauty, which photographs contradict. She was an attractive middle-aged woman who was fastidious about her physical appearance despite what the men suggested. Her weight represented her rejection of the feminine addict—the image of the heroin and morphine habitué that was featured in women's magazines and soft pornography for the elite classes. Her rounded body and face undermined the assumption of authorities that she was a heroin addict—a charge that she continually denied. Her weight and ethnicity ensured that she would attract no sympathy from men such as Anslinger. Physically, she revealed that she was beyond a culture of constraint. Her physical appearance, however, represented to officials a lack of control; her gold-capped teeth displayed her vulgarity, while her chosen profession hinted of "immorality." She had constructed her own concepts of beauty that would have been completely alien to Anslinger because they were uniquely Mexican, although Salazar must have been more accustomed to these representations.

Anslinger's description of la Chata as "Negroid" reflected his suppositions of her sexuality, her morality, and her potential threat. He drew this description from the photos that the Mexican government had supplied. His labeling of her and his distribution of the label ensured that she embodied the sexually lascivious black woman who had to be restrained. Yet, she operated and moved about freely.[84] Other Mexican female peddlers and dealers were described as "white Mexicans" or "notorious," particularly those from northern Mexico.[85] La Chata's "blackness" further emphasized her deviance and her threat to the United States. For Anslinger, her purported ethnicity and her growing success reinforced his view of the dangers of heroin and the inability of Mexican authorities to control the growing drug problem.

In a memo to Henry Morgenthau, secretary of the treasury, about the dangers of heroin and the need for aggressive control of its use and distribution, Anslinger wrote:

> The dangerous nature of heroin from the social point of view overshadows its therapeutic importance; . . . the social dangers of heroin arise from the great reputation this substance possesses among drug addicts and from the illicit traffic which has arisen, its habit-forming properties being much worse than those of other habit-forming narcotics; and . . . the effect of heroin is, in the main, to produce a change in personality characterized by utter disregard for the conventions and morals of civilization which progresses to mental and moral degeneration.[86]

Anslinger's fears regarding the narcotics trade and addiction combined with his thoughts about Mexican justice and nationalism. He grew obsessed with a desire to control not only Mexican smugglers but also those responsible for their capture. Although Mexican authorities lobbied the legislature to strengthen the penal laws against narcotics traffickers and peddlers, to develop programs to treat addiction, and to take measures to stem the flow of drugs in and out of Mexico, U.S. officials constantly questioned Mexican assertions about their seriousness in the war on narcotics.[87]

Anslinger had his own issues with one of his Mexican counterparts, Salazar. In the late 1930s, Anslinger led a campaign against Salazar, who dared to question his narrative about "reefer madness" that was allegedly ravaging the United States and that was, in part, Mexico's fault. Salazar, who publicly questioned the criminalization of addiction, found himself a target of character assassination by the FBN and Mexican criminologists who agreed with Anslinger.[88] Although Salazar sought to undermine Lola la Chata in the 1930s, he was removed from his position in the Ministry of Health after less than two years in office, due in part to the efforts of Anslinger and Washington's chief customs agent in Mexico, H. S. Creighton. Anslinger demonstrated greater success at removing legitimate Mexican officials than Mexican traffickers.

To Anslinger, a woman like la Chata along with others involved in the trade remained a menace to the United States. In his eyes, Mexican officials were weak when it came to dealing with traffickers and addicts. The FBN issued demands that infringed on Mexican national sovereignty. For instance, in 1947 the FBN requested a list of the names of all known traffickers in Mexico. Mexican officials replied that they could not turn over the names of people who were under surveillance, but they *could* provide the names of those who had been convicted of trafficking, one of whom was Lola la Chata.[89] Anslinger hoped to pass the list of suspects to his own agents, who could then independently target traffickers in Mexico. The list provided to the FBN by the Mexican authorities simply gave them information they already knew. In subtle ways like this, Mexican authorities continually sought to outmaneuver Anslinger's efforts to undermine their own control.

Prior to his dismissal, Salazar took a very different approach from Anslinger when engaging Lola la Chata. In his "Open Letter to Lola la Chata," Salazar recognized that her chosen profession may have contributed to her rounded figure, but he did not discuss her complexion or ethnicity, perhaps because he, too, was Mexican. Like Anslinger, Salazar saw la Chata as dangerous because of her physical rejection of elite masculine concepts of feminine beauty, morality, and restraint. Despite her profession as a drug dealer, she was not a fallen woman; and despite her wealth, she had not become an elite moral female crusader. Because of these peculiarities she was more threatening than the run-of-the-mill female addict to constructs of Mexican and U.S. civilization.[90] Instead, she operated on the boundaries of cultural gendered expectations of both nations, and no one knew how to define her or how to approach her.

Although Anslinger and Salazar worried about la Chata's deviations from the constraints of civilization, the American Beat writer William S. Burroughs found her a fascinating person and used her as a character in his writing, thus introducing one of Mexico's most infamous drug traffickers to U.S. popular culture. Burroughs went to Mexico in 1949 to escape a narcotics charge in New Orleans. Accompanied by his wife and young son, Burroughs, like other contemporary urban explorers, sought cheap drugs and easy interracial sex.[91] He found Mexico's perceived acceptance of drug culture fascinating, although he—as well as other Beat writers—indeed misread its cultural meanings. While living in Mexico City, he became mesmerized by the infamous crime boss Lola la Chata.[92] As a character, she appears in his novels and short stories, sometimes with the name of Lupe, Lupita, or Lola.[93] Burroughs specialists have questioned whether he actually met her or not, but his fascination with her continued for years.[94]

Unlike Salazar and Anslinger, Burroughs relished La Chata's deviations from constraint, and he found these departures a source of power that were uniquely tied to the body. In *Cities of the Red Night*, Burroughs described a meeting between his protagonist, Mr. Snide, and a version of Lola la Chata.[95] As Snide arrived at a warehouse owned by la Chata and guarded by a "skull-face *pistolero*," he entered a room richly decorated like a "Mexican country estate." A feast had been prepared for the visitors: "platters of tamales and tacos, beans, rice, and guacamole, beers in tubs of ice, bottles of tequila, bowls of marijuana, and cigarette papers." He pointed to the table with the syringes and "beverages" as well as the curtained booths for later encounters. Then his attention shifted to Lola. As Burroughs wrote:

> Lola la Chata sits in a massive oak chair facing the door, three hundred pounds cut from the mountain rock of Mexico, her graciousness underlining her power. She extends a massive arm: "Ah Meester Snide . . . El Puerco Particular . . . the private pig," she shakes with laughter. . . . And your handsome young assistants . . ." She shakes hands with Jim and Kiki, "You do well by yourself Meester Snide."
>
> "And you Lola . . . You are younger if anything. . . ."
>
> She waves her hand to the table, "Please serve yourselves. . . ."[96]

Burroughs payed homage to his dealer by admiring her power contextualized by her body and physical presence. Basing his literary inventions on reality, Burroughs described her as gracious because of her immensity in presence and power. He elaborated upon her mountainous and massive figure and visibly displayed wealth. In the Beat subculture, he celebrated her deviance as corporal and sexual. To Burroughs, she embodied a natural essence of Mexican culture; he described her as an Aztec, an earth goddess who gave her special clients packets of heroin from between her massive breasts. Burroughs associated her breasts as a site that nurtured his addiction. She suckled her favorite clients to her, via a syringe, just as she did her "kittens." Her femininity and nurturing of her addicts was an integral part of her peddling. Similar to Anslinger, Burroughs's visions of her gender, but also her otherness, offered a potential site of weakness that led even junkies to consider the fragility of her power in the hopes of conquering her heroin franchise.

Salazar also recognized la Chata's power and influence. Both he and Burroughs acknowledged that she knew the desires and needs of her clients. Like any good businesswoman, she provided a hook to expand her clientele—a day when all could be had for free, even for the police.[97] In examining her business acumen, Salazar recognized her intelligence and her hard work in the same letter in which he discusses her physical appearance. He confessed:

> This, I must tell you for your own satisfaction has not diminished my admiration for you. I consider you to be a perfect product of our time. For you, a drug addict is merely a good customer and nothing more. For me, he is an unhappy person dragged in the dust by civilization. As it is, you as a drug dealer have had better luck than those of us who are entrusted with incorporating the addicts [among] active, social, and living [people]. You have accomplished a marvel—and this is a real compliment to your talent and ability—of knowing how to maintain your position and gaining always goodwill of the whole police force. You are a dispenser of graft, a national emblem. No one ever resists your bribes which, according to what I am told are very grand indeed. One thing is surely clearer, you, old in the custom, know how the business can produce even if sometimes the demands are heavy and excessive, with a little more bicarbonate in the heroin and a little more pressure on the client, you are able to make ends meet.
>
> In addition to your business ability, you have a very acute sense of psychology, you know the "when" the "how" and the "how much" of the bribe to be given; you know how to tell if the person involved has his teeth sharpened or not.[98]

Salazar had an ironic admiration for la Chata's ability to glean the needs of her clients as well as her skill in protecting herself; she indeed embodied the entrepreneurial peddler who had matured in the highly competitive and politicized informal economy.[99] She created a plague of addicts, however, whom Salazar struggled to help against insurmountable odds. Like many prostitutes and street vendors, this uneducated mestiza from an impoverished family had few options in life.[100] For many women in her circumstances, their futures were limited to becoming street vendors, waitresses, maids, nannies, prostitutes, or traffickers. Having few opportunities available to her, she overcame traditional constraints on her gender and developed criminal skills that evolved into a public threat because of her success and her ability to bribe.[101] That leap drew the attention of international crime fighters.

On the surface, narcotics abuse is a solitary and private activity, in contrast to the public nature of drinking, which initially takes place in the cantina, bar, or pub (but which may too become a solitary endeavor).[102] Thus, opium and its derivatives appealed to women of the late nineteenth and early twentieth century. It was a private vice that could be indulged in far from the public eye. Moreover, if a doctor provided a user with a prescription for some contrived ailment, the vice could easily be explained away. In Mexico, habitués—elite female opium addicts—were represented as beautiful women, lounging on satin pillows with willowy smoke framing their perfectly made-up faces. Their addiction remained feminine, and a well-kept family secret. Their threat was private; they neglected their feminine duties of child rearing, sexually satisfying their husbands, preparing food, and maintaining their homes. Their beauty may have remained intact, but their addictions disrupted their families. Families easily concealed, explained away, or dismissed these disturbances. As long as a woman's addiction never graduated to illicit or public sexual encounters, her secret remained safe.

Lowly and poor *borrachas*, on the other hand, were public nuisances. Artists, writers, and social workers documented their public shame.[103] Borrachas transgressed acceptable gender boundaries to drink in masculine spaces—bars, cantinas, or streets. Like the borracha, la Chata differed from the addict because she resituated the private location of women's lives and traditional work into the public realm.

Opium addiction as a feminized and private pastime tied to race and gender evolved into a public act when drugs were peddled and trafficked. The marketing and selling of these items represented a common and acceptable historical act on the part of women, except in cases where women became wealthy and powerful from those acts. La Chata used feminine skills as a basis upon which to build a powerful enterprise. Her legal food vending corresponded to a private skill common to all women, on the scale of home production. Once women marketed their wares more broadly, however, that became a public act that potentially led to danger. In-home food production or the street vending of food products denoted the systematic survival of people on the brink in a culture of poverty.[104] Drug peddling, however, permitted certain people, like la Chata, to break away from that poverty by moving into the public realm. The illegality of heroin, and to a lesser degree marijuana, required that these products be more discreetly marketed and used than alcohol. Peddlers subtly created secret networks of distribution for these items. Even the ability to bribe the police became a form of manipulation that was common to women and, as Salazar suggested, la Chata had honed it to a fine art.

The private and informal selling of narcotics developed naturally from Mexican women's traditional work in street vending, prostitution, and other lowly occupations.[105] Lower-class people, particularly poor mestizas like la Chata, struggled against nearly insurmountable odds to break out of the culture of poverty. The legal system, the Department of Health, and the police sought to keep women like la Chata restrained and marginalized. Sexism and racism further ensured that she would not rise above her given lot. Even if she had been able to obtain an education, institutionalized sexism limited job opportunities for women. Instead, she advanced economically through illegal means, which made her a target of the state. The state, elites, and policing agents created the obstacles that she surmounted. La Chata realized how fragile those restraints were. She recognized that the police, judges, and politicians—those responsible for maintaining order and control—were just as easily bought as the junkie in need of a fix.

In her own neighborhood, known as a place of thieves where anything could be purchased, addiction, prostitution, and crime reinforced one another. Like prostitutes around the world, Mexican prostitutes used mind-altering substances that enabled them to perform their jobs.[106] As with food items that are sold to local community members, la Chata found a local market for heroin and marijuana in and around La Merced; local customers are a basic element of a successful business. As Burroughs wrote about his folk hero, la Chata sold "heroin to pimps and thieves and whores."[107]

Her ability to build and maintain a local market for her drugs created a domestic front for Salazar in his battle against narcotics peddling and smuggling, but it also created a place to study those problems associated with addiction. As la Chata and other prominent peddlers rose to the fore, Salazar's attempt to paint Mexico's drug problems as affecting only a minor portion of the population who were fully susceptible to treatment was undermined. At the League of Nations' Advisory Committee on Traffic in Opium and Other Dangerous Drugs, Salazar stated: "In Mexico, the problem of drug addiction is of minor importance. It only exists in the capital and in the port cities, and a few larger cities."[108] When la Chata was based in Mexico City, Salazar's "Open Letter," published in 1938, demonstrated that her threat was more insidious than he had presented at international meetings. At the 1939 League of Nations meeting, Salazar discussed his research on the treatment of addicts in and out of prison with a morphine step-down program, seemingly ignoring Anslinger's view of addiction as an international criminal problem. This notion of "treatment" infuriated

Anslinger, who grew annoyed with Salazar's presentation of Mexico's drug problem as localized in a few areas of the country and not a systematic menacing threat, as perceived by U.S. officials.

Salazar's attempts to combat narcotics revealed a growing recognition of the impact of technology and gender in the trade. Although la Chata used traditional women's networks and vending practices to build her empire, her location in La Merced, her fast-food lunch stand, and her feminine skills became central to Salazar's criticism of her. Like Burroughs, he suspected that her gender would eventually contribute to her competitive weakness. He saw her as evolving into a small-time peddler who would be outmuscled by others in the business. Times were changing, and Salazar's 1938 "Open Letter" seeks to ridicule women like la Chata as slipping into history. He noted that her deputies, many of them men, would continue in her name, but he also noted that the trade was modernizing. He stated:

> You are in spite of your popularity a factor of little importance in the vast network of drug dealing; your stay in the Penitentiary would only greatly increase the traffic therein, without really affecting the traffic outside as you would leave your deputies and temporary substitutes in charge. Moreover and above all, there are your colleagues who, while they do not sell quick lunches, have airplanes at their disposal and descend from the clouds with their infamous cargo.[109]

Among la Chata's top deputies were her husband, Jaramillo, and her rumored lover and accomplice, Enrique Escudero Romano. Her relationships with men ensured that her business moved beyond the borders of La Merced. Jaramillo, a well-known trafficker in his own right, maintained contacts and laboratories in the provinces, as did Escudero.[110] Men offered her protection, since they had a vested interest in her survival and continuation. She was not their dupe. Instead, she constructed and developed a criminal enterprise that served men. That did not mean that there were not other men who hoped to wrestle her market away from her. Like in any business, she faced stiff competition. Her lovers and police agents protected her—many of whom Salazar was well aware of—but she was also victimized by those who worked for her or alongside her.

In 1938, Captain Luis Huesca de la Fuente, chief of the narcotics squad in Mexico City, arrested la Chata and confiscated 250 packets of cocaine that she had on her person.[111] After her arrest, Huesca substituted the cocaine with bicarbonate of soda and sold the cocaine, consequently leading to an investigation of him.[112] He, too, had his price and demonstrated that law enforcement often competed in the drug trade.

Beginning in 1937, the Mexican newspaper *La Prensa* began a series of reports on the heroin trade in Mexico City. Journalists alleged that the Federal Judicial Police and bureaucrats from the attorney general's office were known to traffic heroin within the Federal District.[113] Captain Huesca de la Fuente emerged as one of the primary traffickers in heroin. As scholar Ricardo Pérez Montfort noted, to cover his own association with drug trafficking, Huesca de la Fuente implicated Salazar and the Department of Health in the drug trade at the beginning of 1938.

The "heroin triangle" between Salazar, Huesca de la Fuente, and known heroin dealers such as la Chata that was exposed in the Mexican press drew the attention of U.S. officials, who grew more and more concerned with Mexico's drug problem. The arrest of Huesca de la Fuente and Salazar's "Open Letter" to la Chata attracted wide interest in the United States. This led to increased surveillance of Salazar and the Mexican police. James B. Stewart, U.S. consul general in Mexico, reported to the secretary of state his discussions with H. S. Creighton, supervising customs agent, revealing that Salazar had little interest in acting as a policeman. Stewart reported: "The arrest of the chief of the narcotic squad does not necessarily mean that there is to be inaugurated a campaign against those engaged in drug trafficking."[114] To the U.S. authorities, Mexican officials appeared corrupt or inept, as in this portrayal of Salazar. However, no interpretation of the facts could adequately reflect the complexities of the situation.

While men provided la Chata with protection and their alliances became her alliances, Salazar's "Open Letter" focused on la Chata, not her deputies, as the source of a contagion that demanded to be controlled. While she could be victimized, as when she was arrested by Huesca de la Fuente, Salazar did not see her as a victim. In the documents, her male associates were not the basis of her power but her underlings. If and when she went to jail, Salazar knew that her business would continue. Instead, Salazar sought points of weakness based on her gender and on rapidly modernizing technology. While he congratulated her on the feminine angle of her business expertise, he also expressed that her time was coming to an end. Playing on the age-old theme of the middle-aged woman who gazes in the mirror and fears the loss of her beauty and sexual viability, Salazar noted that traffickers now employed more sophisticated technologies. How could an illiterate mestiza compete? In other words, he used his views of her class and her inability to access new forms of technology to mock her as a has-been whose time was coming to an end.

In 1938, Salazar's gendered assumptions about la Chata's marginality were more wishful thinking than reality. La Chata had developed from local peddler to international trafficker during a time when traffickers were becoming increasingly sophisticated in their use of technology and networks.[115] Moreover, she continued to sell heroin, morphine, and marijuana, whether in or out of prison, for almost another twenty years. This led to a growing crisis between the Mexican and U.S. officials who had repeatedly attempted to arrest and imprison her. Even after Ávila Camacho's presidential decree in 1945, she successfully fought a long-term prison sentence and continued to traffic and peddle for another twelve years—a testament to her ability to maintain networks of powerful friends.

Salazar was not as lucky as la Chata. His public disagreements with Anslinger over marijuana, poppy and marijuana eradication, and the enforcement of more stringent narcotics laws caused great consternation between the United States and Mexico. From the time of Huesca de la Fuente's arrest, Salazar found himself on the front lines of a transnational struggle that ultimately undermined his career. From late 1938 to 1940, the FBN waged a campaign against Salazar to have him removed. Salazar's research on marijuana drew greater and greater criticism and ridicule from the United States but also from within Mexico. James B. Stewart reported on experiments that Mexican doctors conducted to ascertain the links between marijuana and insanity. In his letter, he argued that Dr. Fernando Rosales, a peer of Salazar, also disputed the ties of marijuana to violence and insanity. In both cases, the researchers, examining patients at the Federal Hospital for Drug Addicts in Mexico, reached similar conclusions, that using marijuana combined with alcohol (now a legal commodity in the United States) contributed to increased violence. Stewart went on to write:

> There is no doubt that Dr. Salazar Viniegra has been passing around marijuana cigarettes for some time to persons whom he believes to be interested in the subject of marijuana. In fact on September 6, 1938 when I visited Dr. Almazán, Minister of Public Health, with Mr. A. F. Scharff, U.S. Customs Agent, San Antonio, Texas, Dr. Almázan jokingly remarked that when he called on Dr. Viniegra he would properly offer us marijuana cigarettes. In passing out these cigarettes

Dr. Salazar Viniegra in his capacity as Chief of the Narcotics Section at the Department of Public Health takes the position that he is doing so for experimental purposes and in interest of science.[116]

In this case, Stewart cast Salazar Viniegra as a pusher of marijuana among the upper echelons of the Mexican government. Like some other doctors, he had experimented on himself, which gave pause among the bureaucrats but had been a common practice among researchers. His role as an alleged distributor, compounded with the reaction of the Minister of Health, Dr. Almázan, who found humor in Salazar's self-experiments, illustrated to serious men such as Stewart and Anslinger that the Mexican could not be trusted to respond to the growing drug problem in an efficient way. In turn, Salazar became a prime target.

Stewart and Creighton kept up a correspondence about Salazar's ineptitude and perceived criminality. The embassy translated his articles and distributed them to experts, who disputed and faulted Salazar's findings, particularly his article "The Myth of Marijuana" and his assessment of the Narcotics Farm in Lexington, Kentucky. In "The Myth of Marijuana," Salazar considered the work of a number of his associates, including Dr. Almazán, Dr. Francisco Elizarrarás, Dr. Fernando Rosales, and Salazar's student Jorge Segura Millán.[117] This research built upon earlier studies of marijuana use among soldiers in the Mexican army conducted in the 1920s, and earlier studies of marijuana and its use by Mexican researchers. Although Salazar documented certain changes in human behavior, he discovered that marijuana-induced psychosis was simply the patient's actual psychosis. Those patients who hallucinated during marijuana use already suffered from dementia or acute alcoholism.[118] Marijuana did not cause hallucinations.

Segura Millán's writing more directly targeted the U.S.-instigated hysteria of "reefer madness":

Everybody knows about the very great propaganda started in the United States against marijuana, and that in this neighboring country the most absurd reports are spread, imputing to the plant suicides, acts of madness, terrible assassinations etc. It is enough for this purpose to read the article by H. J. Anslinger (Commissioner of Narcotics in the United States) in the periodical *Excélsior* of this capital city [Mexico City]. In the heaviest type there is published the news that six persons had been wounded by a marijuana addict, and

later it is stated that it cannot be ascertained whether it is a marijuana addict or an alcoholic. . . . The soldier who assassinated three
persons, according to our ascertainments, was not under the influence of marijuana intoxication when he carried out his criminal
acts, but feeling himself caught in the traffic in drugs he tried to flee
and killed those who came to capture him.[119]

The FBN forwarded Segura Millán's dissertation to John Matchett, chief
chemist of the FBN, to read and criticize. In both cases, the documents identified Segura with Salazar. Matchett argued that Segura had concluded that
marijuana did not provoke hallucinations or aggression. Rather, it produced
euphoria, introspection, and gaiety. In his analysis of Segura, Matchett
wrote: "They also insist that use of marijuana has been shown to have a de-
generative effect on mental capacity."[120] Matchett associated Segura's work
with that of Salazar, further adding to the condemnation of the latter.

Salazar paid a heavy price for his insolence toward Anslinger, whom
he criticized for his loose use of science and lack of medical experience. In
November 1939, Dr. Salazar wrote to Stuart Fuller of the Treasury
Department requesting permission to continue his research at Harvard
University and visit the narcotics sanitariums at Lexington and Forth
Worth. In April 1940, Salazar wrote to Anslinger that he had never received
a response from Fuller. In that letter, he disclosed that Anslinger may have
been partially responsible:

> I was inconvenienced by the fact that my government put into effect
> a new regulation concerning narcotics, about which we spoke in
> Geneva as you will remember, and that I proposed to study this
> question again in order to eliminate its disturbing results.
> Unfortunately, upon my return from Geneva I was forced to give up
> my position as chief of narcotics—as you know—in Mexico techni-
> cal matters are tied up with politics—and for this reason I had no
> authority.[121]

The tension between Salazar and the FBN heightened in part due to
Salazar's public persona. His 1938 "Open Letter to Lola la Chata" and her
protectors confirmed certain suspicions of the FBN and the U.S. State
Department. Salazar's medical and scientific training put him at odds with
men such as Anslinger, who saw drugs as a criminal problem rather than a

Figure 17. María Dolores Estévez Zuleta. Serie Mariguana, opio, y drogas, ca. 1935, 14834, Casasola, Mexico City, Fototeca Nacional del Instituto Nacional de Anthropología e Historia (INAH), Pachuca, Hidalgo.

medical one. In turn, Salazar's ability to sway career diplomats to his mode of thinking fell on deaf ears, leading to his marginalization in the global drug debates. The open letter looked to them like he was sympathetic to la Chata. He seemed to court her, when in fact he was attempting to disrupt her business by exposing her, her collaborators, and her protectors to a broad audience.

Salazar's attempt to engage Lola la Chata and her supporters in a dialogue demonstrates a greater knowledge about the power of the narcotics trade. He spoke to a world of power and alliances that few contemplated in the 1940s. Lola la Chata and women like her defied contemporary images of *narcotraficantes*, although the role of women in the trade continues to shock, surprise, and titillate.[122] Like her mother before her, she, and many women of her background, knew how to buy, sell, and create a market whether for food, sex, or narcotics. Using those few spaces within the economy left open to them, women like la Chata resisted the limitations that had been constructed for them. Although a large cadre of men assisted la Chata in her narcotics empire, Salazar, Anslinger, and even President Ávila Camacho acknowledged that she was a boss, a godmother. Her physical presence, criminal mind, and ability to manipulate fascinated the narcotic warriors. She embodied a threat to Mexican and U.S. society, since she ruptured the expectations of what it meant to be a woman. She was not an addict but a shrewd businesswoman who recognized the demand for her product. More dangerous than an addict, her ability to bribe and manipulate the laws and those entrusted to enforce them showcased her danger. Significantly, other women joined la Chata, causing concern in the United States. A woman on the border operating out of Ciudad Juárez, Ignacia Jasso González, "La Nacha," created a multigenerational transnational trafficking family that endured into the 1980s. La Chata died in 1959, and La Nacha in January of 1982. Both women, who had trafficked for years, represent Burroughs's characterization of La Chata's career that, "Selling is more of a habit than using."[123]

CHAPTER FOUR

TRANSCENDING BORDERS

La Nacha and the "Notorious" Women of the North

❧ THE 1940S WERE ALSO EVENTFUL FOR ANOTHER MEXICAN FEMALE criminal boss. Along the U.S.-Mexico border, another familial dynasty took form beginning in the 1920s. The matriarch, Ignacia Jasso la viuda de González, also known as Emma and la Nacha, entered the popular imagination like her more cosmopolitan counterpart, Lola la Chata in Mexico City. Jasso also found herself the target of transnational scrutiny that drew unwanted attention, particularly beginning in the early 1940s.

In 1942, narcotics trafficker Jasso made the critical error of stepping into a planned snare set up by U.S. narcotics officers in El Paso, touching off a four-year firestorm between the United States and Mexico over drug trafficking. Harry J. Anslinger, director of the U.S. Federal Bureau of Narcotics (FBN), demanded her extradition to stand trial in the United States for violation of the Harrison Narcotics Tax Act. As he had done for Lola la Chata, President Ávila Camacho targeted Jasso with a presidential decree on April 27, 1945. The two cases differ, because la Nacha had been in prison since 1942 and a well-known border boss since 1930.

As a product of the border, Jasso understood the cultural constructs of both Mexico and the United States, and she also knew how contraband flowed between the two nations. Borderlanders like Jasso and her family demonstrated a sophisticated knowledge of market demand in the United States, but, more importantly, their location on the border enabled them to take advantage of the illicit as well as legal flows of people, products, and information.[1] With this knowledge, she adeptly manipulated the press, the public, and government officials. Her extradition case heightened tensions between the two countries at a time when opiate use had allegedly declined. Her stature as a transnational trafficker, like la Chata's, rose as World War II cut trade from Asia and Europe. With wartime blockades and increased surveillance by warships and submarines patrolling the waters of the Atlantic and the Pacific, key transportation routes were disrupted. Significantly, European and Asian land routes for trafficking opium and opiate derivatives were also disrupted by the global conflict.

La Chata and la Nacha flourished by stepping into the vacuum created by the war. Organized crime figures in the United States sought alternative sources of narcotics. Mexico was a known supplier, although its heroin was considered lower grade than that from Europe and Asia. After her extradition case, Jasso remained in the public eye for the next thirty years as a primary source of heroin, morphine, and marijuana for the U.S. market. After her release from prison in the 1940s, she maintained a lower profile but reemerged in the 1950s as a threat because of her continued dealing and trafficking along the border.

Jasso remains a pivotal figure in U.S.-Mexican narcotics relations because of her reemergence in contemporary drug literature and the centrality of the border region in the current war on drugs.[2] A product of a city known for its zone of tolerance of legalized gambling and prostitution, she operated out of Ciudad Juárez supplying morphine and heroin to border residents and Americans who traveled there. Eventually, her reach extended as far as Seattle, Detroit, and New York City.[3] Until her death in the early 1980s, la Nacha peddled and trafficked heroin, marijuana, and morphine. She persisted in this dangerous trade for over fifty years, surpassing many of her male peers in longevity.

Jasso and other women of the border involved in drugs remained a focus of the FBN, the Bureau of Narcotics and Dangerous Drugs (BNDD), and politicians. Today, they are drawing greater scrutiny from border scholars and other specialists.[4] Like Lola la Chata and the Texas-based Beland family, Jasso demonstrated the importance of family in building her drug empire, but her location on the border made her appear all the more threatening to the United States and to Mexico's relations with the north. Jasso's lifetime of activities coincides with and exemplifies the shifting attitudes toward and interpretations of the border and its centrality in the wars on drugs. Her life intersects with and informs the evolution of government policy with respect to the policing of narcotics that took place from the 1930s to the 1970s.[5] Despite her longevity, her establishment of a multigenerational dynasty, and her physical location, she was rarely mentioned by name in the historiography on drug trafficking until recently even though the FBN, the FBI, the local police in Ciudad Juárez, journalists, the successive governors of Chihuahua and mayors of Ciudad Juárez, and members of the U.S. Congress saw her as a central threat beginning in the 1930s. More recently, scholars of drug trafficking have rediscovered Jasso, and her dynasty has been reconceptualized as an important nexus between old forms of drug trafficking and the new forms that have triggered such violence in the twenty-first century.[6]

THE EXTRADITION OF LA NACHA

Jasso's 1942 arrest was triggered by two events. In April 1942, the FBN, U.S. Customs, and Mexican authorities set up a sting operation to arrest la Nacha. She had emerged in the early 1930s as a known drug trafficker, and Ciudad Juárez was seen as a city where many were involved in the drug trade. She, her family, and her peers had entered the popular imagination. These "meros gallos" lived lives of luxury with "magnificent houses, cars, and clothes," often with the support of the local police and politicians.[7] Since the 1930s, Jasso's resources had given her these advantages, as demonstrated by her ability to buy her way out of prison.

In the summer of 1942, police in El Paso detained two of Jasso's agents, Teodoro García and Guadalupe Guzmán, in front of the El Paso Laundry shortly after they had crossed the Santa Fe Bridge from Ciudad Juárez. They had planned to deliver nineteen cans of opium (valued at $150 a can; 2012: $2,128 a can) to a buyer who was actually an undercover agent. In interrogations, Jasso's men admitted that the cans belonged to her.

Two "ace" U.S. narcotics agents, H. B. Westover and W. H. Crook, posed as dealers who sold to Oklahoma Indians. They went to Ciudad Juárez to buy large quantities of opium and morphine after Westover initially arranged a meeting with la Nacha. At first, she insisted that they purchase 450 cans of smoking opium and a kilo of gummed opium.[8] Like any good dealer, Westover asked for a sample of her stuff. An assistant and her cleaning lady brought him a fruit jar full of smoking opium and a can of opium.[9] La Nacha told Westover and Crook that she had a chemist who could extract morphine, but he was a five-hour drive from Ciudad Juárez. Westover told la Nacha that he wanted to think it over, but that he would soon contact her.

A couple of weeks later, Westover and Crook returned to Ciudad Juárez to visit la Nacha. She told them that she had a group of smugglers who trafficked her opium into the United States, and that she had customers as far away as New York and San Francisco.[10] Her assertion may have been true. In 1947, the United Nations Commission on Narcotic Drugs reported:

> The Mexican government in its intensified drive to stop the traffic ordered an aerial survey to be made in the spring of 1947 of the poppy cultivation which although prohibited by Mexican law, was increasing year after year. Some 4,500 fields were observed and of them, 200 destroyed. Between twenty and thirty clandestine landing strips for aeroplanes had been constructed in Mexico to handle the illicit transportation of narcotics from Mexico to the U.S. The traffic now appeared to be organized by underworld groups in the U.S. They have representatives in Mexico engaged in promoting the cultivation of opium poppy, purchasing the crop and arranging its transformation into more valuable and less bulky derivatives. It was estimated that at least one half of the raw opium [was] produced in Mexico and processed into morphine and heroin most of which found its way into the United States. . . . The so-called "brown" heroin found in Canada originated in Mexico. It was found in various parts of the country in adulterated form. The traffic in this drug was directed by a syndicate with headquarters in Toronto.[11]

Jasso agreed to sell Westover a can of opium so that he could gauge how quickly she could deliver it to a location in El Paso. Like many dealers located on the border, she guaranteed delivery to the U.S. side. Once delivered, Westover planned to have his own chemists test it.[12] Crook went back to El Paso to await delivery, confident that la Nacha would indeed deliver. She did.[13]

Once the opium was tested, the agents told la Nacha that they could only obtain a small amount of morphine from the opium, but that they remained interested in doing business with her. Over time, they worked to gain her trust. Once she trusted them, she introduced them to her operation. She took them to visit poppy fields in the state of Jalisco and to one of her morphine labs in Guadalajara, where the agents observed chemists working with a ten-pound batch of crude opium. The agents met two of her lieutenants, "the

Chemist," Luis Manuel Vázquez, and "the Lawyer," Alberto Torres Ibarra, who quietly offered to sell directly to the agents and cut la Nacha out of the deal.[14] The four men thus worked out a separate transaction. Vázquez and Torres traveled to San Antonio with fifty-five ounces of morphine hidden in a secret compartment in the gas tank of their car, and they were arrested. They pled guilty in court, and both were sentenced to five years in prison.

Despite the arrests of Vázquez and Torres, la Nacha remained free, but she was now suspicious of cross-border contacts seeking supplies of narcotics. Along with the arrests in the United States, the Ciudad Juárez police also detained many of her runners, yielding seizures of 125 ounces of smoking opium and 78 ounces of morphine.[15] These events led to the search of her café on the morning of November 4, 1942. She was found in the company of two addicts, Mariano Morales ("el chamaco") and Regina Guzmán ("la picuchi"), both of whom she had allegedly injected. A toxicology report showed that Morales and Guzmán were indeed addicted to morphine and heroin, but la Nacha's blood showed no evidence of opiates. The ten-month attempt to arrest her ended with la Nacha in the custody of the Ciudad Juárez police.[16]

Recognizing that she had been the subject of a transnational sting, la Nacha told the Juárez chief of police, Teodoro Pérez Rivas: "I have been in tighter spots before, why shouldn't I be able to get out of this one."[17] In previous arrests, she had merely paid a fine, and probably a couple of bribes. This arrest, however, was a bit more complicated because the United States demanded her extradition.

La Nacha's arrest made national news on both sides of the border. Two days after her arrest, *El Continental Span* reported that the United States wanted to extradite Jasso de González.[18] In Ciudad Juárez and El Paso, rumors persisted that U.S. narcotics and customs agents had orchestrated the raid of her house and her subsequent arrest. Due to these rumors, the municipal president, Antonio J. Bermúdez, issued a public statement in the newspaper *El Mexicano* repudiating such claims. He argued that la Nacha had been arrested by Pérez Rivas because her activities violated Mexican laws, not those of the United States. He further argued that extradition was not a matter decided by the municipal government but by federal authorities.[19] Despite his claims, on November 9, 1942, the U.S. State Department presented the secretary of foreign relations, Ezequiel Padilla, with a request for her extradition for violation of the 1914 Harrison Act.[20]

Figure 18. La Nacha's 1942 mug shot. RG59, box 6, General Records of
Department of State, National Archive College Park, MD.

Bermúdez's statements to the press may not have been completely accurate. On September 2, 1942, Ben Foster, U.S. attorney for the western district
of El Paso, had formally requested Jasso's extradition. On October 22, the
U.S. embassy sent a formal request to Secretary Padilla to detain Jasso in
preparation for extradition proceedings.[21] In the documents, U.S. authorities
described la Nacha as forty-eight years old, standing five feet five inches tall,
weighing 170 pounds, and dressed poorly "when around home." The document reflected that agents from the FBN and other agencies had regularly

observed her and her activities at home. They also may have had informants who gave them information.[22]

The argument for the extradition of Jasso touched off a crisis in Mexico and contributed to heated exchanges between officials on both sides of the border, an example of the historical realities of U.S.-Mexico diplomacy regarding criminal behavior. On January 19, 1943, Anslinger wrote to Municipal President Bermúdez following a meeting about la Nacha:

> We believe that the extradition of Ignacia Jasso González is of utmost importance in suppressing the illicit traffic in narcotics between Mexico and the United States. Mexico has now become the principal source of supply of opium and its derivatives throughout the United States. We find narcotic drugs of Mexican origin in New York, Washington, Chicago, and Detroit and in fact every large center of population. Those narcotics drugs are being distributed by organized gangs which we are sending to prison, but as long as Mexico remains the source of supply and the traffic is not suppressed there, the traffic will increase. Before the war, Japan was the source of these drugs and this traffic was part of the Imperial policy of Japan to poison and weaken our people for conquest. The people of Mexico were also being poisoned by these drugs. We presented sufficient evidence to substantiate our charges before the Opium Advisory Committee of the League of Nations. It is unfortunate that we must now place before the world public the fact that Mexico has now become the source of smuggled narcotics.[23]

To encourage Mexican officials to prevent their country from becoming a promoter of "human slavery" (drug addiction) and to force the extradition of Jasso González, Anslinger threatened that the United States would publicize Mexico as a chief source of narcotics at the League of Nations as well as in its own reports. This caused grave concern in Mexico and added further strains to relations with the United States, already tense because of Mexico's recent nationalization of oil.[24] In February 1943, the case of la Nacha came before the House of Representatives. On the tenth, John J. Cochran, representative from Missouri, recognized the work of Anslinger and his men. He insisted that Anslinger deserved "a medal of honor" for his work in attempting to rid the United States of drugs. Cochran identified Mexican poppy and opiates as the source of narcotics distributed by Dutch Schultz's and Lucky

Luciano's gangs.[25] Whether the "remnants" of Schultz and Luciano actually dealt in Mexican opiates remains subject to debate.

Cochran's declaration, however, markedly highlights the escalation of moral panic that surrounded Mexican drug trafficking and its alleged ties to U.S. organized crime. Cochran read a statement about the case against la Nacha and called her the largest distributor of illicit drugs on the Mexican frontier.[26] His claim thus positioned la Nacha as one of the earliest Mexican drug traffickers to gain public recognition in the United States. She had been called out on the floor of Congress and tied to organized crime in the United States.

In October 1942, Anslinger emphasized la Nacha's and Mexico's growing role in the narcotics trade to George S. Messersmith, U.S. ambassador to Mexico. Anslinger wrote: "This case is of unusual importance at this time because narcotic smuggling from Europe, the Near East, and the Far East has just ceased, and the traffic is switching to Mexico. We feel that potentially large traffic has been destroyed by the apprehension of this ring."[27] Anslinger's letter implies that Mexico had evolved into a key site of production and that it was no longer simply a site of transshipment. La Nacha, like la Chata, had played an important role in that evolution.

In Mexico, Bermúdez immediately forwarded Anslinger's translated letter to President Ávila Camacho, arguing that Mexico had inherited the "sad role" of France and Japan as the world's major drug exporter. He asked what they should do in regard to the extradition request, since the Jasso case could have negative ramifications on Mexico's global standing.[28] In turn, Mexican officials began to investigate how to proceed with the extradition request. The war had severed the opiate lines from Asian and Europe. Mexican drug traffickers had discovered a market advantage that created problems for their government.

The pressure that Anslinger placed on Mexico initially appeared to work in the favor of the FBN.[29] The U.S. embassy in Mexico City reported that the minister of foreign relations, Ezequiel Padilla, was cooperating with U.S. ambassador Messersmith, who had forged a close working relationship with Padilla during World War II. In his correspondence with Padilla, Messersmith echoed the words of Anslinger and argued that the prosecution of Jasso would destroy a significant narcotic smuggling ring that endangered not only the United States but also Mexico. To further persuade Mexico, the United States offered to extradite Americans charged with crimes in Mexico, specifically check fraud.

Notwithstanding the verbal support that Padilla and his legal advisers offered, the Americans expressed concern that Jasso would bribe Mexican authorities. Officials in the FBI, the FBN, and the State Department also noted that corruption existed among the police force along the border.

> The officials of the Health Department of the Mexican government have been co-operating with the officials of the United States Treasury Department in Mexico City . . . in an effort to stamp out the international dope traffic. However, one obstacle to this program is the fact that local officials in the border states and even the municipal police sometimes "have a hand" in the growing of poppies. It has been rumored in several distinct pieces of correspondence that it might be difficult to keep Ignacia Jasso Gonzalez in jail because of the influence of local politicians, and even that the adverse decision of the trial judge in the initial extradition proceedings was strongly influenced by this factor.[30]

Before long, the Mexican national press knew about the proceedings and a campaign opposing the extradition of la Nacha began.

As with the case of la Chata, people in Ciudad Juárez wrote directly to the president. La Nacha had other contacts beyond her drug selling through her small businesses and farming. Her extensive family ties, business relations, and government patronage added to her popularity in the city. That popularity, whether real or contrived, could be found in the support letters. A letter from fellow farmers of Ciudad Juárez asked President Ávila Camacho to cancel the pending extradition order. The farmers recognized that la Nacha's husband, Pablo González, indeed sold and trafficked drugs, but they argued that since his death in 1928 or 1929, Jasso had lived an "absolutely moral" life and supported her children by growing cotton and selling clothes. Her defenders insisted that as a Mexican national, she must not be extradited to the United States on manufactured charges by her enemies in Ciudad Juárez and El Paso.[31] Jasso, they argued, traveled throughout Mexico only to buy clothes that she then sold in Ciudad Juárez, not to distribute drugs or engage in trafficking. The growers asserted that the case not only harmed her and her clothing and farming businesses, but also hurt her "modest but numerous family," the majority of whom were minors.[32]

Just as citizens wrote letters to complain about foreigners who undermined the revolution, the health of the nation, and the general good, some of

Jasso's fellow Ciudad Juárez residents forwarded this letter to the president, positioning Jasso as an upstanding woman who was being attacked by the United States in its relentless antinarcotics crusade.[33] Letters such as these represented the power that citizens felt they could legitimately muster to sway the national government as well as to highlight their own nationalism and belief in the revolution. These exchanges exhibited a continuous dialogue between the masses and the powerful over their respective interpretations and elaborations of the concepts of citizen and state in the postrevolutionary period. The farmers co-opted a language of exceptionalism that became an essential component of Mexican identity. This documentary evidence also suggests contradictory readings of la Nacha on the part of ordinary Mexicans and the American authorities. While the United States presented Jasso as a menace, Mexican citizens interpreted her as a hard-working businesswoman who performed good works for the poor in various pueblos in Chihuahua. She emerged as a true product of the border and of Ciudad Juárez.

Despite the claims of La Nacha and her supporters, Mexican government documents revealed that Jasso's business had been tied to drug trafficking since the 1920s. Ciudad Juárez had a long history of gambling, prostitution, and bootlegging.[34] The first Juárez drug lords, many of them Chinese, emerged in the 1910s, but by the mid-1920s Jasso and her husband had displaced many of the Chinese and aligned themselves with different organized crime entities. Urban myths circulated that la Nacha and Pablo González ("El Pablote") ordered the executions of eleven prominent Chinese distributors and traffickers in the 1920s.[35] Whether the sensational aspects of such stories were true, it appears that the González family succeeded in removing their competition. They created what some have described as the first Mexican drug cartel to emerge on the border, and perhaps the first cartel in the hemisphere. La Nacha and her husband's reputation as drug traffickers was well known on both sides of the border. The Spanish-language newspaper in San Antonio, *La Prensa*, identified her as a drug queen as early as 1930.[36]

Despite these undocumented assertions about the use of violence to wrest control of the Juárez dope trade, it is well documented that by the late 1920s González and Jasso began to move heroin, morphine, and marijuana into the United States. At times, she worked with other traffickers, but later she became independent and was increasingly seen as the one responsible for turning parts of El Paso into a *tecato* (old-time junkie) town whose back alleys were lined with shooting galleries.[37] From El Paso, Jasso and her family branched out into New Mexico and other areas of the United States.

The dynamics between Jasso and González have been duplicated in other drug trafficking families. Their family members, both immediate and extended, played key roles in narcotics distribution. Unlike Lola la Chata, who entered the drug economy working with her mother, and Lucy Beland, who started selling to support her children's addiction, it was la Nacha's marriage that facilitated her rise. While Pablote has been described as loud, boisterous, alcoholic, and lavish with money, la Nacha remained more discreet and respectable.[38]

Jasso's supporters contended that Pablote had forced his wife into the trade. However, evidence suggests that even prior to his death she already controlled the finances of their emerging enterprise, although her home, surroundings, and lifestyle reflected a modest businesswoman and farmer rather than a transnational trafficker. La Nacha may have seen drug smuggling as the best means by which she could maintain her family, and her husband's trade became her own after his death. When male drug traffickers were imprisoned or died, it often happened that their wives sought to maintain their families through the same illicit business. La Nacha also recognized that concealing her real business venture ensured its continuation. Hence, her supporters' letter in 1943 emphasized the points of her life that she wished to be known, although the supporters had come to a vastly different conclusion about la Nacha than that drawn by men such as Bermúdez and Anslinger.

Scholars of women and narcotics suggest that the most successful female drug peddlers exhibit more discretion in their trade than men commonly do, as is represented in popular culture.[39] Women are more likely to maintain a middle-class lifestyle and avoid ostentatious expenditures that would draw unneeded attention to their business and their family.[40] This, in part, may be due to the fact that women rarely appear to grow their businesses to the size of those of most prominent male dealers. Women also avoid drawing attention to their business for fear of the authorities and their competitors.

Some drug peddlers interviewed by U.S. and Australian scholars have described women as less trustworthy in the trade, but that may be because male dealers want to ensure that women remain marginal to the trade. La Nacha, like la Chata, proves that in Mexico, the discreetness of women may have contributed to their ability to remain in the trade for much longer periods than their peers in other parts of the world as well as their male colleagues in Mexico.

The fact that la Nacha and la Chata prospered in illicit trade to such a degree that their names became associated with transnational drug trafficking long before the men of the modern-day cartels offers a possible reading of class and gender relations among the working class as first suggested by anthropologist Oscar Lewis.[41] Scholarly assertions implied that at times, women of working and rancho classes have taken the reins of power from men. La Nacha's marriage to Pablote may have given her an entry into the business, and he may have trained her. However, another scenario may have existed. She may have been as adept as he in acquiring, processing, and moving product. Since she maintained a connection to her home state of Durango and a connection with Jalisco, she may have provided her husband with a direct supply line from the poppy fields.

Both Pablote and Jasso were transplants to Ciudad Juárez, and perhaps they entered the trade as equals. In a 1930 article published by *La Prensa*, their names are listed as equals among border traffickers.[42] Like la Chata's relationship with Jaramillo, Jasso's relationship with Pablote may have enhanced her own abilities rather than simply relegating her to be his accomplice or apprentice. For both women and their respective partners, their personal and sexual relationships may have added to their businesses and their longevity. Could they both have attained perfect business partnerships that endured beyond their emotional relationships? For la Nacha, her elevation to boss of her organization may have been preordained following her husband's early death. Later, her sons, nephews, and grandsons played key roles as partners and mules.

After Pablote's death, la Nacha consolidated and then ran the criminal enterprise until the 1980s. Very early, her reputation as a highly connected boss spread. In 1933, Daniel Minjares Párea and Daniel Rodríguez, leaders of the Confederation of Parents and Teachers in Ciudad Juárez, complained about her to the governor of Chihuahua, Rodrigo Quevedo. They wrote:

> The sale of narcotics is being done shamelessly and with impunity in the house of a woman dubbed La Nacha with the knowledge of the Police chief, a man called Moriel, and the protection of the Municipal President who has exploited this business, not only in that [la Nacha's] house, but in several places where armed men who flaunt their impunity engage in the sale who are nonetheless the employees of the current administration.[43]

The confederation outlined a host of threats to the health of the nation: the showing of banned films, illegal licensing of businesses, prostitution, extortion from tourists, and government corruption. In turn, they demanded that a commission form to study and remedy the numerous problems in the city. Citizens of Ciudad Juárez routinely engaged in dialogues with government officials regarding graft, corruption, and vice.[44] In this petition, la Nacha was identified as a threat but also as a highly connected drug dealer in the city. The petition indicates that by 1933 she had the protection of the police and the local government. Governor Quevedo had also been linked to the drug trade, and he and la Nacha had some sort of working relationship. Quevedo and his brothers actively engaged in the vice trade, whether drugs or gambling. In the 1930s, they battled with a competitor and ally of la Nacha, Enrique Fernández. By 1936, the Quevedos had killed Fernández and merged the two gangs, and la Nacha became part of the Quevedos' organization.[45]

In the 1930s, la Nacha served as a supplier to city employees who sold drugs to tourists. These city employees, like other peddlers in Ciudad Juárez, sold for a commission or as part of a franchise rather than as independent vendors. As discussed in chapter 1, the multifaceted means of peddling created a system of networks and connections rather than small, independent, and self-contained groups of peddlers. In other words, those who worked on commission or were part of a franchise had less invested in the business but could access the profits more easily, although arrest was always a danger.

Despite la Nacha's fierce reputation, men tried to outmuscle her in the trade, particularly when her children were young, which may account for her alliances with rival gangs. In 1939, American vice consul T. L. Lilliestrom wrote to the secretary of state about la Nacha and her ties to powerful men. He pointed out that she had long been the head of a prominent narcotics ring that operated in El Paso–Ciudad Juárez. In October 1939, she fled from Ciudad Juárez due to an impending arrest by Mexican authorities. In Torreón, Coahuila, two plainclothes police officers beat her and told her that she had to pay twenty thousand pesos or General Alatorre, the commander of the garrison at Ciudad Juárez, would use the evidence against her to send her to Islas Marías. A relative of la Nacha approached Alatorre. Lilliestrom wrote: "The General made it clear to this individual that he had no part in the matter, but that to the contrary he deplored the underhanded treatment she had received. He further stated that the only action he could condone would be legal punishment which might be meted out to her as a result of regular judicial procedure."[46]

Lilliestrom further explained that Alatorre deplored the behavior of his men, but he also recognized that la Nacha had a protector, namely the sub-chief of police. This communication further indicates that the police had a dual relationship with traffickers and peddlers, as seen in other cases described in earlier chapters. In this case, la Nacha went to jail, in 1939. In 1940, however, Terry Talent, a customs agent, informed Anslinger that la Nacha was out of jail, lived close to Ciudad Juárez, and operated as "the source of supply for small peddlers."[47] In Talent's report, she was the only confirmed female drug dealer in Ciudad Juárez, but there were five other women who were under suspicion.

Betrayed by men who worked for her or were in her pay, Jasso realized that her antagonism toward Bermúdez, her arrest, and her imprisonment in the local jail in 1942 could lead to her extradition to the United States or, after 1945, her removal to the Mexican penitentiary at Islas Marías. La Nacha remained in prison more than three years, but she was never far from the public eye. In 1944, the *El Paso Herald-Post* reported that the psychological pressure caused by the stress of her possible extradition to the United States or a sentence to Islas Marías had driven la Nacha to become a born-again Christian, who followed the evangelical minister Pablo I. Delgado and his twelve-year-old son, Beto, reportedly a biblical prodigy.[48]

Letters from Delgado's followers and from Jasso's family (including her husband's mother and brother) pleaded for la Nacha to be permitted to attend his revivals. Although she had been permitted to attend family events such as funerals, prison authorities in Ciudad Juárez denied requests to attend the religious services. She then called upon her fellow prisoners to listen to the sermons of Delgado and his son in the prison yard. She stated, "I accepted Christ after I heard the Bible messages. I have also found, through reading the Scripture, a consolation and peace of mind hard to describe."[49] The newspaper published a photo of Jasso peering into the camera holding a Bible.

In spite of la Nacha's alleged conversion and the prayers of her fellow inmates, Mexican president Manuel Ávila Camacho issued a presidential decree on April 27, 1945, that waived constitutional guarantees in cases of narcotics trafficking and permitted the immediate detention of peddlers and smugglers in the federal penitentiary at Islas Marías without first having to be tried in the Mexican courts.[50] She, along with Lola la Chata and other traffickers, were to be sent to Islas Marías. She immediately petitioned for an *amparo* (a protection of an individual's rights for due process) to be released

or permitted to remain in Ciudad Juárez.[51] Jasso may have succeeded in her
pleas, because an attorney for the family claimed that she was never sent to
Islas Marías.[52] Evidence suggests that she was moved to Chihuahua City and
later returned to the penitentiary in Ciudad Juárez without ever being sent
to the island prison. In Chihuahua City and Ciudad Juárez, she received
prominent visitors who were never inspected for contraband prior to entering or leaving the jail. As a result, she continued to sell marijuana and opiates
in and outside the prison.[53] Newspapers, however, reported that she was sent
to Islas Marías in July 1945 and later gained her release in 1946 or 1947. The
family, the evidence, and la Nacha herself disputed what the newspapers
reported.[54]

Ultimately, Ávila Camacho and officials in Ciudad Juárez decided not
to extradite her to the United States. The Mexican government denied the
U.S. request in 1943, but Anslinger continued to press in the courts. In 1946,
U.S. federal judge Charles Boynton dismissed the case on the recommendation of Holvey Williams, assistant U.S. district attorney, because of the
Mexican government's refusal to grant Jasso's extradition on the grounds
that insufficient evidence had been presented. She had never been arrested
in the United States and had not committed a crime there before returning
to Mexico. "We convicted two of La Nacha's confederates on the evidence
the Mexican Government says is insufficient," Mr. Williams explained.
"However, extradition has been refused."[55]

Once released from prison, la Nacha continued to sell and distribute
heroin, morphine, and marijuana, although some U.S. journalists reported
that she returned to selling tortillas from a stall in Guadalajara.[56] This story
made good press for *American Weekly* but was more wishful thinking than
reality. Of course, American journalists embraced the rhetoric of the state
and demanded punishment as a successful deterrent to crime. In 1950, FBN
officials documented Jasso as the likely narcotics source of a prominent
California trafficker and dealer, an ex-prostitute from Ciudad Juárez who
operated in the Los Angeles area.[57]

In 1951 the mayor of Ciudad Juárez, Pedro García, told P. A. Williams,
an FBI agent, that la Nacha lived permanently in Guadalajara. When she
visited her sons in Ciudad Juárez, she always carried an amparo prohibiting
her arrest. Her children, Natividad, Manuel, Pabla, and Ignacia, continued
to live in Ciudad Juárez. Like la Chata, la Nacha too had brought her children
into the drug trade. They ensured that her business interests and access to

Figure 19. "Fall of the Opium Queen," *American Weekly.*
Courtesy of the Hearst Corporations.

the international port of entry in Ciudad Juárez continued whether she was physically present or not. Prison or "exile" did not undermine her smuggling, because her social networks ensured her economic survival. By the early 1950s, she could have very well been the supplier to her own children, who then supplied dealers in El Paso and beyond.

BORDER MENACE

In the mid-1950s, la Nacha and her children reemerged in the United States as one of the primary sources of opiates in the Southwest.[58] In 1955, the U.S. Senate Judiciary Committee created a subcommittee to undertake a study of drugs and the need to change the federal criminal code. Meetings were held in cities across the United States. During what have come to be known as the Price Daniel hearings in Texas in October 1955, the celebrated Chicano journalist Ruben Salazar gave testimony about a notorious border trafficker, la Nacha, thus reintroducing her to the U.S. Congress thirteen years after initial efforts to extradite her.[59] Salazar painted the history of a prominent woman in the trade, but his work also provided insight into other women operating on or close to the U.S.-Mexico border in the 1950s. He also exposed ties between drug traffickers and people in power along the border and the conflicts that emerged between different political figures.

The hearings took place in New York, Pennsylvania, Texas, and California. Beginning a year after the end of the McCarthy hearings, the Price Daniel hearings were overshadowed by the effects of the Red Scare; the House Un-American Activities Committee (HUAC) was still operating. Anslinger routinely associated drug addiction, peddling, and trafficking with communism and behavior deemed un-American or threatening to American values.[60] The purpose of the hearings was to establish the extent of drug use and drug trafficking in the United States, much of it associated with "Red China" and China's attempts to poison Americans.[61]

Anslinger testified in March 1955 to the Senate Judiciary Committee hearing on China and narcotics traffic. In these meetings, he continually alluded to attempts to undermine the United States through drugs and addiction.[62] Anslinger's testimony was a persistent narrative of vice that connected Asia, particularly China, with drugs, prostitution, and other depravities. However, local police forces in the United States did not blame a "yellow menace" as described by Anslinger. Rather, the Price Daniel hearings reflected vastly different approaches to the same problem.

The Price Daniel hearings held in September reflected disagreements between the medical community and policing agencies over what to do about drug addiction. The New York hearings served as a platform to discuss efforts in the struggle against drug addiction; those held outside Washington, D.C., and New York had a regional focus, with an emphasis on the growing drug problems in major U.S. cities and regions. In Chicago and Detroit, the hearings highlighted connections to Canada and the role of organized crime families in major American cities.

During the Texas and California hearings, Mexico was again emphasized as a dangerous site of drugs and drug trafficking. The Mexican government sent representatives to the hearings in California. From Texas, Daniel sent an invitation to Foreign Minister Óscar Rabasa and Attorney General Carlos Franco Sodi.[63] Both declined but outlined their ongoing commitment to the battle against drug trafficking. In part, Rabasa and Franco Sodi's reason for not attending the hearings came from the U.S. State Department, which advised them not to attend and expressed concern then and in later hearings in Los Angeles in 1959 that Rabasa might be used as a political scapegoat. Lower-level Mexican officials attended the hearings in southern California, and in 1959 Rabasa offered to meet in another state.[64]

A close reading of the Daniel Commission Report of 1955 on illicit narcotics traffic challenges conclusions commonly drawn in the drug literature published from the 1970s to the 1990s. The literature situates Mexico as a minor player in the international narcotics trade. In part, this conclusion derived from a lack of appreciation for Mexico's strategic geopolitical position. Instead, scholars studied the Asian and European drug trade because U.S. foreign policy, largely directed by Cold War concerns, focused on those areas of the world. Ever an astute bureaucrat, Anslinger framed his arguments and rhetoric with this in mind to ensure the continuation of his bureau. Throughout the numerous interviews and hearings, Mexico was cast as a major player in the heroin and morphine trade in the 1950s in the southwestern United States. The Texas and California hearings positioned Mexico not as an upstart in the heroin trade but rather as a site of marijuana and heroin supply for years past. This picture emerged in the testimony of Alvin Scharff, who had broken the Loeffelholz-Brandstatter case in the 1930s (chapter 2). By the 1950s, as the treasury agent in charge of Texas, Scharff dramatically depicted Mexico's role, which, to those on the border, remained blatantly obvious.

Jasso came up in many of the hearings and interviews prior to Salazar's testimony. In the days before his appearance, people spoke about "la Noche Queen" (the Night Queen) of Ciudad Juárez and speculated about her reach into Texas and the Southwest. Testimony in the hearings brought up the ties between Ciudad Juárez's drug trade and El Paso's army post, Fort Bliss. Daniel and the other members of the committee heard about soldiers going to Juárez's shooting galleries (*picaderos*) and those in El Paso, many of which were supplied by Jasso, her son Natividad, and her adopted son Gilberto. Clearly, the hearings demonstrated that women such as Jasso posed a national security threat.

The most famous case involving drug use at Fort Bliss concerned twenty-two-year-old paratrooper Daniel Barrera, whose body was found in an El Paso arroyo apparently dead of a heroin overdose. On the evening of August 23, 1955, Barrera had gone to the home of Antonio Tavarez Rodriguez in El Paso, where he purchased and then injected heroin. In an interview, Tavarez claimed that Barrera was already drunk before he injected himself, and he immediately became ill and passed out. Tavarez and Barrera's two female companions assumed that he was asleep. When they failed to wake him the next morning, Tavarez hired a cab to take Barrera to the arroyo on the other side of the border. There, he cut Barrera's throat and arms to hide the track marks that indicated heroin use.[65] The Juárez police later arrested Tavarez, the two women, and the two drivers who had disposed of the body.[66] This case further contributed to a growing fear of drug pushers such as Tavarez, who may have been supplied by women such as Jasso and who in turn got American veterans and active-duty soldiers addicted to heroin.

The issue of soldiers using narcotics had been a concern of the FBN and other U.S. agencies since the Mexican Revolution, when U.S. soldiers sought companionship, alcohol, and drugs in the border cities (chapter 1). The arguments articulated during the efforts to extradite la Nacha kept her imprisoned during World War II to ensure that soldiers remained in good fighting shape. As noted with Lola la Chata, Anslinger continued to put pressure on Mexico regarding its role in drug trafficking, whether along the border or in Mexico's capital city. Despite the focus on Mexico during World War II, with the war's end and the low levels of addiction among returning veterans, Anslinger's attention turned to organized crime and drugs as a communist plot. The attention paid to Mexico diminished in the post–World War II era only to resurface in the mid-1950s.

In 1955, journalists such as Ruben Salazar provided the most insight into Jasso, but they also reported extensively on the drug workings in Ciudad Juárez and along the U.S.-Mexico border. What is striking about Salazar's testimony is that, despite having been a veteran himself, he had to establish his own as well as Barrera's U.S. citizenship.[67] While working with the *El Paso Herald-Post*, Salazar covered El Paso and Ciudad Juárez as a local.[68] Born in Ciudad Juárez and a naturalized American citizen who attended Texas Western College (now the University of Texas at El Paso) on the GI bill, Salazar, like Jasso, knew both sides of the border. His work as a journalist and his observations of addiction in El Paso and Ciudad Juárez gave credence to his testimony. In his statement to the committee, he announced that he had told the mayor of Ciudad Juárez that he was scheduled to appear before them. In other words, Salazar had been honest with the politicians in his hometown about his testimony.[69] Daniel asked how he had come to know la Nacha, and Salazar said that many people in the border region knew her, because she had been trafficking for at least twenty-three years; this information shocked Daniel, who immediately inquired about her operations.[70]

Salazar's articles on Jasso had also drawn the Texas senator's attention. Moreover, Salazar provided the committee with a number of eight-by-ten photographs of places where drugs were sold in El Paso and Ciudad Juárez.[71] Fifty-six other people testified including addicts, small-time traffickers and peddlers, narcotics agents, and customs agents as well as children of addicts.[72] In his newspaper articles, Salazar noted la Nacha's presence on the border. He wrote: "La Nacha is the dope queen of the border. She's big stuff. But she will sell you one papel (paper) of heroin for five dollars just like any other pusher on a street corner."[73]

In one instance, Salazar visited her with a junkie named Hypo.[74] Salazar posed as a *jornear*, a heroin sniffer rather than a mainliner who injects. He described her as "fat, dark, cynical, and around 60." Salazar noted that Jasso's life in Ciudad Juárez was far more modest than that of Lola la Chata, who lived in much grander style. La Nacha lived in a barrio with unpaved roads— "a good house in a bad neighborhood." Her house had all the modern conveniences despite its location on an unpaved street.[75] According to Salazar, she lived quite differently from her client Hypo, who had sold all his furniture to pay for his ten-dollar-a-day addiction. Thus, he shared a filthy mattress on the floor with his wife and children.

From Salazar's articles, readers learned that Jasso's daughters and sons worked with her. Her sons Gilberto and Natividad owned public baths but also controlled shooting galleries on both sides of the border.[76] Her daughters, Ignacia and Pabla, also helped her in the trade. What is distinctive about Jasso is that, despite her success and extensive reach, she also sold papelitos from her home like any other small-scale pusher. She worked as a supplier and distributor but also as a peddler. Perhaps her protection in Ciudad Juárez gave her a sense of comfort, and she did not feel the need to create distance between herself and the sale of the product, as other traffickers did. Instead, she earned a steady cash flow by selling directly from her house in the Bellavista barrio on Violeta Street. Salazar pointed out that her house was close to the official border crossing.

La Nacha's life and career remained an essential topic of the Daniel hearings in Texas because she not only peddled but also supplied key dealers throughout the state. Salazar verified that la Nacha had long been active and that U.S. agencies had previously attempted to control her drug dealing. He originally heard about her because he "got to know some heroin addicts . . . who talked about La Nacha to me. I had heard La Nacha was not selling any more because during World War II, the Mexican government sent her to a penal colony because the United States pressured them to take her out of the border because we feared she would sell narcotics to our soldiers."[77]

He described how easy it was to purchase heroin from Jasso, and how she enjoyed some sort of legal protection. He was referring to the amparo that she obtained from the courts at various times. During Salazar's testimony, Daniel revealed surprise and shock that she enjoyed such protections.

> **Mr. Salazar:** I understand she had gotten an embargo which is an injunction. This I cannot prove but I understand at one time she could buy protection from Federal judges.
> **Senator Daniel:** Now, you mean by injunction that she has had injunctions issued, restraining officers from arresting her?
> **Mr. Salazar:** That is right.
> **Senator Daniel:** Is it common knowledge around there in Juárez that has been the situation in the past?
> **Mr. Salazar:** Yes it is.

Senator Daniel: She has had court orders enjoining officers from arresting her?

Mr. Salazar: That is what I understand. I have never seen them, sir. It is common knowledge.

Senator Daniel: Have you talked to the district attorney across the border of Juárez?

Mr. Salazar: Right, sir. He says he has been district attorney a year and a half. She has not had an amparo during that time.[78]

After this exchange, Salazar told the commission that Humberto Poncinon Solaranzo, the district attorney in Ciudad Juárez, had told him to tell the commission that Mexican president Adolfo Ruiz Cortines had established his own commission to investigate the drug trade in that city. Agents from Mexico City had been sent to Ciudad Juárez to assist the police there in the investigation of narcotics. Senator Daniel expressed his appreciation that the Mexican federal government planned to investigate the narcotic problem in Ciudad Juárez, but he noted that the hearings had caused problems with the Mexican government because some officials denied that la Nacha sold drugs, at the same time that the Mexican federal government was sending federal agents to investigate the border region. This apparent inconsistency drew considerable attention from diverse sectors in the United States and fueled the perception that Mexico was too lax on drug peddlers and traffickers, a theme that had echoed since the early 1900s.[79] Salazar used a map to show the committee the location and numbers of shooting galleries and dope pads in Ciudad Juárez and El Paso, and he provided names of known sellers in the region.

Salazar's testimony set the stage for the other informants who followed. Witnesses continually noted the ease by which narcotic drugs could be purchased in Mexico and hence in the United States.[80] In one exchange, Daniel asked Perry Milton Turner of Austin, Texas, to describe how he found drugs in Mexico. That set the tone throughout the hearings. Turner, clean for years, replied: "A person can go down there, as long as he's got dollars, that's all it takes."[81] Turner explained that he began to use morphine after being hospitalized for an injury. Later, he continued to use it because he enjoyed it. He challenged concepts of reefer madness, an addict's inability to work, and "ballyhoo" and "propaganda" in the newspapers, and he told Daniel that he held jobs while using moderate amounts of the drug. However, as morphine became more difficult to obtain through legal and illegal means, he turned to heroin. Once he became a heroin junkie, he lost his job and resorted to stealing to maintain his addiction.

Daniel established that Turner had been arrested 52 times on narcotics charges, his wife of twelve years had been arrested on similar charges 122 times, and her sister 140 times. Their addictions forced Turner to frequently cross the border into Nuevo Laredo to buy twenty-dollar papelitos, each of which contained twelve to sixteen grams of heroin. To obtain that amount in San Antonio, Turner said that he paid thirty dollars (2012: $256.00) and that this heroin was more likely to be cut to increase profits for a dealer. By going to Nuevo Laredo, he received purer heroin at a lower price. In response to questioning, he confirmed that someone could purchase heroin in Nuevo Laredo and actually have it delivered to the United States for a small fee. The Mexican dealer determined the location of the drop-off and guaranteed delivery upon payment.

The Daniel hearings confirmed that Mexico supplied 90 percent of the heroin in Texas. The abundant supply along the border led to questions about the hierarchy of heroin purity and origin. Members of the committee asked addicts whether they preferred brown Mexican heroin or white Asian heroin. However, W. E. Naylor, chief of the Narcotics Division of the Department of Public Safety, argued that white Mexican heroin was actually available in Houston or anywhere else in Texas.[82] He suggested that the processing led to the differentiation between brown and white heroin, and he insisted that Mexican heroin was not some bastardized variety of Asian opium. Naylor argued that Mexican heroin was far purer than Asian; as Turner had established, it was less likely to be cut so it was far more concentrated for its price.[83] Mexican heroin was not less potent, it was simply not as highly refined. Despite Naylor's arguments, the commissioners continued to ask addicts their preference, which helped create a hierarchy of heroin whereby Asian heroin, trafficked predominantly by Europeans into the United States, was presumed to be purer and more desirable. When questioned, addicts confirmed this distinction.

The questions about the supply and distribution from Mexico rippled through the hearings and disclosed the names of other women on both sides of the border who were active in the drug trade. The hearings revealed the complex roles of women in the drug trade of the 1950s, whether as users, mules, suppliers, or distributors. Women were not simply victims of the trade but actual participants. This included women of different ethnicities and socioeconomic backgrounds. More startling for the commissioners, several women who testified did not seem to be repentant but rather were antagonistic and confrontational. To the commissioners who questioned these women, who were without legal representation, the drugs undermined their ability to understand their proper place in society.

On September 22, 1955, Alvin Scharff, customs agent in charge of Houston, outlined the activities of numerous women smuggling heroin across the border. He mentioned Ester Herrera, who worked with her extended family members to smuggle, on one occasion, sixty-three pounds of marijuana. He also recounted the case of Alma Mouton, Terrell Eva Lee Carradine, and Henrietta McCarty, three African American women who worked for Houston drug dealer Earl Voice. This group of women had gone to Mexico with $4,000 (2012: $34,250) to purchase heroin, smuggle it across the border, and deliver it to Voice, allegedly the major dealer among Houston's black community.[84] Scharff recruited McCarty to be an informant, and she would call Scharff and tell him about Voice's plans. Her tips led to the arrest of the other two women as well as the arrest of another prominent drug peddler who had $405,000 (2012: $3,468,000) worth of heroin in his possession. All were connected to Voice.[85]

Purificación Rodríguez Pérez (also know as Pura) appeared before the committee on September 22, 1955. From the beginning of her testimony, Senator Daniel and C. Aubrey Gasque, the general counsel, treated her as a hostile witness, and she was threatened with imprisonment because of her evasive answers. Her connections to heroin revealed a complex social network of family on a local peddling level. She argued that she had never sold heroin or marijuana but rather ran a legitimate establishment called the Pérez Lounge; she presented this testimony in spite of the fact that she was at the hearing while under a federal bond of ten thousand dollars and a state bond of two thousand dollars. Daniel and Gasque pressed her to confess. She denied that she sold heroin herself, but in the latter part of her testimony she did state that she was present when Johnny López sold heroin to an FBN agent. Daniel asked about her family. In her testimony, Rodríguez acknowledged that her husband had served a two-year sentence for heroin, and her niece Cora Luna had also served a sentence at the federal women's prison in Alderson, West Virginia. Her brother-in-law Raphael Sánchez was still in prison on a heroin charge, as were her two brothers, Pete and Alberto. Daniel finished his interview:

> **Senator Daniel:** Are you the only one left in the family that has not been in prison for heroin?

Mrs. Rodríguez: Yes.

Daniel: And now you have been convicted and given a 4-year sentence, and you are out on bond on a state charge.

Rodríguez: Yes, sir.

Daniel: I want to say this to you, that you would not have been called here today had not witnesses told us that they had bought heroin from you while you had been out on bond and that you were still selling heroin. And in my view of your testimony I am going to direct counsel to turn over this testimony to the Department of Justice, with the recommendation that they take such procedure as they may deem advisable.[86]

Like la Nacha, Rodríguez sold from her house but also at her business. By selling from her home, Rodríguez maintained a smaller operation than that of la Nacha. In her testimony, she revealed an extensive family business that was multigenerational. Houston served as a key destination for heroin that was trafficked through Brownsville, Matamoros, Reynosa, Laredo, and Eagle Pass. Rodríguez and women like her appear to have been equal partners in these family businesses. Like la Nacha, she maintained a legitimate business that helped cover up her illicit business, although she eventually lost her legal establishment. At the hearings, Rodríguez's assertions of her innocence throughout the questioning reflected a certain amount of feminine bravado. She, like many other women who appeared, testified without legal representation. She also demanded not to be photographed.

As discussed, women who owned businesses used them to legitimize the illegal work of their husbands, other family members, and themselves. The 1950s Tijuana dealer Big Mike Barragán Bautista and his wife Ismelda Galindo Barragán (also known as Puchi) provide another example of a fully successful partnership. The Barragáns remained shadowy figures in the testimony provided to the Daniel hearings in California. They never testified, but addicts and narcotics officers did testify in November 1955 about their empire, which extended from Tijuana to Los Angeles and as far east as Texas. Combined with the Jasso network, there appeared to be an overlapping system operating out of Tijuana and Ciudad Juárez that supplied the southwestern United States.

Big Mike's name initially appeared in the joint testimony of Los Angeles sheriff E. W. Biscailuz, undersheriff Peter J. Pitchess, and LAPD narcotics chief K. E. Irving. Also present for the meeting was the Mexican consul general in Los Angeles, Adolfo Domínguez, and his attorney, Bruno Newman.[87] Domínguez was one of a few Mexican officials who attended the hearings. He provided a couple of questions to Daniel to ask the police officers in order to ascertain the quantity of heroin that came from Mexico. Big Mike's name emerged as a prime source for the southern California drug trade, and he was as well known among police as he was among dealers and users.

Bebe Phoenix and Mickey Wallace, two sisters, provided more information about Big Mike in their testimony to the Daniel Commission. Both were prostitutes and grifters and had bought heroin in Tijuana. Phoenix, in her testimony, explained that Big Mike might be Italian and that he had something to do with taxis. The two sisters established a network involving a transnational flow of drugs and sex from Tijuana to Hollywood. The women had found that their work as waitresses in Los Angeles could not support their heroin habit, so they went directly to the drug's source in Mexico. From Wallace, the commission learned that most female addicts in Tijuana were Anglo American women, not Mexican or African American, and they opted to work as prostitutes in the city to be closer to their drug source.[88]

Wallace demonstrated that she was quite entrepreneurial in bankrolling her addiction. As a cocktail waitress in the early 1940s, she had averaged from eighty to one hundred dollars a night (2012: about nine hundred dollars) through tips and by shortchanging her clients. It was while working as a cocktail waitress that she began to mainline heroin with her lover rather than simply smoking opium. Daniel asked Wallace: "Did you break any other laws other than living with this man and knocking down on the customers?"[89] She confessed to prostitution, so that she could buy heroin in Tijuana and sell it in Los Angeles. She would secretly carry seven to eight ounces each time she crossed the border.[90] Wallace had thus served as a low-scale trafficker and dealer in the Los Angeles area in the late 1940s and 1950s. She bought from Big Mike in Tijuana, slipped across the border, and then sold in Los Angeles.

Small-time dealers like Wallace relied on people like Big Mike for a regular drug supply. Wallace's testimony painted Big Mike as a boss and a sophisticated supplier. Oscar Palm, an addict, and Rae V. Vader, the customs agent in charge based in San Diego, developed a fuller picture of Big Mike beyond that of supplier to small-time dealers.[91] As did la Nacha, Big Mike engaged in multiple entrepreneurial activities that were licit, if perhaps not entirely respectable to some.

Figure 20. Women with contraband. H. J. Anslinger Papers, box 14, folder 5, image 227, Eberly Family Special Collections Library, Pennsylvania State University, University Park, PA. This is most likely a staged photo.

A native of El Paso, Palm was a dealer in Los Angeles and perhaps a distributor for Big Mike because he continually pleaded the Fifth Amendment when questioned about his own involvement, although he did admit to purchasing an ounce of uncut heroin at $400 (2012: $3,415) in Mexico. He brought it back to Los Angeles, where he sold it. He also admitted to having business contacts in Mexicali-Calexico and Ciudad Juárez–El Paso. Under pressure from the commission, Palm revealed that Big Mike had interests (perhaps his own poppy fields) in Sinaloa and that he also maintained laboratories in Tijuana. Palm also reported that Big Mike worked closely in his drug business with his brother-in-law Al Galindo.[92]

Agent Vader filled in the rest. Big Mike was reputed to be Mike Barragán Bautista, who owned one of the largest taxi companies in Tijuana as well as the dog-racing track. As some addicts indicated, his taxi drivers sought clients as well as delivered heroin to different locations on both sides of the border.[93] Addicts described crossing into Tijuana and getting a ride in one of the taxis to another destination to purchase drugs. Despite the efforts of U.S. customs and Mexican agents, they were never able to purchase heroin directly from Big Mike, only from his runners. Thus, Big Mike maintained distance between himself and the actual sale of drugs. From undercover informants, Vader had learned that Big Mike supplied dealers as far away as Dallas. In addition, he and his wife, Ismelda Galindo Barragán, owned a large and successful "house of ill repute" in Tijuana. In that bordello, Ismelda also sold heroin. (Consul General Domínguez interrupted Vader's testimony and asked him for specific information regarding the Barragáns; Vader replied as best he could.) Like her husband's taxi company, Ismelda's business gave her an opportunity to exchange pesos and dollars and to mask the sale of narcotics.[94]

All the women mentioned in the testimony had lives unlike those portrayed in the popular literature on drug trafficking that emerged in the 1970s and 1980s, such as Don Henry Ford's *Contrabando*, a picaresque escapade about a gringo trafficker. Don Ford told anthropologist Howard Campbell: "When I operated, few women were involved. . . . It was a more male-dominated [activity] because of their culture, in rural areas women didn't participate in business . . . very much."[95] Ford argued that with the introduction of cocaine, more women entered the trade as traffickers.

Ford's reading of drug trafficking, like many of the biographies and pseudo-memoirs of the narcos, reinforces the sense of masculine bravado surrounding the narcotics trade, which is then repeated by scholars who disregard the involvement of women. The introduction of cocaine brought greater numbers of women into the trade because more profit was available. Women worked as mules to pay off the debts of the men in their lives, or they may have been forced into smuggling because of their impoverishment. Campbell's astute contemporary analysis, however, demonstrates the multifaceted experience of women in drug trafficking on the U.S.-Mexico border. It wasn't only poor women who got involved; upper-class women were drawn to the excitement of illicit activity, as in the case of one of Campbell's informants, whose comfortable and educated background allowed her to rise in the business to become a drug lord. She used her privilege to her advantage.[96]

In the 1950s, the Price Daniel hearings offered compelling evidence that men like Ford had misread the role of women. Their perceptions were informed by their own gendered constructs of masculinity rather than by the realities of the feminine experience within the trade. La Nacha was a crime boss who created a drug empire. Although she was a widow, her sons served as her collaborators and carried on the business as she aged, demonstrating the integral role of her family. Like la Nacha and Lola la Chata, other women in the drug trade such as Pura Rodríguez, Ismelda Galindo Barragán, Bebe Phoenix, and Mickey Wallace demonstrated that women were not necessarily anomalies in the business, and in fact were involved in all aspects of it. Women and men engaged in drug trafficking as part of multiple business interests that they held, whether they were creating multidimensional crime families or using drugs as a tool to supplement their income. Rather than being simply a complement to the men, women had and still have parallel roles, whether as mules, small-time peddlers, or bosses.

CONCLUSION: THE EXTENDED FAMILY BUSINESS

In 1962, FBN agent Thomas W. Andrew recognized Jasso as a source of heroin being smuggled into New Mexico. He wrote to Harry Anslinger that most peddlers in Albuquerque bought directly from her, and her sons and grandsons assisted the purchaser by meeting them on the U.S. side of the border and then accompanying them to the Mexican side. After concluding the purchase, mules crossed the border with the drugs.[97] From Albuquerque, she supplied other parts of the state. More than seven years after the Daniel hearings, la Nacha continued to play a significant role in drug trafficking. Even in the mid-1960s, her age did not inhibit her business, because her children—and her grandchildren and grandnephews—had joined her. Like la Chata, she had created an extended multigenerational peddling and trafficking family.[98]

In 1964, Jasso remained the most recognized supplier for the state of New Mexico. Once again, her name came up in government hearings on organized crime and illicit traffic in narcotics.[99] While various reports argued that Mexico had returned to transshipping European opiates and had emerged as a site of operations for Corsican drug smuggling organizations, two Mexican dealers were listed as prominent in drug trafficking and organized crime: Jasso and Enrique (Henry) Sanchez of Nogales were labeled as international smugglers who trafficked in Mexican opiates.[100]

In 1965, one of Jasso's grandsons, Eduardo Amador González, was arrested for transporting heroin into the United States. He confessed that he helped the Tartaglias brothers of Albuquerque smuggle heroin bought from la Nacha in Ciudad Juárez into Texas.[101] Detectives reported that in 1965 and as late as 1968, Jasso still served as a heroin supplier in the Southwest, and allegedly in this case her grandson served as a mule but against her wishes. His plea reflected his desperation to reach a favorable verdict, but it remains highly unusual considering that his uncles and one of his cousins achieved tremendous success in the trade. Having a grandmother such as Ignacia Jasso gave veracity to such a plea.

Jasso's daughter Pabla was the mother of Héctor González, also known as El Arabe, an infamous heroin dealer in the 1960s and 1970s. González built upon the foundations of his grandparents. He ran the Juárez heroin trade in the late 1960s and early 1970s until he died in an automobile accident on November 25, 1973. The *El Paso Times* reported:

> The victim, known to police as "El Arabe" (the Arab) [was the] grandson of the celebrated and reputed queen of the Juarez "underworld," Mrs. Ignacia "La Nacha" Jasso Vda. de Gonzalez. "La Nacha" is also being sought by federal narcotic police on a fugitive warrant.
>
> Police said Rui [*sic*] Gonzalez was killed instantly when the pickup truck he was driving overturned near Casas Grandes. His wife, Angela, and their two children, also riding in the truck, escaped with minor injuries.[102]

By the time of his death, Jasso was only peripherally involved in the trade due to her age. His death ended her dynasty and created an opportunity for a new boss, Carlos Carrillo Fuentes, to emerge.

Ignacia Jasso was not the first Mexican citizen whom the U.S. government attempted to extradite for a crime committed in the United States. Her case provides some insight into Mexican revolutionary rhetoric and the country's relations with the United States. With the consolidation of the state during the 1930s, the government sought to develop Mexico's economy after years of revolution and displacement. Illegal contraband on the U.S.-Mexico border became a growing concern for Mexican customs officials and police. It undermined attempts to develop legal industries and fill state coffers. Mexican officials' concerns thus focused on goods coming from the United States into Mexico that might compete with the country's own emerging industries. The border was where the laws of the two countries clashed.

These collisions of illegal and legal industries along the border led to constant renegotiations of power, law, and culture. Jasso truly represents the culture of *el ambiente fronterizo* of the twentieth century. With her husband, she recognized the potential of their proximity to America's market for drugs. After her husband's death, she expanded her business beyond the immediate border region. With World War II, the transnational flows of heroin and opium from Asia and Europe were severed, and that gave la Nacha an economic advantage that she had never enjoyed before. Demand remained constant while supply declined. La Nacha, like many other borderlanders, took advantage of economic disparities and other forms of marginalities created along the border by using the region as a site for transnational entrepreneurial activity. In turn, Harry Anslinger, George Messersmith, Ezequiel Padilla, Antonio Bermúdez, and others demanded that she, like the border as a symbolic and rhetorical device, be restrained, controlled, and enclosed. She became a site, like the border, to reinforce the "need" for strengthening policies, laws, and relations, like the physical border with its fences, customs workers, policing agencies, and laws that reinforce such disparities across the region.[103]

Jasso's analysis of the market, her multiple holdings, and her involvement in all aspects of the trade from growing and processing to distribution and even street selling ensured that her presence became an ongoing problem for the Mexican government. La Nacha was perceived as an insidious threat because of her physical location on the border and her acute knowledge of transnational flows, border inspections, customs, and policing. Like la Chata, she diversified her drug business from small-time peddling, to acquiring her own labs and chemists, to supplying places as distant as New York and Detroit. Her success suggests the inability of either Mexico or the United States to control migratory flows, whether of people, ideas, or narcotics. La Nacha, like countless other people along the border, must be located in some place between the United States and Mexico, legal and illegal, and masculine and feminine.

Despite her imprisonments, threats from male dealers and suppliers, the attempt at extradition by the United States, the revealing information aired at the Daniel Commission, and the constant chatter about her role as a supplier, Jasso sold and distributed heroin and marijuana from the late 1920s until her death in the 1980s. The Daniel hearings and other reports demonstrate that other women, too, developed multifaceted businesses to sell drugs and distribute in Mexican cities and across the border. Whether they were small-time peddlers or transnational traffickers, these women combined legitimate and illicit businesses and formed informal and formal networks for their own preservation and expansion. In the 1970s, women developed the drug business further. As cocaine displaced heroin, the U.S.-Mexico border played a smaller role in international drug smuggling for a few years, only to return as a central site for transshipment. Women on both sides of the border and in much of South America continued to play greater roles in the drug trade, from mule to boss. However, women like Jasso and la Chata pioneered women's status as drug lords and rivaled their competitors in longevity. There have been few since who survived in the trade as long as they did, but beginning in the 1970s women, like men, made more money in a far shorter period of time. The profits, heightened competition, and violence of that era forever changed the drug trade.

CHAPTER FIVE

THE WOMEN WHO MADE IT SNOW

Cold, Dirty Drug Wars, 1970s

BY THE 1970S, LA NACHA AND WOMEN LIKE HER WERE VIEWED WITH nostalgia by some narcotics agents, who longed for the "good old days" when traffickers were known entities who stayed along the border. With the Vietnam War, student protests, and the "summer of love" came social discontent and an ever-increasing demand for illicit drugs. The U.S. government responded to the generational shifts and conflicts within the narcotics business with an approach that emphasized policing, even if that hampered its own efforts to control demand for narcotics.

Just as in the early 1910s, the United States waged a drug war directed at multiple enemies. The late 1960s and 1970s marked a pivotal shift in policy with a new war on drugs that led to greater professionalization of enforcement on both sides of the border and throughout the hemisphere.[1] With increased professionalization and the formation of new agencies to fight the drug trade, the United States again embarked on a campaign to control supplies from Asia, Europe, and the Americas while diplomats advocated systematic changes in global policing.[2] With a greater focus on a global struggle to stem the flow of narcotics, the United States and Mexico engaged in certain collaborations—although fraught with mistrust—to combat drug trafficking. Those collaborations ignored the changing dynamics of consumer demand for cocaine.

Richard Nixon's 1968 election to the U.S. presidency and his pledge to combat drug trafficking triggered significant changes escalating the fifty-year drug war. The relationship between the United States and Mexico grew troubled due to Nixon's focus on narcotics and its official targeting of sources of supply. In spite of this, authoritarian Latin American governments appeased the Nixon administration's demand for cooperation. Mexico's geographical proximity to the United States and its historical role as a supplier ensured that it remained a target of suspicion, but Mexican presidents, as well as other Latin American governments, were able to use the drug war and the Cold War to obtain certain financial and military support, a common issue that continues in some guise to the present day.

Despite the escalation of the war on drugs, demand for narcotics and drugs continued to grow in the United States. Urbanites rediscovered cocaine in the 1970s and used it as a "safe" party drug.[3] Traffickers responded to the increased market demand, and to growing diplomatic and policing efforts to stem the flow, with ever more creativity and ingenuity.[4] Their attempts to find new routes and methods to transport drugs ensured continued profits. That escalating profitability contributed to increased competition, which in turn ensured that traffickers used more violence in the 1970s and 1980s than in the near past. Increased demand and its corresponding profits ensured that all sides, whether drug suppliers, distributors, and traffickers or local, state, and federal policing agents, further professionalized their narcotics operations, resulting in complex organizations and operations with overlapping alliances that spread across continents. Increased policing led to an increase in profits because production costs remained more or less the same, but transportation and distribution costs escalated.

Beginning in the 1960s, the counterculture's growing acceptance of drugs challenged society's traditional taboos. Federal, state, and local governments sought to stem the flows of drugs by creating task forces, running advertisements targeting adolescents, and galvanizing parent and civic organizations in order to stop drug use. In the United States, many kids who came of age in the 1970s remember the "after-school specials" that addressed, and solved within sixty minutes, drug problems that had spread from the cities into the suburbs. As national campaigns from after-school specials to "Just Say No," featuring first lady Nancy Reagan during the Reagan administration, sought to expose the dangers of drugs, U.S. officials again cast weary glances south and deemed Mexico, and much of Latin America, as prime culprits in the spread of the popularity of marijuana and heroin among Americans.

Heroin and marijuana, and later cocaine, moved across borders to major U.S. cities in growing volume. From the cities, drugs then flowed to suburbs and small-town America. President Nixon created the Drug Enforcement

No Antiwoman Job Bias In the Narcotics Trade

Women have a prominent place in Latin America's illicit drug traffic, filling every role from "mule" (courier) to head of a criminal organization.

A short, stocky, middle-aged woman of Chilean descent who owns three wig shops in Buenos Aires is considered by American officials to be one of the major sources of narcotics brought into the United States.

Yolanda Sarmiento, who is 46 years old, has a long history of narcotics involvement.

"She's one of the sharpest dealers anywhere," said Rhyn C. Tryal, head of the Federal Drug Enforcement Administration's office in Buenos Aires.

Yolanda Sarmiento

On April 15, 1970, the New York police raided a West Side apartment allegedly used by Mrs. Sarmiento and seized 72 kilograms of heroin and 47 kilograms of cocaine with a wholesale value of $3.5-million.

A few days later, the police arrested Mrs. Sarmiento along with her lover, Emilio Díaz González, who is a native of Spain, and two other men outside a New Jersey motel. Federal agents say they were traveling by car from Miami to claim the narcotics that had been stashed in the apartment.

Escapes City Jail

Mrs. Sarmiento's bail was set at $100,000. She posted the bail and then fled the United States, leaving Mr. Díaz and his associates in custody in New York.

Several months later, on Jan. 24, 1971, Mr. Díaz escaped from the Federal House of Detention in Manhattan. Investigators in New York believe that Mrs. Sarmiento had helped plan and finance his escape.

The pair were next seen in Buenos Aires where Mr. Díaz was seriously wounded in a gunfight with the Argentine police on Dec. 2, 1972. He escaped and his whereabouts are unknown, but Mrs. Sarmiento was apprehended.

The United States tried to have her expelled from Argentina to New York to stand trial. But the Argentine courts ruled that since her children were born in Argentina, Mrs. Sarmiento was entitled to the rights of an Argentine citizen and so could not be expelled.

Unlike Mafia wives who avoid involvement in their husbands' rackets, Latin women often work closely with their men in the narcotics traffic. When two brothers, Juan and Roberto Hernández, were imprisoned in Mexico for drug smuggling in 1970,

their wives continued their work.

On Oct. 17, 1974, the Mexican federal police investigated their activities in the La Mesa State Penitentiary in Tijuana and discovered evidence showing that the Hernándezes had continued to run their drug ring even behind bars. Also busy in the traffic from her cell was Roberto's wife Helen, who had been apprehended earlier.

A month later, Mexican authorities arrested Juan's wife Patricia in a Tijuana motel as she was delivering a kilo of heroin to a customer from the United States. They found in her possession fairly records documenting extensive real-estate holdings and a balance in Hernández bank accounts of about $20-million. She also was convicted.

But the risks for women in the narcotics trade are not always confined to law-enforcement agents. Consider the harsh fate of Ruth Godamez of Chile, who was a dealer in cocaine with her lover, Selim Valenzada. United States narcotics agents had made Miss Godamez a major target and placed her under sueveillance.

Mr. Valenzada saw Miss Godamez speaking to someone whom he thought was a narcotics agent and decided that she had become an informer. He shot her five times in the stomach, but she survived the wounds.

Later Mr. Valenzada was expelled from Chile to the United States, where he had been under indictment on a narcotics charge. As he was led to detention, he asked narcotics agents, "Was she talking or did I waste the bullets?" No one answered his question.

Miss Godamez did not "turn"—become an informant — but after several months in jail, Mr. Valenzada has decided to cooperate with the government.

Administration in 1973 after his overwhelming reelection the year before. With the formation of the DEA, the United States forged cooperation agreements with Mexico, France, and Turkey. Moreover, the U.S.-Mexico border remained a central site of concern. Formalization of the drug war led to the 1974 establishment of the El Paso Intelligence Center staffed by DEA, Immigration and Naturalization Service (INS), and Justice Department representatives who coordinated the gathering of intelligence on the southern border with Mexico.

In the 1970s, the DEA, FBI, and Justice Department decried the marijuana and heroin that arrived across land ports from Mexico and cocaine from the Andean highlands that was flown to rural areas in the United States or passed through U.S. ports only to be moved to major American and Canadian cities. Chileans and Argentines played key roles in the flows of heroin from Asia through Europe to the United States—commonly referred to as the French Connection.[5] Other countries such as Brazil, Panama, and some Caribbean islands became sites of transshipment and money laundering.[6] Although the trade had changed, women remained an integral part of it. As in the 1930s, women showcased an ability to create cross-ethnic alliances for profit, and in the 1970s geopolitical and economic forces ensured that alliances between different groups would emerge.

Roberto Hernández and his wife, Helen, were imprisoned in Mexico for the smuggling of drugs.

Figure 21. "No Antiwoman Job Bias in the Narcotics Trade." *New York Times.*

In 1975, the DEA proclaimed the slogan "No Antiwoman Job Bias in the Narcotics Trade," in response to key arrests of women from Argentina, Chile, Mexico, and Venezuela who were involved in transnational narcotics trafficking to the United States.[7] The titillating and sensationalist headline purported that something new had "transpired," as if it were only then that women appeared as central characters in the drug trade. The DEA's embrace of feminist rhetoric served as an ironic twist to the emergence of new players in drug trafficking and to ever-escalating profits with the reintroduction of cocaine.

Yet the 1970s drug war recycled familiar political, social, cultural, and historical themes. A collective historical amnesia ensured that policy makers made the same demands that they had beginning in the 1910s, although the 1970s drug trade dramatized one profound difference: heightened competition for the lucrative U.S. market triggered greater violence by drug organizations in order to maintain supply routes. Although women historically avoided violence in the drug trade, the 1970s marked a clear escalation of feminine uses of violence as a tool. At times, the use of violence was a demonstration of power that women could brandish against male competitors. At other times, they used it to defend their male partners.

MARIJUANA, HEROIN, AND THE COLD WAR

The U.S. government and state and local officials described the flow of marijuana and heroin from Mexico to the United States during the Price Daniel hearings and follow-up hearings in the 1950s and 1960s. The Mexican government, first under Gustavo Díaz Ordaz (1964–1970) and then under Luis Echeverría (1970–1976), paid greater attention to the flow of narcotics internally and externally because of U.S. demand. In 1968, the Nixon administration launched an offensive on drug use in the United States. This multifront "war" proposed to stop the flows from the French Connection, the Golden Triangle region in Southeast Asia, and Mexico.[8] The French Connection involved the flow of heroin from the Middle East and Turkey to France and then on to the United States, particularly New York. New initiatives and agencies formed to confront the perceived growing drug problem in the United States. This included the formation of the DEA and the Special Presidential Task Force Relating to Narcotics, Marijuana, and Dangerous Drugs.

On September 16, 1968, prior to his election, Nixon pledged to the American people that he would "move against the source of drugs" and "accelerate the development of tools and weapons to detect narcotics in transit."[9] Arguing that "mind-changing" drugs were essentially a problem of youth, the report of the Task Force Relating to Narcotics, Marijuana, and Dangerous Drugs focused on the flow from Mexico as a problem of supply rather than demand. Although the growing demand for drugs crossed classes and ethnicities, the task force downplayed such aspects of the overall problem and instead clamed that the U.S.-Mexico border needed greater control to keep drugs from entering America.

The task force proposed a number of changes to border crossing procedures. For example, it sought to encourage Americans to walk across the border rather than drive their cars. Border control and customs officials viewed motor vehicles as key transporters of contraband (chapter 2).[10] Hence, those citizens who crossed in cars attracted more intense scrutiny than those who crossed on foot. Those on foot would be observed for any unusual behavior or appearances; surveillance of pedestrians is easier to achieve than surveillance of travelers sitting in or driving a car. The task force also suggested that border cities be declared off limits to military personnel. This suggestion echoed similar recommendations of the Price Daniel Commission in the 1950s as well as earlier discussions going back to the Mexican Revolution. Suggestions for infrastructural changes at the border, such as fences and easements, were far easier to implement.

Along with the infrastructure changes, which altered the movement of traffic for easier inspection, the task force wanted more detection capabilities along the border, using dogs and sensors. Much of the border control that is evident today came about through these recommendations. The report also recommended substantial budget increases for customs, border patrol, and the Bureau of Narcotics and Dangerous Drugs (BNDD) to hire more personnel and to purchase more equipment such as airplanes for aerial surveillance.[11]

Following the report, White House adviser John Ehrlichman encouraged Nixon to force Mexico to defoliate marijuana and poppy fields and implement stricter enforcement on the Mexican side of the border.[12] Again, these demands echoed the same requests American presidents had made to Mexican presidents beginning with Plutarco Calles in the 1920s. Defoliation programs had been requested and complied with by every Mexican president. With Ehrlichman's encouragement, Nixon embraced a language of warfare to take "immediate steps calculated to make a frontal attack on the narcotic, marihuana [sic] and dangerous drug traffic across the Mexican border."[13] With a stalemate in the war in Vietnam, perhaps Nixon believed that a war on drugs in Mexico offered a more likely achievement in the first few short months of his presidency.

Nixon and Ehrlichman's plans to engage in a "frontal attack" met with reservations within the State Department. The U.S. ambassador to Mexico, Robert McBride, warned President Díaz Ordaz about Nixon's growing concern about the flow of drugs from Mexico. Before Nixon's meeting with Díaz Ordaz to inaugurate the Friendship Dam on the Rio Grande River that took place in September 1969, National Security Advisor Henry Kissinger briefed the U.S. president to ensure that the United States would not initiate any new protocol without first informing the Mexican side. Ambassador McBride again attempted to convey the seriousness of the issue and strongly encouraged the Díaz Ordaz administration to enact some changes. Despite the State Department's and other agencies' hesitancy to implement a unilateral action, Operation Intercept began on September 21.[14]

Two thousand customs agents working around the clock stopped cars and pedestrians for inspection at thirty-one border crossings. Motorists, pedestrians, business owners, and even customs agents vented their frustrations as businesses lost money and people waited six to eight hours to cross. G. Gordon Liddy described it as follows:

> Operation Intercept has been called a failure—only by those who never knew its objective. It was actually a great success. For diplomatic reasons the true purpose of the exercise was never revealed. Operation Intercept, with its massive economic and social disruption could be sustained far longer by the United States than by Mexico. It was an exercise in international extortion, pure, simple and effective, designed to bend Mexico to our will. We figured Mexico could hold out for a month; in fact they caved in after two weeks and we got what we wanted. Operation Intercept gave way to Operation Cooperation.[15]

Liddy's revisionist reading of the event did match many opinions expressed across the United States and in Mexico at the time. The *New York Times* reported that it had resulted in "a minor haul of marijuana," while business leaders on both sides of the border complained.[16] The Mexican newspaper *Excélsior* argued that Operation Intercept "can only be new grounds for the mistrust over the position that the United States will take on improving commercial and financial conditions for Latin American development.[17] President Díaz Ordaz echoed this, stating that it had created a "wall of suspicion" in U.S.-Mexican relations.[18] Díaz Ordaz's criticism mirrored those denunciations leveled at the United States when the George W. Bush administration insisted that other nations adopt similar policing protocols and strategies during his war on terror.

The drug war met the Cold War in 1969, but in this case, Nixon and Kissinger may have miscalculated. Díaz Ordaz, a rather conservative Mexican politician, may have been more receptive to some sort of cross-border initiative with regard to drugs had he been directly consulted. He, like Nixon, was no fan of the emerging youth culture, and during his presidency he consistently, and at times violently, stood his ground against hippies, striking medical students, and student protesters.[19] He sought to create a fiscally responsible and modern Mexico, which should have endeared him to Republican leaders in the United States.

Operation Intercept as a show of strength ensured criticism not only from Mexicans but also from Americans. The border searches caused havoc and generated myriad complaints from businesspeople on both sides of the border, who loudly protested to local politicians and to their national representatives. Then, as now, Mexicans and Americans crossed the border to visit family members, shop, work, and go to school. Journalist Ruben Salazar, who testified about the border drug trade in the Price Daniel hearings, reported about the disruptions that Operation Intercept caused for many border residents. In his articles, he argued that Operation Intercept "hurt the pride of southwest Mexican-Americans who feel the United States is trying to blame Mexicans for a problem which is to a large extent uniquely 'Anglo.'"[20] The operation turned up very little dope but stirred up resentment among borderlanders, Mexican Americans, commuters, and customs and government officials.

Although Nixon undertook Operation Intercept unilaterally, its poor results ended up forcing negotiations with Díaz Ordaz. Perhaps to make amends, Nixon extended greater military aid to Mexico in the form of helicopters. Moreover, this period marked a closer relationship between the two countries to battle antigovernment guerrilla groups that had emerged in Mexico during the 1960s. Like in many other Latin American countries, the United States feared the success of guerrillas, who drew inspiration from Cuban revolutionaries as well as Mexican figures.[21]

Operation Intercept did yield one significant outcome for the Mexican government. Whether marijuana or heroin, drugs threatened the security of the nation, and the war on drugs met the Cold War and contributed to Mexico's dirty war. Americans who crossed the border to purchase marijuana found themselves subjected to greater harassment. Hippies, who came to Mexico not necessarily to traffic but to smoke some pot and enjoy the beaches, encountered harassment and at times arrests. Mexican young people, whether in the guerrilla movements or not, found themselves, like their American counterparts, associated with drugs and trafficking. The international aid, particularly aerial equipment for crop eradication and border surveillance, became instruments of repression that ended up targeting young people.

In March 1970, the attorney general for the United States, George Mitchell, and the attorney general for Mexico, Julio Sánchez Vargas, approved what became known as Operation Cooperation.[22] Immediately following Mexican approval of this initiative, Mexican agents and agents of the BNDD worked jointly in numerous raids and arrests of prominent and not-so-prominent drug traffickers and dealers.[23] In the 1960s, the FBN, followed by the BNDD, opened offices in Mexico City (1963),Guadalajara (1969), and Hermosillo (1971) to facilitate collaboration between Mexican and U.S. officials.[24] Joint operations and arrests took place, and official agencies shared information. Internally, the BNDD reported its own apprehension about Mexico's ability to work jointly with the United States in stemming the flow of heroin. BNDD officials believed that Mexican antinarcotics agents could not be trusted, as U.S. agents had believed for sixty years.

The 1970s ushered in a time of social turmoil in Mexico. The Cold War and national issues intersected with the evolving drug policies of the United States. In the wake of the 1968 Mexican student movements, some young Mexicans fled to the guerrilla movements or took up arms against the government. Moreover, Mexican society was entering a modern age that seemed to contradict the perception of control exhibited by the Mexican government in the summer of 1968. Increasingly discontent, young people who recognized that civil actions did not lead to democratic change sought more rapid transformation, sometimes through violence.

Genaro Vázquez Rojas was the leader of Comité Cívico Guerrerense (Civic Committee of the People of Guerrero), which opposed government corruption, poverty, and violence in the state of Guerrero.[25] During the 1960s, Guerrero was a hotbed of activity, with Vázquez Rojas's CCG and Lucio Cabañas's Partido de los Pobres (Party of the Poor).[26] Educators and students joined the rural struggle. Vázquez Rojas and Cabañas served as intellectual mentors to disenchanted youth around the country who were captivated by the struggle in the mountains of Guerrero.[27]

In the northern Mexican city of Monterrey, Ignacio Salas Obregón, a student at the Monterrey Institute of Technology and Higher Education, an elite private university, was an activist in the Professional Student Movement, a lay Catholic organization. He came into contact with communists while working with the urban poor. Salas Obregón would later lead a number of activists into armed struggle. In 1973, various guerrilla groups formed the Liga Comunista 23 de Septiembre (Communist League of September 23, or LC-23), led by Salas Obregón.[28] LC-23 took its name from the 1965 guerrilla assault on a military compound in Chihuahua led by Arturo Gamíz and medical doctor Pablo Gómez, similar to Fidel Castro's attack on the Moncada Barracks in Santiago de Cuba twelve years earlier. On September 23, 1965, the guerrillas issued a formal statement that directly challenged the corruption of the Chihuahua state government. The following day, a group led by Gamíz and Gómez assaulted the Madera military compound; both of these leaders as well as six soldiers died in the resulting battle.

Vázquez Rojas, Cabañas, and La Liga all became tied to the emerging drug trade in the 1970s, whether or not they had anything to do with drugs and trafficking. In 1970, Mexican police arrested American James Lee Daniels with $6,000 (2012: $35,500). He planned to buy marijuana from Manuel Priedo Llaguno of Huachinantla, Puebla. The police raided Priedo's home and found 150 kilos of Acapulco Gold, a common strain of marijuana from Mexico known for its toffee scent. Along with the marijuana, the police also found propaganda from Vázquez Rojas and Cabañas.[29] In 1971, Sabino Rodriguez Pérez was arrested with his friend Pascual Olais Alvarado in the port of Veracruz in an unrelated case. They had in their possession two thousand firearms, twenty-two thousand bullets, and twenty-five thousand pesos in cash. Despite the guns and ammunition, the police asserted that they were engaged in the sale of opium. Rodriguez's house was searched, and the police found 150 kilos of Acapulco Gold and materials related to Vázquez Rojas and Cabañas.[30] In the reports, Rodriguez and Olais had met with "an American" potential buyer.

In 1973, the Federal Security Directorate (DFS) also reported the arrest of Emilia "Mily" Peña Contreras. She had suitcases that contained forty kilograms of marijuana. The DFS documented that she carried literature from the Liga Comunista.[31] Modeled on the U.S. Federal Bureau of Investigation, the DFS formed in the 1940s to combat subversion by foreign and revolutionary groups; later it became the investigative arm of narcotics policing.[32]

By the early 1970s, LC-23 as well as other guerrilla groups were kidnapping and holding business leaders hostage for money to finance their activities.[33] LC-23's kidnapping and murder of Eugenio Garza Sada, a prominent Monterrey businessman, did little to enhance the Echeverría administration's reputation among the business elites of northern Mexico.[34] Under Echeverría, disappearances and state-sponsored torture became tools of repression, resulting in the murder of at least 275 people and perhaps as many as 1,500, including the intellectual architects of LC-23.[35] The government considered youth suspect and dangerous, as it had in 1968. Like in the United States, some young men and women who were actively opposed to the Vietnam War also became associated with drugs and drug trafficking. The DFS's role to protect the state from terrorism and subversion also extended to drugs. Like Raúl Camarago, the chief of the narcotics police in Mexico City who worked for the Lung Sung tong in the 1920s, DFS agents accidentally stumbled onto drug safe houses while in pursuit of antigovernment guerrillas; and, like Camarago's targets, drug traffickers knew the economic weaknesses of many police officers and DFS agents. For some DFS members, the financial rewards that could be acquired through the drug trade were too significant to ignore.[36] Over time, the DFS evolved into protectors for the drug traffickers, which contributed to the growth of narcotics organizations and their connections to people in power. From the few accessible documents, evidence suggests that some DFS agents planted drugs on terror suspects while others planted propaganda on drug peddlers and smugglers.

This subterfuge worked for corrupt DFS agents in two ways. By connecting drugs and guerrillas, they gained greater support from Washington. At the same time, as top policing agents they could control multiple situations and information regarding arrests and raids. Drug traffickers sought out corrupt but highly trained DFS agents, and the "war" became a lucrative arrangement for both the DFS and drug dealers while it targeted young people. Some of the young people arrested for possession or distribution did confess to being part of the guerrilla movements, but one document suggests that the DFS forced a confession from a young man who possessed marijuana but was also mentally ill.[37] How many forced confessions did the DFS obtain from young men and women who simply passed a couple of joints or from young people who circulated propaganda and later found that their cars or backpacks also contained marijuana or heroin? And how many of the images of young men and women standing beside confiscated marijuana and propaganda were staged by corrupt DFS agents? We may never know, but it is not entirely implausible to assume that such incidents occurred.

The role of women in political subversion was not as threatening as that of men to officials.[38] The narconarratives that emerged in the United States during the 1960s and early 1970s again served the Mexican government as justification for the detention of certain people. The guerrilla uprisings, increasing demand for drugs in the United States, and lucrative drug flows contributed to strange collaborations. Guerrillas interested in overthrowing a corrupt government might have trafficked marijuana, and elite policing agents seeking to snuff out guerrillas wanted to profit from the drug trade. As in 1968, the government cast the young members of guerrilla organizations as drug addicts or drug traffickers. The government used images of young men with longish hair and counterculture-influenced clothing to establish connections between drugs and criminality.

Although women were rarely depicted as drug runners and marijuana traffickers, the government tied those who were to the guerrilla movements, building the model of the new Mexican trafficker on the legacy of women like Lola la Chata and la Nacha. This new female trafficker was not ideologically opposed to the government. More likely, she never considered the government as a hindrance or threat until it targeted her, her family, and her business. The woman trafficker of the 1970s still used familial networks, but she became far more mobile and used multiple means—whether cars, planes, or human mules—to move marijuana, heroin, and cocaine through international ports of entry.

ANOTHER PERFECT COUPLE

It was in Tijuana where Mexican and U.S. agents worked together to arrest Roberto Hernandez, his wife Helen, his brother Juan, and Mercedes Coleman, the owner of the home where the raid took place. The BNDD described the group as "the most sophisticated and efficient of all clandestine drug trafficking operations in U.S.-Mexican channels today." The BNDD went on to argue that Hernandez supplied much of the illicit drug supply to the United States, smuggling over twenty kilograms of heroin per week through Tijuana to San Diego and beyond.[39] The transnational cooperation and arrests made national news in the United States and Canada. Reports claimed that Roberto Hernandez resisted arrest and had to be dragged from the home.[40] Other reports stated that the police found drugs, fifteen pounds of cocaine, grenade launchers, a bazooka, a machine gun silencer, and small arms.[41] Newspapers also reported that the members of the Hernandez group had in their possession $25,000 cash (2012: $149,000) and thirty-one un-cashed money orders from customers in the United States. Those arrested included two other women who served as couriers and six other men.

Because of their location in Tijuana, the Hernandez family acted in much the same fashion as their predecessors, Big Mike and Ismelda Galindo Barragán. Customers placed orders by telephone in coded messages and then paid via money order from the United States. In turn, the Hernandezes de-livered to the other side of the border using female couriers. Because Operation Intercept had curtailed the flow of drugs through increased sur-veillance and other measures, the Hernandez network had grown more cre-ative. As depicted in the 2000 Steven Soderbergh film *Traffic*, the Hernandezes used Mexican folk art to enclose the heroin for the purpose of transport across the border.

With the arrest of the Hernandez ring, the BNDD had a huge case, and the FBI identified Helen Hernandez specifically as a woman who had bene-fited from the narcotics trade.[42] Because she was a partner in the illegal en-terprise, the FBI recognized that whether her husband was in or out of jail, the smuggling and selling of heroin and marijuana would continue. Four years later, the Hernandez family provided the DEA, the successor to the BNDD, with another case. On Thursday, October 17, 1974, Mexican federal police and army units raided the La Mesa Penitentiary in Tijuana. The newly formed DEA participated in the case. Police officials and army soldiers searched the cells of Roberto, Helen, and Juan, who had served four years of their eleven-year sentences by that date.

Despite being in jail, the Hernandez ring had operated without disruption. The raids of their cells yielded $30,000 (2012: $140,000) in cash and over $41,000 (2012: $469,000) in jewelry. Coded messages were also found.[43] The DEA and Mexican authorities described the messages as documenting a multi-national ring with connections to France, the United States, Mexico, and Canada. They argued that there were "strong indications" that the Hernandezes had replaced the French Connection for the purpose of smuggling heroin to the United States and Canada via Europe. Moreover, certain journalists al-luded to the Hernandez connection to the U.S.-based prison gang known as the Mexican Mafia.[44] The tie to the Mexican Mafia came at a time when that organization was gaining greater recognition as an influential prison gang.[45]

The Hernandez case confirmed Mexico's ongoing role in illicit flows of drugs into the United States and the ability of Mexican organized crime to create transnational alliances with criminal entities in the United States. The DEA's hopes, however, seem almost naïvely unrealistic in retrospect. By removing the Hernandez prison control, the DEA argued that the French Connection would finally be snuffed out, as would the Mexican flow of drugs. Plus, Mexican and U.S. authorities had dealt a heavy blow to the Mexican Mafia. Both of these claims as presented to the press in 1974 were simply another fictitious narconarrative of vice; they did not address the reality of an ever-responsive and changing business model of drug trafficking, an approach that would require policing strategies to finally focus on the ever-present demand side of trafficking.

The DEA and the U.S. Justice Department, however, did provide evidence to the Mexican authorities that resulted in the successful prosecution of Helen and Roberto. According to Glen E. Pommerening, the acting assistant attorney general in the Justice Department, Mexican authorities requested that the United States initiate extradition hearings because that would allow them to prosecute the couple for drug trafficking and not simply localized prison peddling.[46]

The Hernandez ring operated as an extensive family enterprise in which all three partners seemed to have equal power within the organization. With their proximity to one of the most important ports of entry, Roberto, Helen, and Juan mimicked their Tijuana predecessors, the Barragáns, and other borderlanders such as la Nacha. In fact, they were almost identical to the Barragáns. All the border organizations conformed to the prototype of Mexican organized crime as defined by Article 2 of the Ley Federal contra la Delincuencia Organizada:

> When three or more persons agree to organize themselves or to be organized to carry out, in an ongoing or repeated way, actions which themselves or related to others, have as a goal or result, to commit [certain specified] crimes, they will be prosecuted for that very fact, as members of organized crime.[47]

The Hernandez organization shared certain characteristics with other Mexican traffickers. The family served as the nucleus of an organized crime entity. As with Sicily's Cosa Nostra, family and blood relatives made up the organization. The fact that women in Mexico operated as jefes and capos from the 1930s to the 1970s offers a striking difference from popular perceptions of Italian organized crime families. In all Mexican cases, women played key leadership roles. They held equal positions of power—at times greater than that of their male partners—and they acculturated their children and other family members into the business. Helen Hernandez, like Lola la Chata and la Nacha, was one of the *madrinas* of the 1970s. By the mid-1970s, she had the company of other women who also ranked as bosses or capos, contributing to what the FBI described as the lack of "antiwoman" bias in the Latin American drug trade.

THE LATIN AMERICAN TRIANGLE

With the onset of a multifront drug war led by the Nixon administration in the early 1970s, the transnational routes used by traffickers evolved into more sophisticated operations that connected the Americas to European and Asian networks. In that decade, cocaine reemerged as a recreational drug of choice, leading to greater sophistication of its transnational flows and networks. During the 1970s and 1980s, women proved to be innovators in the global heroin and cocaine trade. Along with Helen Hernandez, two women served as early test cases for the newly formed DEA. Yolanda Sarmiento and Griselda Blanco dominated the South America–New York City drug connection in the early 1970s. Although drug use became more common in the United States overall, distributors preferred to work in major cities such as New York, Los Angeles, Detroit, and Chicago.[48] These cities served as hubs for distribution to the suburbs and other cities.

Rhyn C. Tryal, head of the DEA office in Buenos Aires, described Sarmiento as "one of the sharpest dealers" anywhere. A Chilean by birth, Sarmiento moved to Argentina when she was twenty-two years old.[49] By the 1970s, she owned a fashionable wig and hat shop close to the U.S. embassy in Buenos Aires. Beyond her vending of fashionable hats, she worked with Corsican drug traffickers who operated out of Argentina. From their base in Marseille, Corsicans first started trafficking heroin in the post–World War II economy.[50] From Marseille, they developed distribution networks that reached to Montreal and New York, and the resulting "French Connection" established itself in the popular imagination with the novel and film of the same name.[51]

With the advent of greater airport controls on the American east coast in the late 1960s and early 1970s, Corsican traffickers encountered difficulties smuggling into international airports and other familiar ports of entry. And with additional controls and enhanced surveillance along the U.S-Mexico border, smuggling into the United States became more difficult all around. Responding to the tighter security, traffickers sought alliances in the Americas to assist in the movement of European heroin into the United States.[52] Sarmiento was one of a few women who emerged as a direct link in the heroin trade between Europe, South America, and the United States. Her initial organization of a couple of people later expanded to more than twelve members from across the globe.

At first, Sarmiento shipped cocaine and heroin in Chilean and Argentine wine bottles because South America's wine industry had expanded its exportation and entered global markets beginning in the early 1970s.[53] Sarmiento placed sealed packets of heroin in the wine. Thus, wine offered a perfect disguise for inspectors; however, a wine bottle could only hold limited amounts of heroin or cocaine because it also had to contain the liquid it was meant to carry. In 1970, Sarmiento, Alfred Mazza, Juan Carlos Franco (also known as Miguel Aspilche), and Wladimir Bandera devised a plan to ship heroin to Rodolfo Ruíz, a painter based in New York City. They used false backs and frames around paintings, hollowing them out and packing them with cocaine and heroin. The art was sent to Ruíz, and Mazza and Franco would then pick up the contraband for distribution. Mazza and Sarmiento's scheme enabled the group to smuggle an estimated 170 kilos of heroin and cocaine worth some $250–$500 million (2012: $1.47–$2.95 billion).[54]

Mazza and Sarmiento traveled back and forth from Argentina to the United States to receive the drugs from Ruíz and also to sell them. On April 15, 1970, police raided Sarmiento's west side New York City apartment and seized heroin and cocaine worth an estimated $3.5 million (2012: $20.9 million). She had gotten word before the raid and fled Manhattan. A few days later, police arrested Sarmiento, her lover and accomplice Emilio Díaz González, and two other men in New Jersey en route to Miami. With her arrest, Sarmiento posted $100,000 bail and immediately fled the United States to Argentina, thus becoming a fugitive.[55] Díaz González would later escape from the Metropolitan Corrections Center (MCC), a fortress-like building in Manhattan, in an operation allegedly financed by Sarmiento. Once free, he joined her in Buenos Aires.[56]

When Buenos Aires police attempted to arrest the pair after being pressured by U.S. officials, a gun battle broke out between Sarmiento, Díaz, their neighbors, and the police. Díaz escaped, but the police arrested Sarmiento.[57] The United States requested her extradition. Initially, Argentina balked because Sarmiento had children who were Argentine citizens by birth. Moreover, existing treaties between the United States and Argentina did not contain any specific extradition clauses.

Although Sarmiento resided in Argentina, her name continued to come up in legal proceedings that took place in the United States. In 1974, grand juries in Brooklyn and Manhattan handed down indictments against twelve current and former New York City police officers, including detectives and two lieutenants whose responsibilities included gathering evidence against narcotics dealers and traffickers.[58] The officers stole narcotics from police property clerks in 1972, and they had stolen money during various raids, including those of Sarmiento and her partners. They divided among themselves $235,000 in cash (2012: $1.3 million) that they took from Sarmiento's partners Luis Torres and Wladimir Bandera. During the raid on Sarmiento's west side apartment, officers took cash and five kilos of heroin to resell. Besides stealing from Sarmiento's organization, police stole narcotics and money on other raids. Allegedly, police also stole $80,000 (2012: $442,000) from Nicodemus Olete and Justo Quintanilla in Queens, Chilean traffickers who used frogmen to move cocaine from freighters anchored in the harbor into Brooklyn.[59]

With the rise of the military junta in Argentina in 1975, the Nixon administration saw an opportunity. The United States and Argentina entered an era of greater cooperation over drugs and Cold War policies. The DEA trusted that Argentina now would expel Sarmiento. In his 1993 book *The Big White Lie*, DEA Agent Michael Levine wrote about his arrest of Miguel Russo, Sarmiento, and François Chiappe.[60] Chiappe and the others were not legally extradited; instead, they were expelled. Chiappe was an infamous Corsican trafficker who had fled to Buenos Aires in 1965 on a false passport after being accused of two murders in France. As a leading member of Corsican organized crime, he and others had been responsible for the creation of the French Connection. DEA press releases hailed the expulsions of Chiappe, Russo, and Sarmiento as "among the most sought after among criminal narcotics organizers in the world."[61] The assistant U.S. district attorney of the Eastern District, David DePetris, celebrated the expulsions as proof that the "last haven for narcotics smugglers" in South America had now been breached.[62] Sarmiento's relationship to Chiappe in Buenos Aires is difficult to ascertain from her available U.S. documents, but it does appear that they had some connection.

The DEA agents sent to Argentina remained on the plane as the Argentine secret police delivered the hooded and manacled prisoners. Levine recounted that he guarded Chiappe, who smelled of perspiration, blood, and excrement. When Levine removed his prisoners' hoods during the flight, he noticed that Chiappe and the others had been badly beaten. On Chiappe's arrival in New York, journalists described that his body was covered with bruises and his teeth were broken at the gum line.[63]

Halfway back to the United States, Levine shifted duties and sat with Sarmiento. He wrote:

> Yolanda Sarmiento [was] a middle-aged Chilean drug dealer and the only one of the three who had ever been in the United States. She told me that the Argentine police had killed her son. "I don't care what happens to me now," she sobbed, laying her head on my shoulder. "I have nothing to live for."
>
> I felt her sorrow enter me for a moment and put my arm around her. She looked so sweet and helpless; she reminded me of my grandmother. She had been indicted for murdering a drug dealing competitor on the Upper West Side of Manhattan, and was alleged to have hacked the body to pieces in a bathtub by herself because her husband didn't have the stomach for it. I tried to picture her doing it, but couldn't.[64]

Upon arrival at Kennedy Airport, the prisoners were formally arrested, and Sarmiento, accompanied by Chiappe and Russo, returned to the MCC in New York City, the same jail from which she had helped Díaz escape earlier.[65] In New York, Sarmiento's case turned even more dramatic, and she remained in the media because of her own attempted escape. To plan her escape, she needed help. While in the MCC, she befriended another inmate, Joseph Martinez-Carcano, who was a trustee. Meeting Sarmiento, however, created more problems for Martinez-Carcano than his Puerto Rico and Bronx drug convictions ever did.

When he met Sarmiento, Martinez-Carcano was close to his release date. Of Puerto Rican descent, Martinez-Carcano was a professional engineer who had worked for major defense contractors such as Grumman

Aircraft and Pratt & Whitney.[66] His brother had served in Vietnam, returned as a heroin addict, and then died. The grieving family decided to return to Puerto Rico. Martinez-Carcano thought that with his high-level security clearance, his education, and his savings, he would easily find a job or start a business. In spite of his skills, he could not find work in Puerto Rico. Eventually, an acquaintance asked him to deliver a package. He was subsequently arrested with four ounces of cocaine. Fleeing the conviction, he returned to the Bronx as a fugitive and worked off the books in a Bronx bar. During a police raid at the bar, Martinez-Carcano was arrested again for possession of cocaine. At his trial, Martinez-Carcano stated that some of the patrons at bar were involved in narcotics distribution. He argued that he had been holding misplaced cocaine, hoping for a tip, when the bar was raided. He pled guilty and was given a three-year term at the MCC for both the Bronx and the Puerto Rican cases.[67]

Martinez-Carcano made good use of his time at the MCC. He gained the trust and respect of social workers, prison guards, and prisoners by teaching English to Spanish speakers, creating a law library, chartering buses for families of inmates, and getting book donations from local publishers.[68] Because of his trustee status, he was allowed to visit many of the MCC's different areas. One day, he was asked to deliver a card to Yolanda Sarmiento shortly after her arrival.[69]

As they became friends over the next few months, she told him that she had been beaten, tortured, and raped for eight days while awaiting her secret extradition from Argentina. She also told him that the U.S. government would not stop punishing her for helping her husband escape. In his later testimony, Martinez-Carcano reported that she cried for her murdered son and that she was afraid for her life. Not knowing that she was lying about her son's murder, Martinez-Carcano felt sympathy for the grieving mother, just as DEA agent Levine had. She also told him that she had over $300,000 (2012: $1.22 million) in banks in New York City.[70] After months of her pleading for his assistance, he told her that he could not help her escape but he might know some people who could. In her testimony, Sarmiento argued that Martinez-Carcano approached her and said: "I was talking to one of the officers and he told me that for $50,000 he will take you out of prison."[71] She contacted her attorney, who contacted the DEA and the district attorney's office.

Regardless of who approached whom, Martinez-Carcano contacted two corrections officers he knew who needed money: George Philip and Yasin Wahib. The latter took the leadership role in the planned breakout; he and his wife were to receive $15,000 (2012: $61,000), while Philip would receive $8,000 (2012: $32,500). Martinez-Carcano's wife received a "finder's fee" of $1,000 (2012: $4,050). Sarmiento had asked other inmates to help, even Armando Cardona, who had been convicted of first-degree murder. He turned her down. She told all who asked that her brother would help with the payment and assist with the escape. What Martinez-Carcano did not realize was that Sarmiento had been working as a government informant for months, even prior to his arrest.[72] In her defense, Sarmiento argued that Martinez-Carcano approached her after he delivered a message to her from Roberto Rivera, who was at the MCC and who used to buy heroin from her in 1969 and 1970.[73]

Simply by delivering the Rivera letter, Martinez-Carcano became involved with three of the most prominent drug traffickers in the hemisphere, who made up what became known as the Latin American Triangle: Sarmiento, Dominique Orsini, and Chiappe.[74] In fact, the message he delivered to Sarmiento from Rivera was written on the back of Gino Gallina's business card, the attorney for Orsini and Chiappe. Gallina would later represent Martinez-Carcano (who translated for Gallina while he worked with Orsini and Chiappe). Like Chiappe, Orsini was part of the Corsican mafia, and he, too, was extradited to the United States following an arrest in Senegal while on a layover from Buenos Aires to Nice, France.[75]

Sarmiento's testimony against Martinez-Carcano offers insight into her criminal record. Beginning in the early 1960s, she traveled back and forth from Argentina to the United States, using false passports and names. She had been arrested in the United States for an array of charges, from shoplifting to possession of dangerous drugs and weapons.[76] In 1976, she was charged with trafficking over nine hundred of pounds of heroin into the United Sates.[77]

When Philip, Wahib, and Zulma Amy, Martinez-Carcano's wife, met Sarmiento's brother, Ricardo Lopez, and Rafael Rodriguez at a Ramada Inn in Manhattan on September 21, 1976, they had no idea that the latter pair were NYPD undercover detectives. They hatched a plan to smuggle Sarmiento from the prison disguised as a bilingual teacher. Wahib had created a false identification card at the MCC, and he showed it to the two undercover agents. The escape occurred on October 4, 1976. Sarmiento testified that she went to the medical unit, where Martinez-Carcano had hidden the fake ID card, a wig, and clothing in the bathroom. She changed, put on the wig, and walked out of the MCC. A car was waiting for her. Once she got in, they drove about a block until they were surrounded by police.

Martinez-Carcano had fewer than three months to serve when the escape occurred. Once Sarmiento was apprehended after her escape, the NYPD arrested Wahib, Philip, and their accomplices, including Martinez-Carcano. Philip and Wahib received two-year prison sentences, fines of two thousand dollars, and three years' probation. Sarmiento's cooperation ensured relative leniency. She entered a plea of conspiracy to import narcotics, and she received a five-year sentence. She was also indicted for income tax evasion.[78] Prior to pleading guilty, she faced a maximum of eighty years on four indictments. Representing Martinez-Carcano, Gino Gallina asserted that Sarmiento had made a deal for her testimony. In Gallina's cross-examination, she claimed that she had assisted the government because she wanted to straighten out her life, although her actions continued to provide evidence to the contrary.

Sarmiento was directly associated with violence in both the United States and Argentina. She attempted to escape from prison and turned against a confidant in prison to obtain greater leniency on her other charges. As a nexus between European, South American, and New York–based organized smuggling rings, she traveled extensively to move heroin. She had ties to the Corsican mafia: her secret "extradition" and incarceration with Chiappe, Orsini, and Russo alludes to her ties to their organization. They may have been her suppliers. Like Lola la Chata and la Nacha, she acted as an innovator in smuggling, using the opportunities that emerged with the expanding South American wine industry. She also maintained a legitimate and successful business front—her hat business—that possibly served to launder money and provide a site for meetings, processing, and packing.

THE MEDELLÍN COWGIRL: GRISELDA BLANCO

The career of Yolanda Sarmiento overlapped with that of the infamous cocaine trafficker Griselda Blanco. Both were indicted at approximately the same time and both supplied the New York City drug market. Blanco, an innovator in cocaine trafficking, captured the attention of narcotics agents in the early 1970s and then led them on a chase for over a decade. Perhaps she consciously took advantage of the greater policing of heroin, which allowed cocaine to reemerge. In 1974, Dr. Peter Bourne wrote: "Cocaine . . . is probably the most benign of illicit drugs currently in widespread use. At least as strong a case could be made for legalizing it as for legalizing marijuana. Short acting—about 15 minutes—not physically addicting, and acutely pleasurable, cocaine has found increasing favor at all socio-economic levels in the last year."[79] Bourne's analysis of cocaine continues to be debated, because the presumption that cocaine was harmless only fueled its use.[80] With the growth of cocaine use in the 1970s and 1980s, Americans' appetite for it triggered a new drug war.

For women like Blanco, the fact that cocaine was highly pleasurable and illegal ensured an accumulation of capital. Similar to Sarmiento, Blanco created alliances with wealthy and highly connected men, and she relied on violence. Sarmiento had used violence to defend her lover and ensure their escape from custody and prison. Broadening such tactics, Blanco employed violence as an offensive tool against male competitors and men who were employed by her. Her use of violence served to display her power and to strike fear in her competitors. Her ruthlessness contributed to a growing transnational "gangsta" popular-culture hagiography that continues to surround her and the men connected to her even after her murder by a motorcycle assassin (*sicario*) on September 3, 2012, in Medellín. The documentary evidence detailing Blanco and her New York years exhibits a complex and sophisticated organization in which many women played active roles in all areas of the drug trade. Blanco was a boss, but she employed other women who worked as mules, couriers, and distributors.[81] Significantly, women in Blanco's organization testified against her during her 1985 trial, and one woman within her organization was a star witness.

Twenty-seven years before her murder, DEA agent Bob Palombo arrested a Venezuelan housewife for conspiring to distribute large amounts of cocaine and marijuana in the United States. Arrested on Sunday morning, February 15, 1985, while in bed reading the Bible, Blanco identified herself as Lucrecia Adarmez. She had used a Venezuelan identity off and on for close to twenty years.[82] Since the formation of the DEA, Palombo had been involved in tracking the cocaine flows from Colombia to New York, and in the early 1970s he was able to arrest some Colombians involved in this trafficking. He and his DEA colleagues eventually uncovered a sophisticated organization that far exceeded their initial encounters with male drug mules smuggling cocaine in their shoes or baggage.[83] Palombo's search for Blanco and the DEA's investigation to unravel her organization are recounted in Richard Smitten's 1990 *The Godmother*.[84]

Sixteen years later, Blanco surfaced in popular culture with the October 27, 2006, release of Billy Corben and Alfred Spellman's sensational film documentary, *Cocaine Cowboys*. Corben, who directed the film, retells the cocaine wars of South Florida in the late 1970s and early 1980s, depicting the rise and fall of key Colombian smugglers and their American compadres who together flooded the United States with cocaine. It juxtaposes interviews with U.S.-based traffickers Jon Roberts, a distributor, Mickey Munday, a pilot, and Jorge "Rivi" Ayala, one of Blanco's lieutenants, with those of Miami-Dade police officers such as Al Singleton and DEA agent Palombo, many of whom Smitten had earlier interviewed. The protagonists relive the days when cocaine transformed Miami from a mid-size southern city with Latin flair into one of the economic engines of Florida and much of Latin America. The film release of *Cocaine Cowboys* came two years after Blanco was released from jail and deported to Colombia.[85] In his review of the film in *Entertainment Weekly*, critic Owen Gleiberman described Blanco as "a homicidal Colombian 'Godmother' who, no lie, makes Tony Montana (Al Pacino's Scarface) look like Mother Teresa."[86]

For over a decade, Blanco served the Medellín cartel as a key distributor, first in New York City and then in Miami. She was the only female distributor affiliated with the cartel not related to the Ochoa family. She developed and maintained her own crime network, which distributed countless kilos of cocaine and allegedly contributed directly to the deaths of more than two hundred people. More recently, Colombian journalists have associated her activities with the rise of sicarios, young male motorcycle assassins in Colombia.[87] Her alleged callousness has captivated journalists, writers, television executives, and filmmakers, inspiring the hit television series *Miami Vice* and the film *Scarface* in the United States as well as recent telenovelas in Latin America.[88] Similarly, Blanco constructed her own narcodrama based on an Al Pacino character; she named her youngest son Michael Corleone.

Like Lola la Chata, who emerged in popular culture in the 1940s and 1950s, Blanco has been the muse for countless narcodramas, whether in true crime literature, documentary film, or popular magazines. She typically appears as an out-of-control, coked-out, bazooka-smoking (heroin and cocaine combined) murderess. Yet, she had a large cadre of accomplices. Miami police arrested Florida engineer Max Mermelstein on charges of smuggling cocaine on June 5, 1985. His arrest facilitated Blanco's entry into the popular imagination, exposing one of the most successful female drug traffickers. Mermelstein told PBS's Frontline in 2005:

> I was the only American that ever sat on the council of the Medellin cartel. Living undercover and wearing disguises is

necessary. There's still an, in effect, $3 million contract on my head. I'm personally responsible for bringing 56 tons of cocaine into the United States, shipped out $300 million of their profits. I also paid out over $100 million in their expenses here in the United States. And when I decided to cooperate with the government, Escobar wanted me dead.[89]

Mermelstein's testimony led to the dismantling of one of the most lucrative drug-smuggling enterprises in the hemisphere and the arrests of key members of the Ochoa family, including Pablo Escobar in Colombia and men such as Roberts and Munday in the United States. In 1990, Mermelstein's biography, *The Man Who Made It Snow*, hit the bookstores, in which he told his story to Robin Moore, author of *The French Connection*, and the novelist Richard Smitten, who, after his work with Mermelstein, turned to the genre of true crime.[90] In turn, Mermelstein served as a key witness in federal cases against his fellow traffickers, but he also provided much of the background for Smitten's book *The Godmother*.

In *The Man Who Made It Snow*, Mermelstein explained that he became involved in drug trafficking through his wife, a Colombian native.[91] Originally from Brooklyn, Mermelstein worked as a building and facilities engineer in resort hotels. While working in Puerto Rico, he met his future wife. After they married, he was introduced to many of her friends. He started smuggling her relatives, and then later other Colombians, into the United States by plane. His growing circle of Colombian friends, his fluency in Spanish, and his human smuggling business drew the attention of cocaine traffickers. A street hood from Bogotá, Rafael (Rafa) Cardona Salazar, understood that the Spanish-speaking Mermelstein could serve an important role for the Medellín cartel because of his contacts with American pilots through his human smuggling.[92]

In his testimony to Moore and Smitten, Mermelstein argued that his entry into the cartel did not stem from his personal greed but rather resulted from his fear of Rafa. On Christmas Day, Rafa shot another drug trafficker at a party, fled to Mermelstein's house, and forced him to assist in disposing of the body. Although Mermelstein had grown up in a working-class neighborhood in Brooklyn, his New York toughness did not prepare him for the brutality of the men and women he encountered in Colombia. While the Ochoa family's upper-middle-class background protected them from suspicion in the early years of the trade, they relied on men like Rafa to perform their dirty work. Rafa's elevation of Mermelstein to an essential position in the Ochoa organization brought him into contact with Colombia's survivors of violence, including Griselda Blanco, who became his friend and associate. Like Rafa, Blanco wore murder as a badge of honor. She did it to preserve her status in the organization.

Smitten found that Mermelstein's true-life tales were as compelling as the best of detective crime fiction. After the publication of *The Man Who Made It Snow*, Smitten turned his attention to the center of the Miami drug wars, to Blanco. His work on Blanco construes the contest between the criminal (Blanco) and the police (Palombo) as a struggle between good and evil. What is missing in the sensationalist accounts of Blanco's life is an appreciation of her ability to survive in a highly masculine and dangerous criminal environment that was rapidly changing in the 1970s due to Nixon's newly ignited war on drugs.

The NYPD issued its first arrest warrant for Blanco in 1972. In 1975, a grand jury indictment charged her and thirty-seven others with conspiring to manufacture, import, and distribute cocaine and conspiring to import and distribute marijuana. This indictment also included charges of gun smuggling, possession of drugs, and money laundering.[93] Although the indictment was issued in 1975, the court case files are extensive because many of those indicted became fugitives, and some eluded police until the 1990s. Of the thirty-eight, only fifteen were initially prosecuted.

Although the collection of materials spans two decades, members of the NYPD and the DEA identified Blanco as instrumental to and innovative within the cocaine trade by 1973. It was because of the indictment that Blanco fled to Colombia as a fugitive, using her old skills in document forgery to invent a new identity. DEA agents tracked her in Colombia for three years, confident that she could not travel to the United States.[94] In this time period, Colombian law did not permit the extradition of its citizens to another country, and international law dating to the 1800s did not require Colombia to extradite.[95] As a result, U.S. authorities never filed an extradition request for Blanco.

A HISTORY OF VIOLENCE, DISPLACEMENT, AND BUSINESS

On April 9, 1948, the assassination of populist Jorge Eliécer Gaitán marked the end of Colombia's democratic stability and beginning of *La violencia*.

Colombians experienced social disarray due to epidemic criminality, political violence, and general impunity triggered by the fighting of political factions.[96] Young men took to the streets to wage war for political factions, to join guerrilla movements, or to commit crimes. Women also found themselves drawn into the violence, joining the guerrillas and engaging in social and political protests. The hostilities affected both men and women, and women found themselves to be targets of all factions. Although the violence and social upheaval led to opportunities for some women, many more women experienced these battles as victims. Scholar Donny Meertens has argued that rape became a political tool because "combatants viewed women exclusively in their status as mothers, that is as actual or potential procreators of the hated enemy."[97]

In *The Godmother*, Smitten provides a narrative that rape was a significant event in Blanco's life, but he does not connect it to the historical instability in Colombia. Instead, it is part of a litany of personal difficulties and traumas that molded Blanco's later life. Her rape serves as a personal experience of violence rather than something more systemic and daunting. Smitten opens his book with two anecdotes that take place when Blanco was thirteen. The first occurred, Smitten argues, when she returned to her shack one day to find it empty except for her mother's boyfriend, who attacked her. After the attack, Blanco went to find her mother at the place where she worked as a domestic and found her in the kitchen cleaning the floor. Upon telling her what happened, her mother got up from the floor and stared at her daughter. Smitten writes:

> The first blow almost knocked her out. Her eyes were so full of tears she didn't see it coming. It drove her all the way across the kitchen to the edge of the sink. Then her mother was flailing at her unmercifully. "You lying little puta, he would never do such a thing. It is you, you puta. You are trying to take my man away."[98]

Blanco fled from her mother's house, turned to a life of prostitution, and ultimately befriended Carlos Trujillo, a barrio hoodlum who had organized a successful human trafficking business. He specialized in creating false papers and transporting illegal immigrants from his old barrio in Medellín to the Colombian neighborhood of Jackson Heights in Queens, New York. Smitten writes that Trujillo, Blanco's future husband, saw potential in the young girl. Blanco was beautiful, smart, quick, and a survivor. He fathered her three eldest sons and introduced her to the man who ultimately replaced him.[99]

Smitten employs the alleged rape, her mother's assumed rejection, and her subsequent survival as an explanation for Blanco's control issues and also her sociopathic tendencies. This view is repeated in Mermelstein's autobiography and in *Cocaine Cowboys* and *Cocaine Cowboys 2: Hustlin' with the Godmother*. Blanco's ability to defend herself against her enemies with corresponding violence and metaphoric castration foreshadows her future use of violence against men.

From La violencia's legacy, power frequently came through violent acts. From violence-induced societal disarray, however, economic opportunity also emerged. Blanco and Trujillo succeeded in human smuggling in part because of the violence that drove people to flee the country. Once exiled, they sought opportunity, whether legitimate or illicit. Thus, Trujillo, Blanco, and others involved in falsifying papers and trafficking people established an early network for human cargo that later evolved into the use of mules to smuggle cocaine.

Blanco, like la Chata, la Nacha, the Barragáns, and the Hernandezes, accessed power though a number of different channels. Trujillo introduced her to document forgery, which would prove to be an invaluable skill. Like la Chata's relationship with Castro Ruiz Urquizo, who introduced her to the border, Blanco encountered men and women who had a profound impact on her life. Her informal social network served to construct a new business when Trujillo introduced her to another man involved in human smuggling, Luis Alberto Bravo. As the civil unrest in Colombia calmed, falsifying papers was not as lucrative as it had been in the past. By the early 1970s, U.S.-style discos and clubs were growing in popularity, and in those spaces cocaine was consumed. DEA crackdowns on the heroin and marijuana trade contributed to the growing demand for cocaine. Bravo grew interested in cocaine as an alternative source of revenue, although Trujillo was skeptical. Blanco and Bravo collaborated to distribute cocaine, and their business relationship turned romantic. When Trujillo found out, Smitten asserts, he badly beat her, but he died soon after of cirrhosis of the liver, leaving Blanco and Bravo to consolidate and build their emerging business in cocaine.[100]

Whether Smitten's biography and analysis are completely accurate or not, Blanco and Bravo created a business that became phenomenally successful. Their experience in human trafficking ensured that they had a network of reliable Colombian workers in New York City. Essentially, they benefited from perfect timing. They were in the right place, with the right contacts, at the right time. Like the Barragáns and Hernandezes, Bravo and Blanco also had a nearly perfect partnership that endured separations, affairs, economic losses, and law enforcement. Their impact on the modern drug trade is indisputable. Colombian journalists have argued that Blanco may have mentored Pablo Escobar. In her home, she had a painting that featured her children and Escobar, as well as herself, gathered around a table.[101]

Because of Blanco's ties to the Medillín cartel, her case generated substantial interest in New York City. Numerous attorneys represented the government, including Attorney General Rudolph Giuliani. For Giuliani and his later tough stance on crime and drugs as New York's mayor from 1994 to 2001, Blanco's case surely fit the image of the depraved and corrupt New York of the 1970s. Blanco's wealth allowed her to assemble a formidable defense team. Frank Mandel and Nathan Diamond, Blanco's attorneys, questioned every aspect of the case and the indictment, and even demanded that their client be granted permission to hire her own translator rather than use the one provided by the government.[102] In their cross-examinations, they expertly sought to discredit the witnesses for the prosecution as paid informants who were only trying to discredit a successful businesswoman. However, the evidence against Blanco that had been compiled over ten years proved to be insurmountable for the defense.

Attorney Arthur Mercado opened the case by referring to the past:

> It was in a country called Colombia. They were in a city called Medellin. Pepe was there, Alberto was there, Dona Gris was there, and they were talking about how to get merchandize from Dona Gris in Colombia to Pepe in New York where Pepe could sell it. Pepe said, "Let's bring it in a cage," and Dona Gris said, "Let's bring it in bras and girdles. Pepe's name is Jose Cabrera, They call him El Tio. Alberto's name is Alberto Bravo, Albertico, Trapito they call him. Dona Gris's name Griselda Blanco. They called her La madrina, the Godmother, or Dona Gris.[103]

Mercado explained to the jurors that this was a conspiracy case between Pepe (José Antonio Cabrera-Sarmiento), Alberto, Griselda Blanco, "and a host of others." He argued that the jurors would hear many names, dates, and places, but that they must consider the conspiracy as a whole and Blanco's role in it because the leaders did not carry the cocaine across borders themselves, but rather they employed others to bring cocaine into the United States, as the money from cocaine sales went back to Colombia.[104]

One of the first witnesses called was Charles W. Cecil Jr., a DEA agent. In Colombia, Cecil had tracked Blanco using informants.[105] He contacted her attorneys in Colombia and asked for their assistance in convincing her to surrender to authorities. His attempt to reach Blanco through her attorneys proved unsuccessful, but his informants told him that Blanco had a legitimate passport under the name Ahichel Vence López, and that she continued to travel. According to court documents, Cecil attempted to get his informants to persuade her to travel to Costa Rica, where the DEA hoped they had a greater chance of extraditing her.

As in 1942, when U.S. authorities tried to lure Ignacia Jasso across the border, Blanco avoided traveling to places where she might be extradited. If she did travel, which she did often during this time, she used false documents. Stories circulated about Blanco. She was rumored to have entered the United States or to have been killed in Miami or in Medellín.[106] The DEA considered such stories rumors, but their circulation had the purpose of shielding Blanco, her travels, and her ongoing business. Cecil's investigation was part of Operation Banshee, a large-scale initiative to dismantle Bravo and Blanco's cocaine networks.[107]

Despite the numerous DEA agents who testified, the prosecution's key witness was Gloria Cabán. Cabán, whose real name was Amparo Atehortua, used more than twenty aliases while involved in petty crime and the drug trade in Colombia, Puerto Rico, and New York.[108] She became Gloria Cabán when she worked at a bar called Intermezzo at Seventy-Fourth Street and Columbus Avenue in Manhattan. A patron sold her a Puerto Rican birth certificate and social security card. This allowed her to apply for a U.S. passport and travel there despite her earlier arrests and deportation. While at Intermezzo, she met Edgar Restrepo and Pepe Cabrera, part of the Bravo-Blanco organization, who sold kilos of cocaine to her boss, "Mr. Morris." When police raided Morris's bar and closed it for drugs, he simply opened a series of others. Cabán continued to work for Morris.[109]

Under oath, she testified how Morris bought kilos from Restrepo and Cabrera, which he then resold, but she also described the transnational operation. Eventually, Restrepo approached Cabán, and she began working for him. At his apartment close to LaGuardia Airport, she observed numerous cocaine purchases and also the arrival of the supply. Suitcases and shoes would be carefully broken apart, and the valuable contents weighed and bagged for sale. On one occasion, while on an outing to Rockefeller Center, Restrepo and Cabrera asked Cabán to carry money to Colombia and to give it to Bravo, Blanco, and another partner. She returned to Colombia with the cash and money orders. Cabrera, who worked as a loan officer in a bank, and Restrepo had purchased money orders at numerous banks in the city. Cabán stated that they would visit more than ten banks in one day to purchase money orders, and these she took to Colombia.[110]

While on her first money courier trip to Colombia, Cabán heard and observed a conversation between Bravo, Blanco, and Cabrera about people getting caught smuggling cocaine.[111] Gloria's sister Carmen, who was in Colombia, was also recruited to become a courier.[112] During this time, Gloria became the lover of Restrepo and then of Cabrera, whose wife and family lived in Colombia.[113] The sisters often flew directly from Bogotá to JFK Airport in New York; other times, they flew to New York from Colombia via Puerto Rico. After a number of arrests, the Cabán sisters worked closely with the DEA to build a case against Blanco.

Other women involved included Olga Perdomo, a college-educated musician who had played for the Bogotá Philharmonic Orchestra.[114] She, as well as other highly educated women, worked with Blanco. They smuggled drugs under false names and false passports, which Perdomo thought were obtained from people working in the U.S. embassy.[115] She met Blanco in 1974 at the U.S. embassy via an acquaintance who worked in security. They would later meet at the embassy and then go out to have lunch or coffee at luxury hotels in the city.

In his autobiography, Max Mermelstein described how Blanco sought female friends to accompany her on shopping trips, to parties, and to beauty salons. DEA agents observed this quite early in Colombia. Blanco recruited and employed attractive young women to transport cocaine into the United States. Many of these women were fair skinned and more accomplished than her friends from her old neighborhood, Barrio Antioquia, a rough part of Medellín. Women also worked as distributors for her and Bravo in New York City. These included Lilia Parada and Gloria and Carmen Cabán. These women, who testified against Blanco, described her and Bravo's extensive businesses and their partners. Even early in the 1970s, Blanco owned ranches and real estate in Colombia.

Mermelstein and the men interviewed in *Cocaine Cowboys*—Jorge Ayala, Mickey Munday, and Jon Roberts—saw Blanco's close female friendships, her shopping trips, and her lavish gifts to female friends as further displays of her insatiable vanity. However, she was using these women to manipulate the men in her business. By getting close to the women associated with her comrades and competitors, she gained an edge over the men. Her vanity in a sense masked her uncanny ability to read the strengths and weaknesses of the men she associated with, whether competitors or colleagues. Mermelstein noted his increasing discomfort with Blanco's friendship with his wife, Cristina.[116] Blanco also understood masculinity at its most elemental, the compulsion to protect women and children. By courting the wives and girlfriends of her lieutenants and competitors, she further inspired fear and even hatred among the men, who realized that she could eliminate their families as she had already done with those who had betrayed her.

Before moving to Miami, Blanco and Bravo set up the "biggest Colombian narcotics organization" in the United States, but the NYPD worked to expand upon the initial arrests and close in on the bosses.[117] The 1975 arrests of members of Blanco's organization eventually implicated those at the top. Gustavo Restrepo and Lilia Parada were arrested by the NYPD; they were compared with other major drug groups, including members of the Italian mob and Harlem heroin boss Leroy "Nicky" Barnes's organization.[118] Parada was the only woman arrested.

The NYPD described Parada as "a major importer and supplier."[119] In 1973–1974, the NYPD placed her under surveillance and wiretapped her phones; it was the wiretaps that led police to Blanco and Bravo. In those conversations, Parada and her coconspirators talked about what appeared to be mundane subjects such as laundry, chores, and home life. They discussed dropping off shirts and skirts at the dry cleaner's or picking up their children. The "children," it turned out, were one-eighth-kilo packets of cocaine. The wiretaps captured Parada talking to her children while arranging deliveries of "children." "Beautiful children with good bones" referred to high-quality pure cocaine with crystal rocks.[120] The NYPD also learned that the cocaine entering New York City came from a number of locations. Most often it was flown into Kennedy Airport, but one of the coconspirators, "Ruben" drove to the U.S.-Mexico border and smuggled the cocaine into the United States in small statuettes each stuffed with half a kilo. He would then drive to New York City. From the wiretaps, it appears that the Colombians operating in New York in the early 1970s were already working with Mexican drug organizations to move cocaine.[121]

Police officer Frank Iturralde recorded and transcribed the conversations of Parada and five other Colombians. Of Spanish decent and educated in Puerto Rico, he was a new recruit who was brought into the huge narcotics case because he was bilingual.[122] Dalays Rossi translated the recordings into English. She and Iturralde noted that the Colombians never used their true names, and they used coded language. Rossi, an interpreter for the state supreme court in Manhattan and the Bronx, testified: "I have also come across other types of Pig Latin, syllables, which were used during conversations by participants."[123] The Colombians inserted "cun" rather than English Pig Latin's "chi" to create nonsense words. In cross-examination of Rossi, one of Blanco's defense attorneys asked how she could correctly translate nonsense. Rossi assured the court that, just as a native English speaker can immediately pick out alterations in the language, so too, could a native Spanish speaker when the same practice occurs in Spanish. Blanco's defense attorneys forced both witnesses to confirm that Blanco's voice was never heard on the wiretaps.

Like other female drug bosses, Blanco created distance between herself and the actual distribution and sale of her drugs. She had contact with countless women who worked for her, and ultimately they assisted in her prosecution. Parada's and the Cabán sisters' experiences show the diversity of roles women play in contemporary drug organizations. Parada was a New York distributor for Bravo and Blanco. The Cabán sisters and many other women ran stash houses and worked as mules, couriers, processors, and local transporters. The NYPD detectives soon realized that the people they had under surveillance in New York City were connected to a far more sophisticated global network, and the newly formed DEA pursued Blanco and Bravo.[124] The Cabán sisters cooperated with the police after they were arrested in 1973. Amparo and Gilman Atehortua, the real identities of the Cabán sisters, both received seven-year prison sentences. Gilman (Carmen) initially told her sister that she planned to cooperate with the police because she had children whom she wished to see.[125] As Blanco's attorney Nathan Diamond demonstrated, Amparo and Gilman appeared to be paid informants who had offered assistance because of their involvement in drugs through the early 1970s.[126]

DEA agent Heather Campbell confirmed that Amparo and Gilman's family members received visas, and that Amparo (Gloria, the key informant) received approximately $3,300 (2012: $7,000) a month in 1985 from the DEA for lodging, food, and other expenses.[127] Despite Diamond's efforts to portray the Atehortua sisters as paid informants who created a false case against a prominent Colombian businesswoman, Blanco was found guilty of crimes in New York. She was sentenced to fifteen years and fined twenty-five thousand dollars.[128] After her conviction, Miami district attorneys also hoped to prosecute Blanco for murder, but the case was plagued with problems.

MASCULINE BRAVADO VIA THE GODMOTHER

Blanco's career and her reemergence in popular culture offers a vehicle to consider representations of crime with a historian's more skeptical approach. Blanco's New York City court documents show a complex illicit business enterprise that employed many people. Her reappearance in popular culture came in the documentary film *Cocaine Cowboys*, which juxtaposed interviews with news reports and images. In the film and the true crime biographies, Mermelstein, Smitten, and Rivi claimed that her heavy drug use and bisexuality were indicators of her decline into insanity.[129] Although her success in drug trafficking rivaled that of many men, her former colleagues ascribed Blanco's drug addiction and sexuality as signs of her weakness, vulgarity, and hysteria. To the DEA and NYPD, however, she was a force to be reckoned with for many years. The DEA agents and NYPD detectives had a difficult time understanding her organization, and their testimonies bordered on showing respect. Charles Cecil, Bob Palombo, and others spent years unraveling an illicit transnational enterprise that operated in three countries. Their careful work, however, seemed futile once the case reached Miami. There, film director Billy Corben found a story that he could relish.

Blanco's story is retold in Corben's *Cocaine Cowboys* documentaries. In the second film, *Hustlin' with the Godmother*, the documentary style gives way to greater sensationalism. Murderous confrontations are in black-and-white graphic comic in a single-shot format, except when characters fire semiautomatic weapons and bodies fall mutilated, splashing red blood. Female characters have chiseled facial features, cinched waists, and enormous breasts. In these depictions, Blanco appears more masculine and svelte rather than as the stylish, chubby, middle-aged woman she was.

The added animated sequences, in the style of graphic novels, and the sounds of South Florida rappers Trick Daddy and Pitbull in *Hustlin' with the Godmother* serve to heighten Blanco's "gangsta" hagiography. In 1985, Charles Cosby, a street dealer in Oakland, California, watched the news about Blanco's arrest. As he describes it, Blanco mesmerized him due to the amount of cocaine she trafficked and her power. He wrote a fan letter to her and ultimately became a prison groupie. In his autobiography, available online, he writes: "Throughout my life, I've always been an opportunist, what better opportunity than to fuck with Griselda Blanco. . . . [One] could call it groupie or whatever, no muthafucka in his right mind is gonna wanna pass up that chance."[130] He wrote to her, she replied, and they began a courtship. He recalls: "We developed a bond from the very first phone call. Griselda was like John Gotti, receiving mail from all over the world. I was the only person she ever wrote back."[131]

They allegedly became lovers, and Cosby reported paying the prison guards $1,500 for each sexual encounter. However, he also worked for her and her sons as a distributor. As he tells it, Blanco's network enriched him, and she elevated him to a high position, which no other African American man held in her organization. He continued to work for Griselda until her legal situation spiraled further out of control. After her trial in New York, she was to be tried for her crimes in Miami. In building a murder case against her that could lead to the death penalty, the DEA and the district attorney's office in Florida offered Rivi Ayala, her enforcer, a deal of life in prison rather than the death penalty for his crimes if he testified against her. Once Blanco knew that Rivi had cut a deal, she was desperate to return to Colombia, where her sons had been deported, as Cosby describes. She turned to Cosby to help her kidnap John F. Kennedy Jr. in 1994 in order to hold him for ransom in exchange for her release and passage to Colombia. Despite his devotion to Blanco, Cosby was now working with law enforcement and agreed to wear a wire in his prison conversations with her.

Blanco never stood trial for murder because Rivi engaged in phone sex with the secretaries in the district attorney's office in Miami, thus tainting the case. Cosby alleged that he, too, had sex with one of the secretaries when he went to a deposition in Miami in 1997. Because of the sexual relationships between Rivi and members of the office staff, Blanco served her New York City sentence until 2004, when she was deported to Colombia. Corben closes *Hustlin' with the Godmother* with a photograph of Blanco taken in 2007. The men's magazine *Maxim* republished that image along with a story about Blanco:

> The woman in the photo hardly resembles the Black Widow of legend. By all accounts Blanco has been out of the cocaine business for more than a decade and is living a quiet existence in Bogotá. Without her makeup, hair dye, or designer clothes, at 65 the Godmother looks more like a Grandmother these days. But the eyes remain cold and in looking at them one can't forget that this is a woman allegedly responsible for more than 200 murders, who rose from the slums of Bogotá to the pinnacle of the crime world, who killed three husbands, and sacrificed three sons to her limitless ambition. And on her face as

she gazes into the camera, is that trademark smirk, which seems to gloat: I played the game, and I'm still here. That means I won.[132]

What *Maxim* neglected to address is that Blanco continues to make money for men whether in true crime publications or documentary films, or simply by association. While they assert their control over her in interviews, she was the vessel for their performative gangster masculinity whether as hotshot pilots, multimillionaire entrepreneurs, true crime writers, or drug gangsters. To Cosby as street dealer turned gangsta with a Colombian network, to Rivi who uses his insider knowledge to save himself from the death penalty, to Mermelstein, Smitten, and Corben who have a great story to exploit, and even to her son Michael Corleone who uses the family name to promote his music label in Colombia and Miami, Blanco is a remarkable muse who "made" all the men who survived her.[133]

William Burroughs created a fictional Lola la Chata so he could imagine what it would be like to assume her power. Neither Cosby, Rivi, nor Mermelstein ever usurped Blanco's power. What strikingly differs between Burroughs and Blanco's former employees is that Burroughs created a fictionalized fantasy world to portray la Chata's drug empire, while the men featured in *Cocaine Cowboys* created parallel narconarratives to shift the focus to themselves and away from their boss, whom they feared.

Had Corben followed Blanco's life to the bitter end, it would not have been a fascinating masculine epic set to a hip-hop soundtrack but rather a feminized story. Her life did not end in a blaze of bullets between her gang and the DEA or Colombian police, like her old associate Pablo Escobar. Instead, she lived a quiet life of retirement in a lavish neighborhood in Medellín. She routinely passed the afternoons sipping coffee and visiting her friends in her old barrio. Two of her children were dead, one she did not raise, and her eldest son became an addict. In her final years, she turned to performing good works for her neighbors and family members in Barrio Antioquia, like many good Catholic women as well as her neighborhood friend Pablo Escobar. Neighbors and friends remembered a ladylike elderly woman who did not swear and who maintained a circle of friends who were well aware of her past.[134] She lived a quiet life in a comfortable house, surrounded by portraits of her younger self and commissioned paintings. After her murder, her well-attended mass was followed by her burial.[135] In her lavish neighborhood of El Poblado, her neighbors observed her old friends from Barrio Antioquia who drank aguardiente and sent her off with wails of grief.[136]

The 1975 *New York Times* article "No Antiwoman Job Bias in the Narcotics Trade" misrepresented women in drug trafficking and organized crime by arguing that Latin American women were somehow unique in organized crime and drug trafficking. Perpetuating the gendered images of women found in Mario Puzo's novel and Francis Ford Coppola's film of the same name, *The Godfather*, a journalist wrote: "Unlike Mafia wives who avoid involvement in their husband's racket, Latin women often work closely with their men in narcotics traffic."[137]

It is true that women worked closely with their lovers, partners, and fathers in the drug trade, but they also created and worked within sophisticated organized crime networks in which they were not intimately involved with men. Where women had few options for employment or encountered obstacles to legitimate business ownership, they used the distribution of drugs as a vehicle for socioeconomic advancement. Journalists often ignored the complexity and continuity of women's roles, whether as equal partners with their husbands or as high-ranking distributors and suppliers in global trafficking organizations.

In the 1970s, women such as Helen Hernandez, Yolanda Sarmiento, and Griselda Blanco operated as suppliers. They were not street vendors, peddlers, or dealers. They ensured their own safety and wealth by maintaining a distance between themselves and their sales, and their work as suppliers led them to embrace new forms of technology. All of them added new methods and innovations to the trafficking of drugs. They relied on men and women to work for them and with them in their pursuit of profit. Whether using picture frames, wine bottles, undergarments, false-bottom suitcases, or human mules; whether working with existing banking laws or manipulating them; all the women demonstrated that constant shifts in government policies must be followed by further innovations in their own businesses.

Sarmiento and Blanco operated in New York City in the 1970s. They lived fairly comfortable lives, although fraught with danger. They had nice apartments whether in New York, Colombia, or Argentina; substantial bank accounts; and legitimate, although falsified, passports that permitted them to travel about the hemisphere. NYPD narcotics agent Kathy Burke argued that, in her experience, women in their position were rare. Global conspiracy cases fell under the domain of federal agencies such as the DEA. Burke experienced the local trappings of the drug trade, and she suggested that the drug life of women in New York City in the 1970s was far from glamorous. It was a cycle of poverty, prostitution, and violence.[138] That poverty and violence had developed into a fifty-billion-dollar industry by 1985, and it continues to grow, affecting the lives of more women and their families far beyond the era of Hernandez, Sarmiento, and Blanco.[39] All three served as architects of the modern drug trade and played significant roles in organizations that were supposed to be the exclusive domains of men. Like their predecessors and successors, they found a space in a male industry, an industry that for decades accepted women as lovers, mules, couriers, partners, and bosses.

GANGSTERS, NARCS, AND WOMEN

A Secret History

IN 2003, THIS PROJECT TOOK FORM WITH A SIMPLE QUESTION: IF women dominate the informal (secondary) labor market, why are they missing from most historical studies on drug peddling and trafficking? By researching from this perspective, I uncovered countless women who have operated at transnational levels throughout the Americas since the passage of the 1914 Harrison Narcotics Tax Act in the United States, which marked the beginning of the modern drug war. Those few scholars who work on the history of narcotics have long recognized the roles of women in the illegal business, but usually as burros or mules who are portrayed as tangential rather than central to the trade. Recently, popular culture and news accounts have served as the primary evidence to document the rise of *las narcas* such as the Mexican María "Chata" León and U.S. customs agent Martha Garnica.

Dubbed the gangster matriarch, León built an empire that included both human and drug trafficking.[1] An undocumented immigrant from the state of Guerrero, León led a family business with ties to the Mexican Mafia. She settled on Drew Street in Los Angeles, a neighborhood of California bungalows and low-rise apartments, There, she raised her family of thirteen children, some of whom also entered the drug trade.[2] León, like la Chata and la Nacha, was in and out of prison, and Los Angeles police monitored her house and her neighborhood as a central site of drug distribution, particularly crack cocaine.[3] Her case triggered public declarations that she and her family contributed to the moral decline of Los Angeles without considering the demand that ensured she always had a market.[4]

In the case of Garnica, also known as la Estrella (the Star), *Washington Post* journalists fueled public fear north of the Rio Grande by demonstrating that the lure of the drug trade even influenced U.S. agents.[5] Garnica had been an El Paso police officer who transferred to U.S. Customs and Border Protection. Once at Customs, it appeared that she knowingly allowed massive amounts of marijuana to pass into the United States. Like Sandra Ávila Beltrán, Garnica was characterized by journalists on both sides of the border as sexually insatiable, with a similar appetite for the good life. Ávila Beltrán, la Reina, sashayed into her arrest wearing tight designer jeans and demanding time to fix her hair and makeup for her mug shots. Before her arrest, customs agent la Estrella, "a brassy looker," appeared to live above her means, donning designer clothes, vacationing in Europe, and driving a Hummer, all on her modest civil servant's salary.

These cases of contemporary women traffickers demonstrate a continuation of women's involvement in the drug trade as it changed over time. In the twentieth century, women intersected with the complexity of those changes that were marked by the introduction of new forms of technology, global flows of people, innovation in banking and communications, and continuous demand for new, and cheaper, drugs. León reinforces the image of the local dealer as Mexican and a foreign menace operating inside the United States. She is portrayed as a contagion that must be removed to protect society.

Media depictions of León are similar to those of Ignacia Jasso, la viuda de González, la Nacha, whose drug trafficking activities directly on the border ensured that she held the attention of U.S. lawmakers for over fifty years. Harry Anslinger used her and María Dolores Estévez Zuleta, "Lola la Chata," as examples with which to threaten the Mexican government and demand greater border control. Seventy years later, León's tale serves to justify stricter immigration laws and border enforcement in a time of a crescendo of anti-immigrant sentiment. And yet, this same society that views itself as a victim has increasingly demanded León's products, just as it desired those of la Nacha and la Chata. Garnica's arrest exemplified the intersection of the policing of globalized crime and the lure of the narcolifestyle. As a customs agent posted at an international port of entry, Garnica and her corruption evolved into a cautionary tale. Despite receiving greater media attention, these women have been portrayed as gendered caricatures or appendages of

Figure 22. Woman in a marijuana field. Photo by José Carlos Cisneros Guzmán.

more important masculine figures such as players in the Mexican Mafia, León's adult sons, and Garnica's cartel connections, but the truth is very different.

In the historiography of drugs, women still remain marginal if mentioned at all. Most works on drugs that address women focus on them as victims of drugs and addiction. I do not dispute the analysis of women as addicts, and I recognize that they do sell cocaine, narcotics, pharmaceuticals, and their bodies to support their drug habits. The connections between women and the drug trade, however, are far more complex. Thinking historically and using historical methods, I have exposed women's long-term ties to the industry as active agents in the flow of drugs in all levels, from mule to jefa.

In this study, I have argued that most women bosses preferred to remain anonymous and on the fringes of criminality, because being on the margins allowed them to operate and generate greater profits without the disruptions of prison or greater competition. Becoming a known trafficker disrupted business with legal proceedings, imprisonment, and exile. Exposure also led to separation from family, harassment, and competition. By staying unacknowledged for most of the twentieth century, the largely anonymous women traffickers ensured their own longevity in the trade. Women such as Ignacia Jasso, María Dolores Estévez Zuleta, Ismelda Barragán, and Griselda Blanco all trafficked drugs for years.[6] During their eras, police officials and politicians routinely recognized their existence and used legal and extralegal means to undermine them.

By not problematizing the role of women in the narcotics trade, scholars have undervalued women and ignored the importance of family and informal social networks that exist within drug trafficking and organized crime. The great male epic narrative, whether of the capo or the cop, is only a small part of the story. Frankly, it is rarely the metanarrative of these modern tales or histories. Indeed, the majority of women participate in the drug trade as mules, addicts, and victims. And despite the ever-increasing attention paid to capos, bosses, and godfathers, most men in the trade operate and exist in those very same roles: mule, low-level worker, addict, and victim. Exceptional women, like exceptional men, formed cross-class, cross-ethnic partnerships to build organizations to facilitate transnational illicit flows. The masses who eke out a living and die in the drug trade rarely merit articles or books. Instead, they enter into the trade, perhaps recognized only as a statistical estimate. They then leave with little formal or historical notice, except for maybe an arrest warrant, a prison record, or a death certificate.

The historical importance of mules and the centrality of couriers are essential to understanding drug flows. Maria Wendt's arrest in 1936 triggered the collapse of one of the largest drug trafficking empires of its time. Her role as a highly skilled and educated mule portrays a completely different scenario from the common representation of the mule as a poor woman desperate to change her circumstances. What does it mean if women chose to become mules to achieve socioeconomic advancement or experience excitement rather than pursuing it for economic survival? In my work with José Carlos Cisneros Guzmán, we argued that young upper-middle-class women are drawn to the drug trade for the same reason as their male peers.[7] They enjoy the quick money but also the power that they wield over other men and women who work for them. In prison interviews conducted by the Rockefeller Foundation in the 1920s, women reported the same type of draw: money and glamour.[8] Cisneros Guzmán's ongoing work with these women demonstrates that their interest in the trade is far more insidious than that of the poor woman who feels forced into the trade.[9] These young women make a conscious decision to build an illicit business rather than a legal one.

The centrality of women in laundering money is more difficult to document but remains a historical continuity. The businesses that women started or used to cover their true professions or to assist their husbands', fathers', or brothers' drug businesses must be analyzed to understand the flow of revenues. Boutiques, hair salons, nail salons, bars, and restaurants have always been businesses where women could find employment or become proprietors, since the clientele was predominantly female or female presence was welcomed. The fact that women such as Estévez, Jasso, Ismelda Galindo Barragán, Yolanda Sarmiento, and Griselda Blanco owned businesses like these demonstrates the fluidity between illicit and licit enterprises. Like immigrant men who found themselves on the margins of the economy, women used those few economic openings to create other businesses. They did not control masculine venues such as waterfronts, unions, or construction companies that frequently became associated with organized crime. Yet, female bosses, too, realized the importance of having diversified holdings, and they used these business types that were not unusual to women.

Sandra Ávila Beltrán and the women in this study demonstrate that kinship remains an important factor to their success in trafficking drugs. Ávila Beltrán described to Julio Scherer García, a prominent Mexican journalist, how she gained credentials through her relationships with powerful men.[10] As defined by criminologist Howard Abadinsky, credentials are essential to building trust, protection, and profit.[11] Those credentials allowed her to thrive and to create a protective circle around her. Like Ávila Beltrán, la Chata, la Nacha, Galindo Barragán, Helen Hernandez, Sarmiento, and Blanco all used their credentials with criminal organizations to promote their own legitimate businesses. Yet they, too, encountered betrayals from men in their organizations or difficulties with policing agents.

The evidence is clear that women of such families have been able to successfully launder money through their legitimate businesses. However, this ability remains largely unacknowledged because few consider the importance of women involved in finances or as partners. For example, Enedina Arellano Félix ran the Tijuana cartel once the police and DEA arrested her brothers. An accountant and businesswoman, she was always a partner in the criminal organization, and she groomed her son Luis to succeed her and her brothers, just as Ciudad Juárez drug boss Ignacia Jasso had prepared her own sons.[12] Arellano's ability to survive in the trade is the latest chapter in a Tijuana historical continuum, beginning with Ismelda Galindo Barragán in the 1950s and followed by Helen Hernandez in the 1970s, both of whom played equal roles along with male family members.

This study positions drug trafficking as an undocumented part of women's and gender history, and it draws some conclusions about women's political, social, and economic power in environments in which they were presumed to remain economically, socially, and politically disempowered. Instead, they partnered with men to build powerful transnational trafficking organizations from the 1910s to the present. Here, I shed light on how they intersected with the state and its policing efforts. By looking at the connections between women, their families, and transnational criminal organizations, I question contemporary accounts and studies of organized crime. The continued distortion of organized crime as an exclusive men's club is a misreading of the historical roles and practices of women. A close reading of journalistic literature and documentary evidence reveals that women who were the wives, sisters, mothers, and daughters of organized crime figures did not simply sit by the stove stirring the sauce. They frequently worked as couriers, confidants, or partners.[13] In examining Sarmiento and Blanco, DEA and NYPD agents recognized their power and contacts as significant.

Returning to Nancy Campbell's assertion that drugs threaten to level the naturalized hierarchy between the sexes and the state,[14] I argue that women have used the skills they gained from the informal market such as prostitution and street vending to develop business in transnational organized crime. Women employed their social networks such as family and friends to construct sophisticated organized crime entities, just as men have done whether in Chinese, Jewish, Irish, Italian, or Mexican organized crime or in biker or prison gangs. Contemporary women in the drug trade have their preferences. Some prefer to work exclusively with men while others prefer to work with women. Some rely on their children and train them to enter the trade, and some employ violence to defend their business interests against potential competitors, as Blanco did. Other women who see themselves as bosses send their children abroad to boarding school to protect them and keep them far from the business, like the iconic Michael Corleone character in *The Godfather*, who was supposed to be the son who followed a legitimate path to success and prosperity.

While many contemporary journalists and writers remain blind to the complexity of gender roles in crime, many others have long pursued this topic in depth. Present-day scholars—both anthropologists and criminologists—such as Tammy Anderson, Alan Block, Howard Campbell, Barbara Denton, Eloise Dunlap, Bruce Johnson, Lisa Maher, and Ric Curtis all challenge the universalizing and tautological constructs of women in the drug business as mule or victim. Their theoretical approaches and methodologies are essential to this work.

In this book, I engage their research by offering a study of the past that positions women as modern innovators, as demonstrated by their fluid responses to political, social, and economic shifts.[15] For example, I consider Block's analysis of legitimate fronts to illicit ventures undertaken by female Jewish criminals in the early 1900s when I analyze Galindo Barragán. In the 1940s and 1950s, Galindo ran a successful bordello in Tijuana where she distributed heroin. She and her husband, Big Mike, operated legitimate businesses such as boutiques, hair salons, taxi services, and a dog racing track, all of which facilitated the distribution of heroin and the laundering of money gained from supplying numerous cities in the United States.

In the case of Anderson's analysis of multiple economic arrangements utilized by women in the drug trade, I found evidence of women in New Jersey selling heroin on commission or purchasing franchises to sell it from organized crime entities beginning in the 1920s. Along the U.S.-Mexico and U.S.-Canada borders, evidence from the 1930s suggests that women traffickers and suppliers also sold franchises to female dealers in major cities.

To ignore masculinity, though, is intellectually perilous. After all, men have done most of the policing, diplomacy, and governing as well as trafficking. In some ways, this situation has contributed to women remaining bit characters in a great masculine epic. In doing this work, I built upon Hermann Herlinghaus's theory regarding narconarratives. He argues that these narratives designate a multiplicity of dramas expressed in antagonistic language and articulated along the border through fantasies that revolve around the depravity and deterritorialization of individual and communitarian life.[16] I employed Herlinghaus's construct of the narconarratives in some of its complexities and mediums to demonstrate historical continuities and contingencies that both men and women experienced. For example, treasury agent Alvin Scharff demonstrates the antagonism that exists along borders and frontiers. His criminal tendencies made him a successful agent because he easily moved between the two worlds, just as drug bosses do. He was in many ways a classic American man's man. He embraced the freedom of the frontier and moved between the illicit and the licit with a skill that rivaled that of most of his fellow agents. Despite his antagonism with Harry Anslinger, he persevered, but he never could quite capitalize on his fame as he attempted to dramatize his life by working with fictional Western writer Garland Roark.[17]

Scharff's and Maria Wendt's cases demonstrate that the massive displacement of people during the interwar years led certain professional men to build a successful four-continent criminal network. War, displacement, access to heroin, and the changing technologies of the twentieth century contributed to the rise of the Loeffelholz-Branstatter organization. Although the 1930s gave rise to a sensationalized drug problem, similar to the problem prompting the present-day drug war, Herlinghaus's analysis offers a means to depart from hypermasculine journalistic accounts of violence—considered "expert"—by seeking out and analyzing other forms of evidence to develop knowledge that engages the symbolic and metaphorical transfer of information about everyday life and change over time. By mining sources and piecing together the histories of diverse criminal organizations from an array of archives, I was able to establish the flows between illicit and licit business, and where and how men and women connected to those enterprises.

In the Americas, as in much of the world, the informal and illicit economy has long flourished and has been tolerated as a form of social safety net to replace or supplement those services offered only inadequately by the government, the Church, or other legitimate organizations. Those unique economic structures combined with the incomplete democratic reforms implemented in Colombia, Argentina, and Mexico in the twentieth century. In Mexico, the breakdown of the gentleman's agreement between the drug traffickers and the Partido Revolucionario Institucional (Institutional Revolutionary Party, PRI) ensured that Mexico regained centrality in the narconarratives.

Narconarratives coexist in sites, and times, of violence, but these are also sites of profit, legitimate business, and even socioeconomic advancement for those on the margins. For example, the Hongkong and Shanghai Banking Corporation (HSBC) recently issued a public apology for laundering money for drug cartels.[18] A skeptical historian realizes that other legitimate businesses must also be involved. These narratives have long been "open secrets," a cultural dynamic in which much is known but little publicly acknowledged except at certain times for economic, social, or political reasons.[19] For years, drugs have—borrowing Avery Gordon's words—"haunted North America[,] exhibiting a seething presence, acting on and meddling with the taken for

granted realities." It is exactly this type of haunting in Mexico that led soci-
ologist Luis Astorga, writer Élmer Mendoza, and artist Lenin Márquez, all
Sinaloans, to take on the muse of drugs and violence in their work.[20] As
skeptical observers, they too wondered why their daily lives, and those of
their fellow Sinaloans, were not studied, depicted, or recognized. These were
not ethereal speculations but rather unique realities that spilled across state
and national boundaries.

The war on drugs, whether one places its beginning in the 1930s with the
formation of the FBN in the United States (intended to both coordinate with
and apply pressure on the Mexican government), with Richard Nixon's war
on drugs and the formation DEA, or with the expansion of that war under
Ronald Reagan's "Just Say No" campaign, has a long history on both sides of
the border that emerges in certain periods of time, during acute power struggles between policing agents and drug traffickers. We are currently in one of
these periods of time. In Mexico, the assassinations did not begin with former Mexican president Felipe Calderón's 2006 declaration of a drug war.
However, the growing numbers of the dead finally captured public attention
as those numbers increased every year to horrific levels. The century-old
open secret finally grabbed our attention. As I discuss, the issue had risen to
prominence earlier, only to fade from our collective memory.

As in the past, narcos have always been as adept as the police in using
the tools of technology to further their work. Before the Harrison Act, people
celebrated cocaine, morphine, heroin, and marijuana as modern medical
miracles that were widely embraced by health practitioners, governments,
and industry.[21] With illegality, things changed. Michael Kenney documented
that contemporary drug traffickers have always maintained nimble organizations that easily respond to technological, criminological, cultural, and
market shifts far more quickly than bureaucracies.[22] This is evident from the
1910s, immediately following the Harrison Act, and into the 1920s and 1930s.
Trafficking organizations readily adopted new tools in banking, the use of
airplanes, and early telecommunications, as evidenced by the Loeffelholz-
Brandstatter crime organization, which first realized the meaning of the globalization of narcotics trafficking in the 1930s and which also left a heap of
corpses in its wake. Traffickers such as François Chiappe, Yolanda Sarmiento,
Alberto Bravo, and Griselda Blanco repeated the sophistication of
Loeffelholz-Brandstatter forty years later. All four of these traffickers and
their organizations yielded narconarratives that had a profound effect on
contemporary popular and political culture.

The recent terror unleashed by Calderón's (2006–2012) war on drugs led to the death of more than sixty-five thousand people during his six-year term. This war shifted the focus away from the struggles of everyday people trying to go to school or work, simply living their lives, to a heroic masculine epic struggle that again marginalizes women and children. This struggle between men escalated the spectacle of violence, as in every narco-melodrama. As debates circulate in Mexico about what to do regarding the escalating violence, U.S. policing agencies encounter skeptical Latin American politicians who are becoming more vocal in their criticism of the demand for drugs in the United States, and the U.S. government's ongoing militarized response. Recently, Mexico's new president, Enrique Peña Nieto, questioned the access that the DEA and other U.S. agencies have had in Mexico. While U.S. agencies collaborated with the Calderón government, the victims of the melodrama struggle to flee from the violence, with asylum requests from Mexicans increasing to a staggering forty thousand a year. They flee to the very same country whose demand for cocaine, heroin, marijuana, methamphetamines, and pharmaceutical drugs contributes to the terror in their home cities and states.

That demand and desire has triggered increased spending on diplomacy and enforcement, but as the recent HSBC case revealed, the revenue derived from drugs spreads from country to country and into the pockets not only of criminals but also of elite businessmen and women. As film director Felipe Aljure vividly acknowledged in his film *El colombian dream*, the money is far more intoxicating than the drugs.[23] Whether narc or narco, mule or boss, politician or banker, there is no secret: the money is alluring. And, it knows no gender.

NOTES

ACKNOWLEDGMENTS

1. The Bushwacker is a rum and coffee drink. The owner of the patent was the source of a lawsuit. See *Sandshaker Lounge and Package Store, LLC v. Quietwater Entertainment, Inc.*, U.S. Patent and Trademark Office, 92051664, October 25, 2012.
2. Tamara Lush, "Cocaine, Sand, and a Bunch of Friends," *Tampa Bay Times*, December 4, 2004; Associated Press, "Panhandle Lounge Owner Gets 2 Years in Drug Case," *Herald-Tribune* (Sarasota), July 29, 2004; and "Sandshaker House Sells for $1,043,800," *Pensacola News Journal*, June 22, 2005.

INTRODUCTION

1. "Por narco, capturan a la llamada Reina del Pacífico," *La Jornada*, September 29, 2007; and Arturo Pérez-Reverte, *La reina del sur* (Madrid: Alfaguara, 2002). Pérez-Reverte's book was also adapted into a miniseries of the same title; *La reina del sur* began airing in the fall of 2011.
2. Miguel Ángel Félix Gallardo and Juan José Quintero Payán, along with Ernesto Fonseca Carillo, worked closely with Colombian cocaine traffickers creating what became known as the Guadalajara cartel. In the 1990s, their organization split into two other organizations, one based in Tijuana led by the Arellano Félix family and the other in Sinaloa led by Joaquín "El Chapo" Guzmán Loera.
3. "Ejecutan a siete personas en Guerrero," *La Jornada*, October 9, 2007. Pancho Villa launched his invasion of Columbus, New Mexico, from Palomas, also known as Puerto Palomas de Villa.
4. For an interview with a female boss, see Howard Campbell, *Drug War Zone: Frontline Dispatches from the Streets of El Paso and Juárez* (Austin: University of Texas Press, 2009).
5. Following a practice from colonial times, narcos use their daughters to create alliances by marrying them into other drug families. For a brief discussion of

this, see Elaine Carey and José Carlos Cisneros Guzmán, "The Daughters of La Nacha: Women, Drugs, and the Border," *NACLA Report on the Americas* (May–June 2011): 23–24.

6. Steven Soderbergh, *Traffic*, Bedford Falls Productions, 2000; Joshua Marston, *María Full of Grace*, HBO Films, 2004; Ted Demme, *Blow*, New Line Cinema, 2001; and Brian De Palma, *Scarface*, Universal Pictures, 1983.

7. See Susan Boyd, *From Witches to Crack Moms: Women, Drug Law, and Policy* (Durham, NC: Carolina Academic Press, 2004). Boyd examines the shifts and distinctions of policies that focus on women in Canada, Great Britain, and the United States. In *Using Women: Gender, Drug Policy, and Social Justice* (New York: Routledge, 2000), Nancy Campbell historicizes the shifts of policy on cultural meanings of drug use in the United States. Much has been written on mothers' use of drugs from various disciplines. For a legal and policy perspective, see Laura Gómez, *Misconceiving Mothers: Legislators, Prosecutors, and the Politics of Prenatal Drug Exposure* (Philadelphia, PA: Temple University Press, 1997), who studies drug policy in California from 1983 to 1996 as directed at crack mothers. Sheigla Murphy and Marsha Rosenbaum, *Pregnant Women on Drugs: Combating Stereotypes and Stigma* (New Brunswick, NJ: Rutgers University Press, 1999), provide a sociological study of mothers who use opiate and coca derivatives. Boyd's earlier work, *Mothers on Illegal Drugs: Transcending Myths* (Toronto: University of Toronto Press, 1999), questions why the numbers of using mothers is so high in North America when compared to Europe, while analyzing the impact of anti-narcotics legislation and maternal behavior in Canada. See also Mara L. Keire, "Dope Fiends and Degenerates: The Gendering of Addiction in the Early Twentieth Century," *Journal of Social History* 3 (1998): 809–22.

8. For contemporary analysis of women and drug peddling, see Howard Campbell, *Drug War Zone*; Eloise Dunlap, Gabriele Stürzenhofecker, and Bruce D. Johnson, "The Elusive Romance of Motherhood: Drugs, Gender, and Reproduction in Inner-City Distressed Households," *Journal of Ethnicity and Substance Abuse* 5, no. 3 (2006): 1–27; Barbara Denton, *Dealing: Women in the Drug Economy* (Sydney: University of New South Wales Press, 2001); Eloise Dunlap and Bruce D. Johnson, "Family and Human Resources in the Development of a Female Crack Seller: Case Study of a Hidden Population," *Journal of Drug Issues* 26, no. 1 (1996): 175–98; and Patricia Adler, *Wheeling and Dealing: An Ethnography of an Upper-Level Drug Dealing and Smuggling Community* (New York: Columbia University Press, 1993).

9. See peripheral role in drug research, Valli Rajah, "Intimacy, Time, Scarcity: Drug Involved Women Account for Secretly Withholding Financial Capital in Violent Intimate Relations," *Journal of Contemporary Ethnography* 39, no. 131 (2010): 131–58.

10. "Smuggling of Dope Alarms," *Los Angeles Times*, August 21, 1922. Mexicali-Calexico was second only to the ports in Los Angeles and San Francisco as a gateway for narcotics flowing into the United States.

11. Kimberley L. Thachuk, "An Introduction to Transnational Threats," in *Transnational Threats: Smuggling and Trafficking in Arms, Drugs, and Human Life*, ed. Kimberley L. Thachuk (Westport, CT: Praeger Security International, 2007), 3–20. These entrepreneurs should also include what Peter Andreas and Ethan Nadelmann call "transnational moral entrepreneurs," who generally work to convince foreign elites to adopt the moral codes of one society as if they were universal truths. See Peter Andreas and Ethan Nadelmann, *Policing the Globe: Criminalization and Crime Control in International Relations* (Oxford: Oxford University Press, 2006); and Michael Kenney, *From Pablo to Osama: Trafficking and Terrorist Networks, Government Bureaucracies, and Competitive Adaptation* (University Park: Penn State University Press, 2007).

12. For a contemporary analysis of these trends, see Enrique Desmond Arias, *Drugs and Democracy in Rio de Janeiro: Trafficking, Social Networks, and Public Security* (Chapel Hill: University of North Carolina Press, 2006). One of Arias's categories of analysis is that of informal networks with civic and political actors.

13. Anthony Giddens, *Modernity and Self-Identity: Self and Society in the Late Modern Age* (Stanford, CA: Stanford University Press, 1992).

14. Hermann Herlinghaus, *Violence Without Guilt: Ethical Narratives from the Global South* (New York: Palgrave Macmillan, 2009), 4. The theme of narconarratives was widely discussed at the conference Narco-Epics Unbound: New Narrative Territories, Affective Aesthetics, and Ethical Paradox, University of Pittsburgh, April 4–5, 2008.

15. Paul Gootenberg, *Andean Cocaine: The Making of a Global Drug* (Chapel Hill: University of North Carolina Press, 2008).

16. Samuel Truett and Elliott Young, "Introduction: Making Transnational History; Nations, Regions, and Borderlands," in *Continental Crossroads: Remapping U.S.-Mexico Borderlands History*, ed. Samuel Truett and Elliott Young (Durham, NC: Duke University Press, 2004), 6–32; Roger Rouse, "Mexican Migration and the Social Spaces of Postmodernism," in *Between Two Worlds: Mexican Immigrants in the United States*, ed. David Gutiérrez (Wilmington, DE: Scholarly Resources, 1996), 247–64 and Michiel Baud and Willem van Schendel, "Toward a Comparative History of Borderlands," *Journal of World History* 8, no. 2 (Fall 1997): 211–42. For a contemporary study of the impact of drugs on borderlanders and on a particular border site, see Howard Campbell, *Drug War Zone*. Also see Elaine Carey and Andrae Marak, "Introduction," *Smugglers, Brothels, and Twine: Historical Perspectives on Contraband and Vice in North America's Borderlands*, ed. Elaine Carey and Andrae Marak (Tucson: University of Arizona Press, 2011), 1–9.

17. Itty Abraham and Willem van Schendel, "Introduction: The Making of Illicitness," in *Illicit Flows and Criminal Things: States, Borders, and the Other Side of Globalization*, ed. Willem van Schendel and Itty Abraham (Bloomington: Indiana University Press, 2005), 4–25; and David Kyle and Christina A. Siracusa, "Seeing the State Like a Migrant: Why So Many Non-criminals Break Immigration Laws," in Van Schendel and Abraham, eds., *Illicit Flows and Criminal Things*, 153–76.

18. Gretchen Kristine Pierce, "Sobering the Revolution: Mexico's Anti-alcohol Campaigns and the Process of State-Building, 1910–1940" (PhD diss., University of Arizona, 2011).

19. Luis Astorga, *Drogas sin fronteras: los expedientes de una guerra permanente* (Mexico City: Grijalbo, 2003); Luis Astorga, *El siglo de las drogas: el narcotráfico, del Porfiriato al nuevo milenio* (Mexico City: Plaza y Janés, 2005); Nancy Campbell, *Using Women*; Gootenberg, *Andean Cocaine*; Joseph Spillane, *Cocaine: From Medical Marvel to Modern Menace in the United States, 1884–1920* (Baltimore, MD: Johns Hopkins University Press, 2000); and William O. Walker III, *Drug Control in the Americas* (Albuquerque: University of New Mexico Press, 1989).

20. Rosemary Hennessy, "Open Secrets: The Affective Cultures of Organizing on Mexico's Northern Border," *Feminist Theory* 10, no. 3 (December 2009): 310–22.

21. Avery Gordon, *Ghostly Matters: Haunting and the Sociological Imagination* (Minneapolis: University of Minnesota Press, 2008).

22. Nancy Campbell, *Using Women*, 71.

23. Denton, *Dealing*.

24. Women in both Mexico and the United States made up the greater percentage of addicts, their addictions inadvertently induced by physicians or through medical treatments.

25. Bingham Dai's study of addiction in 1935 demonstrated that 15 percent of the women addicts whom he studied were traffickers. See Bingham Dai's *Opium Addiction in Chicago* (1937; repr. Montclair, NJ: Patterson Smith, 1970). For a definition of organized crime and how it intersects with economic structures, see Max Weber, *The Theory of Social and Economic Organization*, trans. A. M. Henderson and T. Parsons, (New York: Oxford University Press, 1947).

26. Joan W. Scott, "Unanswered Questions," *American Historical Review* 113, no. 5 (December 2008): 1422–29.

27. Isaac Campos, *Home Grown: Marijuana and the Origins of Mexico's War on Drugs* (Chapel Hill: University of North Carolina Press, 2012); Carlos Aguirre and Robert Buffington, eds., *Reconstructing Criminality in Latin America* (Wilmington, DE: Scholarly Resources, 2001); Pablo Piccato, *City of Suspects: Crime in Mexico City, 1900–1931* (Durham, NC: Duke University Press, 2001); Robert M. Buffington, *Criminal and Citizen in Modern Mexico* (Lincoln: University of Nebraska Press, 2000); Lyman Johnson, ed., *The Problem of Order in Changing Societies: Essays on Crime and Policing in Argentina and Uruguay, 1750–1919* (Albuquerque: University of New Mexico Press, 1990); and Paul Vanderwood, *Disorder and Progress: Bandits, Police, and Mexican Development* (Lincoln: University of Nebraska Press, 1981).

28. Nancy Leys Stepan, *The Hour of Eugenics: Race, Gender, and Nation in Latin America* (Ithaca, NY: Cornell University Press, 1991); and Katherine Elaine Bliss, *Compromised Positions: Prostitution, Public Health, and Gender Politics in Revolutionary Mexico City* (University Park: Penn State University Press, 2001).

29. "Mexico to Join U.S. in Fight on Drugs," *New York Times*, May 10, 1925. Calles remained the de facto leader of the country until 1935.

30. Carolyn Nordstrom, *Global Outlaws: Crime, Money, and Power in the Contemporary World* (Berkeley: University of California Press, 2007), xix.

31. Anne Hyde, *Empires, Nations, and Families: A History of the North American West, 1800–1860* (Lincoln: University of Nebraska Press, 2011). Hyde documents the role of women in diverse economic activities.

32. See Stephanie Mitchell and Patience A. Schell, *The Women's Revolution in Mexico, 1910–1953* (Lanham, MD: Rowman and Littlefield, 2006); Jocelyn Olcott, *Revolutionary Women in Postrevolutionary Mexico* (Durham, NC: Duke University Press, 2005); and Mary Kay Vaughan, *Cultural Politics in Revolution: Teachers, Peasants, and Schools in Mexico, 1930–1940* (Tucson: University of Arizona Press, 1997).

33. Michael Taussig, *Defacement: Public Secrecy and the Labor of the Negative* (Stanford, CA: Stanford University Press, 1999).

34. Theodore Levitt, "The Globalization of Markets," *Harvard Business Review*, May–June 1983. Levitt popularized the use of the term. See Rawi Abelal and Richard S. Tedlow, "Theodore Levitt's 'The Globalization of Markets': An Evaluation After Two Decades," Harvard Business School Working Paper no. 03–0802, at http://papers.ssrn.com/so13/papers.cfm?abstract_id=383242, accessed April 8, 2011.

35. This is still the case. The Arellano Félix cartel was a family business operated by seven brothers and four sisters. See Public Broadcasting Service, "The Family Connection," Frontline, *Drug Wars*, October 9–10, 2000, at http://www.pbs.org/wgbh/pages/frontline/shows/drugs/business/afo/afosummary.htm, accessed April 8, 2011.

36. Nordstrom, *Global Outlaws*.

CHAPTER ONE

1. Letter to J. de D. Bojórquez, April 1935, n.d., Dirección General de Gobierno: Estupefacientes Drogas, vol. 2, file 3, Archivo General de la Nación, Mexico City (hereafter AGN).

2. Leopoldo Alvarado to Secretario de Gobernación, June 21, 1935, Dirección General de Gobierno: Estupefacientes Drogas, vol. 2, file 3, AGN.

3. The Porfiriato is a term used to describe Mexico from 1876 to 1910, when José de la Cruz Porfirio Díaz held power either by direct rule or by indirect rule through a puppet president. During this time, Mexico modernized with electric lights, rail lines, new ports, and modern cities with boulevards and department stores modeled on those in Paris.

4. For an excellent history of the Cristero rebellion and its impact on the modern state, see Jean Meyer, *The Cristero Rebellion: The Mexican People Between Church and State, 1926–1929* (Cambridge: Cambridge University Press, 2008).

5. Stepan, *The Hour of Eugenics*; Bliss, *Compromised Positions.*

6. Gootenberg, *Andean Cocaine*, 7. For concepts of disease in Latin America, see Diego Armus, ed., *Disease in the History of Modern Latin America: From Malaria to AIDS* (Durham, NC: Duke University Press, 2003).

7. Andreas and Nadelmann, *Policing the Globe.*

8. Edward Said, *Orientalism: Western Conceptions of the Orient* (London: Pantheon Books, 1978).

9. See Fray Bernardino de Sahagún, *A History of Ancient Mexico, 1547–1577: Anthropological, Mythological and Social* (New York: Blaine Ethridge, 1931).

10. Early work such as Francisco Guerra, *The Pre-Columbian Mind: A Study into the Aberrant Nature of Sexual Drives, Drugs Affecting Behaviour and the Attitude Towards Life and Death, with a Survey of Psychotherapy in Pre-Columbian America* (New York: Seminar Press, 1971) examines the attempts of Spanish laws to control the use of psychotropic drugs.

11. See Richard Evans Schultes, "Teonanacatl: The Narcotic Mushroom of the Aztecs," *American Anthropologist* 42, no. 3 (July–September 1940): 429–33; and Gastón Guzmán, "Hallucinogenic Mushrooms in Mexico: An Overview," Special Mushroom Issue, *Economic Botany* 62, no. 3 (2008): 404–12.

12. Isaac Peter Campos-Costero, "Marijuana, Madness, and Modernity in Global Mexico, 1545–1920" (PhD diss., Harvard University, 2006). Also see Campos, *Home Grown.*

13. David F. Musto, *The American Disease: Origins of Narcotic Control* (New York: Oxford University Press, 1987).

14. Peter H. Reuter and David Ronfeldt, "Quest for Integrity: The Mexican-U.S. Drug Issue in the 1980s," Special Issue: Drug Trafficking Research Update, *Journal of Interamerican Studies and World Affairs* 34, no. 3 (Autumn 1992): 93.

15. Ibid. Beginning in the 1940s, as Mexico's war on drugs escalated, officials became concerned about trafficking across the southern border. See letter to Manuel Nájera Días, Viceconsul of Mexico in Guatemala, from Secretaría de Relaciones Exteriores, Archivo Histórico "Genero Estrada," Secretaría de Relaciones Exteriores (hereafter AHSRE), III-1650–52. Mexican customs officials patrolled the southern border for opium from Guatemala. Poppy was also grown in the southern United States.

16. Campos-Costero, "Marijuana, Madness, and Modernity," 105–7. Also see Reverend William Bingley, *Travels in North America* (London: Harvey and Darton, 1821); and Mathieu de Fossey, *Viaje a Méjico* (Mexico City: Imprenta de Ignacio Cumplido, 1844). During the colonial era, Spaniards argued that the poor climate of the Americas produced laziness. Criollos also employed similar rhetoric to criticize mestizos' and indigenous peoples' lack of productivity and their backwardness.

17. Federal Narcotic Control Board. *Traffic in Opium and Other Dangerous Drugs with Respect to the Philippine Islands.* Report by the Government of the United States, 1927/1928/1929 (Washington, D.C.: Government Printing Office, 1929).

18. James Thayer Addison, *The Episcopal Church in the United States, 1789–1931* (New York: Charles Scribner's Sons, 1951); and James Thayer Addison, *Memorial Sermons Commemorative of Charles Henry Brent* (Buffalo: Diocese of Western New York, 1929).

19. Appendix 1, Second International Opium Conference, Senate doc. 733, 62nd Congress, 2nd session.

20. Beginning in the late 1800s, Mexico and the United States exchanged information regarding the Chinese in Mexico. By the 1930s, Mexican consuls in Asia were reporting on ships illegally bringing heroin and Chinese workers to Mexico. Port masters along the coasts had to respond to the secretary of foreign relations as well as the Department of Health regarding the illegal transport of heroin and people. Concerns about international crime grew during this same period. See Paul Knepper, *The Invention of International Crime: A Global Issue in the Making, 1881–1914* (London: Palgrave Macmillan, 2010).

21. See Buffington, *Criminal and Citizen in Modern Mexico*; and Piccato, *City of Suspects*.

22. Carlos Roumagnac, *Los criminales en México: ensayo de psicología criminal* (Mexico City: Tipografía "El Fénix," 1904), 159.

23. Ibid.

24. There are many books about the Mexican Revolution, but the most comprehensive is Alan Knight, *The Mexican Revolution*, 2 vols. (Cambridge: Cambridge University Press, 1990). The Constitutionalist army led by Carranza fought against Victoriano Huerta after the murder of President Francisco Madero, whose election had led to the end of Porfirio Díaz's dictatorship but triggered the fighting. Later, the Constitutionalist would turn on his generals, Pancho Villa and Emiliano Zapata.

25. See Olga Cárdenas de Ojeda, *Toxicomanía y narcotráfico: aspecto legales* (Mexico City: Fondo de Cultura Económica, 1976); and Ricardo Pérez Montfort, "Los orígenes del narco: historias primigenia," Centro de información para la prensa, at http://web.cip.etecsa.cu, accessed April 2000.

26. José María Rodríguez, "La profilaxis de la sífilis en del Departamento de Salubridad Pública," *Boletín del departamento de salubridad pública* 4 (January 31, 1919), 1–5.

27. John D. Rockefeller, like other business titans turned philanthropists, was concerned about health, both physical and moral. He funded studies on prostitution and eugenics as well as studies to eradicate diseases. See E. Richard Brown, *Rockefeller Medicine Men: Medicine and Capitalism in America* (Berkeley: University of California Press, 1979); Marco Cueto, ed., *Missionaries of Science: The Rockefeller Foundation and Latin America* (Bloomington: Indiana University Press, 1994); Edwin Black, *War Against the Weak: Eugenics and America's Campaign to Create a Master Race* (New York: Four Walls Eight Windows, 2003); and Harry Bruinius, *Better for All the World: The Secret History of Forced Sterilization and America's Quest for Racial Purity* (New York: Alfred A. Knopf, 2006).

28. *Excélsior,* July 8, 1919. Because of the perceived connection between poppy pro-
    duction and the Chinese, Chinese immigrants were targeted for attack. See José
    Jorge Gómez Izquierdo, *El movimiento anti-chino en México (1871–1934): prob-
    lemas del racismo y el nacionalismo durante la Revolución Mexicana* (Mexico
    City: Instituto Nacional de Antropología e Historia, 1991).

29. "La resolución tomada por el Consejo S. de Salubridad relativa a la ratificación
    de la Convención Internacional sobre el Opio celebrada en la Haya el año de
    1912," Fondo Presidentes Obregón-Calles, AGN.

30. League of Nations, *Advisory Committee on Traffic in Opium and Other Dangerous
    Drugs: Revised List Drawn Up by the Sub-Committee of Experts on Drugs,
    Preparations and Proprietary Medicines Coming Under the Hague (1912) and
    Geneva (1925) Opium Conventions and the Limitation Convention* (Geneva, 1931),
    1940.

31. Mexico was one of thirteen nations that signed but did not ratify the convention.

32. Letter to the president, vol. 311, document 812–5-8, AGN.

33. When Franklin D. Roosevelt was a state senator, he received a number of letters
    that protested the passage of various bills that would limit the sale of cocaine and
    narcotic medicines. Edmond Congar Brown, attorney, to Franklin D. Roosevelt,
    February 22, 1913; and Charles B. Towns to Franklin D. Roosevelt, March 31, 1913;
    New York State Senator, box 8, FDR Presidential Library, Hyde Park, New York
    (hereafter FDR Library).

34. Charles Edward Terry, "Further Study and Report on the Use of Narcotics Under
    the Provision of Federal Laws in Six Communities," Bureau of Social Hygiene,
    New York, 1927, box 219 114504, New York Academy of Medicine, New York,
    (hereafter NYAM). Additionally, heroin and other opiate derivatives were used
    to treat respiratory ailments.

35. Quoted in California Legislature, Joint Narcotic Committee, 1925, "Report on
    Drug Addiction in California by the State Narcotic Committee" (Sacramento:
    California State Printing Office, 1926), 20–21, box 230, 105014, NYAM.

36. Ibid., 24–28. See also Nancy Campbell, J. P. Olsen, and Luke Walden, *The Narcotic
    Farm: The Rise and Fall of America's First Prison for Drug Addicts* (New York:
    Abrams, 2008); and "American's First Drug Treatment Prison," National Public
    Radio, November 1, 2008, at http://www.npr.org/templates/story/story.php
    ?storyId=96437766, accessed May 19, 2011.

37. Terry, "Further Study and Report on the Use of Narcotics Under the Provision of
    Federal Laws in Six Communities," Bureau of Social Hygiene, New York, 1927,
    box 219 114504, NYAM, 36.

38. The Canadian Opium and Drugs Act of 1911 covered opium and cocaine; mari-
    juana was added in 1923. For more information, see Catherine Carstairs, *Jailed
    for Possession: Illegal Drug Use, Regulation, and Power in Canada, 1920–1961*
    (Toronto: University of Toronto Press, 2006). Bruce Davis and Ian Hamilton,
    "Lady in the Heat: A True Story of Underworld Drugs and Undercover Cops,"
    Narc Officer: Official Publication of the International Narcotics Enforcement

Officers Association (1986); "Lady in the Heat" is a serialized work of nonfiction demonstrating a growing fear among Canadians that the United States served as a drug transshipment point. See also Marcel Martel, "Preventing the Invasion: LSD Use in Canada in the Sixties," in *Smugglers, Brothels, and Twine*, ed. Carey and Marak, 160–76. Martel demonstrates the fear among Canadians that they would be swamped by drugs from America.

39. Terry, "Further Study and Report on the Use of Narcotics Under the Provision of Federal Laws in Six Communities," Bureau of Social Hygiene, New York, 1927, box 219 114504, NYAM, 36.

40. "Estimated Average Annual Drug Addiction Among Violators of the Harrison Narcotic Act, 1922–1928," table, reprinted in Dai, *Opium Addiction in Chicago*, 39.

41. Secretaría de Relaciones Exteriores de México, Informe sobre la "Prohibition" en Estados Unidos de America, 1917. Legajo 523.16/41, Archivo de la Embajada de México en Estados Unidos de América, AHSRE.

42. Convención celebrada entre los Estados Unidos Mexicanos y los Estados Unidos de Norte América sobre importación illegal de mercancias, narcóticos, y otros productos, migración illegal de extranjeros y pesca, 1922–1926, part I, AHSRE.

43. James R. Sheffield, ambassador, to Aáron Saenz, Secretario de Relaciones Exteriores, February 7, 1927, 2.015.4(1–4)-1, Caja 3, Bebidas Embriagantes (Cantinas), Dirección General de Gobierno–Ramo Gobernación, AGN; and Pitman B. Potter, "The Positions of Canada and the United States in the Matter of Trade in Alcoholic Beverages," *American Journal of International Law* 24, no. 1 (January 1930): 131.

44. The reports may be found in box 35, documents 104-2-20, Fondo Obregon y Calles, AGN.

45. "Mexico to Join US in Fight on Drugs," *New York Times*, May 10, 1925; Reuter and Ronfeldt, "Quest for Integrity," 89–153. In examining contemporary drug trafficking, Peter H. Reuter and David Ronfeldt of the RAND Corporation argue that corruption *and* nationalism are instrumental in the growth of drug trafficking in Mexico.

46. Reuter and Ronfeldt, "Quest for Integrity," 89–153. By the mid-1940s, Mexico was producing thirty-two to forty metric tons of opium annually.

47. *Diario Oficial* 35, no. 33 (April 10, 1926).

48. H. S. Middlemiss, "Narcotic Drugs in Mexico: Testimony of Don Basilio Bulnes," Narcotic Education: First Report of the Proceedings of the First World Conference on Narcotic Education, Philadelphia (Washington D.C.: H. S. Middlemiss, 1926), 113–17. In 1926, the ports designated for narcotic importation in the United States were Detroit, Indianapolis, New York, Philadelphia, Saint Louis, and San Francisco. U.S. Department of the Treasury, "Traffic in Opium and Dangerous Drugs" (Washington, D.C.: Department of the Treasury, 1926).

49. H. S. Middlemiss, "Narcotic Drugs in Mexico: Testimony of Don Basilio Bulnes," Narcotic Education: First Report of the Proceedings of the First World

Conference on Narcotic Education, Philadelphia (Washington D.C.: H. S. Middlemiss, 1926), 113–17.

50. Ibid., 115.

51. Ibid., 115–16.

52. See Eric Michael Schantz, "All Night at the Owl: The Social and Political Relations of Mexicali's Red-Light District, 1909–1925," in *On the Border: Society and Culture Between the United States and Mexico*, ed. Andrew Grant Wood (Lanham, MD: SR Books, 2004), 91–144; and Luis Astorga, "Organized Crime and the Organization of Crime," in *Organized Crime and Democratic Governability: Mexico and the U.S.-Mexican Borderlands*, ed. John Bailey and Roy Godson (Pittsburgh: University of Pittsburgh Press, 1999), 58–82. Even into the late 1930s, residents of Baja California complained about drug and alcohol smugglers, who had started to use airplanes. Antonio Castro to President Lázaro Cárdenas, June 15, 1938, box 997, 5633/339, Fondo Lázaro Cárdenas, AGN.

53. Narcotics Questionnaire, series 4, box 2, Bureau of Social Hygiene, Rockefeller Foundation Archive, Tarrytown, NY.

54. Ibid.

55. Demetrio López to C. Jefe de Departamento de Salubridad, December 21, 1927, file 8, box 8, Servicio Jurídico, Archivo de Secretaría de Salud, Mexico City. It should be noted that many analogous drugs were just as addictive as those they sought to replace, as is the case today.

56. See Beatriz Urías Horcasitas, *Historias secretas del racismo en México (1920–1950)* (Mexico City: Tusquets, 2007).

57. Harry J. Anslinger and William F. Tompkins, *The Traffic in Narcotics* (New York: Funk and Wagnalls, 1953); Harry J. Anslinger and Will Oursler, *The Murderers: The Shocking Story of the Narcotic Gangs* (New York: Farrar, Straus and Cudahy, 1961); Carstairs, *Jailed for Possession*; Julio Guerrero, *La génesis del crimen en México: estudio de psiquiatría social* (Paris and Mexico City: Vda de C. Bouret, 1901); and Julio Guerrero, *Causas de la transformación monetaria de México: disertación de economía política presentada a la Academia de Ciencias Sociales en México* (Mexico City: Impr. del Gobierno Federal, 1905).

58. The Harrison Act required physicians and pharmacists to register with the Treasury Department, pay a tax, and keep records of the narcotic drugs they prescribed or dispensed. David T. Courtwright, *Dark Paradise: A History of Opiate Addiction in America* (Cambridge: Harvard University Press, 2001), 2–4.

59. "Nab Alleged Heads of Drug Syndicate Here," *Los Angeles Times*, June 13, 1917. When arrested, Kirshon and Singer had over $500,000 (2012: $8,969,000) worth of morphine, heroin tablets, and opium.

60. Eva Silverstein was from a long list of "queens" who had earned their "royal titles" from narcotics. In the early twentieth century, male smugglers were rarely referred to as "kings"; the term "kingpin" came later.

61. "Nab Alleged Heads of Drug Syndicate Here," *Los Angeles Times*, June 13, 1917.

62. For a discussion of the border as a site of vice, see Eric Michael Schantz, "From the Mexicali Rose to the Tijuana Brass: Vice Tours of the United States–Mexico Border, 1910–1965" (PhD diss., University of California, Los Angeles, 2001). See also Wood, *On the Border*.

63. "Accused Drug Dealers Free," *Los Angeles Times*, August 6, 1924. For the role of Calexico-Mexicali, see Gabriela Recio, "Drugs and Alcohol: US Prohibition and the Origins of the Drug Trade in Mexico, 1900–1930," *Journal of Latin American Studies* 34, no. 1 (2002): 38–40.

64. "Accused Drug Dealers Free," Mexicali consul to secretary of state, April 24, 1927, National Archives, 812.114, Narcotics 98.

65. Daniel Bailey, customs agent in charge, *Intelligence Bulletin*, no. 8, September 19, 1936, Henry Morgenthau Papers, FDR Library.

66. For a discussion of Jewish organized crime in drug distribution, see Alan A. Block, "The Snowman Cometh: Coke in Progressive New York," *Criminology* 17, no. 1 (May 1979): 75–99; and David T. Courtwright, Herman Joseph, and Don Des Jarlais, *Addicts Who Survived: An Oral History of Narcotic Use in America, 1923–1965* (Knoxville: University of Tennessee Press, 1989).

67. State of California, State Senate Narcotic Committee, "Report on Drug Addiction in California" (Sacramento: California State Printing Office, 1926).

68. Ibid., 18.

69. Ibid. See also New York Academy of Medicine, "Second Annual Report to the Legislature of New York," April 7, 1920; and Carleton Simon. *Control of Narcotics* (New York: n.p., 1923).

70. H. H. Dubs, "The Chinese in Mexico City in 1635," *Far Eastern Quarterly* 1, no. 1 (1942): 387–89. Dubs argues that a small colony was established in Mexico City in 1635 to trade luxury goods. I want to thank Ray Pun for this source. National origin is always difficult to ascertain due to the often ambiguous use of the term "chino." However, the evidence suggests that these immigrants were Chinese.

71. Evelyn Hu-DeHart, "Coolies, Shopkeepers, and Pioneers: The Chinese of Mexico and Peru, 1849–1930," *Amerasia Journal* 15, no. 2 (1989): 91–116.

72. Ibid.

73. For a specific reference to controlling pharmacists as well as street vendors, see Rafael Grisi Quintano, "El tráfico de drogas," *Criminologia* 3 (December 1936): 1–12.

74. Lamberto Hernández to C. Jefe del Departamento de Salubridad Pública, August 27, 1927, and Emilio Kentler to C. Jefe del Departamento de Salubridad Pública, August 27, 1927, file 10, box 4, Servicio Jurídico, Archivo de Secretaría de Salud (hereafter SJASS), Mexico City.

75. "Dr. Hugo Schroeder, comerico ilícito de drogas," file 5, box 17, SJASS, Mexico City.

76. Dr. A. Perales Vegas to Jefe del Departamento de Salubridad Pública, August 11, 1931, box 4, SJASS, Mexico City.

77. It must be noted that foreign doctors in the United States also aroused suspicion as "dope doctors." For example, in 1936 in Richmond, Virginia, two physicians,

five pharmacists, and forty users were arrested by U.S. narcotics agents. The doctors and pharmacists involved in the case drew addicts from other states including Georgia and Tennessee. U.S. Department of the Treasury, "Traffic in Opium and Other Dangerous Drugs" (Washington, D.C., 1936), 50–53.

78. Telegram to presidente de la república from Departamento de Salubridad, B. J. Gastelum, May 25, 1925; and telegram to Gral. J. Amaro, subsecretario de guerra, from P. Elías Calles, May 26, 1925, vol. 295, exp. 241, D2-B-10.

79. Mary Roth Walsh, *Doctors Wanted, No Women Need Apply: Sexual Barriers in the Medical Profession, 1835–1975* (New Haven, CT: Yale University Press, 1977); Regina Markell Morantz-Sanchez, *Sympathy and Science: Women Physicians in American Medicine* (New York: Oxford University Press, 1985); and Leslie J. Reagan, *When Abortion Was a Crime: Women, Medicine, and Law in the United States, 1867–1973* (Berkeley: University of California Press, 1997).

80. Olcott, *Revolutionary Women in Postrevolutionary Mexico.*

81. Dr. Ulises Valdez to Lic. Francesco Vázquez Pérez, May 29, 1931, file 12, box 4, SJASS, Mexico City.

82. These tinctures can be purchased today in certain Mexican markets.

83. Pérez Montfort, "Los orígenes del narco."

84. Consul Henry C. A Damm, "Opium Poppy Planted in Northern Sonora," August 16, 1927, file 8, Manchuko, Mexico Special File, 1936, RG 170, Record of Drug Enforcement Administration and Bureau of Narcotics and Dangerous Drugs (hereafter DEA-BNDD), NAII.

85. Robert Chao Romero, *The Chinese in Mexico, 1882–1940* (Tucson: University of Arizona Press, 2010), 26–27.

86. Hyung-chan Kim, *A Legal History of Asian Americans, 1790–1990* (Westport, CT: Greenwood Press, 1994).

87. Chao Romero, *The Chinese in Mexico*, table 3.2. In 1926, Chinese were in every state; the largest populations were in Chihuahua, 1,037; Sonora, 3,758; Tamaulipas, 2,918; Veracruz, 1,908; Baja California, 5,889; Sinaloa, 2,019; and the Federal District, 1,062.

88. José Román Valez to secretario de gobernación, "Expulsión y quejas contra extranjeros," September 1930, 2.362.22, vol. 5, Dirección General de Gobierno, AGN.

89. Secretario general de Sindicato Nacional Pro-Raza to secretario de gobernación, August 20, 1926, "Expulsión y quejas contra extranjeros," 362.2 (721.1), 5, Dirección General de Gobierno, AGN.

90. Secretaría de Gobernación, *El servicio de migración de México* (Mexico City: Talleres Gráficos de la Nación, 1930), 36–38.

91. Campaña Anti-Chino, advertisement, "Expulsión y quejas contra extranjeros," vol. 5, Dirección General de Gobierno, AGN.

92. Hu-DeHart, "Coolies, Shopkeepers, and Pioneers"; and Chao Romero, *The Chinese in Mexico*, 43–45.

93. For a discussion of the use of popular culture to influence women to avoid interracial relationships, see Robert Chao Romero, "El destierro de los chinos: Popular

Perceptions of Chinese-Mexican Intermarriage in the Twentieth Century," *Aztlán* 32, no. 1 (Spring 2007): 113–44.

94. José Mendiola, secretario de Liga Nacional Pro-Raza, to Ministro de Gobernación, Campana Anti-Chino, January 14, 1927, file Manuel Chen, 362.2 (1–1), expulsión y quejas contra extranjeros, vol. 5, Dirección General de Gobierno, AGN.

95. Carstairs, *Jailed for Possession*, 32–33.

96. See Chao Romero, *The Chinese in Mexico*, 67–96.

97. The testimonies of wives were included in a number of cases in Expulsión y quejas contra extranjeros, Dirección General de Gobierno, AGN. All East Asian men in Mexico regardless of national origin were assumed to be Chinese.

98. M. M. Chen to secretario de gobernación, September 1930, 2.362.2 (24), Expulsión y quejas contra extranjeros, 5, Dirección General de Gobierno, AGN.

99. Carstairs, *Jailed for Possession*, 16–34.

100. Chao Romero, *The Chinese in Mexico*, 43–45.

101. Ibid., 136–41.

102. José Luís Trueba Lara, *Los chinos de Sonora: una historia olvidada* (Hermosillo: Instituto de Investigaciones Historicas, University of Sonora, 1990), 73; and Chao Romero, *The Chinese in Mexico*, 136–37.

103. J. Meza Terán, el jefe de los servicios confidenciales, to secretario de gobernación, July 19, 1929, vol. 14, box 17, Fondo Salubridad Pública, Sección Servicios Jurídicos, Archivo de Secretaría de Salud, Mexico City. Citizens' complaints connected the Chee Kung tong to opium dens and gambling in Sinaloa, but Meza Terán disputed these allegations. C. F. Ramirez to Plutarco Calle, April 10, 1928, Dirección General de Gobierno, Estupefacientes Drogas, vol. 2, file 24, AGN.

104. Ibid.

105. Ties between the police and organized crime is not a new phenomenon.

106. C. M. Goethe, "The Influx of Mexican Amerinds," *Eugenics: A Journal of Race Betterment* 1, no. 3 (December 1928): 6–9.

107. Francisco E. Balderrama and Raymond Rodríguez, *Decade of Betrayal: Mexican Repatriation in the 1930s* (Albuquerque: University of New Mexico Press, 2006).

108. See, for example "Weeds That Cause Insanity," *Washington Post*, June 15, 1914. Carlota (1840–1927) was the wife of Emperor Maximilian, who was executed by Mexican Republicans in 1867.

109. "Plants Cause Madness," *Washington Post*, May 9, 1913.

110. "Kills Six in Hospital: Mexican, Crazed by Marihuana, Runs Amuck With Butcher Knife," *New York Times*, February 21, 1925.

111. "Mexican Family Go Insane," *New York Times*, February 6, 1927.

112. "Mexico to Join US in Fight on Drugs" and "Mexico Bans Marihana," *New York Times*, December 29, 1925.

113. William O. Walker III, ed., *Drug Control Policy: Essays in Historical and Comparative Perspective* (University Park: Penn State University Press, 1992), 16–18.

114. Anslinger was not the only public official or criminologist to document reefer madness. See also Carleton Simon, *Plants That Incite to Crime* (New York: n.p., 1940).

115. Harry J. Anslinger, "Marijuana: Assassin of Youth," *American Magazine* 124, no. 1 (July 1937).

CHAPTER TWO

1. Marston, *María Full of Grace*.

2. Gootenberg, *Andean Cocaine*; and Paul Gootenberg, "'Blowback' Cocaine Commodity Chains and Historical Origins of the Mexican Drug Crisis, 1910–2010," World History Lecture, presented at St. John's University, October 15, 2012.

3. Images may be found in the Anslinger archive and in David Courtwright, *Forces of Habit: Drugs and the Making of the Modern World* (Cambridge, MA: Harvard University Press, 2001). More recently, a photograph circulated on the Internet of an elderly Mexican woman arrested with kilos of narcotics strapped to her thighs. The woman, who was well beyond seventy years of age, was photographed in her underwear and bra alongside police officers. In this case, humiliation rather than sexual titillation was the prime objective.

4. See Frances Heidensohn, *Women in Control?: The Role of Women in Law Enforcement* (Oxford: Clarendon Press, 1992); Susan Ehrlich Martin and Nancy C. Jurik, *Doing Justice, Doing Gender: Women in Legal and Criminal Justice Occupations* (Thousand Oaks, CA: Sage Publications, 2007); and Dorothy Moses Schulz, *Breaking the Brass Ceiling: Women Police Chiefs and Their Paths to the Top* (Westport, CT: Praeger, 2004).

5. In 1866, the U.S. Congress passed an act allowing women to be customs inspectors. Most of the first women in customs worked on the northern border between the United States and Canada in the Great Lakes region. Women also worked in customs in the western territories. The first female deputy collector on the U.S.-Mexico border was Mary C. Devine in Laredo, Texas. The first female customs guard at an international crossing was Daisy U. Holder in El Paso. U.S. Customs Today, at http://www.cbp.gov/cU.S.today/mar2000/womhist.htm, accessed December 12, 2009.

6. Tammy Anderson, "Dimensions of Women's Power in the Illicit Drug Economy," *Theoretical Criminology* 9, no. 4 (November 2005): 371–400. A good contemporary analysis can be found in the chapter "Why Do Drug Dealers Still Live with Their Moms," in Steven D. Levitt and Stephen J. Dubner, *Freakonomics: A Rogue Economist Explores the Secret Side of Everything* (New York: HarperCollins, 2005), 114–52.

7. Lisa Maher and Ric Curtis, "Women on the Edge of Crime: Crack Cocaine and the Changing Contexts of Street-Level Sex Work in New York City," *Crime, Law, and Social Change* 18, no. 2 (1992): 221–58.

8. Dunlap and Johnson, "Family and Human Resources."

9. See for example the television series *Breaking Bad*, Sony Pictures Television, 2008–2013.

10. Soderbergh, *Traffic*.

11. Howard Campbell, "Female Drug Smugglers on the U.S.-Mexico Border: Gender, Crime, and Empowerment," *Anthropological Quarterly* 81, no. 1 (Winter 2008): 235.

12. Howard Campbell, *Drug War Zone*, 60–75.

13. Tracy Wilkinson, "Mexico Under Siege: Women Play a Bigger Role in Mexico's Drug War," *Los Angeles Times*, November 10, 2009.

14. Studies that do exist include Barbara Denton and Pat O'Malley, "Gender, Trust, and Business: Women Drug Dealers in the Illicit Economy," *British Journal of Criminology* 39, no. 4 (1999): 513–60; James Inciardi, Anne Pottieger, and Charles Faupel, "Black Women, Heroin and Crime: Empirical Notes," *Journal of Drug Issues* 12 (1982): 241–50; James Inciardi, Dorothy Lockwood, and Anne Pottieger, *Women and Crack-Cocaine* (New York: Macmillan, 1993); and Maher and Curtis, "Women on the Edge of Crime."

15. Courtwright, *Dark Paradise*, 2–4, 142. For a detailed history of the Harrison Act, see Musto, *The American Disease*, 54–68. For a policy history of cocaine, see Spillane, *Cocaine*. For a global approach, see Paul Gootenberg, ed., *Cocaine: Global Histories* (New York: Routledge, 1999); and Gootenberg, *Andean Cocaine*. For a policy history of marijuana, see Rudolph Joseph Gerber, *Legalizing Marijuana: Drug Policy Reform and Prohibition Politics* (Westport, CT: Praeger, 2004). For studies on drug control in the Americas, see William Walker, *Drug Control in the Americas*; and William O. Walker III, ed., *Drugs in the Western Hemisphere: An Odyssey of Cultures in Conflict* (Wilmington, DE: Scholarly Resources, 1996).

16. *Webb et al. v. United States*, 239 U.S. 96 (1919); *United States v. Doremus*, 249 U.S. 86 (1919); and *Jin Fuey Moy v. United States*, 254 U.S. 189 (1920). All three cases dealt with medical doctors who, while they maintained records as required by the Harrison Act, wrote prescriptions for opiates to known users in violation of the Harrison Act.

17. Stephen R. Kandall, *Substance and Shadow: Women and Addiction in the United States* (Cambridge, MA: Harvard University Press, 1999); and Caroline Jean Acker, "Portrait of an Addicted Family: Dynamics of Opiate Addiction in the Early Twentieth Century," in *Altering American Consciousness: The History of Alcohol and Drug Use in the United States, 1800–2000*, ed. Sarah W. Tracy and Caroline Jean Acker (Amherst: University of Massachusetts Press, 2004), 165–81. For historical studies of addiction, see Abraham Myerson, *The Nervous Housewife* (1920; repr. New York: Arno Press, 1972); and Sara Graham-Mulhall, *Opium: The Demon Flower* (New York: H. Vinal, 1926). Graham-Mulhall served as New York City's first deputy state narcotic control commissioner.

18. See Edmond Congar Brown, attorney, to Franklin D. Roosevelt, February 22, 1913, and Charles B. Towns to Franklin D. Roosevelt, March 31, 1913, New York State Senator, box 8, FDR Library.

19. For personal letters regarding the use of heroin to treat asthma and other respiratory problems, see Franklin D. Roosevelt, New York State Senator, box 8, FDR Library.

20. George Pettey, "The Heroin Habit: Another Curse," *Alabama Medical Journal* 15 (1903): 174–80.

21. See Courtwright, *Dark Paradise*, 85–109; and Lawrence Kolb, *Drug Addiction: A Medical Problem* (Springfield, IL: Charles Thomas, 1962).

22. Historical studies about the U.S.-Mexico border inform current perceptions of it as a place of danger, violence, and vice since the time of the revolution. For diverse approaches, see Ana María Alonso, *Thread of Blood: Colonialism, Revolution, and Gender on Mexico's Northern Frontier* (Tucson: University of Arizona Press, 1995); David E. Lorey, *The U.S.-Mexican Border in the Twentieth Century: A History of Economic and Social Transformation* (Wilmington, DE: Scholarly Resources, 1999); Robin E. Robinson, "Vice and Tourism on the U.S.-Mexican Border: A Comparison of Three Communities in the Era of U.S. Prohibition" (PhD diss., Arizona State University, 2002); and Benjamin Heber Johnson, *Revolution in Texas: How a Forgotten Rebellion and Its Bloody Suppression Turned Mexicans into Americans* (New Haven, CT: Yale University Press, 2003).

23. W. D. Hornsday, "Bootleggers on the Border," *Los Angeles Times*, August 6, 1916.

24. Dean F. Markham, executive director of the President's Advisory Committee on Narcotics and Drug Abuse, 963, James Roosevelt Papers, Legislation Subject File, 1963, box 483, FDR Library.

25. For a historiographical study of the family, see Ann S. Blum, "Bring It Back Home: Perspectives on Gender and Family History in Modern Mexico," *History Compass* 4, no. 5 (2006): 906–26.

26. Initial works of scholarship to contemplate gendered constructs and differences in Latin America include Ann Pescatello, *Female and Male in Latin America: Essays* (Pittsburgh, PA: University of Pittsburgh Press, 1973); and Asunción Lavrin, *Latin American Women: Historical Perspectives* (Westport, CT: Greenwood Press, 1978). More contemporary literature reveals how women become public figures and how they interact with the state or other institutions. For the colonial period, scholars have examined constructs of honor and how men and women conform to or rebel against those constructs. See Ann Twinam, *Public Lives, Private Secrets: Gender, Honor, Sexuality, and Illegitimacy in Colonial Spanish America* (Stanford, CA: Stanford University Press, 1999); and Sonya Lipsett-Rivera and Lyman L. Johnson, eds., *The Faces of Honor: Sex, Shame, and Violence in Colonial Latin America* (Albuquerque: University of New Mexico Press, 1998). For the modern period, scholars have examined how women of diverse classes engage in public life. See Thomas M. Klubock, *Contested Communities: Class, Gender, and Politics in Chile's El Teniente Copper Mine, 1904–1948* (Durham, NC: Duke University Press, 1998); Karin A. Rosenblatt, *Gendered Compromises: Political Cultures and the State in Chile, 1920–1950* (Chapel Hill: University of North Carolina Press, 2000); Heidi Tinsman, *Partners in Conflict: The Politics of Gender, Sexuality, and Labor in the Chilean Agrarian Reform, 1950–1973* (Durham, NC: Duke University Press, 2002); and Elaine Carey,

Plaza of Sacrifices: Gender, Power, and Terror in 1968 Mexico (Albuquerque: University of New Mexico Press, 2005).

27. Mary Murphy, "Bootlegging Mothers and Drinking Daughters: Gender and Prohibition in Butte, Montana," *American Quarterly* 46 (June 1994): 174–94.

28. Tanya Marie Sanchez, "The Feminine Side of Bootlegging," *Journal of the Louisiana Historical Association* 41, no. 4 (2000): 403–33. For Russian women bootleggers, see Patricia Herlihy, *The Alcoholic Empire: Vodka and Politics in Late Imperial Russia* (New York: Oxford University Press, 2002), 90–111.

29. José M. Alamillo, *Making Lemonade out of Lemons: Mexican American Labor and Leisure in a California Town, 1880–1960* (Urbana: University of Illinois Press, 2006), 57–78; Julia Kirk Blackwelder, *Women of the Depression: Caste and Culture in San Antonio, 1929–1939* (College Station: Texas A&M University Press, 1984), 166–67; and Diane C. Vecchio, *Merchants, Midwives, and Laboring Women: Italian Migrants in Urban America* (Urbana: University of Illinois Press, 2006), 71.

30. Giovanni Ferrucci, *Bootlegger* (New York: Independent Publishing Company, 1932), iv.

31. See Alamillo, *Making Lemonade out of Lemons*, 72; and George Díaz, "Twilight of the Tequileros: Prohibition-Era Smuggling in the South Texas Borderlands, 1919–1933," in *Smugglers, Brothels, and Twine*, ed. Carey and Marak, 59–79. For a novelistic account of bootlegging and socioeconomic advancement along the border and in California, see Victor Villaseñor, *Rain of Gold* (Houston, TX: Arte Publico Press, 1991).

32. Much has been written about the business of organized crime. For example, see Tom Behan, *The Camorra: Political Criminality in Italy* (New York: Routledge, 1996); Anton Blok, *The Mafia of a Sicilian Village, 1860–1960: A Study of Violent Peasant Entrepreneurs* (New York: Harper and Row, 1974); Rich Cohen, *Tough Jews: Fathers, Sons, and Gangster Dreams* (New York: Simon and Schuster, 1998); Steven Erie, *Rainbow's End: Irish-Americans and the Dilemmas of Urban Machine Politics, 1840–1985* (Berkeley: University of California Press, 1988); and Diego Gambetta, *The Sicilian Mafia: The Business of Private Protection* (Cambridge, MA: Harvard University Press, 1993).

33. Díaz, "Twilight of the Tequileros."

34. "A Informe sobre cajas de alcohol," Archivo Histórico "Genero Estrada" 627, exp. 22, AHSRE, 523.16/41. The Mexican embassy was one of many foreign missions in the United States that held that Prohibition did not apply to their buildings and property on U.S. soil.

35. "Capital Jury Indicts 'Man in the Green Hat,'" *New York Times*, December 18, 1929; "'Dry' Agents Search for Congress Liquor as Alleged Capitol Bootlegger is Arraigned," *New York Times*, March 26, 1926; "Sleuth Was Sent to Catch Senate Bootlegger; Curtis 'Approved' Watch on Office Building," *New York Times*, November 1, 1930.

36. Even today, street vending yields greater profits than working, for example, in a factory job. See John C. Cross, *Informal Politics: Street Vendors and the State in*

Mexico City (Stanford, CA: Stanford University Press, 1998). Cross argues that a street vendor in the late 1990s could earn over $2,000 dollars a month in the informal market. Many professionals in Mexico City in the 1990s earned far less than that.

37. John J. Rumbarger, *Profits, Power, and Prohibition: Alcohol Reform and the Industrializing of America, 1800–1930* (Albany: State University of New York Press, 1989).

38. The Blaine Act passed on February 17, 1933, ending Prohibition in the United States.

39. "Traffic of Opium and Other Noxious Drugs," résumé for the Mexican delegation at the League of Nations, by Dr. Leopoldo Salazar Viniegra, 1938. Salazar wrote: "In respect to the traffic in opium, it can be briefly said that in our country it has two aspects: Those who promote and encourage the use of drugs by our inhabitants, and that which is destined for the United States coming through our country merely in transit."

40. William O. Walker III, "Control Across the Border: The United States, Mexico, and Narcotics Policy, 1936–1940," *Pacific Historical Review* 47, no. 1 (February 1978): 93.

41. Ethan Nadelmann, *Cops Across Borders: The Internationalization of U.S. Criminal Law Enforcement* (University Park: Penn State University Press, 1993), 105. For a discussion of the contemporary exchange of information as well as DEA activities in Mexico, see María Celia Toro, "The Internationalization of Police: The DEA in Mexico," *Journal of American History* 86, no. 2 (September 1999): 623–40. For a discussion of Mexican and U.S. enforcement in the 1920s and 1930s, see William Walker, "Control Across the Border."

42. For an international focus on policing, see Andreas and Nadelmann, *Policing the Globe.*

43. Much of the recent literature on drug trafficking focuses on security issues; see Tony Payan, *The Three U.S.-Mexico Border Wars: Drugs, Immigration, and Homeland Security* (Westport, CT: Praeger Security International, 2006); and Peter Andreas, *Border Games: Policing the U.S.-Mexico Divide* (Ithaca, NY: Cornell University Press, 2006). Journalists have continued to question the U.S. war on drugs. See Elaine Shannon, *Desperados: Latin Drug Lords, U.S. Lawmen, and the War America Can't Win* (New York: Viking Press, 1988); Sebastian Rotella, *Twilight on the Line: Underworlds and Politics at the U.S.-Mexico Border* (New York: W. W. Norton, 1988); and Charles Bowden, *Down by the River: Drugs, Money, Murder, and Family* (New York: Simon and Schuster, 2002). Mexican journalistic approaches include María Idalia Gómez and Darío Fritz, *Con la muerte en el bolsillo: seis desaforadas historias del narcotráfico en México* (Mexico City: Planeta, 2005), which documents the different cartels and individuals operating in Mexico; and Jesús Blancornelas, *El Cártel* (Mexico City: Random House, 2002), which focuses on the rise of the Arellano Félix family as it emerged as one of the most powerful organized crime families in the country. Ricardo

Ravelo has written a number of books on those involved in drug trafficking in Mexico: *Los capos: las narco-rutas de México* (Mexico City: Plaza y Janés, 2005); *Los narcoabogados* (Mexico City: Grijalbo 2007); and, in light of the escalated drug war, *Herencia maldita: el reto de Calderón y el nuevo mapa de narcotráfico* (Mexico City: Grijalbo, 2007).

44. As noted in chapter 1, Harry J. Anslinger directed the Federal Bureau of Narcotics for thirty-two years. The FBN became the Bureau of Narcotics and Dangerous Drugs in 1968 under the U.S. Justice Department. In 1973, the BNDD was reorganized into the Drug Enforcement Administration.

45. "Luisa Primero Mendoza," file 1244, Dirección General de Servicios Coordinados de Prevención and Readaptación Social, AGN.

46. Class distinctions over perceptions of crime have been well documented; see Piccato, *City of Suspects*, 132–37. Much of the crime involves banditry; see Vanderwood, *Disorder and Progress*.

47. "Anastasia Serna Mendoza la viuda de Mendoza," vol. 361, exp. 498, folio 11, Dirección General de Servicios Coordinados de Prevención y Readaptación Social, AGN.

48. "Eloisa Cárdenas Benavides de Guerra," vol. 354, exp. 128, Dirección General de Servicios Coordinados de Prevención y Readaptación Social, AGN.

49. "Natalía Ortíz Ramos la viuda de Cerda," vol. 361, exp. 507, Dirección General de Servicios Coordinados de Prevención y Readaptación Social, AGN.

50. "Manuela Ortíz Rodríguez de Caballeros," vol. 354, exp. 903, Dirección General de Servicios Coordinados de Prevención y Readaptación Social, AGN.

51. "Carmen Cantú de Garza," vol. 354, exp. 235, Dirección General de Servicios Coordinados de Prevención y Readaptación Social, AGN.

52. "Raquel Katz de Frenkel," vol. 359, exp. 376, Dirección General de Servicios Coordinados de Prevención y Readaptación Social, AGN.

53. "Emilia Fabris Guica," vol. 357, exp. 228, Dirección General de Servicios Coordinados de Prevención y Readaptación Social, AGN.

54. "Soledad González Sandoval," vol. 359, exp. 383, Dirección General de Servicios Coordinados de Prevención y Readaptación Social, AGN.

55. "Daniel Curiel Rodríguez," vol. 356, exp. 144, Dirección General de Servicios Coordinados de Prevención y Readaptación Social, AGN.

56. See Elliott Young, *Catarino Garza's Revolution on the Texas-Mexico Border* (Durham, NC: Duke University Press, 2004); and B. Carmon Hardy and Melody Seymour, "Importation of Arms and the 1912 Mormon 'Exodus' from Mexico," *New Mexico Historical Review* 72, no. 4 (October 1997): 297–318.

57. Elizabeth Salas, *Soldaderas in the Mexican Military: Myth and History* (Austin: University of Texas Press, 1990), 53–54.

58. Steven Topik, Carlos Marichal, and Zephyr Frank, eds., *From Silver to Cocaine: Latin American Commodity Chains and the Building of the World Economy, 1500–2000* (Durham, NC: Duke University Press, 2006). During the 1920s and 1930s, many popular magazines in Mexico focused on the smuggling and at times

glorified the Border Patrol. See Frederick Simpich, "Along Our Side of the Mexican Border," *National Geographic* 38, no. 1 (1920): 61–80; "The Border Patrol," *Popular Science Monthly* (June 1928): 933–35; and "Border Guard Wages War on Smugglers," *Popular Science Monthly* (November 1934): 26–28.

59. It is difficult to tell what happened to the confiscated merchandise.

60. "Guadalupe Navarro de Cons," vol. 359, exp. 327, Dirección General de Servicios Coordinados de Prevención y Readaptación Social, AGN.

61. "Ola McDonald," vol. 361, exp. 465, Dirección General de Servicios Coordinados de Prevención y Readaptación Social, AGN.

62. See also "Lauren O. Scott," vol. 361, exp. 475, Dirección General de Servicios Coordinados de Prevención y Readaptación Social, AGN.

63. "Guadalupe Chavez," vol. 361, exp. 466, Dirección General de Servicios Coordinados de Prevención y Readaptación Social, AGN.

64. "Winnifred Chapman, C. & N. D. Act, Vancouver BC," report by C. J. Harwood, file 21, correspondence, box 2, Anslinger archive, Penn State University Special Collections.

65. Ibid.

66. Ibid.

67. Bureau of Social Hygiene, series 3, box 1, folder 105, Rockefeller Archive Center (hereafter RAC), Tarrytown, New York.

68. This was a highly sensational case due to the involvement of the police with organized crime. Rosenthal had gone public with the fact that Becker was extorting from his bookmaking business. In response, Becker hired Rosenberg, Harry "Gyp the Blood" Horowitz, and other members of the Lenox Ave Gang to take care of Rosenthal. At the time of their capture, they were photographed in the police station. See "Gyp and Lefty Caught at Last Here in Town," *New York Times*, September 15, 1912. Also see their trial transcripts, *New York Supreme Court v. Whitey Jack, Dago Frank, Frank Cirofisi, Howard Horowitz, Frank Muller, Louis Rosenberg*, 10/07/1912, trial 3200, reels 387–388; and mug shot of Louis Rosenberg, Lewis Lawes Collection, at http://dig.lib.jjay.cuny.edu /Greenstone/collect/newcrime/index/assoc/HASH828d.dir/1100051a.jpg, Lloyd Sealy Library, John Jay College of Criminal Justice, New York (hereafter LSL). Rosenberg, Horowitz, and Becker were executed in 1915.

69. Bureau of Social Hygiene, series 3, box 1, folder 105, Rockefeller Archive, Tarrytown, New York.

70. The term "moll" refers to prostitutes who were associated with male criminals. Early studies on such women were highly sensational and moralistic in tone. See Otto Pollak, *The Criminality of Women* (Philadelphia: University of Pennsylvania Press, 1950); and Otto Pollak and Alfred Friedman, eds., *Family Dynamics and Female Sexual Delinquency* (Palo Alto, CA: Science and Behavior Books, 1969).

71. This continues to be a common practice today. Anthropologist Patricia Tovar has noted a similar trend among Colombian women who work in the drug business that echoes what Campbell described in Ciudad Juárez and El Paso. Tovar argues

that, like women who followed male guerrilla fighters for love, women in the drug industry also may begin their careers as mules and carriers of drugs for men in their families or lovers. Conversation with Patricia Tovar, May 13, 2009, John Jay College of Criminal Justice, New York.

72. H. J. Anslinger, "Notice to District Supervisors and Others Concerned, attached is Amelia B. de G. to Immigration Office, San Isidro CA," Censorship Office of the United States, "Mexican Border Resident Reveals Names of Persons Alleged to Be Smuggling Drugs into the U.S," folder Mexico no. 4, 1944, RG 170, BNDD–DEA, NAII.

73. "Josefina Lara Paredes," vol. 1059, exp. 1560, Dirección General de Servicios Coordinados de Prevención y Readaptación Social, AGN.

74. Ibid.

75. "María Albina Flores," vol. 1053, exp. 455, Dirección General de Servicios Coordinados de Prevención y Readaptación Social, AGN.

76. "Queria meter droga a la prison militar," *El Nacional*, February 23, 1940, DEA-BNDD.

77. "C. Zepeda Morantes," vol. 4, exp. 8, Estupefaciantes Drogas, Dirección General de Gobierno, AGN.

78. Dr. José Siroub, "The Struggle Against Toxicomanlas," *Pacific Coast International* (November–December 1939): 19–25.

79. Alvin F. Scharff, U.S. Customs agent, memorandum for Consul General James B. Stewart concerning conversation with LSV, file Leopoldo Salazar Viniegra, RG 170, DEA-BNDD.

80. Scharff maintained a close relationship with José Siroub, minister of public health, and Ignacio Téllez, attorney general of Mexico, during the early and mid-1930s.

81. "Traficante de drogas sorprendido," *El Nacional*, January 20, 1940.

82. *People of New York v. Lulu Hammond*, February 2, 1914, no. 1828, reel 231, Crime in New York, 1850–1950, LSL.

83. Walter C. Smith File, Anslinger archive, Penn State University Special Collections.

84. See Howard Abadinsky, *Organized Crime* (Chicago, IL: Nelson Hall, 1985), 13; and Donald Cressey, *Theft of the Nation: The Structure and Operations of Organized Crime in America* (New York: Harper and Row, 1969), 175–76.

85. Eloise Dunlap, Bruce Johnson, and Lisa Maher, "Female Crack Sellers in New York City: Who They Are and What They Do," *Women and Criminal Justice* 8, no. 4 (1997): 25–55.

86. Terry R. Furst, Richard Curtis, Bruce Johnson, and Douglas S. Goldsmith, "The Rise of the Middleman/Woman in a Declining Drug Market," *Addiction Research* 7, no. 2 (1999): 103–28.

87. "La Esposa de Uriquijo y Pascual Miravete, presos, son traficantes de drogas," James B. Stewart, American Consul General, to Secretary of State, February 28, 1940, translated new clippings, RG, 170, DEA-BNDD, NAII.

88. Dai, *Opium Addiction in Chicago*, 44–46.

89. "A Marijuana Addict Is Injured," *Excélsior*, December 24, 1939.

90. Nancy Campbell, *Using Women*, 71.

91. H. J. Anslinger to Francisco Vásquez Pérez, November 16, 1934, file 20, box 39, SJASS, Mexico City.

92. Loeffelholz-Brandstatter's name also appeared in the documents and newspapers as Loefelholz-Brandstaner and Lefenholtz Branstatter.

93. See Garland Roark, *The Coin of Contraband: The True Story of United States Customs Investigator Al Scharff* (Garden City, NY: Doubleday, 1964), 326. Scharff, a smuggler turned customs agent, worked closely with Roark on this biography.

94. H. J. Anslinger to Francisco Vásquez Pérez, October 1934, file 20, box 39, SJASS.

95. To H. J. Anslinger, 1934, file 20, box 39, SJASS.

96. The MV *Heiyo Maru* routinely appeared in the files of the Federal Bureau of Narcotics as a drug-transporting vessel in the 1930s. The ship's reputation may have contributed to a closer inspection of its passengers.

97. "Questioned in Smuggling," *Los Angeles Times*, August 8, 1936.

98. Daniel Bailey, customs agent in charge, Intelligence Bulletin, report 9, September 26, 1936, Henry Morgenthau Papers, FDR Library. Wurthmueller's name also appears as Wirthmueller.

99. Ibid.

100. *United States v. Maria Wendt*, statement of Maria Wendt taken at Los Angeles Hospital, Los Angeles, California, December 1936, RG 21, Record of the United States District Courts, Criminal Case Files, box 738, file 12845 (hereafter Maria Wendt testimony). "Jews in Shanghai," audio tapes, Dorot Jewish Division, Stephen A. Schwarzman Building, New York Public Library. The expatriate Jewish community in Shanghai emerged after the Bolshevik Revolution in Russia. By the 1930s, newly arrived Jews from various origins argued that the Russian Jews who had preceded them had an agreement with the Japanese, who by then had occupied Shanghai, allowing them to maintain their businesses. According to German, Polish, and Austrian Jews, the older Russian Jewish community was composed of wealthy business owners.

101. Maria Wendt testimony.

102. Ibid.

103. Memorandum of Conference in Secretary's Office, August 12, 1936, Morgenthau Diary, FDR Library. See also "Net Closes in Dope Hunt," *Los Angeles Times*, August 11, 1936.

104. *United States v. Maria Wendt*, Reporter's Transcript of Proceedings.

105. Ibid.

106. Maria Wendt testimony.

107. Memorandum of Conference in Secretary's Office, August 12, 1936, Morgenthau Diary, FDR Library.

108. "Net Closes in Dope Hunt," *Los Angeles Times*, August 11, 1936.

109. Scharff asked novelist Garland Roark to write his biography when Scharff came to investigate a screenplay that Roark was researching. Roark had written a number of novels that were adapted to the screen, with John Wayne playing lead roles.

With Roark, Scharff formed a company, Al Scharff, Inc., hoping that his biography, *The Coin of Contraband*, would end up on the screen. That didn't happen, and the company was disbanded when it looked as though the book would never be optioned. Garland Roark Papers, East Texas Research Center, Stephen F. Austin State University, Nacogdoches, Texas; and ongoing conversations with Harrison Reiner, 2010–2013.

110. Philip Nichols Jr., preface to Roark, *The Coin of Contraband*, xix.

111. See Friedrich Katz, *The Secret War in Mexico: Europe, the United States, and the Mexican Revolution* (Chicago, IL: University of Chicago Press, 1984); and Charles H. Harris and Louis R. Sadler, *The Secret War in El Paso: Mexican Revolutionary Intrigue, 1906–1920* (Albuquerque: University of New Mexico Press, 2009).

112. Douglas Valentine, *The Strength of the Wolf: The Secret History of America's War on Drugs* (London: Verso, 2004), 25.

113. Gene Fowler and Bill Crawford, *Border Radio: Quacks, Yodelers, Pitchmen, Psychics, and Other Amazing Broadcasters of the American Airwaves* (Austin: University of Texas Press, 2002), 199–200.

114. Gary Cartwright, *Galveston: A History of the Island* (Forth Worth: Texas Christian University Press, 1998), 210–11.

115. Valentine, *The Strength of the Wolf*, 24.

116. Al Scharff, deposition, Departamento de Salubridad Pública, Fondo Lázaro Cárdenas, exp 22, September 21, 1936, AGN.

117. José Siroud to the President of Mexico, Fondo Lázaro Cárdenas, exp. 422, October 30, 1936, AGN.

118. Due to the Chinese Exclusion Act, Wendt could not remain in the United States; however, like all Chinese in transit, she could disembark in the United States and take a train or another ship to Mexico. For a discussion of the Chinese and Mexico, see Robert Chao Romero, "Chinese Immigrant Smuggling to the United States via Mexico and Cuba," in *Smugglers, Brothels, and Twine*, ed. Carey and Marak, 13–23.

119. "Wendt Girl Tells Dash," *Los Angeles Times*, August 19, 1936.

120. The *Heiyo Maru* was built in 1930 for the NYK Line. The vessel's ports of call in 1936 were listed as "Hong Kong, Moji via Japan, Ports Honolulu, Hilo, San Francisco, Los Angeles, Manzanillo, La Libertad, Balboa, Buona Venture, Callao, Piso, Mollendo, Iquique, and Valparaiso." "N.Y.K. Line," *Straits Times* (Singapore), January 13, 1936.

121. "Smuggler Pursuit Ended by Suicide," *New York Times*, September 5, 1936.

122. "Dope Case Up Today," *Los Angeles Times*, August 24, 1936.

123. "Fete in Nanking Is Staged by Japan," *New York Times*, March 29, 1938.

124. "Accused in Narcotic Plot," *New York Times*, August 30, 1936.

125. "Smuggler Pursuit Ended by Suicide," *New York Times*, September 5, 1936.

126. Kenney, *From Pablo to Osama*; and Moisés Naím, *Illicit: How Smugglers, Traffickers, and Copycats Are Hijacking the Global Economy* (New York: Anchor Books, 2005).

127. Abraham and Van Schendel, "Introduction: The Making of Illicitness," 14.

128. Ibid., 15.

129. For a brief discussion of the Wendt case, see Valentine *The Strength of the Wolf,* 23–24. Robert Stevenson, *To the Ends of the Earth,* Columbia Pictures, 1948.

130. To view the trailer and a brief clip of *To the Ends of the Earth,* see http://www.tcm .com/tcmdb/title/3733/To-the-Ends-of-the-Earth/, accessed November 4, 2013.

CHAPTER THREE

Note to Title: A version of this article was previously published as "'Selling Is More of a Habit Than Using': Narcotraficante Lola la Chata and Her Threat to Civilization, 1930–1960," *Journal of Women's History* 21, no. 2 (Summer 2009). The "white lady" reference comes from a published open letter written by Dr. Leopoldo Salazar to Lola la Chata, James B. Stewart, American Consul General to Secretary of State," Head of Narcotics writes open letter to Lola la Chata," box 22, RG 170, DEA-BNDD.

1. S. C. Peña, special employee to the commissioner of customs, July 7, 1945, Drug Enforcement Administration, Subject Files of the Bureau of Narcotics and Dangerous Drugs, 1916–1970, box 161, RG 170, DEA-BNDD.

2. The history of crime and women as an academic topic has developed in the past fifteen years. In many of these pioneering works, it has been observed that when female offenders—whether prostitutes, street vendors, or violent criminals—are perceived as not absorbing the cost of their deviance, their actions constitute a disproportionate threat to themselves, to other people, and to their nation. For example, see Bliss, *Compromised Positions;* Buffington, *Criminal and Citizen in Modern Mexico;* Nancy Campbell, *Using Women;* Donna Guy, *White Slavery and Mothers Alive and Dead: The Troubled Meeting of Sex, Gender, Public Health, and Progress in Latin America* (Lincoln: University of Nebraska Press, 2000); and Judith Walkowitz, *City of Dreadful Delight: Narratives of Sexual Danger in Late-Victorian London* (Chicago, IL: University of Chicago Press, 1992).

3. Marston, *María Full of Grace;* Arturo Pérez-Reverte, *The Queen of the South,* trans. Andrew Hurley (New York: Putnam, 2004; originally published as *La reina del sur,* Madrid: Alfaguara, 2002). The arrest of Sandra Ávila Beltrán, "la reina del Pacífico," and the death of "la güera polvos," Rosa Emma Carvajal Ontiversos, in 2007 reveal that the facts are ever closer to fiction. See "Por narco, capturan a la llamada Reina del Pacífico," *La Jornada,* September 29, 2007.

4. The production and distribution of alcohol and narcotics has long been an economic activity that is shared by men and women. See, for instance, Astorga, *Drogas sin fronteras;* Gootenberg, ed., *Cocaine;* and George Peter Murdock, *Social Structure* (New York: Macmillan, 1949).

5. For a discussion of the reasons for feminine addiction in the United States in the 1930s, see E. Mebane Hunt, executive secretary, Women's Prison Association of

New York, "The Experience of the Women's Prison Association with Women Drug Addicts," paper presented at the American Prison Congress, October 5, 1938, box 42, File Female Addicts, DEA-BNDD. For a discussion of feminine addiction and behavior in Mexican prisons, see H. J. Anslinger, commissioner of narcotics, to James Bennett, attachment "Letter to the President from the prisoners of the penitentiary, Mexico City," May 18, 1948, Drug Enforcement, box 23, DEA-BNDD. For a contemporary discussion of women falling prey to the vices of narcotrafficking, see Gabriela Vázquez, "La población feminina, escudo de narcotraficante," *La Jornada*, March 25, 2002; and Margath A. Walker, "Guada-narco-lupe, Maquilarañas, and the Discursive Construction of Gender and Difference on the U.S.-Mexico Border in Mexican Media Representations," *Gender, Place, and Culture* 12 (March 2005): 95–110.

6. Judith Butler, *Gender Trouble: Feminism and the Subversion of Identity* (New York: Routledge, 1999).

7. See Nancy Folbre, *Why Pay for Kids? Gender and the Structure of Constraint* (New York: Routledge, 1994). For a discussion of women's addiction as a threat to U.S. civilization and "structure of constraint," see Nancy Campbell, *Using Women*. The concept of constraint and restraint within the bourgeois class in Mexico and its support of the creation of working-class "family values" may be found in Mary Kay Vaughan, *The State, Education, and Social Class in Mexico, 1880–1928* (DeKalb: Northern Illinois University Press, 1982); and William French, "Prostitutes and Guardian Angels: Women, Work, and the Family in Porfirian Mexico," *Hispanic American Historical Review* 72, no. 4 (1992): 529–53. In 1933, the Academia Mexicana de Ciencias Penales published *Criminalia*, which reflected a growing concern over crime and policy.

8. For a discussion of the FBN's agents in Mexico, see William Walker, "Control Across the Border," 92–93. See also Josephus Daniels's autobiography, *Shirt-Sleeve Diplomat* (Chapel Hill: University of North Carolina Press, 1947). Daniels was the U.S. ambassador to Mexico in the 1930s.

9. Biographical material on la Chata is available in Jorge Robles García, *La bala perdida: William S. Burroughs en México, 1949–1952* (Mexico City: Milenio, 1995); and Michael Spann, *William S. Burroughs' Unforgettable Characters: Lola la Chata and Bernabé Jurado* (Providence, RI: Inkblot Publications, 2013). Leopoldo Salazar Viniegra, "Open Letter to Lola la Chata," box 22, DEA-BNDD.

10. Piccato, *City of Suspects*, 30.

11. For a study of La Merced, see Enrique Valencia, *La Merced: estudio ecológico y social de una zona de la ciudad de México* (Mexico City: Instituto Nacional de Antropología e Historia, 1965). Valencia noted that as the commercial activity grew, so too did the criminal element. The increasing markets also brought *pulgerías, piqueras* (illegal alcohol vendors), cantinas, billiard halls, cabarets, and "hoteles de paso" that offered prostitutes (92).

12. Peter Landesman, "The Girls Next Door," *New York Times Magazine*, January 25, 2004. Landesman's article covered contemporary human trafficking in La Merced.

13. Market scene in Mexico City, circa 1920, photo 73001, Casaola, Fototeca, Pachuga Hidalgo, reprinted in Ricardo Pérez Montfort, *Yerba, goma, y polvo: Drogas, ambientes, y policía en México, 1900–1940* (Mexico City: Ediciones Era, 1999), 31.

14. Mule in Mexico City, circa 1920, photo 70646, Casaola, Fototeca, Pachuga Hidalgo, reprinted in Pérez Montfort, *Yerba, goma, y polvo*, 27.

15. U.S. Consulate, Nuevo Laredo, to Treasury Department, translation of "Inducía su hijo a vender drogas," *La Prensa*, December 22, 1939, box 22, DEA-BNDD. Margarito Oliva was arrested for selling marijuana. His son was also turned in by one of his schoolmates for selling marijuana cigarettes at school. C. E. Terry, Report on Field Studies to the Committee of Drug Addiction, December 1926, folder 555, box 1, series 4, Bureau of Social Hygiene Records, RAC. This study examined six cities in the United States, including El Paso, the only city examined that reported high rates of addiction and peddling among schoolchildren. The study's author associated this disturbing trend with Mexicans in El Paso. Interestingly, the study also showed that the adult Mexican population in El Paso had lower rates of addiction compared to adult Anglos.

16. For a discussion of familial connections, see Dunlap, Stürzenhofecker, and Johnson, "The Elusive Romance of Motherhood," 1–27; Denton, *Dealing*; Dunlap and Johnson, "Family and Human Resources," 175–98; and Adler, *Wheeling and Dealing*.

17. Roumagnac, *Los criminales en México*, contains reports on children's addiction in Mexico.

18. Carey and Cisneros Guzmán, "The Daughters of La Nacha," 23–24. In the interviews, contemporary drug peddlers described marrying the suppliers of their mothers, who also sold.

19. Astorga, *Drogas sin fronteras*; and Nicole Mottier, "Organized Crime, Political Corruption, and Powerful Governments: Drug Gangs in Ciudad Juárez, 1928–1933" (master's thesis, Oxford University, 2004). There is little information on who Lola la Chata had contact with in Ciudad Juárez.

20. Attorney general of the republic to commissioner of narcotics, Treasury Department, January 22, 1962, box 161, DEA-BNDD. This document disclosed the arrests of one of her daughters as well as her nieces.

21. Recio, "Drugs and Alcohol," 21–42.

22. Hearings before the Committee on Ways and Means, House of Representatives, Seventy-First Congress, HR 10561, March 7–8, 1930 (Washington, D.C.: Government Printing Office, 1930). The urgency of the problem is illustrated by an attached map of the United States representing the "Estimated Average Drug Addiction Among Violations of the Harrison Narcotic Law (1922–1928)." See also William Walker, *Drug Control in the Americas*.

23. Douglas Clark Kinder and William O. Walker III, "Stable Force in a Storm: Harry J. Anslinger and United States Narcotic Foreign Policy, 1930–1962," *Journal of American History* 72, no. 4 (March 1986): 919.

24. Information regarding Anslinger, Morgenthau Diary, FDR Archive. Anslinger's phrase is famous and has been widely quoted. See Michael Woodiwiss, *Organized Crime and American Power: A History* (Toronto: University of Toronto Press, 2001), 242; and John C. McWilliams, *The Protectors: Harry J. Anslinger and the Federal Bureau of Narcotics, 1930–1962* (Newark: University of Delaware Press, 1990).

25. Anslinger and Tompkins, *The Traffic in Narcotics*, 257. Anslinger and Tompkins argued that there were 150,000 to 200,000 narcotics addicts in the United States prior to 1914, most of them women.

26. Ibid., 152–53. Diarte was later killed by his associates. Anslinger describes the arrests that followed as one of the biggest drug busts in Mexico to that date.

27. William Walker, "Control Across the Border," 201–16.

28. Consul Henry C. A. Damm, Opium Poppy Planted in Northern Sonora, August 16, 1927, RG 170, DEA-BNDD. In 1927, Damm wrote that he received information from U.S. informants living in Mexico about the Chinese in Sonora. He stated: "The large Chinese population on the Mexican West Coast would undoubtedly offer a market for a large quantity of opium produced, but this consulate has not heard of any attempts to smuggle the drug of Sonora origin into the United States directly across the border." See also H. S. Creighton to the Commissioner of Customs, Treasury Department, United States Custom Service, Houston, December 11, 1940; and translation of an editorial in *El Centinela*, a weekly tabloid in Ciudad Juárez, titled "El escandalo del robo a los Chinos," December 1, 1940, box 22, DEA-BNDD.

29. Benedict Anderson, *Imagined Communities: Reflections on the Origin and Spread of Nationalism* (London: Verso Press, 1991). For a discussion in Spanish of the Chinese in Mexico, see Gómez Izquierdo, *El movimiento anti-chino en México*; Trueba Lara, *Los chinos de Sonora*; and Humberto Monteón González and José Luis Trueba Lara, *Chinos y antichinos en México: documentos para su estudio* (Guadalajara: Gobierno de Jalisco, 1988).

30. Guerrero, *La génesis del crimen en México*; and Roumagnac, *Los criminales en México*.

31. Leopoldo Salazar Viniegra, "El mito de la marijuana," *Criminalia* (December 1938): 206–37.

32. Ibid. In 1931, the Mexican government amended the Federal Penal Code to make the use, buying, and selling of drugs a criminal offense (currently Article 195). For an extensive discussion of the 1930s, see Astorga, *El siglo de las drogas*, 43–60.

33. League of Nations, Advisory Committee on Traffic in Opium and Other Dangerous Drugs, Twenty-Fourth Session, June 2, 1939, box 22, RG 170, DEA-BNDD; Daniel Bailey, customs agent in charge, *Intelligence Bulletin*, no. 8, September 19, 1936, and *Intelligence Bulletin*, no. 9, September 26, 1936, Henry Morgenthau Correspondence, box 206, FDR Library.

34. In studies of drug dealers and traffickers, Patricia A. Adler argues that the most successful traffickers create distance between themselves and the actual sale. Moreover, they avoid unwanted attention that may jeopardize the enterprise. Adler, *Wheeling and Dealing*.

35. Denton, *Dealing*. In Denton's research, la Chata fits the profile of women who grow up in the trade and then forge alliances with men in the business.

36. *La Prensa*, May 1937. The newspaper *La Prensa* published a series of exposés about the federal judicial police, the attorney general, and the narcotics police involvement in the distribution of heroin for Lola la Chata. The articles in *La Prensa* connected her to high levels in the Department of Health and to judges and customs agents. Other arrests of traffickers in the 1940s exposed the ties of police and government officials to traffickers. James B. Stewart, American consul general, to Secretary of State, February 28, 1940, clippings of newspaper articles, "Funcionarios en fabuloso trafico de drogas," *Excélsior*, December 7, 1940; and "Es tremendo el trafico de drogas," *Excélsior*, December 8, 1940, box 22, RG 170, DEA-BNDD.

37. Denton, *Dealing*, 32.

38. Susan Strange, *The Retreat of the State: The Diffusion of Power in the World Economy* (Cambridge: Cambridge University Press, 1996), 91–99.

39. See José Carlos Cisneros Guzmán, "Las tres jefas," in *Las jefas del narco: el ascenso de las mujeres en crimen organizado*, ed. Arturo Santamaría Gómez (Mexico City: Grijalbo, 2012), 125–38. See also Carey and Cisneros Guzmán, "The Daughters of La Nacha."

40. Gabriela Cano, "Unconceivable Realities of Desire: Amelia Robles's (Transgender) Masculinity in the Mexican Revolution," in *Sex in Revolution: Gender, Politics, and Power in Modern Mexico*, ed. Jocelyn Olcott, Mary Kay Vaughan, and Gabriela Cano (Durham: Duke University Press, 2006), 35–56.

41. Javier Piña y Palacios, *La colonia penal de las Islas Marías: su historia, organización y régimen* (Mexico City: Ediciones Botas, 1970). Female Cristeros were the first women imprisoned on Islas Marías. Ernestina Vanegas, "Vivimos en la cárcel con Papa," in *La colonia penal de las Islas Marías*, ed. Piña y Palacios, 97–102 Vanegas, the daughter of a prisoner who had killed his wife, describes the routine of prisoners and their families in 1958. Vanegas's life spanned the time that la Chata was in Islas Marías.

42. George White to H. J. Anslinger, newspaper clipping, "Blow to Narcotic Traffic," box 22, DEA-BNDD.

43. Ibid.

44. For a discussion of the complications of "proletarian virtue" in Latin America, see Klubock, *Contested Communities*; Rosemblatt, *Gendered Compromises*; and Tinsman, *Partners in Conflict*.

45. "Criminal History of the Beland Family," box 42, file "Female Addicts," RG 170, DEA-BNDD. The Belands were a Texas family of addicts and sellers whose arrests for possession and distribution of narcotics extended from the 1910s to the 1960s.

46. Texas Department of Health, *Texas Death Indexes, 1903–2000* (Austin: Texas Department of Health, State Vital Statistics Unit), at http://search.ancestry library.com, accessed July 17, 2012.

47. Federal Bureau of Narcotics, *Traffic in Opium and Other Dangerous Drugs* (Washington, D.C.: Government Printing Office, 1942).

48. Department of the Treasury, "Traffic in Opium and Other Dangerous Drugs" (Washington, D.C.: Government Printing Office, 1940), 39–41.

49. "Dozen Girls of Tender Age Involved in Shoplifting, Detectives Claimed," *Fort Worth Star Telegram*, August 29, 1911.

50. Charlie Beland, Leavenworth inmate no. 68030, and Joe Henry Beland, Leavenworth inmate no. 64288, National Archives and Record Administration–Kansas City (hereafter NARA-KC).

51. "Sitting Hen Proves Faithless Guardian of Morphine Supply," *Fort Worth Star Telegram*, December 10, 1921.

52. "Lure of Drug Traffic Mother and Three Follow Son to Prison," *Fort Worth Star Telegram*, December 12, 1921.

53. Texas Department of Health, *Texas Death Indexes, 1903–2000.*

54. Department of the Treasury, "Traffic in Opium and Other Dangerous Drugs" (Washington, D.C.: Government Printing Office, 1936), 36–37.

55. Department of the Treasury, "Traffic in Opium and Other Dangerous Drugs" (Washington, D.C.: Government Printing Office, 1947), 25–27.

56. Charlie Beland, Leavenworth inmate no. 68030, Admissions Summary, NARA-KC.

57. United States Senate, Illicit Narcotics Traffic: Hearings Before the Subcommittee on Improvements in the Federal Criminal Code of the Committee on the Judiciary, United States Senate, Eighty-Fourth Congress, first session (Washington, D.C.: Government Printing Office, 1955), 3285.

58. "Drug Taste at School." *Fort Worth Star Telegram*, December 17, 1921.

59. Charlie Beland, Leavenworth inmate no. 68030, Parole Report, NARA-KC.

60. Charles Louis Beland, Alcatraz inmate no. 18-AZ, National Archives and Record Administration–San Francisco.

61. Interstate I-35 extends from Laredo, Texas, on the U.S.-Mexico border, north to Duluth, Minnesota.

62. Charles Louis Beland, 618-AZ, NARA–San Francisco. Conversation with Joe Sanchez of NARA–San Francisco, August 2, 2012.

63. S. J. Kennedy, Treasury representative in charge, to supervising customs agent, Treasury Department, July 27, 1944, RG 170, DEA-BNDD.

64. "Detection of Clandestine Narcotics Laboratories," File Mexico Border, RG 170, DEA-BNDD.

65. Arias, *Drugs and Democracy in Rio de Janeiro*, 39–60.

66. Cable no. 134, June 15, 1945, U.S. Department of Justice, Federal Bureau of Investigation, María Dolores Estévez Zuleta, Freedom of Information/Privacy

Act request 1150736-00. Notes on cable document teletypes sent to offices in Philadelphia, San Antonio, and El Paso on June 18, 1945.

67. The Narcotics Division was housed in the Department of Pensions and National Health. Charles Henry Ludovic Sharman, formerly of the Royal Canadian Mounted Police, remained a staunch ally of Anslinger. He represented Canada on many international narcotics commissions.

68. H. J. Anslinger to Colonel C. H. L. Sharman, chief, Narcotics Division, Department of National Health and Welfare, Ottawa, "María Dolores Estévez Zuleta," DEA-BNDD.

69. Office memorandum to Ladd from C. H. Carson, June 1945, U.S. Department of Justice, Federal Bureau of Investigation, María Dolores Estévez Zuleta, Freedom of Information/Privacy Act request 1150736-00.

70. Ibid.

71. Ibid.

72. J. Edgar Hoover to FBI Communications Section, July 14, 1945, U.S. Department of Justice, Federal Bureau of Investigation, María Dolores Estévez Zuleta, Freedom of Information/Privacy Act request 1150736-00.

73. S. J. Kennedy to the supervising agent, Treasury Department, United States Customs Service, DEA-BNDD.

74. Lola la Chata to the president and Soledad Orozco, April 1945, Fondo Manuel Ávila Camacho, AGN.

75. Donna J. Guy, *Women Build the Welfare State: Performing Charity and Creating Rights in Argentina, 1880–1955* (Durham, NC: Duke University Press, 2009); and Kristina A. Boylan, "Gendering the Faith and Altering the Nation: Mexican Catholic Women's Activism, 1917–1940," in *Sex in Revolution*, ed. Olcott, Vaughan, and Cano, 199–222.

76. Anslinger and Oursler, *The Murderers*, 4. This scene was repeated in Steven Soderbergh's film *Traffic* when Caroline (played by Erika Christensen), the daughter of the U.S. drug czar (played by Michael Douglas), becomes a heroin addict.

77. Nancy Campbell, *Using Women*. Also see Anslinger and Oursler, *The Murderers*. Anslinger's nativist views were widely circulated in his talks as well as the press. See Anslinger, "Marijuana," 18–19, 150–53.

78. Lic. Arnulfo Martínez Lavalle, visitador general, Procuraduría General de la República to H. J. Anslinger, February 21, 1950, box 29, RG 170, DEA-BNDD.

79. Nancy Campbell, *Using Women*, 64.

80. H. J. Anslinger to Colonel C. H. L. Sharman, chief, Narcotics Division, Department of National Health and Welfare, Ottawa, "María Dolores Estévez Zuleta"; and Astorga, *Drogas sin fronteras*, 166. The description of la Chata also builds upon Anslinger and the FBN's view of the typical dealer. In his book *The Murderers*, Anslinger focused on the "Negro" drug gangs.

81. Adler, *Wheeling and Dealing*. In her research, Adler noted that women involved with traffickers were very beautiful. She argued that they were drawn to the wealth and the lifestyle of trafficking. The image of the beautiful lover of the drug

dealer is celebrated in popular culture. In Brian De Palma's *Scarface*, Michelle Pfeiffer's character becomes the archetype of the trafficker's companion.

82. Leopoldo Salazar Viniegra, "Open Letter to Lola la Chata."

83. Elaine Scarry, *The Body in Pain: The Making and Unmaking of the World* (New York: Oxford University Press, 1985), 39; and Claudia Schaefer, *Textured Lives: Women, Art, and Representation in Modern Mexico* (Tucson: University of Arizona Press, 1992), 18.

84. Julia Sudbury, "Celling Black Bodies: Black Women in the Global Prison Industrial Complex," *Feminist Review* 80 (2005): 162–79.

85. Foreign Service Dispatch from Embassy in Mexico City to the Department of State, "Visit of Gene Sherman *Los Angeles Times* Correspondent to Mexico City," May 16, 1960, RG 170, DEA-BNDD. Gene Sherman submitted information to the embassy about traffickers.

86. H. J. Anslinger, Memorandum for the Secretary, Treasury Department, Bureau of Narcotics, September, 3, 1936, Henry Morgenthau Papers, FDR Library.

87. William Walker, "Control Across the Border," 94.

88. See box 22, file Leopoldo Salazar Viniegra, DEA-BNDD; James B. Stewart, consul general, to State Department, "Laws and Marijuana," October 27, 1938. Stewart reported that the Mexican press depicted Salazar Viniegra as a "propagandist for marijuana," after a concerted effort by U.S. and Mexican officials to tarnish his image.

89. R. W. Artis to H .J. Anslinger, December 12, 1947, and Terry A. Talent to H. J. Anslinger, Treasury Department, Federal Bureau of Narcotics, El Paso, December 1, 1947, box 23, RG 170, DEA-BNDD. This document contains a list of names of Mexican citizens who had been reported for narcotics violations since 1940. One hundred and twenty-five names were listed; seven were women and six were still active. Lola la Chata was listed as imprisoned.

90. See French, "Prostitutes and Guardians Angels," 530–53.

91. Although focused on the Victorian-era explorers of Africa, see Robert J. C. Young, *Colonial Desire: Hybridity in Theory, Culture, and Race* (New York: Routledge, 1995), for a discussion of transgressive sexual fantasies and interracial sex. Jack Kerouac's semiautobiographical novel *Tristessa* (New York: McGraw-Hill, 1960) exemplifies Young's theories, because it is about an affair between a gringo and a Mexico City heroin-addicted prostitute. Burroughs's own fictional work also shows an interest in interracial sexuality.

92. Burroughs maintained a lifelong fascination with crime in general. His interest in criminals and criminal networks in both Mexico and the United States was evident in the circle of friends that he kept. See Oliver Harris, ed., *Letters of William S. Burroughs, 1945–1959* (New York: Viking Press, 1993).

93. William S. Burroughs, *Naked Lunch* (New York: Grove Press, 1959). Lola la Chata appears in a number of Burroughs's works: *Cities of the Red Night* (New York: Viking Press, 1981); and *The Wild Boys: A Book of the Dead* (New York: Grove Press, 1971).

94. Robles-García, *La bala perdida*. Even shortly before his death, Burroughs was still fascinated by la Chata. Robles-García gave Burroughs a photograph of la Chata in which one could make out her gold-capped, jewel-studded teeth. Burroughs made a mixed-media piece using the photo with the words "Folk Hero" inscribed on the bottom. See the photo in Spann, "Unforgettable Characters," 26.

95. Burroughs, *Cities of the Red Night*, 145.

96. Ibid.

97. William S. Burroughs, *The Burroughs File* (San Francisco: City Lights Books, 1984), 137–39. In this short story, Lola la Chata hosts an annual party on her birthday where everything is free, and during which the police receive their payoffs in drugs. Burroughs wrote: "Yes, it's once a year on her birthday that Lola la Chata gives this party and on that day everything is free. On that day she gives. On other days she takes."

98. Leopoldo Salazar Viniegra, "Open Letter to Lola la Chata."

99. For a contemporary discussion of street vending in Mexico, see Cross, *Informal Politics*.

100. These aspects of life for the unprivileged are depicted in popular culture, such as in the film *María Full of Grace*, in which María decides to become a mule after losing her job in a flower plantation. In Arturo Pérez-Reverte's novel *The Queen of the South*, the protagonist, Teresa Mendoza, is also poorly educated but has a mind for numbers.

101. For a discussion of the intersection between the private and the public in marginal women's lives, see Sandra Lauderdale Graham, *House and Street: The Domestic World of Servants and Masters in Nineteenth-Century Rio de Janeiro* (Austin: University of Texas Press, 1992).

102. Catherine Gilbert Murdock, *Domesticating Drink: Women, Men, and Alcohol in America, 1870–1910* (Baltimore, MD: Johns Hopkins University Press, 1998), 47–49. Murdock argues that, by 1900, middle-aged women made up the majority of opium addicts in the United States. Women made up 40 to 50 percent of addicts in treatment facilities.

103. Tina Modotti, two drunk women, photo 35297, Casaola, Fototeca, Pachuga Hidalgo, reprinted in Pérez Montfort, *Yerba, goma, y polvo*, 36. It should be noted that morphine and heroin were prescribed to treat alcoholism.

104. Oscar Lewis, *Five Families: Mexican Case Studies in the Culture of Poverty* (New York: HarperCollins, 1975).

105. Silvia Marina Arrom, *The Women of Mexico City, 1790–1857* (Stanford, CA: Stanford University Press, 1985), 180.

106. Bliss, *Compromised Positions*, 69.

107. William S. Burroughs, "Tío Mate Smiles," in *The Wild Boys*, 11.

108. League of Nations, Advisory Committee on Traffic in Opium and Other Dangerous Drugs, Twenty-Fourth session, June 2, 1939, box 22, RG 170, DEA-BNDD.

109. Leopoldo Salazar Viniegra, "Open Letter to Lola la Chata."

110. H. J. Anslinger to J. Edgar Hoover, July 28, 1945, RG 170, DEA-BNDD.

111. English translation of an article published in *Excélsior*, April 12, 1938, DEA-BNDD. While the article states that she was arrested with cocaine, a later memorandum described her as a heroin and morphine dealer.

112. Ibid.

113. For a discussion of the coverage, see Ricardo Pérez Montfort, "1937–1939: El extraño caso de Lola 'La Chata' y el Capitan Huesca de la Fuente Contra El Doctor Salazar Viniegra," *Humanidades: un periódico para la universidad*, December 3, 2003, at http://morgan.iia.unam.mx/usr/huamnidades/262, accessed March 3, 2004.

114. James Stewart to Secretary of State, April 15, 1938, box 22, file Leopoldo Salazar, DEA.

115. "Opium Smugglers Are Using Planes," *New York Times*, July 6, 1947.

116. James Stewart to Secretary of State, November 15, 1938, box 22, file Leopoldo Salazar, DEA.

117. Salazar headed the Division of Toxicological Studies at the Federal Hospital for Drug Addicts.

118. Leopoldo Salazar Viniegra, "The Myth of Marijuana," presented at the National Academy of Medicine, October 5, 1938, translated by Norman Christianson, vice consul, box 22, file Leopoldo Salazar Viniegra, RG 170, BNDD-DEA.

119. Excerpt from translation of "Marijuana: A Medical and Social Study" by Jorge Segura Millán, box 22, file Leopoldo Salazar Viniegra, RG 170, BNDD-DEA.

120. John R. Matchett, chemist, to Dr. H. J. Wollner, consulting chemist to the Secretary of Treasury, May 10, 1939, box 22, folder Leopoldo Salazar Viniegra, DEA-BNDD.

121. Leopoldo Salazar Viniegra to H. J. Anslinger, April 29, 1940, box 22, folder Leopoldo Salazar Viniegra, RG 170, DEA-BNDD.

122. "No Antiwoman Job Bias in the Narcotics Trade," *New York Times*, April 22, 1975; and "Los dos mayores cárteles de México son dirigidos por mujeres: UEDO," *La Jornada*, September 3, 2002.

123. Burroughs, *Naked Lunch*, 193.

CHAPTER FOUR

Note to Title: I would like to thank Howard Campbell and Bob Chessey for their help in compiling this chapter. Over the years, Bob has also kept me up to date on current events in Ciudad Juárez.

1. For an understanding of borderlanders, see Oscar J. Martínez, "The Dynamics of Border Interaction: New Approaches to Border Analysis," in *Global Boundaries*, ed. Clive H. Schofield (London: Routledge, 1994), 1–15; and Oscar J. Martínez, *Border People: Life and Society in the U.S.-Mexico Borderlands* (Tucson: University of Arizona Press, 1994).

2. Alfredo Corchato, "Mexico's Drug War Shows a Virulent Feminine Side," *Dallas Morning News*, July 12, 2008; and Rafael Nuñez, "A Not So Secret History of Vice in Juarez," *Newspaper Tree*, March 6, 2006. For more current scholarly work, see Campbell, "Female Drug Smugglers on the U.S.-Mexico Border," 233–67.

3. "Border Dope Queen Is Given Prison Sentence," *El Paso Herald-Post*, April 23, 1943.
4. Campbell, "Female Drug Smugglers on the U.S.-Mexico Border."
5. Andreas, *Border Games*; Nadelmann, *Cops Across Borders*; and Timothy J. Dunn, *The Militarization of the U.S.-Mexico Border, 1978–1992* (Austin: Center for Mexican-American Studies, University of Texas, 1996).
6. Howard Campbell, *Drug War Zone*, 30–52.
7. "La reina de las drogas heroicas quedo ya libre," *La Prensa*, August 28, 1930.
8. Affidavit of H. B. Westover, *United States vs. Ignacia Jasso González et al.*, September 16, 1942, State Department (RG 59) Central Decimal Files, 1940–1944, 212.11, González Ignacia Jasso, box 105, National Archives II, College Park, Maryland. Initially, Westover worked with another agent, but Crook replaced him to become the second agent on the sting.
9. Smoking opium is simply derived from raw opium by boiling it to remove the alkaloids. The resulting liquid is strained. Once stained, the brown liquid is slowly boiled to create a paste that is then dried. Canned opium has a more liquid consistency than the putty-like consistency of smoking opium. Opium was frequently trafficked in small containers, from simple tins to highly decorated cans.
10. Affidavit of H. B. Westover. In 1944, a young woman, Hortensia Díaz, was arrested crossing the bridge from El Paso to Ciudad Juárez carrying $24,000 (2008: $313,000) hidden in her brassiere. She and a friend were later shot in El Paso. Díaz transported the money, a payment for opium, from New York. "Dope Ring 'Dupe' Who Hid $24,000 on Person Shot," *Washington Post*, May 21, 1944.
11. United Nations Commission on Narcotic Drugs, Report to the Economic and Social Council on the First Sessions of the Commission on Narcotic Drugs Held at Lake Success, New York, July 24 to August 8, 1947, 7.
12. Affidavit of H. B. Westover.
13. Affidavit of W. H. Crook, *United States vs. Ignacia Jasso González et al.*, September 16, 1942, State Department (RG 59).
14. Extension of remarks of John J. Cochran, Congressional Record, Proceedings and Debate of the Seventy-Eighth Congress, First Session, vol. 89, no. 23, February 10, 1943, box 2, folder 20, Anslinger Archive. Cochran was a congressman from Missouri.
15. Ibid.
16. "Traficante en drogas ha sido aprehendida," *Excélsior*, November 5, 1942.
17. "La Nacha apuesta que sales en libertad," *Diario de la Mañana*, November 15, 1942.
18. "Una episodio más en la historias local de tráfico fuerte de drogas heroícos," *El Continental Span*, November 6, 1942.
19. "Se dictó la formal prisión ayer en contra de la Nacha," *El Mexicano*, November 11, 1942.

20. Treaty between the United States and Mexico, signed at Mexico City, May 4, 1978, *Treaties and Other International Act Series*, no. 9656, 31 U.S.T. For an overview of contemporary studies on extradition as associated with drug offenses, see Ethan A. Nadelmann, "The Evolution of United States Involvement in the International Rendition of Fugitive Criminals," *New York University Journal of International Law and Politics* (Summer 1993): 813–85; Nadelmann, *Cops Across Borders*, 435–36; Sandi R. Murphy, "Drug Diplomacy and the Supply-Side Strategy: A Survey of United States Practice, *Vanderbilt Law Review* (May 1990): 1259–309; and John Patrick Collins, "Traffic in the Traffickers: Extradition and the Controlled Substances Import and Export Act of 1970," *Yale Law Journal* (March 1974): 706–44.

21. "Ignacia Jasso González W/As La Nacha," Federal Bureau of Investigation, Department of Justice, 64-22536-1, March 25, 1943, 5, obtained under the Freedom of Information Act, July 16, 2009. The request was based on Article 1, Sections 22–24 of the treaty of 1926 signed by Plutarco Calles.

22. Ibid.

23. H. J. Anslinger to Antonio Bermúdez, January 19, 1943, Fondo Presidente Manuel Ávila Camacho, AGN.

24. In 1938, Mexican president Lázaro Cárdenas nationalized Mexico's oil, triggering a fierce battle between foreign oil companies and the country's executive branch. It was only in 1943 that Mexican officials and the foreign oil companies reached an agreement, partly due to Franklin D. Roosevelt's Good Neighbor policy, World War II, and sophisticated arguments on the part of State Department officials. For a history of U.S.-Mexico oil relations, see Linda B. Hall, *Oil, Banks, and Politics: The United States and Postrevolutionary Mexico, 1917–1924* (Austin: University of Texas Press, 1995). Also see John J. Dwyer, *The Agrarian Dispute: The Expropriation of American-Owned Rural Land in Postrevolutionary Mexico* (Durham, NC: Duke University Press, 2008).

25. Extension of remarks of John J. Cochran, Congressional Record, Proceedings and Debate of the Seventy-Eighth Congress, First Session, vol. 89, no. 23, February 10, 1943. Dutch Schultz (born Arthur Flegenheimer) was killed in 1935 by organized crime competitors. Schultz became successful in bootlegging and the numbers racket. Seven years after his death, his gang had allegedly moved into narcotics distribution, along with Lucky Luciano's gang. Organized crime entities purchased opiates in a number of cities along the border. During World War II, Luciano was in prison and later deported to Sicily. There are many sensational accounts about organized crime figures; for example, Paul Sann, *Kill the Dutchman! The Story of Dutch Schultz* (New York: Da Capo Press, 1991); and Hickman Powell, *Lucky Luciano: The Man Who Organized Crime in America* (New York: Barricade Books, 2000).

26. Extension of remarks of John J. Cochran, Congressional Record.

27. "Ignacia Jasso González W/As La Nacha," Federal Bureau of Investigation, Department of Justice, 64-22536-1, March 25, 1943.
28. Antonio Bermúdez to Manuel Ávila Camacho, January 22, 1943, Fondo Presidente Manuel Ávila Camacho, AGN.
29. "Ignacia Jasso González W/As La Nacha," Federal Bureau of Investigation, Department of Justice, 64-22536-1, March 26, 1943.
30. Ibid., 3.
31. Higinio M. Reyes et al. to Manuel Ávila Camacho, January 1, 1943, Fondo Presidente Manuel Ávila Camacho, AGN.
32. Ibid.
33. Letter to Juan de Dios Bojórquez, n.d., Dirección General de Gobierno: Estupefacientes Drogas, vol. 2, file 3, AGN; and Letter to Ministro de Gobernación from José Mendiola, El Srio de Est. Liga Nacional Pro-Raza, Campaña Anti-Chino, January 14, 1927, file Manuel Chen, 362.2 (1-1), Expulsión y quejas contra exantrajeros, vol. 5, Dirección General de Gobierno, AGN.
34. See Oscar J. Martínez, *Border Boom Town: Ciudad Juárez since 1848* (Austin: University of Texas Press, 1978); Oscar J. Martínez, *Troublesome Border* (Tucson: University of Arizona Press, 1988); and Martínez, *Border People.*
35. Howard Campbell, "Female Drug Smugglers on the U.S.-Mexico Border," 249. Despite the lack of evidence to support stories that la Nacha and her husband used brutal methods to take control of the narcotics trade, the stories continue to circulate in the press. See "31 Women on List of Drug Smugglers Sought by DEA and FBI in U.S.," *El Paso Times*, March 9, 2010.
36. "La reina de las drogas heroicas quedo ya libre," *La Prensa*, August 28, 1930.
37. Rafael Nuñez, "A Not-So-Secret History of Vice in Juárez," *Newspaper Tree*, March 6, 2006.
38. Higinio M. Reyes et al. to Manuel Ávila Camacho, January 1, 1943.
39. Denton, *Dealing*; Dunlap and Johnson, "Family and Human Resources," 175–98; and Adler, *Wheeling and Dealing.*
40. Obviously, there are exceptions to this among present-day female drug traffickers, but la Nacha and la Chata were in the trade decades longer than many of their contemporaries.
41. Oscar Lewis, *The Children of Sánchez: Autobiography of a Mexican Family* (New York: Random House, 2011).
42. "La reina de las drogas heroicas quedo ya libre," *La Prensa*, August 28, 1930.
43. Daniel Minjares Párea, Daniel Rodríguez et al. to the Governor of the State of Chihuahua, President of the Republic, Minister of Gobernación, March 2, 1933, Manuel Ávila Camacho, vol. 138, 525.3/189, AGN.
44. See Andrae Marak and Laura Tuennerman, "Official Government Discourses about Vice and Deviance: The Early-Twentieth-Century Tohono O'odham," in *Smugglers, Brothels, and Twine*, ed. Carey and Marak, 101–21.
45. Nicole Mottier, "Drug Gang and Politics in Ciudad Juárez, 1928–1936," *Mexican Studies/Estudios Mexicanos* 25, no. 1 (Winter 2009): 19–46.

46. T. L. Lilliestrom, vice consul, Ciudad Juárez, to the secretary of state, October 13, 1939, Drug Enforcement Administration, Subject Files of the Bureau of Narcotics and Dangerous Drugs, 1916–1970, RG 170, DEA-BNDD.

47. Terry A. Talent to H. J. Anslinger, Treasury Department, Federal Bureau of Narcotics, El Paso, December 1, 1947, box 23, RG 170, DEA-BNDD. Seventeen names were on the list of Mexicans arrested for narcotics violations; la Nacha was the only woman.

48. "'Border Dope Queen' Gets Religion in Juárez Jail," *El Paso Herald-Post*, March 14, 1944.

49. Ibid.

50. S. C. Peña, special employee to commissioner of customs, July 7, 1945, box 161, RG 170, DEA-BNDD.

51. Ignacia Jasso la viuda de González to President Ávila Camacho, Fondo Presidente Manuel Ávila Camacho, AGN.

52. Bob Chessey, interview with Joe Rey, attorney for the Jasso family, El Paso, October 1, 2007.

53. American Consulate at Ciudad Juárez, January 24, 1945, box 23, RG 170, DEA-BNDD.

54. "Fall of the Opium Queen," *American Weekly*, January 4, 1948.

55. "Quash Indictment Against 'La Nacha,'" *El Paso Herald-Post*, February 21, 1946.

56. "Fall of the Opium Queen."

57. Memorandum Report, Bureau of Narcotics, El Paso, March 15, 1950, Consuelo Sanchez de Dovas alias Consuelo Rodriguez, Mexicali, box 29, RG 170, DEA-BNDD.

58. Mexican heroin accounted for 90 percent of the heroin sold in the state of Texas.

59. The Subcommittee on Improvements in the Federal Criminal Code, part of the Senate Committee on the Judiciary, was composed of the following senators: Price Daniel (Texas), Joseph O'Mahoney (Wyoming), James O. Eastland (Mississippi), Herman Walker (Idaho), and John Marshall Butler (Maryland), along with C. Aubrey Gasque (general counsel) and W. Lee Speer (chief investigator).

60. "Soviet Retorts on Heroin: Charges in U.N. that U.S. May Be Behind Smuggling," *New York Times*, May 3, 1952; and "Anslinger Replies to Zakusov Charges," *New York Times*, May 6, 1952.

61. For a discussion of McCarthyism, see Ellen Schrecker, *Many Are the Crimes: McCarthyism in America* (Boston, MA: Little, Brown, 1998); and Richard M. Fried, *Nightmare in Red: The McCarthy Era in Perspective* (New York: Oxford University Press, 1990).

62. U.S. Congress, Senate Committee on the Judiciary, Communist China and Illicit Narcotics Traffic, Hearing Before the Subcommittee to Investigate the Administration of the Internal Security Act and Other Internal Security Laws, Eighty-Fourth Congress, First Session, March 8–13, 1955, 14–17. For a discussion of his testimony, see Valentine, *The Strength of the Wolf*, 152–54.

63. Price Daniels to Óscar Rabasa and Carlos Franco Sodi, October 1, 1955, reprinted in *Hearing Before the Subcommittee on Improvements in the Federal Code of the Committee on the Judiciary, United States Senate, Eighty-Fourth Congress, Illicit Narcotics Traffic (Austin, Dallas, Forth Worth, Houston, and San Antonio, Texas)* (Washington, D.C.: Government Printing Office, 1956).

64. Telegram from consulate of Mexico City to Department of State, December 4, 1959, box 28, file Mexico Border, RG 170, DEA-BNDD.

65. "Two Arrested in Mystery Death of El Pasoan: Prisoner Says Man Was Slashed After Taking Dope," *El Paso Herald-Post*, September 1, 1955.

66. "Five Held in Death Inquiry," *El Paso Herald-Post*, September 2, 1955.

67. Salazar was born in Ciudad Juárez in 1928, but he grew up in El Paso. He entered the military for a two-year tour after he finished high school. After graduating from Texas Western College, he worked for the *El Paso Herald-Post*. He made his way to the *Los Angeles Times*, where he reported on the Vietnam War. He became bureau chief in Mexico City, covering much of Latin America. On August 29, 1970, Salazar, working for the KMEX television station as well as the *Los Angeles Times*, he attended the National Chicano Moratorium Committee to end the Vietnam War. He was killed by a police tear gas canister fired into the café where he and his crew had taken refuge during the riot. No police officer was ever charged. See "One Dead, 40 Hurt in East LA Riot," *Los Angeles Times*, August 30, 1970.

68. Ruben Salazar, *Border Correspondent: Selected Writings, 1955–1970*, ed. Mario T. García (Berkeley: University of California Press, 1995).

69. Urban myths routinely circulate about crime and drug issues. In Ciudad Juárez, there is an urban myth that Salazar was not permitted to return to the city because he had exposed details about its drug trade. In fact, his testimony reveals that politicians in the city knew that he was going to testify.

70. Ruben Salazar testimony, Hearing Before the Subcommittee on Improvements in the Federal Code of the Committee on the Judiciary, United States Senate, Eighty-Fourth Congress, Illicit Narcotics Traffic, 3304–24.

71. Some of the images were published in the report, others were not. Price Daniel Committee, San Antonio Hearings, December 14, 1955, box 9, Daniel Hearings, File Texas, RG 170, BNDD-DEA.

72. Ibid.

73. Ruben Salazar, "La Nacha Sells Dirty Dope at $5 a 'Papel,'" *El Paso Herald-Post*, August 17, 1955.

74. Ibid.

75. Ibid.

76. This may have been an error. Natividad had a closer relationship with his adopted or half brother Gilberto.

77. Salazar testimony, 3306.

78. Salazar testimony, 3317.

79. Appendix 1, Second International Opium Conference, Senate doc. 733, Sixty-Second Congress, Second Session; "La resolución tomada por el Consejo S. de

Salubridad relativa a la ratificación de la Convención Internacional sobre el Opio celebrada en la Haya el año de 1912," Fondo Presidentes Obregón Calles, AGN.

80. Testimony of Colonel Homer Garrison Jr., director of Department of Public Safety, State of Texas, Hearing, Illicit Narcotics Traffic, 2366.

81. Testimony of Perry Milton Turner, Hearing, Illicit Narcotics Traffic, 2371–81.

82. Testimony of W. E. Naylor, chief of Narcotics Division of Public Safety, State of Texas, Hearing Before the Subcommittee on Improvements in the Federal Code of the Committee on the Judiciary, United States Senate, Eighty-Fourth Congress, Illicit Narcotics Traffic, 2381.

83. Testimony of Perry Milton Turner, 2371–81.

84. Bureau of Customs, Memorandum to the Subcommittee on Narcotics of the Senate Judiciary, October 10, 1955.

85. Roark, *The Coin of Contraband*.

86. Statement of Pura Rodríguez Pérez, Hearing, Illicit Narcotics Trade, 2957.

87. Testimony of E. W. Biscailuz, sheriff of Los Angeles County, accompanied by Undersheriff Peter J. Pitchess and Captain K. E. Irving, narcotic chief, Los Angeles Police Department, November 15, 1955, Los Angeles, Hearing, Illicit Narcotics Traffic, 3677–96.

88. The situation has changed; presently, most female addicts in Tijuana are of Mexican descent. Moreover, those who are users engage in riskier behaviors. See Steffanie A. Strathdee et al., "Correlates of Injection Drug Use Among Female Sex Workers in Two Mexico-U.S. Border Cities," *Drug and Alcohol Dependence* 92, nos. 1–3 (January 2008): 132–40.

89. Testimony of Mickey Wallace, Los Angeles, November 15, 1955, Hearing, Illicit Narcotics Traffic, 3713.

90. Ibid.

91. Testimony of Oscar Palm, Los Angeles, accompanied by Harry M. Umann, Los Angeles, his counsel, November 15, 1955, 3594–605 and 3605–19; testimony of Rae V. Vader, customs agent in charge, San Diego, Bureau of Customs, accompanied by Richard L. McCowan, customs inspector, November 15, 1955, Hearing, Illicit Narcotics Trade.

92. Ibid.

93. Taxi drivers on both sides of the border procured drugs and prostitutes for their clients. Historically, they have played a key role in the drug industry and the underworld. See Anthony Joseph Stanonis, *Creating the Big Easy: The Emergence of Modern Tourism, 1918–1945* (Athens: University of Georgia Press, 2006), 117–20; Graham Russell Gao Hodges, *Taxi: A Social History of the New York City Cabdriver* (Baltimore, MD: Johns Hopkins University Press, 2007); and Robert P. Stephens, *Germans on Drugs: The Complications of Modernization in Hamburg* (Ann Arbor: University of Michigan Press, 2007). Trains have a long history as central vessels for drug running. In the 1960s and 1970s, people moved marijuana across the border and loaded it onto trains. Trains and those who worked on them became a focus of drug running early on. In 1916, at a

meeting of the State Association of Judges and Justices held in New York, one judge argued that Pullman Porters were running drugs from Canada into the United States. See "Opiates Shipped Illegally to Canada," *Pharmaceutical Era* 49 (January–December 1916): 493. In Mexico, two railroad conductors wrote to President Adolfo Ruiz Cortines about inspectors using the trains to smuggle heroin into the United States. Alfonso Gutierrez and Marcos Acosta García to Adolfo Ruiz Cortines, box 423, July 30, 1953, AGN. Kathy Burke, an NYPD narcotics agent in 1968, told me that the train routes from south to north were a prime corridor for moving drugs from Mexico to New York. Kathy Burke, telephone interview with the author, February 4, 2011.

94. The role of women involved in prostitution who also sold narcotics appears in many works. See Alan Block, "Aw, Your Mother's in the Mafia: Women Criminals in Progressive New York," *Crime Law and Social Change* 1, no. 1 (December 1976): 5–22, and Timothy Gilfoyle, *City of Eros: New York City, Prostitution, and the Commercialization of Sex, 1790–1920* (New York: W. W. Norton, 1992).

95. Quoted in Howard Campbell, "Female Drug Smugglers on the U.S.-Mexico Border," 238.

96. Howard Campbell, *Drug War Zone*, 60–75.

97. Memo to H. J. Anslinger from Thomas W. Andrew, June 11, 1962, file Mexican Cooperation, box 23, RG170, BNDD-DEA.

98. Wayland L. Speer, acting commissioner of narcotics, to Mr. A. Gilmore Fluez, assistant secretary of the treasury, August 26, 1960; Ernest M. Gentry to H. J. Anslinger, June 7, 1962; Thomas W. Andrew to H. J. Anslinger, June 11, 1962; and George H. Gafiney, "Survey of the Southwest Border," RG 170, BNDD-DEA. See also Astorga, *Drogas sin fronteras*, 91–92. For a discussion about cocaine familial enterprises, see Paul Gootenberg, "The 'Pre-Colombian' Era of Drug Trafficking in the Americas: Cocaine, 1945–1965," *Americas* 64, no. 2 (October 2007): 133–76.

99. Organized Crime and Illicit Traffic in Narcotics, Hearing Before the Permanent Subcommittee on Government Operations, United States Senate, Eighty-Eighth Congress, July 24, 1964, vol. 4, 5, 1145.

100. Ibid., 907.

101. *Eduardo Amador-González v. United States*, no. 2348, United States Court of Appeals, Fifth Circuit, January 10, 1968. Rehearing denied February 23, 1968.

102. "Mexican Crash Victim Identified," *El Paso Times*, November 27, 1973.

103. Josiah McC. Heyman, "U.S. Ports of Entry on the Mexican Border," in *On the Border*, ed. Wood, 222. Peter Andreas notes the symbiotic relationship between smugglers and states, arguing that it is the perception that smuggling (of goods or people) is a "growing threat that is most critical for sustaining and expanding law enforcement." See Peter Andreas, "Smuggling Wars: Law Enforcement and Law Evasion in a Changing World," in *Transnational Crime in the Americas*, ed. Tom Farer (New York: Routledge, 1999), 94. Moisés Naím similarly argues that the focus on supplier countries is "politically profitable," and the required tools

such as "helicopters, gunboats, heavily armed agents, judges, and generals" are more "telegenic" than those tools that would be required to address demand. See Naím, *Illicit*, 234–35.

CHAPTER FIVE

1. Kenney, *From Pablo to Osama*.
2. Nadelmann, *Cops Across Borders*.
3. For a history of cocaine, see Gootenberg, ed., *Cocaine*; Gootenberg, *Andean Cocaine*; and Spillane, *Cocaine*.
4. Kenney, *From Pablo to Osama*.
5. Alfred W. McCoy, *The Politics of Heroin: CIA Complicity in the Global Drug Trade* (Chicago, IL: Lawrence Hill, 2003); and Gootenberg, *Andean Cocaine*.
6. The highly fluid flows of cocaine have been documented in popular culture and scholarly works. See Ted Demme's film *Blow*; Peter Dale Scott and Jonathan Marshall, *Cocaine Politics: Drugs, Armies, and the CIA in Central America* (Berkeley: University of California Press, 1998); and Arias, *Drugs and Democracy in Rio de Janeiro*.
7. "No Antiwoman Job Bias in the Narcotics Trade," *New York Times*, April 22, 1975.
8. See McCoy, *The Politics of Heroin*.
9. *Task Force Report: Narcotics, Marijuana, and Dangerous Drugs*, Special Presidential Task Force report, June 6, 1969. National Archives, Nixon Presidential Materials, White House Special Files: Staff Members and Office Files, Egil Krogh, box 30, "Operation Intercept," at http://www.gwu.edu/~nsarchiv/NSAEBB/NSAEBB86/, accessed July 10, 2012.
10. Kelly Lytle Hernández, *Migra! A History of the U.S. Border Patrol* (Berkeley: University of California Press, 2010); and Rachel St. John, *Line in the Sand: A History of the Western U.S.-Mexico Border* (Princeton, NJ: Princeton University Press, 2011).
11. *Task Force Report: Narcotics, Marijuana, and Dangerous Drugs*, 21–26.
12. White House memorandum, June 18, 1969, White House Central Files: Subject Files, FG 221, box 5, National Archives; see also National Security Archive.
13. *"Action Task Force" Narcotics, Marihuana and Dangerous Drugs*, White House memorandum, June 27, 1969, White House Central Files: Subject Files, FG 221, box 5, National Security Archive.
14. See Lawrence A. Gooberman, *Operation Intercept: The Multiple Consequences of Public Policy* (New York: Pergamon Press, 1974).
15. G. Gordon Liddy, *Will: The Autobiography of G. Gordon Liddy* (New York: St. Martin's Press, 1980), 135. A veteran and former FBI agent, Liddy served in the Nixon administration and was involved in the Watergate scandal.
16. David Brand, "Operation Intercept Turns Up Little Dope and Lots of Resentment," *Wall Street Journal*, October 3, 1969.

17. Editorial, *Excélsior*, October 8, 1969.

18. Felix Belair Jr., "Operation Intercept: Success on Land, Futility in the Air," *New York Times*, October 2, 1969.

19. Carey, *Plaza of Sacrifices*.

20. Salazar, *Border Correspondent*, 238–39.

21. For a discussion of these influences, see Carey, *Plaza of Sacrifices*; Tanalís Padilla, *Rural Resistance in the Land of Zapata: The Jaramillista Movement and the Myth of the Pax Priísta, 1940–1962* (Durham, NC: Duke University Press, 2008); and Fernando Herrera Calderón and Adela Cedillo, eds., *Challenging Authoritarianism in Mexico: Revolutionary Struggles and the Dirty War, 1964–1982* (New York: Routledge, 2012).

22. "Operation Cooperation," *BNDD Bulletin*, May–June 1970. In 1968, the FBN merged with the Bureau of Drug Abuse Control (BDAC) to form the Bureau of Narcotics and Dangerous Drugs (BNDD) under the Department of Health, Education, and Welfare. John Ingersoll directed the new bureau.

23. See "Notable Cases," a regular feature in the *BNDD Bulletin*.

24. DEA History 1970–1975, at http://www.justice.gov/dea/pubs/history/1970–1975 .html, accessed January 28, 2011. See also U.S. Drug Enforcement Administration, "Drug Enforcement Administration: A Tradition of Excellence, 1973–2008" (Washington, D.C: DEA, 2008).

25. See Calderón and Cedillo, eds., *Challenging Authoritarianism in Mexico*; and Alberto Ulloa Bornemann, *Surviving Mexico's Dirty War: A Political Prisoner's Memoir* (Philadelphia, PA: Temple University Press, 2007).

26. For a discussion on contemporary guerrilla groups that sprang from Partido de los Pobres, see Gustavo Hirales Morán, "Radical Groups in Mexico Today," Center for Strategic and International Studies, *Policy Papers on the Americas* 14 (September 2003).

27. Gustavo Hirales Morán, "La guerra secreta, 1970–78," *Nexos* 34 (June 1982): 36. Hirales was a militant with the Liga Comunista 23 de Septiembre (Communist League of September 23). See also his *La liga comunista 23 de septiembre: orígenes y naufragio* (Mexico City: Ediciones de Cultura Popular, 1977).

28. Hirales Morán, "La guerra secreta"; and Barry Carr, *Marxism and Communism in Twentieth-Century Mexico* (Lincoln: University of Nebraska Press, 1992), 267. See also Calderón and Cedillo, eds., *Challenging Authoritarianism in Mexico*.

29. Dirección Federal Seguridad, Narcóticos, Investigaciones Confidencial y asuntos policías, 17-0-1970, H49, AGN. It should be noted that the files on drugs and the guerrillas are heavily controlled. My attempts to see complete files of young people arrested for narcotics violations as well as for having subversive materials were met with obstacles. Having worked with an archivist and having accessed the files previously, I knew that the collection contained material on drug arrests. I was given limited access to certain case files, and I was not permitted to review other relevant case files. When I requested to see other material, I was allowed to review one page of a substantial file. I believe this is due to the recognized link between the Mexican Federal Security Directorate (DFS) and prominent drug traffickers.

30. Dirección Federal Seguridad, Narcoticos, Investigaciones Confidencial y asuntos policías, 17-0-1971, AGN.

31. Dirección Federal Seguridad, Narcoticos, Investigaciones Confidencial y asuntos policías, 11-235-1973, AGN.

32. Paul Kenny, Mónica Serrano, and Arturo Sotomayor, *Mexico's Security Failures: Collapse into Criminal Violence* (New York: Routledge, 2011).

33. Arnoldo Martínez Verdugo, ed., *Historia del comunismo en México* (Mexico City: Grijalbo, 1985). Also see Juan Miguel de Mora, *Las guerrillas en México y Jenaro Vázquez Rojas* (Mexico City: Editora Latino Americana, 1972).

34. Sergio Tamayo, "The Twenty Mexican Octobers: A Study of Citizenship and Social Movements" (PhD diss., University of Texas, 1994), 221.

35. Tim Weiner, "Mexico Indicts Former Chief of Secret Police," *New York Times*, March 30, 2003.

36. Kenny, Serrano, and Sotomayor, *Mexico's Security Failures*. A number of articles in this volume deal with policing and police corruption.

37. Dirección Federal Seguridad, Narcóticos, Investigaciones Confidencial y asuntos policías, 100-23-1-1976, AGN.

38. Carey, *Plaza of Sacrifices*.

39. "Mexico Join, Smash Drug Ring," *Desert News*, May 16, 1970.

40. Ibid.

41. "U.S.-Mexico Force Breaks Drug Ring," *New York Times*, May 17, 1970.

42. "No Antiwoman Job Bias in the Narcotics Trade," *New York Times*, April 22, 1975.

43. "Heroin Smuggling Ring Broken Up in Prison," *Windsor (Ontario) Star*, October 20, 1974.

44. For more information on the FBI's surveillance of the Mexican Mafia in the 1970s, see FBI Freedom of Information and Privacy Act, Mexican Mafia, parts 1–2, at http://foia.fbi.gov/mafia_mexican/mafia_mexican_part01.pdf, accessed December 20, 2010.

45. There are many sensational docudramas about the Mexican Mafia on television. Tony Rafael, author of *The Mexican Mafia* (New York: Encounter Books, 2007), addresses the organization and how it operates, but he does not delve into the historical formation of the gang.

46. Glen E. Pommerening, U.S. Department of Justice, to Victor Love, Director of the U.S. General Accounting Office, August 5, 1970, published in Report to the Congress, Efforts to Stop Narcotics and Dangerous Drugs Coming From and Through Mexico and Central America, December 31, 1974.

47. Article 2, Ley Federal contra la Delincuencia Organizada, 1996. English translation by John Bailey and Jorge Chabat, in "Public Security and Democratic Governance: Challenges to Mexico and the United States," The Mexico Project (Washington, D.C.: Georgetown University, 2001).

48. Law enforcement adapted, too, as more women were recruited to become narcotics agents. Kathy Burke, telephone interview with the author, February 4, 2011. When Burke began to work for the NYPD's Narcotics Division, she was one of three women there. She mentioned that the first female narcotics agents entered

the NYPD in the 1950s. Narcotics served as a place where underrepresented people entered the police force in order to penetrate the organized crime entities of
different ethnic groups. Paul Chu, cofounder, the Jade Society, interview with the
author, February 9, 2011. Asian American officers also worked undercover in
narcotics in Chinatown and other areas of the city.

49. Yolanda Sarmiento testimony, *United States v. Joseph Anthony Martinez-
Carcano*, United States District Court, Southern District of New York, 76 CR-
965; and *United States v. Joseph Anthony Martinez-Carcano*, United States Court
of Appeals for the Second District, folder 77-1041. To understand Sarmiento's role
in transnational trafficking, I relied on these case files. Sarmiento was the subject
of multiple indictments and court cases, such as *United States v. Yolanda
Sarmiento*, Eastern District of New York, 72 CR-1260, 74 CR-492, 74 CR-11, and
74 CR-493; and *United States v. Yolanda Sarmiento*, Southern District of New
York, 74 CR-472. Despite my efforts and those of the archivists at NARA-NYC
and the file clerks at the Southern District Court to locate these files on Sarmiento,
all turned out to be missing.

50. For a discussion of the Corsican emergence in heroin smuggling, see McCoy, *The
Politics of Heroin*, 46–76; and Alexander Stille, *Excellent Cadavers: The Mafia and
the Death of the First Italian Republic* (New York: Vintage, 1996).

51. Robin Moore, *The French Connection: A True Account of Cops, Narcotics, and
International Conspiracy*, 13th ed. (New York: Lyon Press, 2003); and William
Friedkin, *The French Connection*, 20th Century Fox, 1971.

52. For discussion of the Corsican trafficking organizations, see McCoy, *The Politics
of Heroin*.

53. Chile and Argentina always had vibrant domestic wine industries, but the countries' international market was minimal prior to the 1970s.

54. *United States v. Anthony Torres and Roberto Rivera*, no. 751, July 2, 1975.

55. *United States v. Joseph Anthony Martinez-Carcano*, 52.

56. "No Antiwoman Job Bias in the Narcotics Trade," *New York Times*, April 22, 1975.

57. "12 Charged Here in a World Plot to Import Heroin," *New York Times*, December 13, 1972.

58. "12 in Police Narcotic Unit Charged with Corruption," *New York Times*, March 9,
1974. This case led to a series of investigations into the NYPD. New police officers
were recruited and trained to replace those who had been indicted for corruption
in a number of cases in the early 1970s. Many of the new recruits had military experience and either held university degrees or were attending college when they
were recruited by the NYPD. Anonymous former NYPD narcotics agent (active on
the force in the 1970s), interview with the author.

59. Morris Kaplan, "Frogman Is Among 9 Persons Convicted of Cocaine Smuggling,"
New York Times, December 21, 1971.

60. Michael Levine, *The Big White Lie: The Deep Cover Operation That Exposed the
CIA Sabotage of the Drug War* (Emeryville, CA: Thunder's Mouth Press, 1994).

61. Peter Axthelm and Anthony Marro, "The Drug Vigilantes," *Newsweek*, April 16, 1976.

62. "Drug Suspect's Bail Raised $1 Million, up to $3.5 Million," *New York Times*, May 29, 1976.

63. Ibid.

64. Levine, *The Big White Lie*, 20–21.

65. Max H. Seigel, "3 Major Drug Suspects Are Arrested at Kennedy," *New York Times*, May 28, 1976.

66. *United States v. Joseph Anthony Martinez-Carcano*, 387–88. Martinez-Carcano had worked on the Polaris missile while working for Grumman Aircraft.

67. *United States v. Joseph Anthony Martinez-Carcano*; and *United States v. Joseph Anthony Martinez-Carcano*, United States Court of Appeals for the Second District, folder 77-1041.

68. Ibid., stenographer's transcript, 296–302, 547–65.

69. Ibid., 408–9.

70. Ibid., 50–60.

71. Ibid., 58–60.

72. *United States v. Joseph Anthony Martinez-Carcano*, 410–80.

73. Ibid.

74. Quoted in Max H. Seigel, "3 Major Drug Suspects Are Arrested at Kennedy," *New York Times*, May 28, 1976.

75. *United States v. Dominique Orsini*, 424 F. supp. 229, 1976. See also Nadelmann, *Cops Across Borders*, 436–56.

76. *United States v. Joseph Anthony Martinez-Carcano*, stenographer's transcript, 101–9.

77. Ibid., 100–120, 120–25, 128–32.

78. Ibid., 410–80.

79. Peter G. Bourne, "The Great Cocaine Myth," *Drugs and Drug Abuse Newsletter* 5, no. 5 (1974), 37. See also Kevin A. Shabat, "The Local Matters: A Brief History of the Tension Between Federal Drug Policy and Local Policy," *Journal of Global Drug Policy and Practice* 1, no. 4 (Winter 2007), at http://globaldrugpolicy.org/1/4/index.php, accessed January 28, 2011.

80. Richard DeGrandpre, *The Cult of Pharmacology: How America Became the World's Most Troubled Drug Culture* (Durham, NC: Duke University Press, 2006).

81. Blanco was not the first female cocaine boss. Blanca Ibañez de Sanchez, a Bolivian, worked with other traffickers to develop a route from Bolivia to Cuba to New York in the early 1960s. For more information, see Gootenberg, *Andean Cocaine*, 247–86.

82. *United States v. Griselda Blanco*, U.S. District Court of Southern New York, 75-CR-429, stenographer's minutes, 665–92.

83. Ibid., 306–10.

84. Richard Smitten, *The Godmother: The True Story of the Hunt for the Most Bloodthirsty Female Criminal of Our Time* (New York: Pocket Books, 1990). In places, the evidence in the court documents disputes aspects of Smitten's work, but his account remains a comprehensive source on Blanco.

85. The term "cocaine cowboys" was also used by law enforcement officers. See Statement by Michael Horn, chief officer of International Operations, DEA, Senate Foreign Relations Committee, July 19, 1997.

86. Owen Gleiberman, "Cocaine Cowboys," *Entertainment Weekly*, October 25, 2006.

87. José Guarnizo, *La patrona de Pablo Escobar: vida y muerte de Griselda Blanco* (Bogotá: Planeta, 2012). Guarnizo conducted interviews with Blanco's former employees, who argued that she institutionalized the use of sicarios.

88. De Palma, *Scarface*; and *Miami Vice*, television series, Michael Mann Productions, 1984–1989.

89. Public Broadcasting Service, "The Godfather of Cocaine," Frontline, February 14, 1995, transcript at http://www.pbs.org/wgbh/pages/frontline/programs/transcripts/1309.html.

90. Moore, *The French Connection*; and Smitten, *The Godmother*. After his novel *Twice Killed* (New York: Avon Books, 1984), Smitten moved away from fiction following his work with Mermelstein to publish *The Godmother*, followed by his and Ellis Rubin's *Kathy: A Case of Nymphomania* (Hollywood, FL: Lifetime Books, 1993).

91. Max Mermelstein with Robin Moore and Richard Smitten, *The Man Who Made It Snow: By the American Mastermind Inside the Colombian Cartel* (New York: Simon and Schuster, 1990). Smitten used information from Mermelstein in his book on Blanco. Mermelstein argued that Blanco enjoyed having a few drinks and talking about her use of violence. Smitten, *The Godmother*, 96–100.

92. The Medellín cartel was composed of Pablo Escobar, José Gonzalo Rodríguez, and the Ochoa brothers: Jorge, Juan David, and Fabio. Fabio mostly worked in the United States. The Ochoas were an upper-middle-class family who turned to cocaine. The coca came from Bolivia and Peru; the cartel processed it in Colombia, and American pilots flew it from Colombia to a drop island in the Bahamas.

93. Francisco Adriano Armedo-Sarmiento, aka Eduardo Sanchez, aka Pacho el Mono, aka Elkin, aka Francisco Velez, et al., Defendants-Appellants, nos. 1276–82, 1284, and 1309; 76-1113, 76-1119, 76-1124, 76-1127, and 76-1148, United States Court of Appeals, Second Circuit, argued August 20, 1976, decided October 28, 1976. Certiorari denied March 7, 1977. See 97 S.Ct. 1330, 1331, *United States v. Parra, Gomez, Botero, Cabrera, etc.*, United States District Court for the Southern District of New York, 75-CR-429.

94. *United States v. Griselda Blanco*, United States District Court of Southern New York, stenographer's minutes, July 1, 2, 3, 8, 9, 1985, 75 cr. 429.

95. John E. Harris, an expert on extradition, testified at the trial. John E. Harris, director, Office of Internal Affairs, U.S. Department of Justice, International Cooperation in Fighting Transnational Organized Crime: Special Emphasis on

Mutual Legal Assistance and Extradition, in UNAFEI Annual Report for 1999 and Resource Material Series no. 57 (Tokyo: UNAFEI, 2001). See also Huseyin Durmaz, "Extradition of Terror Suspects and Developments in Extradition Process," in *Understanding and Responding to Terrorism*, ed. Huseyin Durmaz et al. (Amsterdam: IOS Press, 2007), 66–83.

96. Marco Palacios, *Between Legitimacy and Violence: A History of Colombia, 1875–2002* (Durham, NC: Duke University Press, 2006); Gonzalo Sánchez and Donny Meertens, *Bandits, Peasants, and Politics: The Case of "La Violencia" in Colombia* (Austin: University of Texas Press, 2001); and Mary Roldán, *Blood and Fire: La Violencia in Antioquia, Colombia, 1946–1953* (Durham, NC: Duke University Press, 2002).

97. Donny Meertens, "Victims and Survivors of War in Colombia: Three Views of Gender Relations," in *Violence in Colombia, 1990–2000: Waging War and Negotiating Peace*, ed. Charles Bergquist, Ricardo Peñaranda, and Gonzalo Sánchez G. (Wilmington, DE: Scholarly Resources, 2001), 153.

98. Smitten, *The Godmother*.

99. The sons were born as follows: Dixon on April 2, 1960; Uber on November 15, 1961; and Osvaldo on May 5, 1962.

100. Smitten, *The Godmother*, 1–19.

101. Photograph from the author's private collection. Guarnizo, *La patrona de Pablo Escobar*; and Alonso Salazar, *Pablo Escobar: el patrón del mal* (Bogotá: Aguilar, 2012).

102. Diamond also represented Blanco's son Michael Corleone in a narcotics arrest in 2011. Francisco Alvarado, "In the Black Widow's Shadow," *Broward New Times*, October 13, 2011.

103. *United States v. Griselda Blanco*, stenographer's report, 75 CR 429, 5–17. In the documents, all accents and tildes are excluded. The quotation appears as it was in the document.

104. Ibid.

105. Cecil was the DEA agent in charge of Chile; he worked numerous cases in South America. See *United States v. Rafael Lira*, no. 716, 74-2567, United States Court of Appeals, Second Circuit, April 14, 1975; and *United States v. Griselda Blanco*, no. 1187, 85-1423, United States Court of Appeals, Second Circuit, November 10, 1988.

106. *United States v. Griselda Blanco*, stenographer's report, 75 CR-429, 7–76.

107. For information on the limited success of Operation Banshee and other conspiracy cases, see Kenney, *From Pablo to Osama*, 91–95.

108. Smitten's book is based on information from Carmen Cabán, yet it was Gloria who was the star witness. Carmen was also arrested. Smitten's account in *The Godmother* differs from the testimony given by Gloria. The surname Cabán was unaccented in the court documents.

109. *United States v. Griselda Blanco*, stenographer's report, 20–30.

110. Ibid., 43.

111. Ibid., 50–60.

112. Smitten's informant was Carmen Cabán, but Gloria testified in 1985, not Carmen.

113. Smitten, for his book, interviewed Carmen, who he argues was also a lover of Cabrera. This was not confirmed in Gloria's testimony. Cabrera was married to a woman named Elsa who lived in Colombia in the 1970s.

114. *United States v. Griselda Blanco*, stenographer's report, 639–948.

115. *United States v. Griselda Blanco*, no. 1187, 85-1423, United States Court of Appeals, Second Circuit, November 10, 1988.

116. Mermelstein, *The Man Who Made It Snow*, 159–61.

117. "Top Drug Dealers Named by Police: One Woman Is Among the 13 Believed to Rule City Narcotics Trade," *New York Times*, December 9, 1975.

118. Ibid. Leroy "Nicky" Barnes and Frank Lucas controlled the Harlem drug trade in the late 1960s and 1970s. Both have been featured in contemporary popular culture. Barnes was the subject of a documentary by Marc Levin, *Mr. Untouchable*, Blowback Productions, 2007. Lucas was the muse for Ridley Scott's *American Gangster*, Universal Pictures, 2007, in which Denzel Washington plays Lucas.

119. "Top Drug Dealers Named by Police: One Woman Is Among the 13 Believed to Rule City Narcotics Trade," *New York Times*, December 9, 1975.

120. Wiretap transcripts, *United States v. Alberto Bravo et al.*, United States District Court, Southern District, S75 CR-429.

121. Ibid.

122. *United States v. Griselda Blanco*, stenographer's report, 75 CR-429, 457–79.

123. Ibid., 75 CR-429, 491–506.

124. *United States v. Francisco Adriano Armedo-Sarmiento.*

125. Judgment and Probation Commitment Order, folder 1, 75 CR-429. Her judgment was passed on March 1, 1976. On December 21, 1976, she was released.

126. *United States v. Griselda Blanco*, stenographer's report, 75 CR-429, 529–609.

127. Ibid., 609–12.

128. Judgment and Probation Commitment Order, November 8, 1985, USDC-SDNY, Criminal Case files, folder 1, 75 CR-429.

129. Terrence E. Poppa, *Drug Lord: The Life and Death of a Mexican Kingpin* (El Paso: Cinco Puntos Press, 2010). Depictions of Blanco in narconarratives differ greatly from those of male drug traffickers such as Pablo Acosta in Terrence Poppa's *Drug Lord*. Acosta's drug and alcohol addiction is a cry for intervention. His sexuality, and those of other traffickers, is rarely mentioned and never associated with alleged psychosis. Rather, these are signs of virility and strength. Instead, Acosta's colleagues ensure that he gets clean so all could return to the lucrative business of trafficking. Although Patrick Radden Keefe wrote about Joaquín Guzmán Loera's (El Chapo) affinity for women as well as Viagra. Patrick Radden Keefe, "The Hunt for El Chapo," *The New Yorker* (May 5, 2014), http://www.newyorker.com/reporting/2014/05/05/140505fa_fact_keefe?currentPage=all

130. Available at www.CharlesCosby.com.

131. Billy Corben, *Cocaine Cowboys 2: Hustlin' with the Godmother*, Magnolia Pictures, 2008.

132. "Searching for the Godmother of Crime," *Maxim*, July 23, 2008, 96–98.
133. Martin A. Berrios, "Michael Corleone Blanco: The Son of Cocaine Cowboys' Griselda Blanco Speaks!" at http://allhiphop.com/2008/08/04/michael-corleone-blanco-the-son-of-cocaine-cowboys-griselda-blanco-speaks, accessed August 4, 2008.
134. Guarnizo, *La patrona de Pablo Escobar.*
135. Journalist Jennie Smith, conversation with the author, October 5, 2012. Smith lives in Medellín. Also see Jennie Erin Smith, *Cocaine Cowgirl: The Outrageous Life and Mysterious Death of Griselda Blanco* (n.p.: Byliner Originals, 2013), Kindle edition, at https://www.byliner.com/originals/cocaine-cowgirl?hbl, accessed October 6, 2013. Smith found that prior to her death Griselda lived with a woman, Carmen, and her family. Carmen and Blanco had known each other for years and were rumored to be lovers. After Blanco's murder, Carmen and her relatives continued to live in Blanco's house until Michael, Blanco's son, forced them from the home.
136. Jenny Smith, conversation with the author, October 5, 2012.
137. "No Antiwoman Job Bias in the Narcotics Trade," *New York Times*, April 22, 1975.
138. Kathy Burke, telephone interview with the author, February 4, 2011.
139. Drug Enforcement Administration and Metro-Dade Police Department, reported in U.S. Congress, Office of Technology Assessment, *The Border War on Drugs* (Washington, D.C: Government Printing Office, 1987), 9.

CONCLUSION

1. "The Gangster Matriarch of L.A.," *Daily Beast*, September 13, 2010. It is not lost on me that León, like the Hernandez family, was rumored to have connections to the Mexican Mafia (la Eme).
2. Christine Pelisek, "Federal Indictment Targets Street Crime Family," *LA Weekly*, June 27, 2008.
3. Ibid.
4. Sam Quiñones, "Outside the Law," *Los Angeles Times*, March 30, 2008.
5. "Woman's Link to Mexican Drug Cartel a Saga of Corruption on U.S. Side of the Border," *Washington Post*, September 12, 2010. The coverage also contained a detailed description of Garnica's contacts. This is not the first female customs agent involved in drugs; I have found such cases dating to the 1950s.
6. See for example, Carey, "'Selling Is More of a Habit than Using'"; and Elaine Carey, "Women with Golden Arms: Narco-Trafficking in North America, 1900–1970," *History Compass* 6, no. 1 (2008): 774–95.
7. Carey and Cisneros Guzmán, "The Daughters of La Nacha," 23–24.
8. Bureau of Social Hygiene, Series 3, Rockefeller Archive, Tarrytown, New York. See also California Legislature, "Report on Drug Addiction in California by the State Narcotic Committee" (Sacramento: California State Printing Office, 1926), box 230, New York Academy of Medicine; and Dr. Charles Winick, "Some

Observations of the Life-Cycle of Addiction and of the Addict," *United Nations Bulletin: Drug Addiction and Narcotics* (January 1964), at http://www.unodc.org/unodc/en/data-and-analysis/bulletin/bulletin_1964-01-01_1_page002.html.

9. Cisneros Guzmán, "Las tres jefas," 125–38.

10. Julio Scherer García, *La reina del Pacífico: es la hora de contar* (Mexico City: Grijalbo, 2008).

11. Abadinsky, *Organized Crime*. Discussion with Elaine Carey, January 20, 2011, Queens, New York.

12. See Rafael Rodríguez Castañeda, ed., *El México narco* (Mexico City: Planeta, 2009), 13–17.

13. James D. Calder, "Mafia Women in Non-Fiction: What Primary and Secondary Sources Reveal," in *Contemporary Issues in Organized Crime*, ed. Jay Albanese (Monsay, NY: Criminal Justice Press, 1995), 111–40.

14. Nancy Campbell, *Using Women*, 71.

15. Anderson, "Dimensions of Women's Power in the Illicit Drug Economy"; Block, "Aw, Your Mother's in the Mafia"; Howard Campbell, *Drug War Zone*; Dunlap and Johnson, "Family and Human Resources," 175–98; Denton, *Dealing*; and Maher and Curtis, "Women on the Edge of Crime." Also, I have relied on informal conversations with colleagues Ellen Boegel, Ric Curtis, Larry Sullivan, and Barry Spunt of John Jay College of Criminal Justice.

16. Herlinghaus, *Violence Without Guilt*, 4.

17. Roark, *The Coin of Contraband*. Garland Roark Papers, box 14, Correspondence and "Coin of Contraband," East Texas Research Center, Stephen F. Austin University.

18. Dominic Rushe, "HSBC Sorry for Aiding Mexican Drug Lords, Rogue States, and Terrorists," *Guardian*, July 17, 2012.

19. Hennessy, "Open Secrets," 310–22.

20. Astorga, *Drogas sin fronteras*; Astorga, *El siglo de las drogas*; and Élmer Mendoza, *Un asesino solitario* (Mexico City: Tusquets, 1999). For information regarding Marquez, see Reed Johnson, "Art in a Gangster's Paradise: Culiacan's Painters and Writers Illuminate the Mythology Surrounding Mexico's Drug Lords," *Los Angeles Times*, March 2, 2003. Gabriela Polit Dueñas, *Narrating Narcos: Culiacán and Medellín* (Pittsburgh, PA: University of Pittsburgh Press, 2013).

21. For arguments made over and over in the history of narcotics, see Courtwright, *Dark Paradise*; Gootenberg, *Andean Cocaine*; and Musto, *The American Disease*.

22. Kenney, *From Pablo to Osama*.

23. Felipe Aljure, "El tercermundo no existe," presentation at Narco-Epic Unbound, April 5, 2008, Pittsburgh; and Felipe Aljure, director, *El colombian dream*, Cinempresa, 2006.

BIBLIOGRAPHY

Archives and Libraries

United States

East Texas Research Center, Stephen F. Austin State University, Nacogdoches, TX
Franklin D. and Eleanor Roosevelt Library, New Hyde Park, NY
Lindesmith Library, New York, NY
Lloyd Sealy Library, John Jay College of Criminal Justice, New York, NY
    Special Collections
    The Trial Transcripts of the County of New York, 1883–1927
National Archives and Records Administration (II), College Park, MD
    Record Group 170, Drug Enforcement Administration
    Record Group 59, State Department
National Archives and Records Administration, Fort Worth, TX
National Archives and Records Administration, Kansas City, MO
    RG 129 Records of the Bureau of Prisons
National Archives and Records Administration, New York, NY
    RG 21.34 Records of U.S. District Court, Eastern Division
    RG 21.34 Records of U.S. District Court, Southern Division
National Archives and Records Administration, Riverside, CA
    RG 21.6 Records of the U.S. District Court, Central Division, Los Angeles, CA
National Archives and Records Administration, San Francisco, CA
    RG 128 Bureau of Prisons
New York Academy of Medicine, New York, NY
New York Public Library, New York, NY
    Dorot Jewish Division
    Manuscripts and Archives
    Science, Industry, and Business
    Stephen A. Schwarzman Building
Rockefeller Archive, Tarrytown, NY

St. John's University
    Kathryn and Shelby Cullom Davis Library
    Rittenberg Law Library

Mexico
Archivo General de la Nación, Mexico City
    Dirección General de Prevención y Readaptación Social
    Dirección General de Gobierno
    Secretaría de Salubridad y Asistencia
    Dirección Federal de Seguridad
    Álvaro Obregón / Plutarco Elías Calles
    Lázaro Cárdenas
    Manuel Ávila Camacho
    Adolfo Ruiz Cortines
    Adolfo López Mateos
    Gustavo Díaz Ordaz
    Luis Echeverría
Archivo Histórico de la Secretaría de la Salud, Mexico City
Archivo Histórico "Genero Estrada," Secretaría de Relaciones Exteriores
Fototeca, Pachuca, Hidalgo
Biblioteca Nacional, Mexico City
Hemeroteca Nacional, Mexico City

Newspapers and Periodicals
Addiction
American Magazine
American Weekly
Annual Report of the Narcotic Drug Control Commission
BNDD Bulletin
Boletín del departamento de salubridad pública
Boletín de salubridad e higiene
Bulletin on Drug Addiction and Narcotics
Bulletin on Narcotics
Chicago Tribune
Crime and Delinquency
Crime Control Digest
Criminalia
Criminal Law Reporter
Eugenesia
Eugenics: A Journal of Race Betterment
Excélsior

FBI Bulletin
Higiene
International Narcotics Control Strategy Report
Jornada, La
Journal of Drug Issues
Law Enforcement Bulletin
Los Angeles Times
Nacional, La
NACLA Report on the Americas
*Narc Officer: Official Publication of the International Narcotics Enforcement Officers
    Association.*
Narcotics Control Digest
Narcotics Education
Narcotics Enforcement and Prevention Digest
Narcotics Law Bulletin
National Geographic
New Yorker
New York Times
Organized Crime Digest
Police Chief
Popular Science Monthly
Prensa, La
Salubridad
Trends in Organized Crime
Universal, El

Fiction

Burroughs, William S. *The Burroughs File*. San Francisco, CA: City Lights Books,
    1984.
———. *Cities of the Red Night*. New York: Viking Press, 1981.
———. *Naked Lunch*. New York: Grove Press, 1959.
———. *The Wild Boys: A Book of the Dead*. New York: Grove Press, 1971.
Kerouac, Jack. *Tristessa*. New York: McGraw-Hill, 1960.
Lee, Harper. *To Kill a Mockingbird*. 1960. New York: HarperCollins, 2010.
Mendoza, Élmer. *Un asesino solitario*. Mexico City: Tusquets, 1999.
O'Neill, Eugene. *Long Day's Journey into Night*. 1956. New Haven, CT: Yale University
    Press, 2002.
Pérez-Reverte, Arturo. *La reina del sur*. Madrid: Alfaguara, 2002. Translated by Andrew
    Hurley as *The Queen of the South*. New York: Putnam, 2004.
Revueltas, José. *El apando*. Mexico City: Ediciones Era, 2005.
Villaseñor, Victor. *Rain of Gold*. Houston, TX: Arte Publico Press, 1991.

Villegas Gómez, Oscar. *La señora: una mujer en el narcotráfico*. Bogotá: D. H. G.
    Impresos, 2002.

Film

Aljure, Felipe, director. *El colombian dream*. Cinempresa, 2006.
Almada, Natalia, director. *Al otro lado*. Public Broadcasting Service, POV series, 2006.
Corben, Billy, director. *Cocaine Cowboys*. Magnolia Pictures, 2006.
——. *Cocaine Cowboys 2: Hustlin' with the Godmother*. Magnolia Pictures, 2008.
Demme, Ted, director. *Blow*. New Line Cinema, 2001.
De Palma, Brian, director. *Scarface*. Universal Pictures, 1983.
Durán Rojas, Fernando, director. *Narcos y perros*. Vanguard Cinema, 2005.
Friedkin, William, director. *The French Connection*. 20th Century Fox, 1971.
History Channel. *Hooked: Illegal Drugs and How They Got That Way*. Vol. 1, *Marijuana
    and Methamphetamine/Opium, Morphine, and Heroin*; vol. 2, *Cocaine/LSD,
    Ecstasy, and the Raves*. 2005.
Levin, Marc, director. *Mr. Untouchable*. Blowback Productions, 2007.
Marston, Joshua, director. *María Full of Grace*. HBO Films, 2004.
Public Broadcasting Service. "The Family Connection." Frontline, *Drug Wars*,
    October 9–10, 2000. At http://www.pbs.org/wgbh/pages/frontline/shows/drugs
    /business/afo/afosummary.html.
Scott, Ridley, director. *American Gangster*. Universal Pictures, 2007.
Soderbergh, Steven, director. *Traffic*. Bedford Falls Productions, 2000.
Stevenson, Robert, director. *To the Ends of the Earth*. Columbia Pictures, 1948.

Primary Sources

Agnew, Derek. *Undercover Agent, Narcotics: The Dramatic Story of the World's Secret
    War Against Drug Racketeers*. London: Souvenir Press 1959.
Anslinger, Harry J. "Marijuana: Assassin of Youth." *American Magazine* 124, no. 1 (July
    1937).
Anslinger, Harry J., and William F. Tompkins. *The Traffic in Narcotics*. New York:
    Funk and Wagnalls, 1953.
Anslinger, Harry J., and Will Oursler. *The Murderers: The Shocking Story of the Narcotic
    Gangs*. New York: Farrar, Straus and Cudahy, 1961.
Ashbrook, Debra L., and Linda C. Solley. *Women and Heroin Abuse: A Survey of Sex-
    ism in Drug Abuse Administration*. Palo Alto, CA: R & E Research Associates,
    1979.
Bailey, Stanley Hartnoll. *The Anti-drug Campaign: An Experiment in International
    Control*. London: P. S. King & Son, 1935.
Baker, D. Keith. *Discipline Is Not a Dirty Word*. Washington, D.C.: U.S. Drug Enforce-
    ment Administration, 1973.
Beard, George Miller. *Stimulants and Narcotics*. New York: Arno Press, 1981.

Bellingham City Schools. "Program for Instruction in the Elementary Grades Concerning the Evils of Narcotics (Alcohol, Tobacco, and Habit-Forming Drugs)." Bellingham, WA: Bellingham City Schools, 1930.

Bingley, Reverend William. *Travels in North America*. London: Harvey and Darton, 1821.

California, State Senate Narcotic Committee. "Report on Drug Addiction in California." Sacramento: California State Printing Office, 1926.

Campbell, Nancy, J. P. Olsen, and Luke Walden. *The Narcotic Farm: The Rise and Fall of America's First Prison for Drug Addicts*. New York: Abrams, 2008.

Castellanos, Israel. *La delincuencia femenina en Cuba: indices filiativos y album identosocópico*. Havana: Dorrbecker, 1929.

Courtwright, David T., Herman Joseph, and Don Des Jarlais. *Addicts Who Survived: An Oral History of Narcotic Use in America, 1923–1965*. Knoxville: University of Tennessee Press, 1989.

Dai, Bingham. *Opium Addiction in Chicago*. 1937. Reprint, Montclair, NJ: Patterson Smith, 1970.

Daniels, Josephus. *Shirt-Sleeve Diplomat*. Chapel Hill: University of North Carolina Press, 1947.

Department of State. "Slave and Coolie Trade: Message from the President." Washington, D.C.: A. O. P. Nicholson, Senate Printer, 1956.

Department of the Treasury. "Traffic in Opium and Other Dangerous Drugs." Washington, D.C.: Government Printing Office, 1940.

Dunham, Lawrence Boardman. *The Geneva Convention of 1931: Convention for Limiting the Manufacture and Regulating the Distribution of Narcotic Drugs*. New York: Bureau of Social Hygiene, 1932.

Einstein, Izzy. *Prohibition Agent No. 1*. New York: Frederick A. Stokes, 1932.

Eisenlohr, L. E. S. *International Narcotics Control*. London: George Allen and Unwin, 1934.

Federal Bureau of Narcotics. "Digest of Court Decisions Under the Harrison Narcotic Law and Other Related Statutes, for Narcotic Agents and Inspectors, United States Attorneys, and Others Concerned." Washington, D.C.: Government Printing Office, 1931.

———. *Traffic in Opium and Other Dangerous Drugs*. Washington, D.C.: Government Printing Office, 1942.

Federal Narcotic Control Board. *Traffic in Opium and Other Dangerous Drugs with Respect to the Philippine Islands*. Report by the Government of the United States. Washington, D.C.: Government Printing Office, 1929.

Ferrucci, Giovanni. *Bootlegger*. New York: Independent Publishing Company, 1932.

Finlator, John. *The Drugged Nation: A "Narc's" Story*. New York: Simon and Schuster, 1973.

Fossey, Mathieu de. *Viaje a Méjico*. Mexico City: Imprenta de Ignacio Cumplido, 1844.

Gay, Robert. *Lucia: Testimonies of a Brazilian Drug Dealer's Woman*. Philadelphia, PA: Temple University Press, 2005.

Goethe, C. M. "The Influx of Mexican Amerinds." *Eugenics: A Journal of Race Betterment* 1, no. 3 (December 1928): 6–9.

González Félix, Maricela. *Viaje al corazón de la península: testimonio de Manuel Lee Mancilla.* Mexicali: Instituto de Cultura de Baja California, 2000.

Graham-Mulhall, Sara. *Opium: The Demon Flower.* New York: H. Vinal, 1926.

Guerrero, Julio. *Causas de la transformación monetaria de México: disertación de economía política presentada a la Academia de Ciencias Sociales en México.* Mexico City: Imprenta del Gobierno Federal, 1905.

———. *La génesis del crimen en México: estudio de psiquiatría social.* Paris and Mexico City: Vda de C. Bouret, 1901.

International Narcotic Education Association and Enoch George Payne. *The Menace of Narcotic Drugs: A Discussion of Narcotics and Education.* New York: Prentice Hall, 1931.

Kelynack, T. N., MD. *The Drink Problem of To-day in Its Medico-sociological Aspects.* New York: E. P. Dutton, 1916.

Kolb, Lawrence. *Drug Addiction: A Medical Problem.* Springfield, IL: Charles Thomas, 1962.

League of Nations. Records of the Conference for the Limitation of the Manufacture of Narcotic Drugs, Geneva, May 27–July 13, 1931.

———. Traffic in Opium and Other Dangerous Drugs: Analysis of the International Trade in Morphine, Diacetylmorphine, and Cocaine for the Years 1925–1929. Records of the Conference on the Limitation of the Manufacture of Narcotic Drugs, Geneva, May 27–July 13, 1931.

———. Records of the Conference for the Suppression of the Illicit Traffic in Dangerous Drugs, Geneva, June 8–26, 1936.

Levine, Michael. *The Big White Lie: The Deep Cover Operation That Exposed the CIA Sabotage of the Drug War.* Emeryville, CA: Thunder's Mouth Press, 1994.

Lewin, Louis, and P. H. A. Wirth. *Phantastica: Narcotic and Stimulating Drugs; Their Use and Abuse.* London: Kegan Paul, Trench, Trübner, 1931.

Liddy, G. Gordon. *Will: The Autobiography of G. Gordon Liddy.* New York: St. Martin's Press, 1980.

Mermelstein, Max, with Robin Moore and Richard Smitten. *The Man Who Made It Snow: By the American Mastermind Inside the Colombian Cartel.* New York: Simon and Schuster, 1990.

Myerson, Abraham. *The Nervous Housewife.* 1920. Reprint, New York: Arno Press, 1972.

Nacaveva, A. *Diario de un narcotraficante.* Mexico City: B. Costa-Amic, 1967.

National Institute on Drug Abuse. "Drug Dependence in Pregnancy: Clinical Management of Mother and Child." Rockville, MD: Department of Health, Education, and Welfare, Public Health Service, Alcohol, Drug Abuse, and Mental Health Administration, National Institute on Drug Abuse, Division of Resource Development, Services Research Branch, 1979.

Pérez Montfort, Ricardo. *Yerba, goma, y polvo: drogas, ambientes, y policía en México, 1900–1940*. Mexico City: Ediciones Era, 1999.

Pettey, George. "The Heroin Habit: Another Curse." *Alabama Medical Journal* 15 (1903): 174–80.

Poniatowska, Elena. *Here's to You, Jesusa!* Translated by Deanna Heikkinen. New York: Penguin, 2002.

Rodríguez Manzanera, Luis. *La drogadicción de la juventud en México*. Mexico City: Ediciones Botas, 1974.

Romero, José María. *Comisión de inmigración: dictamen del vocal ingeniero José María Romero encargado de estudiar la influencia social y económica de la inmigración asiática en México*. Mexico City: A. Carranza e Hijos, 1911.

Roumagnac, Carlos. *Los criminales en México: ensayo de psicología criminal*. Mexico City: Tipografía "El Fénix," 1904.

Saavedra, Alfredo M. *Manual de trabajo social*. Mexico City: Editorial Polis, 1958.

Sahagún, Fray Bernardino de. *A History of Ancient Mexico, 1547–1577: Anthropological, Mythological and Social*. New York: Blaine Ethridge, 1931.

Scherer García, Julio. *La reina del Pacífico: es la hora de contar*. Mexico City: Grijalbo, 2008.

Simon, Carleton. *Control of Narcotics*. New York: n.p., 1923.

———. *Plants That Incite to Crime*. New York: n.p., 1940.

State of New York. *Annual Report of the Narcotic Drug Control Commission*. Albany: J. B. Lyon Company, 1919.

Street, Leroy, and David Loth. *I Was a Drug Addict*. New York: Random House, 1953.

Terry, Charles Edward. *A Further Study and Report on the Use of Narcotics Under the Provisions of Federal Law in Six Communities in the United States of America for the Period of July 1, 1923, to June 30, 1924*. New York: Bureau of Social Hygiene, 1927.

Terry, Charles Edward, and Mildred Pellens. *The Opium Problem*. New York: Bureau of Social Hygiene, 1928.

United States Congress. Hearings Before the Committee on Ways and Means, Bureau of Narcotics, House of Representatives, Seventy-First Congress, second session, 10561. Washington, D.C.: Government Printing Office, 1930.

———. "Illicit Narcotics Traffic." Hearings Before the Subcommittee on Improvements in the Federal Criminal Code, Committee on the Judiciary House of Representatives, Eighty-Fourth Congress. Washington, D.C.: Government Printing Office, 1956.

———. "Oversight of Federal Drug Interdiction Efforts in Mexico: Review of a Rising National Security Threat." Hearings Before the Subcommittee on National Security, International Affairs, and Criminal Justice, Committee on Government Reform and Oversight, House of Representatives, 104th Congress, second session, June 12, 1996. Washington, D.C.: Government Printing Office, 1997.

———. "Women's Dependency on Prescription Drugs." Hearings Before the Select Committee on Narcotics Abuse and Control, House of Representatives,

Ninety-Sixth Congress, first session, September 13, 1979. Washington, D.C.: Government Printing Office, 1979.

United States Senate. "Organized Crime and Illicit Traffic in Narcotics." Report of the Committee on Government. Washington, D.C.: Government Printing Office, 1965.

Walker, William O., III, ed. *Drugs in the Western Hemisphere: An Odyssey of Cultures in Conflict.* Wilmington, DE: Scholarly Resources, 1996.

Woods, Arthur. *Dangerous Drugs: The World Fight Against Illicit Traffic in Narcotics.* New Haven, CT: Yale University Press, 1931.

Viceversa. "Tras la huella de María Sabina." Special edition on María Sabina. *Viceversa* 63 (August 1998).

Secondary Sources

Abadinsky, Howard. *Organized Crime.* Chicago, IL: Nelson Hall, 1985.

Abraham, Itty, and Willem van Schendel. "Introduction: The Making of Illicitness." In *Illicit Flows and Criminal Things: States, Borders, and the Other Side of Globalization,* edited by Willem van Schendel and Itty Abraham, 4–25. Bloomington: Indiana University Press, 2005.

Acker, Caroline Jean. *Creating the American Junkie: Addiction Research in the Classic Era of Narcotic Control.* Baltimore, MD: Johns Hopkins University Press, 2002.

———. "Portrait of an Addicted Family: Dynamics of Opium Addiction in the Early Twentieth Century." In *Altering American Consciousness: The History of Alcohol and Drug Use in the United States, 1800–2000,* edited by Sarah W. Tracy and Caroline Jean Acker, 165–81. Amherst: University of Massachusetts Press, 2004.

Adams, Rachel. "Hipsters and Jipitecas: Literary Countercultures on Both Sides of the Border." *American Literary History* 16, no. 1 (Spring 2004): 58–84.

Addison, James Thayer. *The Episcopal Church in the United States, 1789–1931.* New York: Charles Scribner's Sons, 1951.

———. *Memorial Sermons Commemorative of Charles Henry Brent.* Buffalo: Diocese of Western New York, 1929.

Adler, Freda, and Rita James Simon, eds. *The Criminology of Deviant Women.* New York: Houghton Mifflin, 1979.

Adler, Patricia. *Wheeling and Dealing: An Ethnography of an Upper-Level Drug Dealing and Smuggling Community.* New York: Columbia University Press, 1993.

Aguirre, Carlos, and Robert Buffington, eds. *Reconstructing Criminality in Latin America.* Wilmington, DE: Scholarly Resources, 2001.

Alamillo, José M. *Making Lemonade out of Lemons: Mexican American Labor and Leisure in a California Town, 1880–1960.* Urbana: University of Illinois Press, 2006.

Albanese, Jay, ed. *Contemporary Issues in Organized Crime.* Monsay, NY: Criminal Justice Press, 1995.

Alonso, Ana María. *Thread of Blood: Colonialism, Revolution, and Gender on Mexico's Northern Frontier.* Tucson: University of Arizona Press, 1995.

Álvarez Amézquita, José. *Historia de la salubridad y del asistencia en México*. Mexico City: Secretaría de Salubridad y Asistencia, 1960.

Anderson, Benedict. *Imagined Communities: Reflections on the Origin and Spread of Nationalism*. London: Verso, 1991.

Anderson, Tammy. "Dimensions of Women's Power in the Illicit Drug Economy." *Theoretical Criminology* 9, no. 4 (November 2005): 371–400.

Andreas, Peter. *Border Games: Policing the U.S.-Mexico Divide*. Ithaca, NY: Cornell University Press, 2006.

——. "Smuggling Wars: Law Enforcement and Law Evasion in a Changing World." In *Transnational Crime in the Americas*, edited by Tom Farer, 85–98. New York: Routledge, 1999.

Andreas, Peter, and Ethan Nadelmann. *Policing the Globe: Criminalization and Crime Control in International Relations*. Oxford: Oxford University Press, 2006.

Appier, Janis. *Policing Women: The Sexual Politics of Law Enforcement and the LAPD*. Philadelphia, PA: Temple University Press, 1998.

Arias, Enrique Desmond. *Drugs and Democracy in Rio de Janeiro: Trafficking, Social Networks, and Public Security*. Chapel Hill: University of North Carolina Press, 2006.

Armus, Diego, ed. *Disease in the History of Modern Latin America: From Malaria to AIDS*. Durham, NC: Duke University Press, 2003.

Arrom, Silvia Marina. *The Women of Mexico City, 1790–1857*. Stanford, CA: Stanford University Press, 1985.

Astorga, Luis. *Drogas sin fronteras: los expedientes de una guerra permanente*. Mexico City: Grijalbo, 2003.

——. *El siglo de las drogas: el narcotráfico, del Porfiriato al nuevo milenio*. Mexico City: Plaza y Janés, 2005.

——. "Organized Crime and the Organization of Crime." In *Organized Crime and Democratic Governability: Mexico and the U.S.-Mexican Borderlands*, edited by John Bailey and Roy Godson, 58–82. Pittsburgh, PA: University of Pittsburgh Press, 1999.

Azaola, Elena. *El delito de ser mujer*. Mexico City: Plaza y Valdés, 1996.

——. *La institución correccional en México: una mirada extraviada*. Mexico City: Siglo Veintiuno Editores, 1990.

Azaola, Elena, and Cristina José Yacamán. *Las mujeres olvidadas: un estudio sobre la situación actual de las cárceles de mujeres en la República mexicana*. Mexico City: El Colegio de México, Programa Interdisciplinario de Estudios de la Mujer, 1996.

Bailey, John, and Roy Godson, eds. *Organized Crime and Democratic Governability: Mexico and the U.S.-Mexican Borderlands*. Pittsburgh, PA: University of Pittsburgh Press, 1999.

Balderrama, Francisco E., and Raymond Rodríguez. *Decade of Betrayal: Mexican Repatriation in the 1930s*. Albuquerque: University of New Mexico Press, 2006.

Barenque, Gregorio Oneto. *La mariguana ante la Academia Nacional de Medicina: refutación al trabajo presentado por el Dr. Leopoldo Salazar y Viniegra.* Mexico City: n.p., 1938.

Baud, Michiel, and Willem van Schendel. "Toward a Comparative History of Borderlands." *Journal of World History* 8, no. 2 (Fall 1997): 211–42.

Beckerleg, Susan, and Gillian Hundt. "Women Heroin Users: Exploring the Limitations of the Structural Violence Approach." *International Journal of Drug Policy* 16, no. 3 (June 2005): 183–90.

Behan, Tom. *The Camorra: Political Criminality in Italy.* New York: Routledge, 1996.

Bergquist, Charles, Ricardo Peñaranda, and Gonzalo Sánchez G. *Violence in Colombia, 1990–2000: Waging War and Negotiating Peace.* Wilmington, DE: Scholarly Resources, 2001.

Bishop, Cecil. *Women and Crime.* London: Chatto and Windus, 1931.

Black, Edwin. *War Against the Weak: Eugenics and America's Campaign to Create a Master Race.* New York: Four Walls Eight Windows, 2003.

Blackwelder, Julia Kirk. *Women of the Depression: Caste and Culture in San Antonio, 1929–1939.* College Station: Texas A&M University Press, 1984.

Blancornelas, Jesús. *El Cártel.* Mexico City: Random House, 2002.

Bliss, Katherine Elaine. *Compromised Positions: Prostitution, Public Health, and Gender Politics in Revolutionary Mexico City.* University Park: Penn State University Press, 2001.

Block, Alan A. "Aw, Your Mother's in the Mafia: Women Criminals in Progressive New York." *Crime Law and Social Change* 1, no. 1 (December 1976): 5–22.

——. "The Snowman Cometh: Coke in Progressive New York." *Criminology* 17, no. 1 (May 1979): 75–99.

Blok, Anton. *The Mafia of a Sicilian Village, 1860–1960: A Study of Violent Peasant Entrepreneurs.* New York: Harper and Row, 1974.

Blum, Ann S. "Bring It Back Home: Perspectives on Gender and Family History in Modern Mexico." *History Compass* 4, no. 5 (2006): 906–26.

Bourne, Peter G. "The Great Cocaine Myth." *Drugs and Drug Abuse Newsletter* 5, no. 5 (1974): 37.

Bowden, Charles. *Down by the River: Drugs, Money, Murder, and Family.* New York: Simon and Schuster, 2002.

Boyd, Susan. *From Witches to Crack Moms: Women, Drug Law, and Policy.* Durham, NC: Carolina Academic Press, 2004.

——. *Mothers on Illegal Drugs: Transcending Myths.* Toronto: University of Toronto Press, 1999.

Boylan, Kristina A. "Gendering the Faith and Altering the Nation: Mexican Catholic Women's Activism, 1917–1940." In *Sex in Revolution: Gender, Politics, and Power in Modern Mexico*, edited by Jocelyn Olcott, Mary Kay Vaughan, and Gabriela Cano, 199–222. Durham, NC: Duke University Press, 2006.

Brown, E. Richard. *Rockefeller Medicine Men: Medicine and Capitalism in America.* Berkeley: University of California Press, 1979.

Bruccet Anaya, Luis Alonso. *El crimen organizado: origen, evolución, situación y configuración de la delincuencia organizada en México.* Mexico City: Librería Porrúa: 2001.

Bruinius, Harry. *Better for All the World: The Secret History of Forced Sterilization and America's Quest for Racial Purity.* New York: Alfred A. Knopf, 2006.

Buffington, Robert M. *Criminal and Citizen in Modern Mexico.* Lincoln: University of Nebraska Press, 2000.

Burgess-Proctor, Amanda. "Intersections of Race, Class, Gender, and Crime: Future Directions for Feminist Criminology." *Feminist Criminology* 1, no. 1 (January 2006): 27–47.

Burnham, John C. *Bad Habits: Drinking, Smoking, Taking Drugs, Gambling, Sexual Misbehavior, and Swearing in American History.* New York: New York University Press, 1993.

Butler, Judith. *Gender Trouble: Feminism and the Subversion of Identity.* New York: Routledge, 1999.

Cairns, Kathleen A. *Hard Time at Tehachapi: California's First Women's Prison.* Albuquerque: University of New Mexico Press, 2009.

Calder, James D. "Mafia Women in Non-Fiction: What Primary and Secondary Sources Reveal." In *Contemporary Issues in Organized Crime*, edited by Jay Albanese, 111–40. Monsay, NY: Criminal Justice Press, 1995.

Calderón, Fernando Herrera, and Adela Cedillo, eds. *Challenging Authoritarianism in Mexico: Revolutionary Struggles and the Dirty War, 1964–1982.* New York: Routledge, 2012.

Campbell, Howard. *Drug War Zone: Frontline Dispatches from the Streets of El Paso and Juárez.* Austin: University of Texas Press, 2009.

———. "Female Drug Smugglers on the U.S.-Mexico Border: Gender, Crime, and Empowerment." *Anthropological Quarterly* 81, no. 1 (Winter 2008): 233–67.

Campbell, Nancy D. *Using Women: Gender, Drug Policy, and Social Justice.* New York: Routledge, 2000.

Campos, Isaac. *Home Grown: Marijuana and the Origins of Mexico's War on Drugs.* Chapel Hill: University of North Carolina Press, 2012.

———. "Marijuana, Madness, and Modernity in Global Mexico, 1545–1920." PhD diss., Harvard University, 2006.

Cano, Gabriela. "Unconceivable Realities of Desire: Amelia Robles's (Transgender) Masculinity in the Mexican Revolution." In *Sex in Revolution: Gender, Politics, and Power in Modern Mexico*, edited by Jocelyn Olcott, Mary Kay Vaughan, and Gabriela Cano, 35–51. Durham, NC: Duke University Press, 2006.

Cárdenas de Ojeda, Olga. *Toxicomanía y narcotráfico: aspecto legales.* Mexico City: Fondo de Cultura Económica, 1976.

Carey, Elaine. *Plaza of Sacrifices: Gender, Power, and Terror in 1968 Mexico.* Albuquerque: University of New Mexico Press, 2005.

———. "'Selling Is More of a Habit than Using': Narcotraficante Lola la Chata and Her Threat to Civilization, 1930–1960." *Journal of Women's History* 21, no. 2 (Summer 2009): 62–89.

———. "Women with Golden Arms: Narco-Trafficking in North America, 1900–1970." *History Compass* 6, no. 1 (2008): 774–95.

Carey, Elaine, and Andrae Marak, eds. *Smugglers, Brothels, and Twine: Historical Perspectives on Contraband and Vice in North America's Borderlands.* Tucson: University of Arizona Press, 2011.

Carey, Elaine, and José Carlos Cisneros Guzmán. "The Daughters of La Nacha: Women, Drugs, and the Border." *NACLA Report on the Americas* (May–June 2011): 23–24.

Carlen, Pat, Jenny Hicks, Josie O'Dwyer, Diana Christina, and Chris Tchaikovsky, eds. *Criminal Women.* Cambridge: Polity Press, 1985.

Carr, Barry. *Marxism and Communism in Twentieth-Century Mexico.* Lincoln: University of Nebraska Press, 1992.

Carstairs, Catherine. *Jailed for Possession: Illegal Drug Use, Regulation, and Power in Canada, 1920–1961.* Toronto: University of Toronto Press, 2006.

Cartwright, Gary. *Galveston: A History of the Island.* Forth Worth: Texas Christian University Press, 1998.

Castañón Cuadros, Carlos. *Las dos repúblicas: una aproximación a la migración china hacia Torrerón, 1924–1963.* Torreón, Coahuila: Ediciones del R. Ayuntamiento, 2004.

Cedillo, Juan Alberto. *La cosa nostra en México, 1938–1950.* Mexico City: Grijalbo, 2011.

Chao Romero, Robert. "Chinese Immigrant Smuggling to the United States via Mexico and Cuba." In *Smugglers, Brothels, and Twine: Historical Perspectives on Contraband and Vice in North America's Borderlands,* edited by Elaine Carey and Andrae Marak, 13–23. Tucson: University of Arizona Press, 2011.

———. *The Chinese in Mexico, 1882–1940.* Tucson: University of Arizona Press, 2010.

———. "El destierro de los chinos: Popular Perceptions of Chinese-Mexican Intermarriage in the Twentieth Century." *Aztlán* 32, no. 1 (Spring 2007): 113–44.

Chein, Isidor, Donald L. Gerard, Robert S. Lee, Eva Rosenfeld, and Daniel M. Wilner. *The Road to H: Narcotics, Delinquency, and Social Policy.* New York: Basic Books, 1964.

Chesney-Lind, Meda, and Lisa Pasko, eds. *Girls, Women, and Crime: Selected Readings.* Thousand Oaks, CA: Sage Publications, 2004.

Cisneros Guzmán, José Carlos. "Las tres jefas." In *Las jefas del narco: el ascenso de las mujeres en crimen organizado,* edited by Arturo Santamaría Gómez, 125–38. Mexico City: Grijalbo, 2012.

Cohen, Rich. *Tough Jews: Fathers, Sons, and Gangster Dreams.* New York: Simon and Schuster, 1998.

Collins, John Patrick. "Traffic in the Traffickers: Extradition and the Controlled Substances Import and Export Act of 1970." *Yale Law Journal* (March 1974): 706–44.

Consejo Nacional para la Cultura y las Artes. *China en las californias.* Tijuana: Centro Cultural Tijuana, 2002.

Courtwright, David T. *Dark Paradise: A History of Opiate Addiction in America.* Cambridge, MA: Harvard University Press, 2001.

———. *Forces of Habit: Drugs and the Making of the Modern World.* Cambridge, MA: Harvard University Press, 2001.

Cressey, Donald. *Theft of the Nation: The Structure and Operations of Organized Crime in America.* New York: Harper and Row, 1969.

Cross, John C. *Informal Politics: Street Vendors and the State in Mexico City.* Stanford, CA: Stanford University Press, 1998.

Cueto, Marco, ed. *Missionaries of Science: The Rockefeller Foundation and Latin America.* Bloomington: Indiana University Press, 1994.

DeGrandpre, Richard. *The Cult of Pharmacology: How America Became the World's Most Troubled Drug Culture.* Durham, NC: Duke University Press, 2006.

Denton, Barbara. *Dealing: Women in the Drug Economy.* Sydney: University of New South Wales Press, 2001.

Denton, Barbara, and Pat O'Malley. "Gender, Trust, and Business: Women Drug Dealers in the Illicit Economy." *British Journal of Criminology* 39, no. 4 (1999): 513–60.

Desroches, Frederick J. *The Crime That Pays: Drug Trafficking and Organized Crime in Canada.* Toronto: Canadian Scholars' Press, 2005.

Díaz, George. "Twilight of the Tequileros: Prohibition-Era Smuggling in the South Texas Borderlands, 1919–1933." In *Smugglers, Brothels, and Twine: Historical Perspectives on Contraband and Vice in North America's Borderlands,* edited by Elaine Carey and Andrae Marak, 59–79. Tucson: University of Arizona Press, 2011.

Dubs, H. H. "The Chinese in Mexico City in 1635." *Far Eastern Quarterly* 1, no. 1 (1942): 387–89.

Duffin, Allan T. *History in Blue: 160 Years of Women Police, Sheriffs, Detectives, and State Troopers.* New York: Kaplan Publishing, 2010.

Dugdale, Robert L. *The Jukes: A Study in Crime, Pauperism, Disease, and Heredity.* 4th ed. New York: G. P. Putnam's Sons, 1919.

Dunlap, Eloise, and Bruce D. Johnson. "Family and Human Resources in the Development of a Female Crack Seller: Case Study of a Hidden Population." *Journal of Drug Issues* 26, no. 1 (1996): 175–98.

Dunlap, Eloise, Bruce Johnson, and Lisa Maher. "Female Crack Sellers in New York City: Who They Are and What They Do." *Women and Criminal Justice* 8, no. 4 (1997): 25–55.

Dunlap, Eloise, Gabriele Stürzenhofecker, and Bruce D. Johnson. "The Elusive Romance of Motherhood: Drugs, Gender, and Reproduction in Inner-City Distressed Households." *Journal of Ethnicity and Substance Abuse* 5, no. 3 (2006): 1–27.

Dunn, Timothy J. *The Militarization of the U.S.-Mexico Border, 1978–1992.* Austin: Center for Mexican-American Studies, University of Texas, 1996.

Durmaz, Huseyin. "Extradition of Terror Suspects and Developments in Extradition Process." In *Understanding and Responding to Terrorism,* edited by Huseyin Durmaz et al., 66–83. Amsterdam: IOS Press, 2007.

Durmaz, Huseyin, Bilal Sevinc, Ahmet Sait Yayla, and Siddik Ekici, eds. *Understanding and Responding to Terrorism.* Amsterdam: IOS Press, 2007.

Dwyer, John J. *The Agrarian Dispute: The Expropriation of American-Owned Rural Land in Postrevolutionary Mexico*. Durham, NC: Duke University Press, 2008.

Eburne, Jonathan Paul. "Trafficking in the Void: Burroughs, Kerouac, and the Consumption of Otherness." *Modern Fiction Studies* 43, no. 1 (1997): 53–92.

Edberg, Mark. "Drug Traffickers as Social Bandits: Culture and Drug Trafficking in Northern Mexico and the Border Region." *Journal of Contemporary Criminal Justice* 17, no. 3 (August 2001): 259–78.

Enciso, Froylán. "Drogas, narcotráfico, y política en México: protocolo de hipocresía (1969–2000)." In *Una historia contemporánea de México: las políticas*, edited by Lorenzo Meyer and Ilán Bizberg, 183–242. Mexico City: Océano, 2009.

Erie, Steven. *Rainbow's End: Irish-Americans and the Dilemmas of Urban Machine Politics, 1840–1985*. Berkeley: University of California Press, 1988.

Farer, Tom, ed. *Transnational Crime in the Americas*. New York: Routledge, 1999.

Fiandaca, Giovanni, ed. *Women and the Mafia: Female Roles in Organized Crime Structures*. New York: Springer, 2007.

Findlay, Mark. *The Globalisation of Crime: Understanding Transitional Relationships in Context*. Cambridge: Cambridge University Press, 1999.

Fiorentini, Gianluca, and Sam Peltzman, eds. *The Economics of Organised Crime*. Cambridge: Cambridge University Press, 1995.

Folbre, Nancy. *Why Pay for Kids? Gender and the Structure of Constraint*. New York: Routledge, 1994.

Fowler, Gene, and Bill Crawford. *Border Radio: Quacks, Yodelers, Pitchmen, Psychics, and Other Amazing Broadcasters of the American Airwaves*. Austin: University of Texas Press, 2002.

French, William. "Prostitutes and Guardian Angels: Women, Work, and the Family in Porfirian Mexico." *Hispanic American Historical Review* 72, no. 4 (1992): 529–53.

Fried, Richard M. *Nightmare in Red: The McCarthy Era in Perspective*. New York: Oxford University Press, 1990.

Furst, Terry R., Richard Curtis, Bruce Johnson, and Douglas S. Goldsmith. "The Rise of the Middleman/Woman in a Declining Drug Market." *Addiction Research* 7, no. 2 (1999): 103–28.

Gambetta, Diego. *The Sicilian Mafia: The Business of Private Protection*. Cambridge, MA: Harvard University Press, 1993.

Gerber, Rudolph Joseph. *Legalizing Marijuana: Drug Policy Reform and Prohibition Politics*. Westport, CT: Praeger, 2004.

Giddens, Anthony. *Modernity and Self-Identity: Self and Society in the Late Modern Age*. Stanford, CA: Stanford University Press, 1992.

Gilfoyle, Timothy. *City of Eros: New York City, Prostitution, and the Commercialization of Sex, 1790–1920*. New York: W. W. Norton, 1992.

Glass-Coffin, Bonnie. "Engendering Peruvian Shamanism Through Time: Insights from Ethnohistory and Ethnography." *Ethnohistory* 46, no. 2 (Spring 1999): 205–39.

Gómez, Laura. *Misconceiving Mothers: Legislators, Prosecutors, and the Politics of Prenatal Drug Exposure*. Philadelphia, PA: Temple University Press, 1997.

Gómez, María Idalia, and Darío Fritz. *Con la muerte en el bolsillo: seis desaforadas historias del narcotráfico en México.* Mexico City: Planeta, 2005.

Gómez Izquierdo, José Jorge, ed. *Los caminos del racismo en México.* Mexico City: Plaza y Valdés, 2005.

———. *El movimiento anti-chino en México (1871–1934): problemas del racismo y el nacionalismo durante la Revolución Mexicana.* Mexico City: Instituto Nacional de Antropología de Historia, 1991.

González Salas, Carlos. *Tampico a vuelo de concord.* Tampico, Tamaulipas: Ediciones Mar Adentro, 1996.

Gooberman, Lawrence A. *Operation Intercept: The Multiple Consequences of Public Policy.* New York: Pergamon Press, 1974.

Goodman, Jordan, Paul Lovejoy, and Andrew Sherratt, eds. *Consuming Habits: Drugs in History and Anthropology.* New York: Routledge, 1995.

Gootenberg, Paul. *Andean Cocaine: The Making of a Global Drug.* Chapel Hill: University of North Carolina Press, 2008.

———, ed. *Cocaine: Global Histories.* New York: Routledge, 1999.

———. "The 'Pre-Colombian' Era of Drug Trafficking in the Americas: Cocaine, 1945–1965." *Americas* 64, no. 2 (October 2007): 133–76.

Gordon, Avery. *Ghostly Matters: Haunting and the Sociological Imagination.* Minneapolis: University of Minnesota Press, 2008.

Grisi Quintano, Rafael. "El tráfico de drogas." *Criminologia* 3 (December 1936): 1–12.

Guadalupe García, Clara. *Islas Marías: historia de una fuga.* Mexico City: Planeta, 1991.

Guarnizo, José. *La patrona de Pablo Escobar: vida y muerte de Griselda Blanco.* Bogotá: Planeta, 2012.

Guerra, Francisco. *The Pre-Columbian Mind: A Study into the Aberrant Nature of Sexual Drives, Drugs Affecting Behaviour and the Attitude Towards Life and Death, with a Survey of Psychotherapy in Pre-Columbian America.* New York: Seminar Press, 1971.

Gutiérrez, David. *Between Two Worlds: Mexican Immigrants in the United States.* Wilmington, DE: Scholarly Resources, 1996.

Guy, Donna J. *White Slavery and Mothers Alive and Dead: The Troubled Meeting of Sex, Gender, Public Health, and Progress in Latin America.* Lincoln: University of Nebraska Press, 2000.

———. *Women Build the Welfare State: Performing Charity and Creating Rights in Argentina, 1880–1955.* Durham, NC: Duke University Press, 2009.

Guzmán, Gastón. "Hallucinogenic Mushrooms in Mexico: An Overview." Special Mushroom Issue. *Economic Botany* 62, no. 3 (2008): 404–12.

Hall, Linda B. *Oil, Banks, and Politics: The United States and Postrevolutionary Mexico, 1917–1924.* Austin: University of Texas Press, 1995.

Hardy, B. Carmon, and Melody Seymour. "Importation of Arms and the 1912 Mormon 'Exodus' from Mexico." *New Mexico Historical Review* 72, no. 4 (October 1997): 297–318.

Harris, Charles H., and Louis R. Sadler. *The Secret War in El Paso: Mexican Revolutionary Intrigue, 1906–1920*. Albuquerque: University of New Mexico Press, 2009.

Harris, Oliver, ed. *Letters of William S. Burroughs, 1945–1959*. New York: Viking Press, 1993.

Harris, Robert. *Political Corruption: In and Beyond the Nation State*. London: Routledge, 2003.

Heidenheimer, Arnold J., and Michael Johnston, eds. *Political Corruption: Concepts and Contexts*. 3rd ed. New Brunswick, NJ: Transaction Publishers, 2002.

Heidensohn, Frances. *Women in Control? The Role of Women in Law Enforcement*. Oxford: Clarendon Press, 1992.

Hennessy, Rosemary. "Open Secrets: The Affective Cultures of Organizing on Mexico's Northern Border." *Feminist Theory* 10, no. 3 (December 2009): 310–22.

Herlihy, Patricia. *The Alcoholic Empire: Vodka and Politics in Late Imperial Russia*. New York: Oxford University Press, 2002.

Herlinghaus, Hermann. *Violence Without Guilt: Ethical Narratives from the Global South*. New York: Palgrave Macmillan, 2009.

Hernández, Kelly Lytle. *Migra! A History of the U.S. Border Patrol*. Berkeley: University of California Press, 2010.

Heyman, Josiah McC., ed. *States and Illegal Practices*. Oxford: Berg Publishers, 1999.

———. "U.S. Ports of Entry on the Mexican Border." In *On the Border: Society and Culture Between the United States and Mexico*, edited by Andrew Grant Wood, 221–40. Lanham, MD: SR Books, 2004.

Hirales Morán, Gustavo. "La guerra secreta, 1970–78." *Nexos* 34 (June 1982): 36

———. *La liga comunista 23 de septiembre: orígenes y naufragio*. Mexico City: Ediciones de Cultura Popular, 1977.

Hobsbawm, Eric. *Bandits*. 1969. New York: New Press, 2000.

Hodges, Graham Russell Gao. *Taxi: A Social History of the New York City Cabdriver*. Baltimore, MD: Johns Hopkins University Press, 2007.

Hodgson, Barbara. *In the Arms of Morpheus: The Tragic History of Laudanum, Morphine, and Patent Medicines*. Buffalo: Firefly Books, 2001.

Hopkins, R. Thurston. *Famous Bank Forgeries, Robberies, and Swindlers*. London: Stanley Paul, 1936.

Hornberger, Francine. *Mistresses of Mayhem: The Book of Women Criminals*. Indianapolis, IN: Alpha Books, 2002.

Hu-DeHart, Evelyn. "Coolies, Shopkeepers, and Pioneers: The Chinese of Mexico and Peru, 1849–1930." *Amerasia Journal* 15, no. 2 (1989): 91–116.

Hyde, Anne. *Empires, Nations, and Families: A History of the North American West, 1800–1860*. Lincoln: University of Nebraska Press, 2011.

Inciardi, James, Dorothy Lockwood, and Anne Pottieger. *Women and Crack-Cocaine*. New York: Macmillan, 1993.

Inciardi, James, Anne Pottieger, and Charles Faupel. "Black Women, Heroin and Crime: Some Empirical Notes." *Journal of Drug Issues* 12 (1982): 241–50.

Johnson, Benjamin Heber. *Revolution in Texas: How a Forgotten Rebellion and Its Bloody Suppression Turned Mexicans into Americans.* New Haven, CT: Yale University Press, 2003.

Johnson, Lyman, ed. *The Problem of Order in Changing Societies: Essays on Crime and Policing in Argentina and Uruguay, 1750–1919.* Albuquerque: University of New Mexico Press, 1990.

Jonnes, Jill. *Hep-Cats, Narcs, and Pipe Dreams: A History of America's Romance with Illegal Drugs.* New York: Scribner, 1996.

Kandall, Stephen R. *Substance and Shadow: Women and Addiction in the United States.* Cambridge, MA: Harvard University Press, 1999.

Katz, Friedrich. *The Secret War in Mexico: Europe, the United States, and the Mexican Revolution.* Chicago, IL: University of Chicago Press, 1984.

Katzew, Ilona, and Susan Deans-Smith, eds. *Race and Classification: The Case of Mexican America.* Stanford, CA: Stanford University Press, 2009.

Keire, Mara L. "Dope Fiends and Degenerates: The Gendering of Addiction in the Early Twentieth Century." *Journal of Social History* 3 (1998): 809–22.

Kenney, Michael. *From Pablo to Osama: Trafficking and Terrorist Networks, Government Bureaucracies, and Competitive Adaptation.* University Park: Penn State University Press, 2007.

Kenny, Paul, Mónica Serrano, and Arturo Sotomayor. *Mexico's Security Failures: Collapse into Criminal Violence.* New York: Routledge, 2011.

Kim, Hyung-chan. *A Legal History of Asian Americans, 1790–1990.* Westport, CT: Greenwood Press, 1994.

Kinder, Douglas Clark, and William O. Walker III. "Stable Force in a Storm: Harry J. Anslinger and United States Narcotic Foreign Policy, 1930–1962." *Journal of American History* 72, no. 4 (March 1986): 908–27.

Kingston, Charles. *Remarkable Rogues: The Careers of Some Notable Criminals of Europe and America.* New York: John Lane, 1921.

Klubock, Thomas M. *Contested Communities: Class, Gender, and Politics in Chile's El Teniente Copper Mine, 1904–1948.* Durham, NC: Duke University Press, 1998.

Knepper, Paul. *The Invention of International Crime: A Global Issue in the Making, 1881–1914.* London: Palgrave Macmillan, 2010.

Knight, Alan. *The Mexican Revolution.* 2 vols. Cambridge: Cambridge University Press, 1990.

Kyle, David, and Christina A. Siracusa. "Seeing the State Like a Migrant: Why So Many Non-criminals Break Immigration Laws." In *Illicit Flows and Criminal Things: States, Borders, and the Other Side of Globalization*, edited by Willem van Schendel and Itty Abraham, 153–76. Bloomington: Indiana University Press, 2005.

Lauderdale Graham, Sandra. *House and Street: The Domestic World of Servants and Masters in Nineteenth-Century Rio de Janeiro.* Austin: University of Texas Press, 1992.

Lavrin, Asunción. *Latin American Women: Historical Perspectives*. Westport, CT: Greenwood Press, 1978.

Lea, John. *Crime and Modernity: Continuities in Left Realist Criminology*. Thousand Oaks, CA: Sage Publications, 2002.

Levitt, Steven D., and Stephen J. Dubner. *Freakonomics: A Rogue Economist Explores the Secret Side of Everything*. New York: HarperCollins, 2005.

Levitt, Theodore. "The Globalization of Markets." *Harvard Business Review*, May–June 1983.

Lewis, Oscar. *The Children of Sánchez: Autobiography of a Mexican Family*. New York: Random House, 2011.

————. *Five Families: Mexican Case Studies in the Culture of Poverty*. New York: HarperCollins, 1975.

Lipsett-Rivera, Sonya, and Lyman L. Johnson, eds. *The Faces of Honor: Sex, Shame, and Violence in Colonial Latin America*. Albuquerque: University of New Mexico Press, 1998.

Lorey, David E. *The U.S.-Mexican Border in the Twentieth Century: A History of Economic and Social Transformation*. Wilmington, DE: Scholarly Resources, 1999.

Lucas, Netley. *Crook Janes: A Study of the Woman Criminal the World Over*. London: Stanley Paul, 1926.

————. *Ladies of the Underworld: The Beautiful, the Damned, and Those Who Get Away with It*. Cleveland: Goldsmith Publishing, 1927.

Luibhéid, Eithne. *Entry Denied: Controlling Sexuality at the Border*. Minneapolis: University of Minnesota Press, 2002.

Maher, Lisa, and Ric Curtis. "Women on the Edge of Crime: Crack Cocaine and the Changing Contexts of Street-Level Sex Work in New York City." *Crime, Law, and Social Change* 18, no. 2 (1992): 221–58.

Malkin, Victoria. "Narcotrafficking, Migration, and Modernity in Rural Mexico." *Latin American Perspectives* 28, no. 4 (July 2001): 101–28.

Marak, Andrae, and Laura Tuennerman. "Official Government Discourses about Vice and Deviance: The Early-Twentieth-Century Tohono O'odham." In *Smugglers, Brothels, and Twine: Historical Perspectives on Contraband and Vice in North America's Borderlands*, edited by Elaine Carey and Andrae Marak, 101–21. Tucson: University of Arizona Press, 2011.

Martel, Marcel. "Preventing the Invasion: LSD Use in Canada in the Sixties." In *Smugglers, Brothels, and Twine: Historical Perspectives on Contraband and Vice in North America's Borderlands*, edited by Elaine Carey and Andrae Marak, 160–76. Tucson: University of Arizona Press, 2011.

Martin, Susan Ehrlich, and Nancy C. Jurik. *Doing Justice, Doing Gender: Women in Legal and Criminal Justice Occupations*. Thousand Oaks, CA: Sage Publications, 2007.

Martínez, Oscar J. *Border Boom Town: Ciudad Juárez since 1848*. Austin: University of Texas Press, 1978.

——. *Border People: Life and Society in the U.S.-Mexico Borderlands.* Tucson: University of Arizona Press, 1994.

——. "The Dynamics of Border Interaction: New Approaches to Border Analysis." In *Global Boundaries,* edited by Clive H. Schofield, 1–15. London: Routledge, 1994.

——. *Troublesome Border.* Tucson: University of Arizona Press, 1988.

Martínez Verdugo, Arnoldo, ed. *Historia del comunismo en México.* Mexico City: Grijalbo, 1985.

McCoy, Alfred W. *The Politics of Heroin: CIA Complicity in the Global Drug Trade.* Chicago, IL: Lawrence Hill, 2003.

McWilliams, John C. *The Protectors: Harry J. Anslinger and the Federal Bureau of Narcotics.* Newark: University of Delaware Press, 1990.

Meertens, Donny. "Victims and Survivors of War in Colombia: Three Views of Gender Relations." In *Violence in Colombia, 1990–2000: Waging War and Negotiating Peace,* edited by Charles Bergquist, Ricardo Peñaranda, and Gonzalo Sánchez G., 151–70. Wilmington, DE: Scholarly Resources, 2001.

Meyer, Jean. *The Cristero Rebellion: The Mexican People Between Church and State, 1926–1929.* Cambridge: Cambridge University Press, 2008.

Meyer, Kathryn, and Terry Parssinen. *Webs of Smoke: Smugglers, Warlords, Spies, and the History of the International Drug Trade.* Lanham, MD: Rowman and Littlefield, 1998.

Mitchell, Stephanie, and Patience A. Schell. *The Women's Revolution in Mexico, 1910–1953.* Lanham, MD: Rowman and Littlefield, 2006.

Monteón González, Humberto, and José Luis Trueba Lara. *Chinos y antichinos en México: documentos para su studio.* Guadalajara: Gobierno de Jalisco, 1988.

Moore, Robin. *The French Connection: A True Account of Cops, Narcotics, and International Conspiracy.* 13th ed. New York: Lyon Press, 2003.

Mora, Juan Miguel de. *Las guerrillas en México y Jenaro Vázquez Rojas.* Mexico City: Editora Latino Americana, 1972.

Morantz-Sanchez, Regina Markell. *Sympathy and Science: Women Physicians in American Medicine.* New York: Oxford University Press, 1985.

Morgan, H. Wayne. *Drugs in America: A Social History, 1800–1980.* Syracuse, NY: Syracuse University Press, 1981.

Mottier, Nicole. "Drug Gang and Politics in Ciudad Juárez, 1928–1936." *Mexican Studies/Estudios Mexicanos* 25, no. 1 (Winter 2009): 19–46.

——. "Organized Crime, Political Corruption, and Powerful Governments: Drug Gangs in Ciudad Juárez, 1928–1933." Master's thesis, Oxford University, 2004.

Murdock, Catherine Gilbert. *Domesticating Drink: Women, Men, and Alcohol in America, 1870–1940.* Baltimore, MD: Johns Hopkins University Press, 1998.

Murdock, George Peter. *Social Structure.* New York: Macmillan, 1949.

Murphy, Mary. "Bootlegging Mothers and Drinking Daughters: Gender and Prohibition in Butte, Montana." *American Quarterly* 46 (June 1994): 174–94.

Murphy, Sandi R. "Drug Diplomacy and the Supply-Side Strategy: A Survey of United States Practice." *Vanderbilt Law Review* (May 1990): 1259–309.

Murphy, Sheigla, and Marsha Rosenbaum. *Pregnant Women on Drugs: Combating Stereotypes and Stigma.* New Brunswick, NJ: Rutgers University Press, 1999.

Musto, David F. *The American Disease: Origins of Narcotic Control.* New York: Oxford University Press, 1987.

———, ed. *One Hundred Years of Heroin.* Westport, CT: Auburn House, 2002.

Nadelmann, Ethan A. *Cops Across Borders: The Internationalization of U.S. Criminal Law Enforcement.* University Park: Penn State University Press, 1993.

———. "The Evolution of United States Involvement in the International Rendition of Fugitive Criminals." *New York University Journal of International Law and Politics* (Summer 1993): 813–85.

Naím, Moisés. *Illicit: How Smugglers, Traffickers, and Copycats Are Hijacking the Global Economy.* New York: Anchor Books, 2005.

Naylor, R. T. *Wages of Crime: Black Markets, Illegal Finance, and the Underworld Economy.* Ithaca, NY: Cornell University Press, 2002.

Nordstrom, Carolyn. *Global Outlaws: Crime, Money, and Power in the Contemporary World.* Berkeley: University of California Press, 2007.

O'Callaghan, Sean. *Damaged Baggage: The White Slave Trade and Narcotics Trafficking in the Americas.* New York: Roy Publishers, 1970.

O'Donnell, Elliott. *Women Bluebeards.* London: Stanley Paul, 1928.

Olcott, Jocelyn. *Revolutionary Women in Postrevolutionary Mexico.* Durham, NC: Duke University Press, 2005.

Olcott, Jocelyn, Mary Kay Vaughan, and Gabriela Cano, eds. *Sex in Revolution: Gender, Politics, and Power in Modern Mexico.* Durham, NC: Duke University Press, 2006.

Padilla, Tanalís. *Rural Resistance in the Land of Zapata: The Jaramillista Movement and the Myth of the Pax Priísa, 1940–1962.* Durham, NC: Duke University Press, 2008.

Palacios, Marco. *Between Legitimacy and Violence: A History of Colombia, 1875–2002.* Durham, NC: Duke University Press, 2006.

Parker, Tony. *Five Women.* London: Hutchinson, 1965.

Payan, Tony. *The Three U.S.-Mexico Border Wars: Drugs, Immigration, and Homeland Security.* Westport, CT: Praeger Security International, 2006.

Pérez Montfort, Ricardo. "Los orígenes del narco: historias primigenia." Centro de información para la prensa. At http://web.cip.etecsa.cu, accessed April 2000.

———. "1937–1939: El extraño caso de Lola 'La Chata' y el Capitan Huesca de la Fuente contra El Doctor Salazar Viniegra." *Humanidades: un periódico para la universidad,* December 3, 2003. At http://morgan.iia.unam.mx/usr/huamnidades/262, accessed March 3, 2004.

Pescatello, Ann. *Female and Male in Latin America: Essays.* Pittsburgh, PA: University of Pittsburgh Press, 1973.

Piccato, Pablo. *City of Suspects: Crime in Mexico City, 1900–1931.* Durham, NC: Duke University Press, 2001.

Pierce, Gretchen Kristine. "Sobering the Revolution: Mexico's Anti-alcohol Campaigns and the Process of State-Building, 1910–1940." PhD diss., University of Arizona, 2011.

Piña y Palacios, Javier. *La colonia penal de las Islas Marías: su historia, organización y régimen.* Mexico City: Ediciones Botas, 1970.

Polit Dueñas, Gabriela. *Narrating Narcos: Culiacán and Medellín.* Pittsburgh, PA: University of Pittsburgh Press, 2013.

Pollak, Otto. *The Criminality of Women.* Philadelphia, PA: University of Pennsylvania Press, 1950.

Pollak, Otto, and Alfred Friedman, eds. *Family Dynamics and Female Sexual Delinquency.* Palo Alto, CA: Science and Behavior Books, 1969.

Poppa, Terrence E. *Drug Lord: The Life and Death of a Mexican Kingpin.* El Paso: Cinco Puntos Press, 2010.

Potter, Pitman B. "The Positions of Canada and the United States in the Matter of Trade in Alcoholic Beverages." *American Journal of International Law* 24, no. 1 (January 1930): 131–33.

Powell, Hickman. *Lucky Luciano: The Man Who Organized Crime in America.* New York: Barricade Books, 2000.

Rafael, Tony. *The Mexican Mafia.* New York: Encounter Books, 2007.

Rajah, Valli. "Intimacy, Time, Scarcity: Drug Involved Women Account for Secretly Withholding Financial Capital in Violent Intimate Relations." *Journal of Contemporary Ethnography* 39, no. 131 (2010): 131–58.

Ravelo, Ricardo. *Los capos: las narco-rutas de México.* Mexico City: Plaza y Janés, 2005.

———. *Herencia maldita: el reto de Calderón y el nuevo mapa de narcotráfico.* Mexico City: Grijalbo, 2007.

———. *Los narcoabogados.* Mexico City: Grijalbo, 2007.

Reagan, Leslie J. *When Abortion Was a Crime: Women, Medicine, and Law in the United States, 1867–1973.* Berkeley: University of California Press, 1997.

Recio, Gabriela. "Drugs and Alcohol: US Prohibition and the Origins of the Drug Trade in Mexico, 1900–1930." *Journal of Latin American Studies* 34, no. 1 (2002): 21–42.

Reuter, Peter H., and J. Haaga. *The Organization of High-Level Drug Markets: An Exploratory Study.* Santa Monica, CA: RAND Corporation, 1989.

Reuter, Peter H., and David Ronfeldt. "Quest for Integrity: The Mexican-U.S. Drug Issue in the 1980s." Special Issue: Drug Trafficking Research Update. *Journal of Interamerican Studies and World Affairs* 34, no. 3 (Autumn 1992): 89–153.

Rivera-Garza, Cristina. "Masters of the Street: Bodies, Power, and Modernity in Mexico, 1867–1930." PhD diss., University of Houston, 1995.

Roark, Garland. *The Coin of Contraband: The True Story of United States Customs Investigator Al Scharff.* Garden City, NY: Doubleday, 1964.

Robinson, Robin E. "Vice and Tourism on the U.S.-Mexican Border: A Comparison of Three Communities in the Era of U.S. Prohibition." PhD diss., Arizona State University, 2002.

Robles García, Jorge. *La bala perdida: William S. Burroughs en México, 1949–1952.* Mexico City: Milenio, 1995.

Rodríguez Castañeda, Rafael. *El México narco.* Mexico City: Planeta, 2009.

Roldán, Mary. *Blood and Fire: La Violencia in Antioquia, Colombia, 1946–1953*. Durham, NC: Duke University Press, 2002.

Roman, Caterina Gouvis, Heather Ahn-Redding, and Rita J. Simon. *Illicit Drug Policies, Trafficking, and Use the World Over*. Lanham, MD: Lexington Books, 2005.

Rosemblatt, Karin A. *Gendered Compromises: Political Cultures and the State in Chile, 1920–1950*. Chapel Hill: University of North Carolina Press, 2000.

Rotella, Sebastian. *Twilight on the Line: Underworlds and Politics at the U.S.-Mexico Border*. New York: W. W. Norton, 1988.

Rouse, Roger. "Mexican Migration and the Social Spaces of Postmodernism." In *Between Two Worlds: Mexican Immigrants in the United States*, edited by David Gutiérrez, 247–64. Wilmington, DE: Scholarly Resources, 1996.

Rumbarger, John J. *Profits, Power, and Prohibition: Alcohol Reform and the Industrializing of America, 1800–1930*. Albany: State University of New York Press, 1989.

Said, Edward. *Orientalism: Western Conceptions of the Orient*. London: Pantheon Books, 1978.

Salas, Elizabeth. *Soldaderas in the Mexican Military: Myth and History*. Austin: University of Texas Press, 1990.

Salazar, Alonso. *Pablo Escobar: el patrón del mal*. Bogotá: Aguilar, 2012.

Salazar, Ruben. *Border Correspondent: Selected Writings, 1955–1970*. Edited by Mario T. García. Berkeley: University of California Press, 1995.

Salazar Viniegra, Leopoldo, "El mito de la marijuana." *Criminalia* (December 1938): 206–37.

Salvatore, Ricardo D., Carlos Aguirre, and Gilbert M. Joseph. *Crime and Punishment in Latin America: Law and Society Since Late Colonial Times*. Durham, NC: Duke University Press, 2001.

Sánchez, Gonzalo, and Donny Meertens. *Bandits, Peasants, and Politics: The Case of "La Violencia" in Colombia*. Austin: University of Texas Press, 2001.

Sanchez, Tanya Marie. "The Feminine Side of Bootlegging." *Journal of the Louisiana Historical Association* 41, no. 4 (2000): 403–33.

Sann, Paul. *Kill the Dutchman! The Story of Dutch Schultz*. New York: Da Capo Press, 1991.

Santamaría Gómez, Arturo, ed. *Las jefas del narco: el ascenso de las mujeres en crimen organizado*. Mexico City: Grijalbo, 2012.

Santamaría Gómez, Arturo, Pedro Brito Osuna, and Luis Antonio Martínez Peña. *Morir en Sinaloa: violencia, narco, y cultura*. Culiacán: Autonomous University of Sinaloa, 2009.

Scarry, Elaine. *The Body in Pain: The Making and Unmaking of the World*. New York: Oxford University Press, 1985.

Schaefer, Claudia. *Textured Lives: Women, Art, and Representation in Modern Mexico*. Tucson: University of Arizona Press, 1992.

Schantz, Eric Michael. "All Night at the Owl: The Social and Political Relations of Mexicali's Red-Light District, 1909–1925." In *On the Border: Society and Culture*

Between the United States and Mexico, edited by Andrew Grant Wood, 91–144. Lanham, MD: SR Books, 2004.

————. "From the Mexicali Rose to the Tijuana Brass: Vice Tours of the United States–Mexico Border, 1910–1965." PhD diss., University of California, Los Angeles, 2001.

Schneider, Friedrich, and Dominik H. Enste. *The Shadow Economy: An International Survey*. Cambridge: Cambridge University Press, 2002.

Schofield, Clive H., ed. *Global Boundaries*. London: Routledge, 1994.

Schrecker, Ellen. *Many Are the Crimes: McCarthyism in America*. Boston, MA: Little, Brown, 1998.

Schultes, Richard Evans. "Teonanacatl: The Narcotic Mushroom of the Aztecs." *American Anthropologist* 42, no. 3 (July–September 1940): 429–33.

Schulz, Dorothy Moses. *Breaking the Brass Ceiling: Women Police Chiefs and Their Paths to the Top*. Westport, CT: Praeger, 2004.

Schweber, Claudine, and Hugh E. Teitelbaum. "Criminalization and Incarceration: The Federal Response to Drug Addiction Among Women, 1914–1934." *George Mason Law Review* 4, no. 1 (Spring 1981): 71–98.

Scott, Joan W. "Unanswered Questions." *American Historical Review* 113, no. 5 (December 2008): 1422–29.

Scott, Peter Dale, and Jonathan Marshall. *Cocaine Politics: Drugs, Armies, and the CIA in Central America*. Berkeley: University of California Press, 1998.

Shabat, Kevin A. "The Local Matters: A Brief History of the Tension Between Federal Drug Policy and Local Policy." *Journal of Global Drug Policy and Practice* 1, no. 4 (Winter 2007). At http://globaldrugpolicy.org/1/4/index.php, accessed January 28, 2011.

Shannon, Elaine. *Desperados: Latin Drug Lords, U.S. Lawmen, and the War America Can't Win*. New York: Viking Press, 1988.

Smith, Jennie Erin. *Cocaine Cowgirl: The Outrageous Life and Mysterious Death of Griselda Blanco*. N.p.: Byliner Originals, 2013. Kindle edition. At https://www.byliner.com/originals/cocaine-cowgirl?hb.

Smith, Stephanie J. *Gender and the Mexican Revolution: Yucatán Women and the Realities of Patriarchy*. Chapel Hill: University of North Carolina Press, 2009.

Smitten, Richard. *The Godmother: The True Story of the Hunt for the Most Bloodthirsty Female Criminal of Our Time*. New York: Pocket Books, 1990.

————. *Twice Killed*. New York: Avon Books, 1984.

Smitten, Richard, and Ellis Rubin. *Kathy: A Case of Nymphomania*. Hollywood, FL: Lifetime Books, 1993.

Solomon, Robert, and Melvyn Green. "The First Century: The History of Non-medical Opiate Use and Control Policies in Canada, 1870–1970." In *Illicit Drugs in Canada: A Risky Business*, edited by Judith C. Blackwell and Patricia G. Erickson, 88–116. Scarborough, Ontario: Nelson Canada, 1988.

Spann, Michael. *William S. Burroughs' Unforgettable Characters: Lola la Chata and Bernabé Jurado*. Providence, RI: Inkblot Publications, 2013.

Sparrow, Gerald. *Queens of Crime: Stories of Great Women Criminals*. London: Arthur Baker, 1973.

Speaker, Susan L. "'The Struggle of Mankind Against Its Deadliest Foe': Themes of Counter-subversion in Anti-narcotic Campaigns, 1920–1940." *Journal of Social History* 34, no. 3 (Spring 2001): 591–610.

Spillane, Joseph. *Cocaine: From Medical Marvel to Modern Menace in the United States, 1884–1920*. Baltimore, MD: Johns Hopkins University Press, 2000.

Stanonis, Anthony Joseph. *Creating the Big Easy: The Emergence of Modern Tourism, 1918–1945*. Athens: University of Georgia Press, 2006.

Stares, Paul B. *Global Habit: The Drug Problem in a Borderless World*. Washington, D.C.: Brookings Institution, 1996.

Stepan, Nancy Leys. *The Hour of Eugenics: Race, Gender, and Nation in Latin America*. Ithaca, NY: Cornell University Press, 1991.

Stephens, Robert P. *Germans on Drugs: The Complications of Modernization in Hamburg*. Ann Arbor: University of Michigan Press, 2007.

Stille, Alexander. *Excellent Cadavers: The Mafia and the Death of the First Italian Republic*. New York: Vintage, 1996.

St. John, Rachel. *Line in the Sand: A History of the Western U.S.-Mexico Border*. Princeton, NJ: Princeton University Press, 2011.

Strange, Susan. *The Retreat of the State: The Diffusion of Power in the World Economy*. Cambridge: Cambridge University Press, 1996.

Strathdee, Steffanie A., Morgan M. Philbin, Shirley J. Semple, et al. "Correlates of Injection Drug Use Among Female Sex Workers in Two Mexico-U.S. Border Cities." *Drug and Alcohol Dependence* 92, nos. 1–3 (January 2008): 132–40.

Sudbury, Julia. "Celling Black Bodies: Black Women in the Global Prison Industrial Complex." *Feminist Review* 80 (2005): 162–79.

Tamayo, Sergio. "The Twenty Mexican Octobers: A Study of Citizenship and Social Movements." PhD diss., University of Texas, 1994.

Taussig, Michael. *Defacement: Public Secrecy and the Labor of the Negative*. Stanford, CA: Stanford University Press, 1999.

Thachuk, Kimberley L. "An Introduction to Transnational Threats." In *Transnational Threats: Smuggling and Trafficking in Arms, Drugs, and Human Life*, edited by Kimberley L. Thachuk, 3–20. Westport, CT: Praeger Security International, 2007.

Thelen, David. "Rethinking History and the Nation-State: Mexico and the United States." *Journal of American History* 86, no. 2 (September 1999): 438–52.

Tinsman, Heidi. *Partners in Conflict: The Politics of Gender, Sexuality, and Labor in the Chilean Agrarian Reform, 1950–1973*. Durham, NC: Duke University Press, 2002.

Topik, Steven, Carlos Marichal, and Zephyr Frank, eds. *From Silver to Cocaine: Latin American Commodity Chains and the Building of the World Economy, 1500–2000*. Durham, NC: Duke University Press, 2006.

Toro, María Celia. "The Internationalization of Police: The DEA in Mexico." *Journal of American History* 86, no. 2 (September 1999): 623–40.

Tracy, Sarah W., and Caroline Jean Acker, eds. *Altering American Consciousness: The History of Alcohol and Drug Use in the United States, 1800–2000.* Amherst: University of Massachusetts Press, 2004.

Trueba Lara, José Luís. *Los chinos de Sonora: una historia olvidada.* Hermosillo: Instituto de Investigaciones Historicas, University of Sonora, 1990.

Truett, Samuel, and Elliott Young, eds. *Continental Crossroads: Remapping U.S.-Mexico Borderlands History.* Durham, NC: Duke University Press, 2004.

Twinam, Ann. *Public Lives, Private Secrets: Gender, Honor, Sexuality, and Illegitimacy in Colonial Spanish America.* Stanford, CA: Stanford University Press, 1999.

Ulloa Bornemann, Alberto. *Surviving Mexico's Dirty War: A Political Prisoner's Memoir.* Philadelphia, PA: Temple University Press, 2007.

Urías Horcasitas, Beatriz. *Historias secretas del racismo en México (1920–1950).* Mexico City: Tusquets, 2007.

Valencia, Enrique. *La Merced: estudio ecológico y social de una zona de la ciudad de México.* Mexico City: Instituto Nacional de Antropología e Historia, 1965.

Valentine, Douglas. *The Strength of the Wolf: The Secret History of America's War on Drugs.* London: Verso, 2004.

Vanderwood, Paul. *Disorder and Progress: Bandits, Police, and Mexican Development.* Lincoln: University of Nebraska Press, 1981.

Vanegas, Ernestina. "Vivimos en la cárcel con Papa." In *La colonia penal de las Islas Marías: su historia, organización y régimen,* edited by Javier Piña y Palacios, 97–102. Mexico City: Ediciones Botas, 1970.

Van Schendel, Willem, and Itty Abraham, eds. *Illicit Flows and Criminal Things: States, Borders, and the Other Side of Globalization.* Bloomington: Indiana University Press, 2005.

Van Wert, James M. "The U.S. State Department's Narcotics Control Policy in the Americas." Special Issue: Assessing the Americas' War on Drugs. *Journal of Interamerican Studies and World Affairs* 30, nos. 2–3 (Summer–Autumn 1988): 1–18.

Vaughan, Mary Kay. *Cultural Politics in Revolution: Teachers, Peasants, and Schools in Mexico, 1930–1940.* Tucson: University of Arizona Press, 1997.

———. *The State, Education, and Social Class in Mexico, 1880–1928.* DeKalb: Northern Illinois University Press, 1982.

Vecchio, Diane C. *Merchants, Midwives, and Laboring Women: Italian Migrants in Urban America.* Urbana: University of Illinois Press, 2006.

Wald, Elijah. *Narcocorrido: A Journey into the Music of Drugs, Guns, and Guerrillas.* New York: Rayo, HarperCollins, 2001.

Walker, Margath A. "Guada-narco-lupe, Maquilarañas, and the Discursive Construction of Gender and Difference on the U.S.-Mexico Border in Mexican Media Representations." *Gender, Place, and Culture* 12 (March 2005): 95–110.

Walker, William O., III. "Control Across the Border: The United States, Mexico, and Narcotics Policy, 1936–1940." *Pacific Historical Review* 47, no. 1 (February 1978): 91–106.

——. *Drug Control in the Americas*. Albuquerque: University of New Mexico Press, 1989.

——. *Drug Control Policy: Essays in Historical and Comparative Perspective*. University Park: Penn State University Press, 1992.

Walkowitz, Judith. *City of Dreadful Delight: Narratives of Sexual Danger in Late-Victorian London*. Chicago, IL: University of Chicago Press, 1992.

Walsh, Mary Roth. *Doctors Wanted, No Women Need Apply: Sexual Barriers in the Medical Profession, 1835–1975*. New Haven, CT: Yale University Press, 1977.

Weber, Jonathan. "Angels or Monsters? Violent Crime and Violent Children in Mexico City, 1927–1932." Master's thesis, Florida State University, 2006.

Weber, Max. *The Theory of Social and Economic Organization*. Translated by A. M. Henderson and T. Parsons. New York: Oxford University Press, 1947.

Whiteside, Henry O. *Menace in the West: Colorado and the American Experience with Drugs, 1873–1963*. Denver: Colorado Historical Society, 1997.

Williams, John B., ed. *Narcotics*. Dubuque, IA: William C. Brown, 1963.

Williams, Phil. "The Nature of Drug-Trafficking Networks." *Current History* 97 (April 1998): 154–59.

Wilson, James Q. *The Investigators: Managing FBI and Narcotics Agents*. New York: Basic Books, 1978.

Wood, Andrew. *On the Border: Society and Culture Between the United States and Mexico*. Lanham, MD: SR Books, 2004.

Woodiwiss, Michael. *Organized Crime and American Power: A History*. Toronto: University of Toronto Press, 2001.

Young, Elliott. *Catarino Garza's Revolution on the Texas-Mexico Border*. Durham, NC: Duke University Press, 2004.

Young, Robert J. C. *Colonial Desire: Hybridity in Theory, Culture, and Race*. New York: Routledge, 1995.

INDEX

Page numbers in italic text indicate illustrations.

Abraham, Itty, 5

Acosta, Pablo, 252n129

addiction and addicts: for Blanco, 189; in California, 32–33; in drug families, 101–3; Harrison Act increasing, 57; heroin, 57–58; nation building and, 29; opium, 57, 117, 219n16; Price Daniel hearings on, 143, 147–48, 151; in prisons, 74; social hygiene, health, and, 29, 74; treatment of, 118–19; women, 57, 70–71, 95–96, 109–10, 117, 151, 208nn24–25, 219n16, 224n68, 230n22, 231nn25–26, 236n102

Alamillo, José M., 60

alcohol and alcoholism, 18–19, 26–27, 29, 58–61, 76, 236n103

Amerindian drug use, 17–18

anonymity, 136, 196–97, 240n40

Anslinger, Harry J., 77, 217n114, 223n44; on addiction and women, 95–96, 109–10, 231n25; la Chata for, 91, 98, 106, 108, 110, 112, 114; on drug trade and communism, 142–43, 144–45; on Mexican deviance, 48, 49–50; Mexican drug control, policy, and, 96, 113–14, 118–19, 235n89; on la Nacha, 132, 133; on partnerships of

men and women, 71–72; on race and vice, 95, 109–10; Salazar Viniegra campaigned against by, 113, 123; Scharff for, 83–84; transnational trafficking and, 78, 82, 89, 142–45

anti-Chinese movement: in Canada, 42; Chinese response to, 43, 217n97; commercial competition feeding, 38–39; drug enforcement in, 43–44, 44; in Gulf Coast region, 39–41; in Mexican government, 39–40, 42; Mexican women and Chinese in, 42–43, 217n97; in Mexico, 38–44; sexual predation in, 41–42; in Sonora state, 40

Arellano Félix, Enedina, 198–99, 209n35

Argentina and Argentinean government, 173–75

arrest and imprisonment: of Ávila, Sandra, 1; Blanco, 178, 179, 187, 189–90; of la Chata, 99, 104, 105, 106–7, 108–9, 110, 119–20, 232n41, 237n111; extradition and, 107, 108; of Hernandez family, 168–69; of la Nacha, 128, 130, 131, 138–40, 241n47; of Sarmiento, 172–73, 174–75, 177; of Wendt, 79–80, 226n96, 226n100

attention, 56–57
automobile smuggling, 65–66, 67–68
Ávila Beltrán, Sandra, 1, 2, 195, 198
Ávila Camacho, Manuel, 91, 126, 133
Ayala, Jorge "Rivi," 179, 190, 191

Bailey, Daniel, 79–80
Barragán Bautista, Big Mike, 150–53, 200
Barragán family, 170, 200
Beland family, 100–103, *101, 103,* 232n45
Bermúdez, Antonio J., 130, 131, 132, 133, 139
Blaine Act, 63, 222n38
Blanco, Griselda "The Godmother," 13; addiction for, 189; appearance of, 190–91; arrest and imprisonment of, 178, 179, 187, 189–90; in community, 191; in document forgery, 183, 185, 186; drug enforcement on, 185, 186, 187–88, 189, 190; drug trade distance for, 188; drug trade men partnering with, 182, 183–84, 186–87, 189–90, 198, 251n99; drug trade women under, 178, 186–87, 188; extradition and, 181, 250n95; feminine used on drug trade men by, 186–87; masculinity and, 189–93; in Medellín cartel, 179, 184–88; men profiting from, 191; narco-dramas inspired by, 179–80; power accessed by, 183; in prostitution, 182; rape for, 182, 183; sexuality of, 189, 252n129, 253n135; transnational trafficking of, 177–79, 181, 183–88, 189, 249n81, 252n118; trial of, 184–88, 190, 251n102, 251n108, 252nn112–13; for U.S. government, 184–85; violence from, 190–91, 250n87
BNDD. *See* Bureau of Narcotics and Dangerous Drugs
body cavity searches, 68–69
Bojórquez, Juan de Dios, 14–15
Bonaudo, Felice, 37

bootlegging, 59–61, 221n34
border regions. *See* customs and border patrol; national borders and border regions
Bravo, Luis Alberto, 183–88
Brent, Charles H., 19, 211n11
brutality, in searches, 68–69
Bulnes, Don Basilio, 27, 28
Bureau of Narcotics and Dangerous Drugs (BNDD), 162, 165, 168–69, 223n44, 246n22
Bureau of Social Hygiene, 24–25, 70
Burke, Kathy, 192–93
Burroughs, William S., 114–15, 191, 235nn91–93, 236n94, 236n97
business: la Chata in, 115–16, 236n100; drug trade women and front of, 150, 153, 154, 156–57, 171, 198–99, 244n94; money laundering, 150, 153, 154, 156–57, 171, 198–99

Cabán, Carmen, 186, 188, 251n108, 252nn112–13
Cabán, Gloria, 185–86, 188, 251n108, 252nn112–13
Cabañas, Lucio, 165–66
Cabrera, Pepe, 184, 185–86
Calderón, Felipe, 202, 203
California, 32–33
Calles, Plutarco Elías, 27, 33–34
Camarago, Raúl, 46–47
Campbell, Howard, 56, 153, 200
Campbell, Nancy, 7, 8, 200
Canada, 25–27, 42, 50, 213n38
Cantú, Gen. Esteban, 28
Cantú de Garza, Carmen, 66
Cardona Salazar, Rafael "Rafa," 180–81
Carvajal Ontiversos, Rosa Emma, 1–2
Castillo, Felipa, 37–38
CCG. *See* Comité Civico Guerrerense
Cecil, Charles W. Jr., 185, 189, 251n105
Chapman, Winnifred, 68–69

la Chata, Lola, 6, 9, 191; appearance of, 104, *105*, 106, 110–12, 114, *124*; arrest and imprisonment of, 99, 104, *105*, 106–7, 108–9, 110, 119–20, 232n41, 237n111; Beland family and, 103; in business, 115–16, 236n100; community for, 98, 108–9; discretion of, 136–37; drug family and street market for, 92–95, *94*, 97–98, 100, 231n15; drug trade men partnering with, 97, 119, 137, 232n35; drug trade power of, 92, 98, 115–16, 124–25; feminine danger of, 110–12, 114–15; gender assumptions of, 120–21; laboratories of, 104; for Mexican government, 95, 104–5, 125; Mexican government connection to, 11–12, 97–99, 108, 118, 121, 123–24; police corruption and, 97–98, 232n36; in popular culture, 236n94, 236n97; real name of, 11, 93; Salazar, Leopoldo, on, 111–12, 114, 115–16, 120–21, 123–24; sexual power of, 115; trafficking stereotypes and, 99–100; transnational trafficking of, 91–93, 97, 100, 107–8, *111*, 120–21; for U.S. government, 95, 104, 106–8, 125; Wendt compared to, 91–92

Chee Quen Towan, 46

Chen, M. M., 43, 44

Chiappe, François, 173–77

children, in smuggling, 66

Chinese: anti-Chinese movement response of, 43, 217n97; immigrants and immigration, 45, 215n70, 216n87; men as feminine, 41–42; in Mexican opium production, 44–45, 96, 212n28, 217n103, 231n28; Mexican women associated with, 42–43, 217n97; mutual aid societies, 46; power struggles, 45–46; racism against, 30, 33, 38–44, *44*, 96, 217n97; as sexual predators, 41–42; in

smuggling, 39, 211n20. *See also* anti-Chinese movement

Ciudad Juárez, 94–95, 128, 134, 135

class, 10, 69, 86–88

cocaine: "cowboys," 250n85; medical professionals on, 177–78; Mexican drug trade in, 19; Mexico transshipment of U.S., 12–13; North American focus on, 12; profit from, 178; transnational trafficking of, 160, 171, 172, 177, 178–88, 189, 245n6; U.S. demand for, 159, 171, 183

Cocaine Cowboys, 178–79, 189

Cochran, John J., 132, 133

Cold War, 164, 173–74

Colombia, 53–54, 181–88

Comité Civico Guerrerense (Civic Committee of the People of Guerrero, CCG), 165–66

commerce and commercial competition, 38–39, 60, 64–65. *See also* business

communication, in transnational trafficking, 85

communism, 142–43, 144–45

community, 98, 108–9, 134–35, 136, 137–38, 191

Corben, Billy, 189, 190, 191

Corsica, 171–72, 176

Cosby, Charles, 189–90

crime, criminality, and criminalization: in Ciudad Juárez, 135; drug use and, 28, 30, 96, 97, 118–19; foreigners associated with, 30–38; gender roles in, 199–200; organized, 132–33, 170–71, 199, 217n105; racializing, 14–16, 20–21, 30–38; scholarship on women and, 92, 228n2; U.S. history of, 8; U.S.-Mexico border and drug, 58

customs and border patrol, 54, 56–57, 68–69, 79, 163–64, 218n5. *See also* U.S. Customs

Dai, Bingham, 76, 208n25
Damm, Henry C. A., 39
danger, 12, 25, 58–59, 110–15, 220n22
Daniels, Josephus, 83
DEA. *See* Drug Enforcement Agency
demand: drug control and policy on,
    156, 162, 170, 203, 244n103; trans-
    national trafficking driven by, 57;
    U.S. cocaine, 159, 171, 183
Department of Health, Mexico
    (Consejo de Salubridad General): on
    addiction, 29; drug control and pol-
    icy from, 22–23, 35, 74, 118–19; on
    drug use, 22, 29, 96–97, 118–19, 121–
    22, 231n32; on foreign medical pro-
    fessionals, 35–37; women in
    healthcare targeted by, 37–38
deviance, 30–31, 47–52
DFS. *See* Federal Security Directorate
Diario Oficial, 27
Díaz, George, 60, 61
Díaz González, Emilio, 172–73
Díaz Ordaz, Gustavo, 161, 163, 164
di Birón, C. L. H. Medici, 36
discretion, 136–37
distance, 66–67, 69–70, 188, 192, 232n34
document forgery, 183, 185, 186
domestic production, Mexican, 8
drug control and policy: extradition in,
    106–7; in law, 23–24, 29–31, 106–7,
    139–40, 231n32; of medical profes-
    sionals, 34–35, 35, 212n33, 214n58;
    from Mexican Department of
    Health, 22–23, 35, 74, 118–19; of
    Mexican government, 21–22, 26–28,
    29, 50–52, 62, 74, 78–79, 91, 96, 113–
    14, 118–19, 126, 139–40, 143, 147, 158–
    59, 161, 162–65, 203, 222n39, 231n32,
    235n89; professionalism in, 4, 158;
    race in, 29–31, 33–34, 96–97, 110;
    shared narconarratives and, 17; on
    supply and demand, 156, 162, 170,

203, 244n103; transnational, 26–27,
    33–34, 77–79, 89, 91–93, 159–60, 163–
    65, 168–69; of U.S. government, 23–
    24, 106–7, 158–59, 161–65, 170, 203;
    U.S.-Mexico border, 12, 16–17, 26–27,
    83, 126–27, 130, 142–54, 162, 163–65,
    168–69. *See also* drug war
Drug Enforcement Agency (DEA), 51;
    Blanco for, 185, 188, 189, 190; forma-
    tion of, 159–60; Garnica corruption
    in, 195; on Latin American Triangle,
    173–74; on women's equality in drug
    trade, 12, *160*, 161
drug enforcement and enforcement
    agencies: in anti-Chinese movement,
    43–44, *44*; on Blanco, 185, 186, 187–
    88, 189, 190; body cavity searches by,
    68–69; collaboration of, 12–13, 63, 64,
    77–79, 104, 106–7, 113–14, 126, 160,
    165, 168–69, 235n89; international,
    63–64; marijuana, *49*; la Nacha sting
    by, 128–30, 238n8, 238n10; of opium,
    27; professionalism and profession-
    alization of, 4, 158; surveillance
    from, 79–80, 120, 131–32, 162, 187–88;
    U.S.-Canada border, 25–26; U.S. gov-
    ernment on, 24–25, 162; women in,
    56, 247n48. *See also* police, drug en-
    forcement, and security force cor-
    ruption; *and specific agencies*
drug family: addiction and, 101–3; of
    Ávila, Sandra, 1, 2; Beland, 100–103,
    101, *103*, 232n45; la Chata use of, 92–
    95, 97–98, 100, 231n15; drug trade
    women's role in, 12, 94, 100–104,
    106–25, 150, 199, 205n5, 230n18;
    Hernandez, 168–71; of León, 194–95;
    of la Nacha, 127, 136, 137, 140, 142,
    146, 154–57, 242n76; Ochoa, 179, 180–
    81; Price Daniel hearings on, 149–51;
    women peddlers and connection to,
    76, 149–50

drug trade: Blanco distance from, 188; Ciudad Juárez in, 128; class transcended in, 10, 88; communism associated with, 142–43, 144–45; community relationship to, 98, 108–9; at Fort Bliss, 144; gender in, 92, 98, 119, 120–21, 124–25; geographical sources of, 6; globalization of, 4, 8–9, 89, 171–77; Latin American Triangle in, 171–77; modernization of, 78–79, 87–88; money laundering, 201, 203; as "open secret," 6, 10, 201–2; power from, 92, 98, 115–16, 124–25; in prisons, 74–75, 169–70; profit, 30, 88; race, sexuality, and, 109–10, 111–12, 235n91; as social safety net, 201; technology, 5, 79, 87, 88, 119, 120–21, 192, 202. *See also* men, in drug trade; Mexican drugs and drug trade; transnational and transnational trafficking; women, in drug trade; *and specific drugs*

drug use: in California, 32–33; criminality and, 28, 30, 96, 97, 118–19; deviance and, 30–31, 48–49; gender roles infringed upon by, 76–77, 109–10; Mexican criminologists and Porfiriato, 20–21; Mexican Department of Health on, 22, 29, 96–97, 118–19, 121–22, 231n32; of Mexican people, 18–19, 20, 25–26, 29, 151, 243n88; in prisons, 73–74; after Prohibition, 63; prostitution and, 109, 118, 151, 243n88; race and, 29–30; religion conflicting with, 17–18; as sickness, 96, 97, 118–19; social change and acceptance of, 159; as solitary or private, 116–17; by U.S. soldiers, 144–45

drug war: Cold War meeting, 164, 173–74; language, 162–63; politics in, 202, 203, 210n15; Scharff in, 82; U.S.

government and, 12, 16, 63, 158–60; violence from, 203

Echeverría, Luis, 162, 167
economy, informal: family in, 61; in Mexico, 61–62, 93, 229n11; profit of, 61–62; women exploiting, 7, 59–60, 116, 194, 236n100
economy, smuggling impact on, 155
Ehrlichman, John, 162–63
equality, 12, 160, *160*, 192
Escobar, Pablo, 180, 184, 191, 250n92
Escudero Romano, Enrique, 104, *105*, 106, 119
eugenics. *See* race and racism
European superiority, 16, 210n16
extradition: Argentinean government and, 173–75; arrest, imprisonment, and, 107, 108; Blanco and, 181, 250n95; in drug control and policy, 106–7; Harrison Narcotics Act and, 130; Mexican and U.S. government collaboration in, 132, 133–34; of la Nacha, 128–40, *141*, 142, 155, 241n59; of Sarmiento, 173

family, 10, 61, 65–66. *See also* drug family
Federal Bureau of Narcotics (FBN), 48, 50, 51, 64; BNDD from, 223n44, 246n22; on drug trade men and women as partners, 71–72; establishment of, 95; in Mexico, 93; Salazar Viniegra campaigned against by, 113, 121–24, 235n88; on transnational trafficking, 154. *See also* Anslinger, Harry J.
Federal Security Directorate (DFS), 166–68, 246n29
feminine and feminism, 9, 41–42, 110–12, 114–15, 186–87
food, marijuana in, 72–73

Ford, Don Henry, 153
foreigners and foreign enemies: crime associated with, 30–38; hierarchy of, 41; medical professionals and, 35–37, 215n77; modernity and technology associated with, 37; narcotics linked to, 17, 42, 49–50, 96–97, 195, 214nn59–60, 231n28; national identity and, 14–16; politicians blaming, 11, 27, 33–34, 42; women in drug trade as, 32. *See also* race and racism
Fort Bliss, 144
franchises and franchising, trafficking, 200
French Connection, 160, 161, 170, 171, 173
Fuller, Stuart, 123

Galindo Barragán, Ismelda, 150, 153, 198, 200
Gallardo, Ángel Félix, 1
Gamboa, Federico, 23
Garnica, Martha, 194, 195–96, 253n5
gender and gender roles: in crime, 199–200; in drug trade, 92, 98, 119, 120–21, 124–25; drug use and infringement on, 76–77, 109–10; trafficking stereotypes of, 32, 85–86, 99–100, 174, 175, 195–96; transnational concepts relation to, 6–7. *See also* masculinity and masculine world
geography, drug trade, 6
globalization, of drug trade, 4, 8–9, 88, 171–77
The Godmother (Smitten), 182
Goethe, C. M., 47–48
González, Héctor, 155
González, Julio M., 35–36
González, Pablo "El Pablote," 135
Gootenberg, Paul, 4–5
Gordon, Avery, 6
Gorman, Thomas, 80
Great Depression, 47–48

Guadalajara cartel, 205n2
Gulf Coast region, 39–41
guns, smuggling of, 67

Halperin, Jorge, 78, 79, 80
Hammond, Lulu, 75
Harrison Narcotics Tax Act, 11–12, 23–24, 31–32, 202; addiction and transnational trafficking from, 57; extradition for violation of, 130; medical profession and requirements of, 214n58
healers, traditional, 38
health. *See* social hygiene and health
healthcare, 37–38, 216n82
Herlinghaus, Hermann, 4, 200, 201
Hernandez family, 168–71, 183, 192, 193
heroin: addiction, 57–58; danger of, 113; media on trade in, 120; medical professionals prescribing, 57, 219n16; in Mexican drug trade, 19, 133, 147–48, 154–55, 241n58; processing, 148; transnational trafficking in, 79–80, 150, 154–56, 168–69, 171–72
Hornsday, W. D., 58–59, 61
Huesca de la Fuente, Luis, 119–20
human trafficking, 89, 180, 182, 183, 194–95
Hurley, Alice, 75
Hustlin' With the Godmother, 189–90

identity, 14–16, 86–87
illicit or illegal flows: in Ciudad Juárez, 135; globalization and, 8–9; in local controlled spaces, 72–77; mules' importance in drug, 197–98; into prisons, 72–77; along U.S.-Mexico border, 152–53, 155–56; women as mules in, 54–55
immigrants and immigration, 45, 47–48, 60–61, 215n70, 216n87. *See also* foreigners and foreign enemies

Immigration and Naturalization Service (INS), 53, 160
imports and importation, 27, 28, 213n48. *See also* smuggling; transnational and transnational trafficking
imprisonment. *See* arrest and imprisonment; prisons
INS. *See* Immigration and Naturalization Service
international drug trade. *See* transnational and transnational trafficking
Iturralde, Frank, 187–88

Jaramillo, Enrique, 97–98, 119, 137
Jasso González, Ignacia, 125, 126–28. *See also* la Nacha

kinship, 198, 199. *See also* drug family; men, in drug trade

laboratories, drug, 24, 85, 104, 108, 119, 152
language, 162–63, 187–88
Latin American Triangle, 171–77
law, legal, and legality: contraband smuggling, 67–68, 69–70, 223n58, 224n59; drug policy in, 23–24, 29–31, 33–34, 106–7, 139–40, 231n32; healers not addressed in, 38; individuals, nation-states, and, 5; legitimacy compared to, 5; for medical professionals, 34; race in drug policy and, 29–31, 33–34, 96–97, 110. *See also* drug control and policy; Harrison Narcotics Tax Act; illicit or illegal flows
LC-23. *See* Liga Comunista 23 de Septiembre
legitimacy and legitimate, 5
León, Maria "Chata," 194–95, 253n1
Levine, Michael, 173–74
Licata, Victor, 49–50, *51*

Liddy, G. Gordon, 163, 245n15
life and lifestyle, of drug trade women, 192–93
Liga Comunista 23 de Septiembre (Communist League of September 23, or LC-23), 166, 167
Lilliestrom, T. L., 138–39
local controlled spaces, 72–77
Loeffelholz-Brandstatter, Naftali, 78, 79, 80, 87, 226n92
Loeffelholz-Brandstatter ring, 78–80, 83, 84–85, 87–89, 201
López, Demetrio, 29
Lung Sung, 45–46

Man in the Green Hat scandal, 61
The Man Who Made It Snow (Mermelstein), 180, 181
María Full of Grace, 53–54, 68
marijuana, 162; Department of Health on, 97, 121–22; drug enforcement, *49*; in food, 72–73; healthcare application of, 37–38, 216n82; Mexican criminologist on, 20; Mexican deviance and, 48–50; in Mexican drugs, 18; in Mexican prisons, 20–21, 72–73, *73*; origins of, 18; Prohibition and, 63; violence and "reefer madness" from, 20, 48, 50, 121, 122–23, 217n114
Martinez-Carcano, Joseph, 174–77
masculinity and masculine world: Blanco and, 189–93; in bootlegging, 61; drug trade women and, 13, 53–54, 59, 153–54, 200–201, 220n26
Maxim, 190–91
MCC. *See* Metropolitan Corrections Center
Medellín cartel, 179, 180–81, 184–88, 250n92
media: drug trade women narconarratives from, 195–96; on equality for drug trade women, 160, *160*, 192;

media (*continued*)
on gender roles in crime, 199–200;
on heroin trade, 120; on Mexican deviance and marijuana, 48–50; on la
Nacha, 130, 134, 140, *141*, 145–46,
240n35; on police corruption and
trafficking, 232n36; on Wendt, 81
medical profession and professionals:
on cocaine, 177–78; drug policy and
control of, 34–35, *35*, 212n33, 214n58;
as foreign enemies, 35–37, 215n77;
healers competing with, 38; heroin
and opium prescribed by, 57, 219n16
men: in bootlegging, 59–60; feminine
in Chinese, 41–42; U.S.-Mexico border smuggling by, 67
men, in drug trade: common roles of,
197; drug trade women and profit of,
191; drug trade women partnering
with, 7–8, 71–72, 97, 119, 125, 136, 137,
138–39, 154, 178, 182, 183–84, 185–87,
189–90, 192, 198–99, 232n35, 251n99;
feminine for manipulating, 186–87;
violence of, 161, 180–81, 203
La Merced, 93
Mermelstein, Max, 179–81, 186–87
Metropolitan Corrections Center
(MCC), 172, 174–75
Mexican: criminologists, 20–21; immigrants, 47–48; Mafia, 169–70, 194,
247n45, 253n1; shipping and ports,
19–20, 206n10
Mexican drugs and drug trade: cocaine in, 19; domestic production
hampered by, 8; heroin in, 19, 133,
147–48, 154–55, 241n58; history of,
17–22, *21*; importation of, 27, 28; international drug trade and, 77;
marijuana in, 18; Mexican
Revolution and, 8; mind-altering
substances in, 17–18; nationalism in,
213n45; poppy in, 18, 44–45;

Prohibition impacting, 26; student
movements linked to, 166–68; U.S.
organized crime and, 132–33, 170
Mexican government and authorities,
post-revolutionary: anti-Chinese
movement in, 39–40, 42; la Chata
connection to, 11–12, 97–99, 108, 118,
121, 123–24; la Chata for, 95, 104–5,
125; drug control and policy from,
21–22, 26–28, 29, 50–52, 62, 74, 78–
79, 91, 96, 113–14, 118–19, 126, 139–
40, 143, 147, 158–59, 161, 162–65, 203,
222n39, 231n32, 235n89; Mexican
immigrant repatriation by, 48;
modernization attempts of, 16; la
Nacha and relationship with, 134–
35, 137–39, 146, 156; opium control
and policy, 23, 27, 63, 222n39;
Prohibition, "tolerance zones," and,
47; social hygiene and health from,
15–16, 21–22, 29; student movements
opposing, 165–67; surveillance of,
120; U.S. government and drug policy of, 28, 50–52, 126, 143, 147, 158–
59, 161, 162–65, 203, 222n39; U.S.
government collaboration with, 63,
64, 77–79, 96, 104, 106–7, 132, 133–
34, 140, 147, 158–59, 163–64, 170, 203,
239n24; youth culture of 1960s and,
164, 165, 167
Mexican people and populace: alcoholism and vice of, 18–19, 25, 29, 47–52;
crime and racism impacting, 30; deviance among, 47–52; drug use of,
18–19, 20, 25–26, 29, 151, 243n88; social hygiene and health of, 25–26
Mexican Revolution, 211n24; for lower
class women, 9; Mexican drug trade
and, 8; Mexican government social
hygiene and health after, 15–16; nationhood after, 15; racism after, 8,
10–11, 14, 16, 38–44, 96; social impact

of, 94. *See also* Mexican government and authorities, post-revolutionary Mexico, 212n31; anti-Chinese movement in, 38–44; Chinese immigrants in, 45, 215n70, 216n87; FBN in, 93; foreigners and national identity of, 14–16; informal economy in, 61–62, 93, 229n11; international drug enforcement response of, 63–64; opium use in, 45; poppy cultivation in, 28, 44–45, 129; smuggling role of, 10–11, 19–20, 26–27, 58–59, 62–64; street market peddling in, 93–94, 117; in transnational trafficking, 12–13, 77, 87, 132–33, 143–44, 150; U.S. government narconarrative on, 50–52, 195–96; women peddlers in, 74–75

Meza Terán, J., 46

militarization, of U.S.-Mexico border, 16

mind-altering substances, 17–18

mobility, of drug trade women, 70

modernity and modernization, 16, 22, 37, 78–79, 87–88

money laundering: drug trade, 201, 203; drug trade women in, 150, 153, 154, 156–57, 171, 198–99

Morgenthau, Henry, 80

motivations, of drug trade women, 56, 197–98

mules and couriers, 197–98. *See also* women, as mules

mutual aid societies, 44–47

la Nacha: arrest and imprisonment of, 128, 130, *131*, 138–40, 241n47; community response to, 134–35, 136, 137–38; discretion exercised by, 136–37; drug enforcement agency sting of, 128–30, 238n8, 238n10; drug family of, 127, 136, 137, 140, 142, 146, 154–57, 242n76; drug trade men partnering with, 136, 137, 138–39; extradition of, 128–40, *141*, 142, 155, 241n59; media on, 130, 134, 140, *141*, 145–46, 240n35; Mexican authorities and relationship with, 134–35, 137–39, 146, 156; in Price Daniel hearings, 142, 144, 145–47, 242nn69–71; real name of, 12, 126; religion for, 139; transnational trafficking of, 126–29, 133, 135–37, 142, 154–56; for U.S. government, 130–32, 140, 154, 155; U.S.-Mexico border drug policies and, 12, 126–27, 130

Nahum Altaled, Vida, 14–15

narconarratives and narcodramas: Blanco inspiring, 179–80; on drug trade as "open secret," 6, 10, 201–2; drug trade women in media, 195–96; on drug use and deviance, 30–31; historical, 4–5, 200–201; Mexico and U.S. government, 50–52, 195–96; shared drug policy and, 17; student movements and Mexican drug trade, 168; of vice in North America, 10; of women peddlers, 75

narcotics: foreigners linked to, 17, 42, 49–50, 96–97, 195, 214nn59–60, 231n28; national security and, 16–17, 100, 165; transnational policing of, 11; U.S. history of, 8

narcotics farms, 24

nation, nationhood, and nationalism: addiction impacting, 29; crime racialized in, 15–16, 30; foreigners and identity of, 14–16; legality from individuals and, 5; Mexican drug trade and, 213n45; after Mexican Revolution, 15; narcotics and security of, 16–17, 100, 165; social hygiene and health in building, 21, 29

national borders and border regions, 4–5, 12–13, 25–26

Nixon, Richard, 158–60, 162–63, 164
Nordstrom, Carolyn, 8, 10
North America, 5, 10, 12, 29–30

Ochoa family, 179, 180–81, 250n92
"open or public secret," of drug trade, 6, 10, 201–2
Operation Cooperation, 163–64, 165
Operation Intercept, 163–65
opium and opiates, 40, 238n9; addiction, 57, 117, 219n16; Chinese in Mexican, 44–45, 96, 212n28, 217n103, 231n28; drug enforcement of, 27; Mexican government control of, 23, 27, 63, 222n39; post-revolutionary Mexico and use of, 45; Prohibition and, 63; in U.S., 24, 213n48; U.S. government on, 19, 24
organized crime, 132–33, 170–71, 199, 217n105
Orsini, Dominique, 176

Padilla, Ezequiel, 133–34
Palm, Oscar, 151–52
Palombo, Bob, 178, 189
Parada, Lilia, 186, 187, 188
Partido de los Pobres (Party of the Poor), 165–66
peddling, 6–7, 74–76, 93–94, 117–18, 149–50
police, drug enforcement, and security force corruption, 16; DFS, 166–68; of Garnica, 195–96, 253n5; mutual aid societies and, 44–47; organized crime and, 217n105; in trafficking, 46–47, 97–98, 104, 119–20, 137, 173, 232n36, 248n58
policing. See drug enforcement and enforcement agencies
politics, politicians, and political subversion: on drug trade and foreign

enemies, 11, 27, 33–34, 42; in drug war, 202, 203, 210n15; student movements and, 165–68; violence and, 181–82; women in, 168, 182
poppy, 18, 28, 44–45, 129. See also opium and opiates
popular culture, 2, 55–56, 89, 218n3, 236n94, 236n97
Porfiriato, 20–21, 209n3
Porter, Stephen G., 24
poverty, of drug trade women, 192–93
power: of Ávila, Sandra, and Carvajal, 2; Blanco's access to, 183; Chinese struggles over, 45–46; from drug trade, 92, 98, 115–16, 124–25; mutual aid societies struggling for, 46; through sexuality and woman's body, 115; through violence, 183
Price Daniel hearings: on addiction, 143, 147–48, 151; on drug families, 149–51; on drug trade women, 148–50, 242n71; on Mexican heroin, 148; Mexican transnational trafficking in, 143–44; la Nacha in, 142, 144, 145–47, 242nn69–71
prisons: addiction in, 74; drug trade and use in, 73–74, 169–70; illicit flows into, 72–77; as local controlled space, 72; marijuana in Mexican, 20–21, 72–73, 73; MCC in, 172, 174–75. See also arrest and imprisonment
privacy or private, 116–18
processing, drug, 104, 148
professionalism and professionalization, 4, 158
profit: from cocaine, 178; drug trade, 30, 88; of informal economy, 61–62; of men from drug trade women, 191; street market, 61–62, 221n36; transnational trafficking, 59, 88; of

U.S.-Mexico border smuggling, 66; violence relationship to, 159, 161

Prohibition: bootlegging during, 59–61, 221n34; drug use after, 63; history following, 4–5, 11; Mexican drugs and alcohol impacted by, 26; Mexican government, "tolerance zones," and, 47; WCTU and, 60

prostitution, 224n70; Blanco in, 182; for drug trade women, 153, 192–93, 244n94; drug use and, 109, 118, 151, 243n88

Pure Food and Drug Act, 23–24

Quintero Payán, Juan José, 1

race and racism: against Chinese, 30, 33, 38–44, 44, 96, 217n97; crime linked to, 14–16, 20–21, 30–38; in drug policy and law, 29–31, 33–34, 96–97, 110; drug trade, sexuality, and, 109–10, 111–12, 235n91; drug use and, 29–30; of European superiority, 16, 210n16; against Mexican immigrants, 47–48; after Mexican Revolution, 8, 10–11, 14, 16, 38–44, 96; trafficking stereotypes of, 32, 85–86; in vice, 41, 95, 109–10

rape, 182, 183

recidivism, 102

"reefer madness," 20, 48, 50, 121, 122–23, 217n114

religion, 17–18, 139

Restrepo, Edgar, 185–86

Roark, Garland, 226n109

Rockefeller, John D., 211n27

Rodríguez, José María, 22

Rodríguez Pérez, Purificación, 149–50

Román Valdez, José, 39–40

Roosevelt, Franklin D., 219n19

Rosas Trejo, Margarita, 71–72

Rossendahl, Francis, 80

Rossi, Dalays, 187–88

Roumagnac, Carlos, 20–21

Ruffin, James E., 106–7

Said, Edward, 17

Salas Obregón, Ignacio, 166

Salazar, Ruben, 142, 145–47, 242n67, 242nn69–71

Salazar Viniegra, Leopoldo, 74, 98, 222n39; on la Chata, 111–12, 114, 115–16, 120–21, 123–24; on drug use, 96–97, 118–19, 121–22; FBN campaign against, 113, 121–24, 235n88

Sánchez Velázquez, Teresa, 77

Sarmiento, Yolanda, 13, 192; arrest and imprisonment of, 172–73, 174–75, 177; escape of, 174–77; extradition of, 173; as informant, 176, 177; police corruption and, 173; trafficking stereotypes and, 174, 175; transnational trafficking of, 171–72, 176, 177, 248n49; violence from, 174, 178

Scharff, Alvin: on drug trade women, 149; personal history of, 82–83, 200–201, 226n109; transnational trafficking exposed by, 81–82, 83–85, 89; in U.S. Customs, 82–85, 83–84, 225n80; for U.S. government, 83–84

scholars and scholarship: on crime and women, 92, 228n2; on drug trade women, 56, 195–97; on gender roles in crime, 199–200; on la Nacha, 128; in research and studies, 6

Schroeder, Hugo, 35–36

Schultz, Dutch, 239n25

Schwartz, Sam, 81–82

searches, 3, 54, 56–57, 68–69, 79, 163–64

Segura Millán, Jorge, 122–23

sexuality and sexual predation: of Chinese, 41–42; of drug trade women, 189, 195, 252n129, 253n135;

sexuality and sexual predation (*continued*)
power through, 115; race, drug trade, and, 109–10, 111–12, 235n91
Sherman, Henry, 68–69
shipment methods, transnational trafficking, 172
sickness, drug use as, 96, 97, 118–19
Silverstein, Eva, 31, 32, 214n60
Sindicato Nacional Pro-Raza (Pro-race National Syndicate, SNPR), 40–41
Smitten, Richard, 180, 181, 182, 250n84, 250n90, 252nn112–13
smuggling: of alcohol, 26–27, 58–59; by automobile, 65–66, 67–68; Chinese in, 39, 211n20; family's role in, 10, 65–66; guns, 67; human, 89, 180, 182, 183, 194–95; by immigrants, 60–61; of legal contraband, 67–68, 69–70, 223n58, 224n59; Mexican economy impacted by, 155; Mexican role in, 10–11, 19–20, 26–27, 58–59, 62–64; over distance, 66–67, 69–70; U.S.-Mexico border, 64–68, 214n52; women in, 64–68; work-related, 64–65. *See also* trafficking; women, as mules
SNPR. *See* Sindicato Nacional Pro-Raza
social hygiene and health, 211n27; addiction and, 29, 74; from Mexican government, 15–16, 21–22, 29; of Mexican people, 25–26; modernization through, 22; in nation building, 21, 29; in U.S., 22
society. *See* student and social movements, Mexican; youth culture, 1960s
soldiers, U.S., 144–45
solitary. *See* privacy or private
Sonora state, 39
Spanish colonists, 17–18
State Department, 163

stereotypes, of drug trade women, 8, 86, 87, 174, 175
Stewart, James B., 121–22
Stock, Sadie, 31–32
street market, 61–62, 92–95, *94*, 117–18, 221n36, 231n15
student and social movements, Mexican: Mexican drug trade linked to, 166–68; Mexican government opposed by, 165–67; political subversion and, 165–68; violence from, 167; youth culture of 1960s and, 165–66, 167
supply, drug policy on, 156, 162, 170, 203, 244n103
surveillance, 79–80, 120, 131–32, 162, 187–88

Task Force Relating to Narcotics, Marijuana, and Dangerous Drugs, 162
technology: in bootlegging, 61; of customs and border control, 68; drug trade, 5, 79, 87, 88, 119, 120–21, 192, 202; foreigners associated with, 37
Terry, Charles Edward, 25–26
"tolerance zones," 47
To the Ends of the Earth, 89
trafficking: from Corsica, 171–72, 176; distance in successful, 232n34; franchises and franchising, 200; gender and racial stereotypes of, 32, 85–86, 99–100, 174, 175, 195–96; gender and transnational concepts in, 6–7; human, 89, 180, 182, 183, 194–95; by León, 194–95; police corruption in, 46–47, 97–98, 104, 119–20, 137, 173, 232n36, 248n58. *See also* transnational and transnational trafficking; *and specific traffickers*
transnational and transnational trafficking: Anslinger and, 78, 82, 89,

142–45; of Blanco, 177–79, 181, 183–88, 189, 249n81, 252n118; of la Chata, 91–93, 97, 100, 107–8, *111*, 120–21; of cocaine, 160, 171, 172, 177, 178–88, 189, 245n6; coded language used in, 187–88; communication in, 85; demand driving, 57; drug policy and control, 26–27, 33–34, 77–79, 89, 91–93, 159–60, 163–65, 168–69; drug trade women in, 31–32, 100, 160, 194, 199; gender relation to concepts of, 6–7; in heroin, 79–80, 150, 154–56, 168–69, 171–72; of Mermelstein, 179–81; Mexico in, 12–13, 77, 87, 132–33, 143–44, 150; of la Nacha, 126–29, 133, 135–37, 142, 154–56; narcotics policing, development of, 11; popular culture impacted by, 89; profit, 59, 88; of Sarmiento, 171–72, 176, 177, 248n49; Scharff exposing, 81–82, 83–85, 89; shipment methods, 172; state challenged in, 88–90; along U.S.-Mexico border, 62–63, 126–27, 135, 142–56, 243n93; in Wendt case, 85–86; women as mules in, 53–57, 71, 77–90, *86*, 197–98, 224n71; during World War II, 127, 144–45

"transnational moral entrepreneurs," 207n11

transshipment, national borders for, 12–13, 25

treatment, for addiction, 118–19

Trujillo, Carlos, 182, 183

Turner, Perry Milton, 147–48

United Nations Commission on Narcotic Drugs, 129

United States (U.S.): Canada border with, 25–26; cocaine demand in, 159, 171, 183; crime and narcotics history, 8; international drug enforcement from, 63–64; on Mexican deviancy and vice, 47–52; Mexican transshipment of cocaine to, 12–13; opium and opiates in, 24, 213n48; social hygiene and health in, 22; soldiers' drug use, 144–45; white women and drug threat in, 7

U.S. Customs: Scharff in, 82–85, *83–84*, 225n80; searches, 3, 68, 79, 163–64; women smuggling and, 65

U.S. government: Argentina government cooperation with, 173–74; Blanco for, 184–85; la Chata for, 95, 104, 106–8, 125; drug control and policy of, 23–24, 106–7, 158–59, 161–65, 170, 203; on drug enforcement, 24–25, 162; drug war from, 12, 16, 63, 158–60; Mexican government collaboration with, 63, 64, 77–79, 96, 104, 106–7, 132, 133–34, 140, 147, 158–59, 163–65, 170, 203, 239n24; Mexican government's drug policy and, 28, 50–52, 126, 143, 147, 158–59, 161, 162–65, 203, 222n39; on Mexican port control, 19–20; la Nacha for, 130–32, 140, 154, 155; narconarratives of, 50–52, 195–96; on opium and opiates, 19, 24; Scharff for, 83–84. *See also* Price Daniel hearings

U.S.-Mexico border: as danger and vice site, 12, 25, 58–59, 220n22; drug control and policy, 12, 16–17, 26–27, 83, 126–27, 130, 142–54, 162, 163–65, 168–69; drug criminalization along, 58; drug trade women along, 127–28, 153–54; illegal flows along, 152–53, 155–56; militarization of, 16; Scharff personal history on, 82–83; smuggling along, 64–68, 214n52; transnational trafficking along, 62–63, 126–27, 135, 142–56, 243n93

Vaca Cordella, Gastón, 104

Vader, Rae V., 151, 152–53
van Schendel, Willem, 5
Vásquez Pérez, Francisco, 78
Vásquez Rojas, Genaro, 165–66
Vega, A. Perales, 36
vice: in Mexican people, 18–19, 25, 47–52; narconarrative of North American, 10; race in, 41, 95, 109–10; U.S.-Mexico border as site of, 12, 25, 58–59, 220n22; women peddlers and narconarrative of, 75
Villa, Pancho, 205n3
violence: in Colombia, 181–83; of drug trade men, 161, 180–81, 203; drug trade women and, 161, 174, 178, 179, 190–91, 192–93, 250n87; from drug war, 203; from marijuana, 20, 48, 50, 121, 122–23, 217n114; politics and, 181–82; power through, 183; profit relationship to, 159, 161; through rape, 182; student movement, 167
La violencia, 181–83

Wallace, Mickey, 151
war on drugs. *See* drug war
WCTU. *See* Woman's Christian Temperance Union
Wendt, Maria, 11, 201; arrest and confession of, 79–80, 226n96, 226n100; la Chata compared to, 91–92; class and identity of, 86–87; communication in transnational trafficking of, 85; contemporary women mules compared to, 90; drug trade women stereotypes used by, 86, 87; escape and recapture of, 80–81, 85, 227n118; international drug trade in case of, 85–86; media on, 81; as transnational mule, 77–90, 86; trial of, 85; U.S. Customs search of, 79; women as mules and, 55, 77–90, 86

Woman's Christian Temperance Union (WCTU), 60
women: addiction for, 57, 70–71, 95–96, 109–10, 117, 151, 208nn24–25, 219n16, 224n68, 230n22, 231nn25–26, 236n102; in bootlegging, 59–60, 61; Chinese association with Mexican, 42–43, 217n97; commerce for lower class, 60; in customs and border patrol, 68, 218n5; Department of Health targeting, 37–38; in drug enforcement, 56, 247n48; drug use and gender roles of, 76–77, 109–10; family and role of, 10; informal economy exploited by, 7, 59–60, 116, 194, 236n100; Mexican Revolution for lower class, 9; in organized crime, 171, 199; as peddlers, 74–76, 149–50; in political subversion, 168, 182; power through body of, 115; rape for, 182, 183; scholarship on crime and, 92, 228n2; in smuggling, 64–68; street markets for, 117–18; U.S. and drugs as threat to white, 7
women, as mules: attention and searches of, 54, 56–57; in cocaine trafficking, 185–86; in international drug trade, 54–55, 77–90, 86; in *María Full of Grace*, 53–54; nature and function of, 54, 55–56, 197–98; popular culture and detained, 55, 56, 218n3; in transnational trafficking, 53–57, 71, 77–90, 86, 197–98, 224n71; Wendt compared to contemporary, 90
women, in drug trade, 152, 196, 228n4; addiction for, 70–71, 208n25, 224n68, 231n26; anonymity for, 136, 196–97, 240n40; appearance of, 234n81; under Blanco, 178, 186–87, 188; business fronts and money laundering for,

150, 153, 154, 156–57, 171, 198–99, 244n94; common roles of, 197; contemporary depictions of, 13; discretion exercised by, 136–37; distance maintained by, 188, 192; drug enforcement women to counteract, 56; drug family role of, 12, 94, 100–104, 106–25, 150, 199, 205n5, 230n18; drug trade men partnering with, 7–8, 71–72, 97, 119, 125, 136, 137, 138–39, 154, 178, 182, 183–84, 185–87, 189–90, 192, 198–99, 232n35, 251n99; equality for, 12, *160*, 161, 192; feminine redefined by, 9; as foreigners, 32; history of, 3–13, 195–97; importance of, 2; kinship and, 198, 199; lifestyle of, 192–93; masculinity and, 13, 53–54, 59, 153–54, 200–201, 220n26; media narconarratives of, 195–96; men profiting from, 191; in Mexico narconarratives, 51–52; mobility of, 70; motivations for, 56, 197–98; North American border regions and, 5; popular culture on, 2; power of, 92, 98, 115–16, 124–25; Price Daniel hearings on, 148–50, 242n71; in processing, 104; prostitution for, 153, 192–93, 244n94; research and studies on, 3, 6; scholars on, 56, 195–97; sexuality of, 189, 195, 252n129, 253n135; stereotypes of, 8, 86, 87, 174, 175; transnational trafficking by, 31–32, 100, 160, 194, 199; U.S. Customs and searching of, 3, 68; along U.S.-Mexico border, 127–28, 153–54; violence and, 161, 174, 178, 179, 190–91, 192–93, 250n87. *See also* Blanco, Griselda "The Godmother"; la Chata, Lola; la Nacha; Sarmiento, Yolanda; Wendt, Maria

work, smuggling related to, 64–65

World War I, 82–83

World War II, 127, 144–45

youth culture, 1960s, 159, 164, 165–66, 167. *See also* student and social movements, Mexican